MY SIXTY YEARS AS A
PUBLIC CONTRACT LAWYER

THE ENRICHING LIFE OF GEORGE MARTIN COBURN

1923-2011

ISBN: 147000867X
ISBN-13: 9781470008673

To Gregory Linwood Watson

PREFACE

This account of 88 years of my life as an American from 1923 to 2011 is one enriched by love, friendships, excellent health, privileged family upbringing and educational opportunities, a challenging life of over sixty years in law practice, primarily public contract law, and happiness. I have written it for family and friends as a record of most of my life, and for members of the public contract bar, practitioners and judges as significant portions of the text recall some of the more challenging matters I experienced. I have chosen to end it by my 88th birthday on December 15, 2011. This does not foreclose my writing further about public contract law and policy of the federal government should I live several more years as now appears likely.

This autobiography is organized into seven parts. Part One, Beginnings, covers growing up until I went into the Army early in 1943 during WW II. Part Two is about the nearly three years of Army life here and abroad. Part Three is the college and law school experience after the war. Part Four is the 12 years as a lawyer in the Navy Office of the General Counsel (OGC), beginning in 1949, mostly concerned with Navy procurement contracts and related issues. Parts Five and Six recount my life while in private law practice, primarily public contract law, in Washington, D.C., from 1962 to 2011; and Part Seven is a summing up with a principal focus on how much has changed here and abroad during my lifetime, some for the better, much for the worse.

I have been inspired to write this by the example of Leonard Woolf (1880-1969), the husband of Virginia, who wrote the magisterial six volumes of his life during his eighties long after her death in 1941. Superbly educated at Cambridge and thereafter, he achieved greatness as a writer, editor, senior advisor to the Labor Party on foreign affairs, and much else. He and his wife moved in the highest intellectual political and literary circles in Britain throughout his lifetime. Of course my life is insignificant by comparison but perhaps worth telling, as the reader will decide. An epigraph comes from his autobiography.

Except for the published decisions of the courts and agency boards of contract appeals as well as statutes and regulations which I discuss, almost everything else I write comes from fallible memory and searches on Google as I have kept no records of my life or work until 1992 when I first began with a computer.

I am publishing this through Amazon, to be available either digitally or as a paperback book at a reasonable price as the reader chooses. I welcome comments addressed to me as indicated below.

George Martin Coburn
1661 Crescent Place NW #208
Washington, DC 20009-4047
202-234-2054 (p&f)
george.tim.coburn@gmail.com
April 2012.

CONTENTS

PREFACE v

PART ONE: BEGINNINGS 2

   1. Forebears. 2

   2. Greenwich 1923-33 9

   3. Summers at Camp Kieve 1933,1934 and 1936 28

   4. New York 1933-36. 34

   5. Brooks School 1936-42. 42

   6. Life Away from Brooks 61

   7. Freshman at Harvard College 69

PART TWO: ARMY LIFE 1943-46 72

   1. USA 1943-44 72

   2. England, France, Germany 1944-45 84

PART THREE: COLLEGE AND LAW SCHOOL 1946-49 . . . 99

   1. Harvard College 1947-47 99

   2. Harvard Law School 1947-49 107

PART FOUR: NAVY PUBLIC CONTRACT
LAWYER 1949-62 122

1. Assistant Counsel, the Aviation Supply Office 1949-51 122

2. Assistant Counsel to the Bureau of Supplies &
   Accounts 1951-54 136

3. Attorney in the Office of the General Counsel Central Office
   1954-62 144

PART FIVE: PRIVATE LAW FIRM PRACTICE 1962-92 ... 174

1. Associate with Hensel, vom Baur & Heller 1962 174
   -Financing the Watergate Construction Project 174
   -Life Beyond the Office 176
   -The Departure of Struve Hensel 177

2. vom Baur, Beresford & Coburn 1963-66 178
   -Practice Before the Patent Office 178
   -Representing Bath Iron Works and Hiring Bill Simmons .. 181
   -The Western Electric Past Services Pension Case 183
   -Erroneous Government Testing and Condemnation of Mizokami's
   Colorado Spinach Crop 185
   -Clients in Chicago; Working with Alan Peterson
   of Arthur Andersen 187
   -Constructive Change Order Claims 188
   -The Impact of Robert McNamara on Navy Shipbuilding
   Claims 191
   -New Partners 192

3. vom Baur, Coburn, Simmons & Turtle 1967-79;
   Gage, Tucker & vom Baur 193
   -Building the Firm 193
   -Life Away from the Office 195
   -Birth of Federal Contracts Report 196
   -Early American Bar Association Activities;
   Birth of the Section of Public Contract Law 196
   -Visits to Barbados, Mexico and Hawaii 197
   -New Homes on Capitol Hill and Connecticut Avenue;
   Don's Business 199

-A Vacation Home near Berkeley Springs, West Virginia . . 201
-Bath Iron Works: The "Crash Astern" Test of a Destroyer
  for the West German Navy. 203
-The Todd $110 Million Shipbuilding Claim on the DE-1052
  Program 204
-Martha's Vineyard. 206
-An ABA Amicus Brief in the S&E Contractors Case in the
  Supreme Court 209
-The Lockheed Shipbuilding Claims and Deputy Secretary of
  Defense David Packard. 212
-The Lockheed Blue River Dam Litigation 221
-The ABA Annual Meeting in August 1971 and
  Travel in Europe 225
-Life in Seattle and Elsewhere 229
-Mother's Last Years. 232
-The Lockheed Icebreaker Pricing Litigation 234
-Teaching Law for Engineers 244
-Return to Key West 246
-Litigating Leasing the Hunter's Point Naval Shipyard 252
-Other Shipbuilding Claims: American Shipbuilding
  and Defoe Shipbuilding, Two Great Lakes Shipyards 254
-Developments at the vom Baur Firm 1977-84 256
-Saving an Iranian Student from Deportation. 258
-Departures from the Firm. 260
-ABA Public Contract Law Section Activities 1976-79 263
-The Anatomy of Unsuccessful Litigation for Ray
  Clairmont and the Logans of Bismarck, North Dakota 266
-McCarney Ford v. Ford Motor Company 276
-Life at 2101 Connecticut Avenue 1976-84 278
-A Project To Reform Government Debarment
  of Contractors. 280

4. Working at Sachs, Greenebaum &Taylor 1984-88 282
-Litigating the Protest of Maryland Shipbuilding & Drydock
  against a Navy Contract Award 284
-Overturning the Debarment of Two Officers of a Debarred
  Contractor 285
-Moving to 1661 Crescent Place in 1984 288

5. On to Ropes & Gray 1988-92 293
 -The General Electric Litigation. 294
 -Joining the National Security Industrial Association. 304
 -Final Years at Ropes & Gray 306

PART SIX: SOLO LAW PRACTICE 1992-2011 308

1. The Kiplinger-Bay Litigation: EPCO v. United States. 309

2. The Slingsby Aviation Litigation 313

3. Family and Friends 1992-2011 315
 -March 18, 1995: Sally Dies. 315
 -May 1995: Chych Waterston Dies 316
 -Bob Fulton at Ninety 317
 -Pat at Ninety 323
 -November 2, 2002: Pat Dies 324
 -Mike at 85 325
 -June 10, 2004: Mike Dies. 326
 -Bob Fulton at Ninety-Five 328
 -May 2004: Bob Fulton Dies 328
 -Selling the Key West House in 1999 330
 -Dick Cassedy and Chapin Leinbach. 330
 -Dick Howland 333
 -Robert Manson Myers. 334
 -Cappy Shannon. 336
 -January 3, 2005: Don Dies 340
 -Ode to Agnes 345
 -May 29, 2006: Robert Manson Myers at Eighty-Five 347
 -October 24, 2006: Dick Howland Dies. 352
 -April 2008: Rawn Harding Dies 355
 -Manson at Ninety. 356

4. Participation of the National Defense Industrial Association 360

5. Allocation of Costs in Government Contracts 363

6. Protecting Contractor Confidential Pricing Information 368

PART SEVEN: A SUMMING UP 374

   1. Some of the Principal Changes in My Lifetime 374

   2. Mostly About Me 390

CITATIONS 397

   Cases: Board of Contract Appeals and Court Decisions 397

   U.S. Constitution 400

   Statutes 400

   Executive Order 402

   Regulations 402

   Authors 403

MY SIXTY YEARS AS A PUBLIC CONTRACT LAWYER
The Enriching Life of George Martin Coburn
1923-2011

"I rarely think of my past or my future, but the moment one contemplates writing an autobiography... one is forced to regard oneself as an entity carried along for a brief period in the stream of time, emerging suddenly at a particular moment from darkness and nothingness and shortly to disappear at a particular moment into nothingness and darkness." Autobiography of Leonard Woolf (1880-1969), Vol. I, *Sowing (1880-1904)* at 1 (1960).

Throughout what follows I shall digress occasionally from a chronological sequence. I am persuaded what Leonard Woolf also wrote about this in the final volume of his autobiography:

"I digress deliberately. Life is not an orderly progression, self-contained like a musical scale or a quadratic equation. For the autobiographer to force his life and his memories of it into a strictly chronological straight line is to distort its shape and fake and falsify his memories. If one is to try to record one's life truthfully, one must aim at getting into the record of it something of the disorderly discontinuity which makes it so absurd, unpredictable, bearable." Autobiography of Leonard Woolf, Vol. V, *The Journey Not The Arrival Matters (1939-1969)* at 69 (1969).

Part One Beginnings 1923-42

1. Forebears.

My parents, Ralph George and Katherine Rawn Coburn, conceived me in April 1923. Perhaps they did this in celebration of their 16th Wedding Anniversary on April 6, 1907, and perhaps accidentally as Mother was then late in her 40th year and this would be her fifth child after an interval of almost 7 years since the birth of her fourth. In any event I arrived by Caesarean section, so Mother told me many years later, and according to my State of New York birth certificate #51320, a Dr. Harold Bailey at the Nursery and Children's Hospital, 161 W. 61st Street, New York, NY, delivered me on December 15, 1923. I was named George Martin Coburn for my paternal grandfather. He was born in Boston on September 22, 1846, the son of Jonas Coburn (born in Weston, MA, March 20, 1810) and Sarah Freeman Sampson Coburn (born in Duxbury, MA, March 1, 1813). The Coburns descend from Edward Coburn who came to Massachusetts from England in 1635. The name is probably Scandinavian suggesting that the Coburns, however the name was spelled, came to England with the Danish invasion that began in 835 and continued for several centuries as more Danes arrived and settled in Northumbria and Eastern England.[1]

---

1   *Genealogy of the Descendants of Edward Coburn*, by Silas R. Coburn and Published by Walter Coburn, Courier-Citizen Company Press, Lowell, MA 1913, at 1-6. For the Danish invasion, *see* Winston S. Churchill, *A History of the English Speaking Peoples*, Vol. One, *The Birth of Britain* at 97-103 (1956).

George Martin Coburn married Louise Gage on October 16, 1879. She was born on October 3, 1859, the daughter of Charles Otis and Charlotte Reed Gage of Arlington, a suburb of Boston. The Coburns lived comfortably in a town house on Marlboro Street in Boston. They had three children: Louise, July 2, 1880, Ralph George, February 23, 1882, and Dorothy, March 21, 1886. Louise Gage Coburn died of a stroke on October 14, 1905 and George Martin Coburn survived her until 1927. He did not go to college and eventually had a prospering shoe machinery manufacturing company until driven into bankruptcy by the predatory practices of the United Shoe Corporation in 1904, probably causing his wife's fatal stroke the next year.

Regrettably, we know too little about the Gage family. My father had a cousin with the biblical name of Vashtie Gage Thompson who lived in New York. She visited us in Greenwich and later in New York City as I dimly remember. Mother would speak of Grandmother Gage, my father's grandmother who long survived her daughter's death in 1905. Many years later, my law partner, Francis Trowbridge vom Baur, told me that as a boy he visited his Trowbridge grandparents in Arlington and their friends and neighbors next door were the Gage family.

Ralph Coburn grew up in Boston, and attended Noble & Greenough School then in Boston. His upbringing was strict and formal in his relationships with his parents and sisters with little demonstration of affection. He entered Harvard College in 1900 and graduated in 1904. He majored in history and would speak highly of President Charles Eliot and Dean Briggs. Ralph played guard on the varsity football team. A lasting disappointment was that he was ill on the day of the Yale game and thus did not get his "H". For each of his three sons he had a nursery prayer: "Grow up to be a good boy. Go to Harvard, play football and BEAT YALE !"

One of his classmates was Franklin Delano Roosevelt whom he knew with slight regard unlike his distant cousin and his wife's Uncle Theodore who was one of Ralph's heroes. Like many of his friends he later thought that as president FDR and his New Deal betrayed the cherished capitalist values of their class by deficit spending and excessive regulation of business.

The reality was that FDR preserved them against the growing threats of revolutionary uprisings from the hopeless despair of many millions whose lives were ruined by the prolonged Great Depression that began in 1929 when there was no governmental safety net such as we enjoy today. While the New Deal failed to overcome the Depression it nevertheless employed millions on public works projects, restored the banking system and gave the public hope. It was war production, however, beginning with the British and French munitions orders in 1939 and American rearmament following the fall of France in June 1940 and the massive deficit government procurement spending after Pearl Harbor until the end of the war in 1945, that finally put America back to work and ended the Depression. This is an unheeded lesson that remains relevant as I write this in 2011 to overcoming the deep recession that began in 2008.

Another of my father's Harvard classmates was George Upton. He asked Ralph Coburn to be one of his ushers for his wedding to Lorna Graydon in 1906 whom he had met at one of the seaside resorts on the north shore of Boston where the Graydons would spend their summers. The wedding was in Cincinnati early that summer. At the bridal dinner Ralph sat next to a Katherine Rawn, a friend of the bride and whose older sister Elizabeth was one of the bridesmaids. Ralph then lived in Pittsburgh and worked there as a superintendent for a glue manufacturing company. Following his father's bankruptcy in 1904 there was little family money and Ralph had to go to work.

Romance blossomed between Ralph and Katherine beginning at that bridal dinner. They married in Lake Forest, a suburb of Chicago, where her parents then lived, on April 6, 1907. His father-in-law, Ira Griffiths Rawn, got Ralph a job in a railroad passenger car lighting company in Des Moines, IA, and they lived there until he was transferred to the company's home office in New York about 1910 whereupon they moved to Greenwich, Connecticut.

In briefly recounting the lives of my maternal grandparents Ira Griffiths Rawn (1855-1910) and Florence Willis Rawn (1862-1944) and their forebears, I am mostly basing what follows on the privately published research of my cousin by marriage George C. Nickum and his son

George C. Nickum, Jr.[2] Ira Rawn was a fifth generation descendant of one of two German brothers, Conrath and Georg von Rahn, who as young men emigrated together from Hamburg to Coatesville, near Philadelphia, Pennsylvania in 1737. They anglicized their name to Rawn. Ira's father was Peter Rawn, 1815-1898. He married Sarah Houston (1818-1892), daughter of Anne Griffiths Houston, in 1844.They had four sons and a daughter, Ira being the youngest son. The family lived in Ohio.

I met the son of Ira's eldest brother Able Milizer Rawn (1845-1912), William Rawn (1910s-?) and his cousin Peter Rawn (1922-?), in Los Angeles and Seattle, respectively, in the 1970s when working in those cities in the course of my law practice. William's son, Bill Rawn, born in the early 1940s, my second cousin, a graduate of Yale and Harvard Law School in 1969, after practicing law for a few years, switched to architecture and based in Boston since the early 1980s has been recognized as one of the leading architects in the U. S., having designed the Ozawa Center for the Boston Symphony at Tanglewood, MA, among his many other landmark achievements, as the William Rawn & Associates website confirms.

My maternal grandfather Ira Rawn married Florence Willis (1862-1944) in 1879 in Delaware, Ohio. They had three daughters, Sarah Elizabeth (1879-1958), my Mother Katherine (1884-1974), and Florence (1886-1944). Ira began at 16 as a telegrapher for an Ohio-Indiana railroad rising to superintendent some 15 years later. From 1887 to 1903 he worked for the Baltimore & Ohio in various positions of increasing responsibility in Cincinnati until he was selected in 1903 to be the General Superintendent of the Illinois Central Railroad. He was promoted to be Vice President of Operations in 1907 requiring the family to move

---

2   *The Rawn-Nickum Genealogy* by George C. Nickum (June 21, 1982); *Ira G. Rawn Death by Gunshot in Chicago* by George C. Nickum, Jr., published in a Nickum family newsletter *Children's Hour* (January 1994). George Nickum (1910-1990s?) was the leading naval architect in Seattle and had a distinguished career. In 1937 he married my cousin Elizabeth Rawn Brinkley ((1912-66), the daughter of my mother's older sister Elizabeth. They had 5 children, 3 daughters and 2 sons. His son George Jr.(1945-) and called "Nick" and his wife Margaret ("Peg") live on Bainbridge Island on Eliott Bay, a short ferry ride west of Seattle and he practices law there.

to Chicago. The Illinois Central was then a major railroad with some 40,000 employees and 4,500 miles of track.

Surprisingly, in November 1909, he resigned this important position to accept the lesser one of the presidency of the Chicago, Indianapolis and Louisville Railroad, also known as the Monon RR, and primarily a freight carrier. He shot himself at the family rented summer home in Winnetka, a Chicago suburb on Lake Michigan, in the early hours of July 21, 1910, whether accidentally or deliberately will never be known.

In the Spring of 1910 attorneys for the Illinois Central had sued three firms repairing the railroad's cars, alleging fraud and kickbacks to Illinois Central officials who contracted for the repair work and who also held stock in these firms. As the vice president for operations Ira Rawn was responsible for contracting out this work. At the trial he denied knowledge of the fraud and testified that he had no stock in the repair firms and knew of no Illinois Central official who did. His further testimony was scheduled for July 26.

On the evening of July 20 he dined with his wife and all three of his married daughters and their husbands.[3] My parents and their two children as well as Florence and David Bigelow were staying in the house. About 1:30 the next morning Ira and Florence Rawn were awakened by noises downstairs similar to ones they had heard before late at night. Rejecting

---

3   Mother's older sister Elizabeth Rawn married Robert Campbell Brinkley (1887-1935) of Memphis on November 30, 1907. They moved to Seattle in 1909 where he founded the Webster-Brinkley Co., a manufacturer of conveyor equipment for the timber, pulp and paper industry in the Pacific Northwest. They had three children: Rawn Brinkley (1909-73), Elizabeth Brinkley Nickum (1912-66), and Robert C. Brinkey, Jr. (1913-67). Mother's younger sister, Florence Rawn, known as "Shonny" or "Aunt Shonce", first married David Bigelow before 1910 who died of a brain tumor several years later. They had no children. In 1927, after several years of running a successful interior design business in New York, she married Francis Goodwin Smith, a widower with 3 young sons and a daughter, all of whom like their mother succumbed to cancer in middle age. He was president of the Hartford Empire Company, primarily a holder of patents of glass manufacturing machinery. They lived in West Hartford and I visited them occasionally from Greenwich and New York. I believe Uncle Goodwin died in the 1960s after marrying Dorothy Carpenter, a New York widow and the mother of Tim Carpenter, a Brooks School friend of mine who died in January 2011.

his wife's pleas to remain in their bedroom, he took his loaded pistol and went downstairs. Shortly thereafter she and Ralph Coburn heard noises and at least one gunshot and both went downstairs. He turned on the light and they found Ira Rawn lying on his back with a bullet wound through his chest and bleeding, struggling to turn over and speak. He could not and died a few minutes later before the summoned doctor could arrive. Ralph Coburn told an inquiring reporter from the *Chicago Tribune* that he had heard two shots and that Ira Rawn was murdered by a burglar attempting a robbery as evidenced by the open door into the front porch, all of which made front-page headlines that also noted other burglaries in that neighborhood and the need for more police protection.

The next day the paper reported that the police concluded that Ira Rawn had committed suicide since he was killed from the bullet in his own gun at very close range and no other bullet was found and citing his scheduled further testimony in the ongoing suit. The family totally rejected this conclusion based on their knowledge of him and his character and their certain belief that he was innocent of any fraud against the Illinois Central.

A week later a coroner's jury of 6 persons was impaneled in Winnetka as required by Illinois law to investigate and render a verdict as to the cause of death. Some 30 witnesses testified including the family members and the Chief of Police who testified that the cause of death was either suicide or accidental. He rejected the burglary-murder testimony of Ralph Coburn as there was no evidence of a second shot or bullet. The jury also rejected the burglary-murder testimony and rendered a verdict that Ira Rawn's death was "caused by a bullet from his own revolver fired by his own hand, but whether this was accidental or with suicidal intent this jury is unable to determine, except that the location of the wound and the type of revolver render the accident theory less probable."

Not counting about $131,000 in life insurance, the inventory of assets filed in the probate of Ira Rawn's estate showed assets of about $125,000, principally stock in 32 companies and minimal liabilities. Significantly, the Illinois Central never asserted a claim against the estate or the life insurance proceeds to recover any of its estimated $1.5M loss from the railroad car repair scam. My cousin Nick Nickum, an attorney who has carefully investigated this matter in a far more detailed account on which the foregoing is based, concluded that his great grandfather did not commit suicide, and that he accidentally shot himself while slipping as he went downstairs in the darkness to investigate the noise. I agree with this conclusion.

It also is noteworthy that my father's older sister, Louise Coburn, as she neared the end of her life in the 1960s, told me that her brother Ralph many years before had sworn her to secrecy that he arranged the scenery to make it look like a burglary murder and that he had perjured himself in so testifying to the coroner's jury in order to save his mother-in-law's recovery of the life insurance which would not have been paid had there been a verdict of suicide. My father probably had no personal knowledge as to the cause of death and however we may regard his actions they do not undermine the foregoing conclusion that Ira Rawn's death was more likely accidental than suicidal.

My maternal grandmother Florence Willis, born in Delaware, Ohio, September 9, 1862, was the daughter of Cynthia Elizabeth Crandall (1838-1893 born in Lebanon, CT) and William Warren Willis (1832-1908 born in Groton, CT.). Her parents married in 1852 and apparently lived their married life in Ohio, each dying in Cincinnati. The Crandalls trace their ancestry to a Bryan Pendelton born in Birmingham, England, in 1619 who arrived in Massachusetts by 1636 and his progeny who mostly settled in Stonington, CT. Florence Willis Rawn and Ira Rawn are buried in the cemetery in Mystic, CT, near the graves of her parents. I have no information about the life of William Willis or his forebears. Florence Willis had a younger brother, Harry, whom I remember meeting in my childhood.

There is importantly an unmistakable Cherokee connection in the Crandall-Willis and/or Rawn genes. This is evidenced by the beautiful Cherokee aquiline shape of the noses of Florence Willis Rawn, her daughters, my sisters, and the daughters of my sister Louise. The family gossip traces this to a Cherokee squaw who gave birth to a daughter said to have been fathered by the young Sam Houston in Tennessee in the 1820s or earlier. We may never know if and how this baby girl grew up to become a Crandall or a Willis or a Rawn. My Mother and Grandmother never discussed this with me or my siblings so far as I know as they would have regarded this connection as scandalous. It is also possible that Sarah Houston, who was born in 1818 and married Peter Rawn in 1844, is the daughter of the Cherokee squaw allegedly fathered by Sam Houston as well as the mother of Ira Rawn. If Florence Rawn also had the Cherokee nose that my mother and sisters had which she supposedly did, that would eliminate Sarah Houston as the Cherokee connection or as the sole connection. I relish this as it importantly establishes a part of our origin as Native American.

2. Greenwich 1923-33.

My parents moved to Greenwich, Connecticut, about 1910 and a year or two later purchased a spacious three-storey house and five-car garage on about an acre at 329 Lake Avenue, four or five miles north of the village and then very much in the country. The driveway to the house and to the large garage in back of the house was from Woodside Road a dirt road perpendicular to Lake Avenue and going east in wooded, hilly countryside for several miles. The place had lovely tall elm and maple and other trees along Lake Avenue and elsewhere. This was to be my home for almost my first ten years.

I had four siblings: Louise, born in Chicago July 14, 1908; Ralph George, Jr., born in Chicago October 11, 1909; Florence Rawn, born in Greenwich September 24, 1912; and John, born in Greenwich April 8, 1917. My father, whom we were brought up to call "Papa" as he had called his father, nicknamed all his children: Louise was "Slippery

Slim"; Ralph George, Jr. became "Pat" because he was Christened on St. Patrick's Day; Florence Rawn "Sally Toad" because she hopped about; John, "Mr. Mike" because of "Pat"; George Martin, "Timothy Tim" to follow "Pat" and "Mike". With the exception of Louise's, all these nicknames lasted for our lifetimes, and we were known as Pat, Sally, Mike, and Tim instead of our given names which we used primarily in signing documents. Few know me as George Coburn.

In 1911 my parents travelled to Broadway, England, to furnish the house. They acquired some lovely pieces, some of which I have. Mine include two lovely oval carved china lamps with pedestals, four antique tables of different sizes, a large antique gate-leg folding dining table, a 16th century joint stool, and two bedroom bureaus.

We were blessed with neighbors who became friends. South on Lake Avenue were the Reginald Coombs whose children were much younger. Next to them were Dorothy and Harold Baker. Their children grew up with some of my siblings, and much later I knew Harold who grew to at least 6' 5" at Brooks School where he was about three years ahead of me. Above us on Lake Avenue adjoining Woodside Road that also abutted our property were the Alfred Fergusons whose children also grew up with my older siblings.

My siblings were so much older than I that it would be many years before I knew them. Louise and Pat were then away at boarding schools: Louise at Miss Porter's in Farmington, CT, until graduating in 1927 and Pat at Groton School in Groton, MA, graduating in 1929. Sally was at Rosemary Hall in Greenwich until going to Farmington in 1926 and graduating in 1930. Mike was at Greenwich Country Day School and then at the Shaw School until he went away to Brooks School in North Andover, MA, in 1930 as a second former until graduating in 1935.

By the time I arrived Papa was a vice president of the Post Cereal Company with offices at 250 Park Avenue in New York. The company was founded by C. C. Post in Battle Creek, Michigan, in the late 19th Century. Mr. Post had been employed by the Kellogg cereal company from which he resigned to form his own company for the manufacture and sale initially of "Grape-Nuts" which he created followed by "Post Toasties" and the beverage "Postum". My parents knew his daughter Marjory Post socially in Greenwich when she was married to her first husband Edward Close. They also were friends with Colby ("Clair") Chester, president of the Post Cereal Co., and his wife Jesse Chester. These contacts led to Papa's being asked after World War I to join the company.

Marjory Post Close's two daughters Adelaide and Eleanor were friends of my sister Louise. Marjorie Post later divorced Edward Close and married Edward F. Hutton who had the E.F. Hutton stock brokerage firm in New York. She made him chairman of the Post Cereal Co. They had a daughter Edwina who was about my age and for a time was a childhood playmate. She later became prominent as the actress Dina Merrill. I remember visiting Mrs. Post with my parents at her grand ocean villa in Palm Beach in 1931 or 1932 when she was married to Ned Hutton and also going aboard her large, magnificent yacht, "The Hussar" with its gold fixtures in her bathroom. Some 20 years later while visiting Louise in Palm Beach Mrs. Post invited us aboard "The Sea Cloud"[4] as she renamed the ship was after divorcing Ned Hutton in 1935.

Over the next several years Papa was instrumental in transforming the Post Cereal Company into the General Foods Corporation. He did this by persuading Marjory Post and Ned Hutton, and president Colby Chester to acquire a family of disparate food product lines; and he was put in charge of accomplishing these acquisitions. They included, among others, Baker's Chocolates, Jello, Log Cabin Maple Syrup, Maxwell House

---

4   As explained in The Sea Cloud's website, Ned Hutton ordered the ship built in 1931 for his wife by the Krupp shipyard in Kiel, Germany. The New York firm of Gibbs and Cox of New York were the naval architects. It was then the largest 4-masted barque sailing yacht ever built: length 360', beam 50', displacement 2,500 tons; diesel engines max. speed 10 knots; cruising range 10,000 nautical miles. It reeked with luxury and required a large crew. Having divorced Ned Hutton in 1935, later in December of that year Marjorie Post married Joseph E. Davies whom FDR named Ambassador to the USSR early in 1937. For the two years he was Ambassador, The Sea Cloud was based in Lenningrad and he and she entertained the Soviet leaders on board. During World War II, the ship became a weather station for the Coast Guard. After the war Mrs. Post had restored it at great expense by 1950. She sold it in 1955 to the Dominican Republic Dictator Trujillo. Much later it became a cruise ship available for private charter and so it remains.

and Sanka[5] Coffee, and Swans Down Flour. In the early 1930s Papa met Clarence Birdseye of Gloucester, MA, who had developed a process for freezing fish. Papa encouraged him to do this with peas. About a year later he succeeded whereupon General Foods acquired his invention and began to market "Birdseye Frozen Peas". This became a huge success and led to other frozen vegetables as it coincided with the advent of electric refrigerators as home appliances. Papa became an executive vice-president of General Foods and was likely to succeed Claire Chester as its next president. He would be impeccably attired for work: a hand-made Dunne suit, white shirt, stiff collar and silk necktie, highly polished English leather black or brown laced shoes, overcoat and fedora or bowler. He spoke with a proper Bostonian accent.

During these Greenwich years Papa's annual earnings exceeded $100,000. We lived very comfortably. We were well served by Idine the superb Swedish cook, by Martha the meticulous German parlor maid, by Cecille the tidy French chamber maid, by Antoinette, the caring Polish laundress, and by Alec the East European chauffeur and gardener who later married Antoinette. Except for Alec, they all lived on the third floor of the house, and he and later he and Antoinette lived in the apartment above the garage.

Early in 1924 Mother through an employment agency in New York engaged Bertha Drews as my nurse. She had emigrated from Berlin after WW I and had relatives in Wilkes-Barre, PA. She was to be my nurse until April 1932 when she moved to Long Island to take care of my sister Louise's first child, Florence Rawn Harding. Bertha, whom I called "Baba", was a surrogate mother to me, and I adored her. She was probably then in her 40s, tall and thin, dressed in black and wore a pince-nez and her dark hair tied in a bun. I suspect she had anglicized her name from "Druse" to "Drews". She was entirely in charge of my upbringing. Combining her own strict Lutheran code of deportment for her "Georgie" with a loving sensitivity, she insisted on my conforming to her upright standards. Mother, prejudiced against the Germans by World War I,

---

5   Mother takes some credit for naming this product. When Papa explained that one of the Maxwell House coffees was made without caffeine, she replied, "Ah, sans kaffeine". Hence "Sanka".

foolishly ordained that Bertha not teach me German. Bertha fortunately interpreted that not to exclude her saying her prayers and singing her songs to me "auf Deutsch". Not surprisingly, I knew the Lord's Prayer in German before I did in English. Her doing this was to benefit me greatly in World War II as we shall see.

In the early, formative years, Baba was the center of my life, far more so than my parents or siblings. Except for Sunday lunch later on, Baba and I ate our meals in the nursery, apart from the rest of the family who happened to be home. For breakfast from an early age Baba served me Grape-Nuts which she softened in hot water until my teeth could chew them. Pancakes and maple syrup became a Sunday breakfast treat. When home, Mother, like the English, had tea served later in the afternoon to which Baba and I were summoned and at which I soon had a taste for Idine's cucumber sandwiches and cookies.

Sunday lunch, to which I was admitted starting when I was about five, was very special and English: roast beef, Yorkshire Pudding, fresh vegetables and baked potatoes in season from the garden and local market, popovers, and vanilla ice cream with butterscotch or chocolate sauce. As I grew older I would help churn the ice cream. At the dining table Papa insisted that all his children sit up very straight, eat all the food before them, and for the younger ones speak only when spoken to by him or Mother or other grown up. Disobedience meant being sent to one's room at once. Also he would not allow any of his children to be interrupted by a telephone call during a family meal in the dining room. Nor would he tolerate prolonged talking on the telephone by his children when he was home.

At bedtime Mother would often read to me and Baba would put me to bed with her prayers and on occasion Papa would say them too. Papa was a strict disciplinarian, and I recall his spanking me a few times for what I thought were trivial instances of disobedience. The result was that I became mostly afraid of him, there being little demonstration of affection by him to me or to my siblings.

Among my earliest memories is that of Mother practicing in the mornings for her weekly piano lesson with Mr. Squire. In the living room we had a baby grand, perhaps a Chickering or Weber but definitely not a Steinway, to which the tuner periodically was summoned. In her youth Mother had become quite an accomplished violinist having begun at an early age. She had a very good ear and nimble fingers. At age 16 she performed the slow movement of the Mendelssohn E minor violin concerto at a student concert of the Cincinnati Symphony Orchestra. Her mother then put her foot down and said "Katherine, you are giving up the violin and coming out in Society." Mother dutifully obeyed. Had she not, one might not be reading this.

Indeed, she foreswore playing a musical instrument until after I was born when she decided to study the piano with the weekly help of Mr. Squire. Papa provided no encouragement, had no interest in music and was tone deaf. This sadly was also true of my brothers but not Louise and Sally who were musically gifted and played the piano quite well. Later, thanks to Mother's piano playing, I developed a great, lasting love for classical music.

Mother's tastes were for the 19th century romantic composers Brahms, Chopin, Liszt and Schumann, many pieces of whom she loved and practiced daily for Mr. Squire's weekly lesson. He seemed pleased with her progress. When I hear any of them now I am reminded how well she played, suffused with a warm glow of happy remembrance.

Mother also loved opera, particularly some of Gounod, Massenet, and Puccini, and would often go in town for a matinee at the Metropolitan Opera or an afternoon concert of the Philharmonic under Toscanini as well and which we later listened to on the Sunday afternoon broadcasts. When Flagstadt sang Isolde Mother was enthralled as she was with many other great voices.

Starting in 1931, listening to the broadcasts of the Metropolitan Opera Saturday afternoons, so informatively announced for many years by Milton Cross, for her, me and Baba was wonderful despite the primitive sound quality then of the transmission and the radio speakers. About that time we received a large electric phonograph to play her 78 rpm 12" records of opera arias by Caruso. Gigli, Ponselle, and other leading

Metropolitan Opera artists. This further awakened my interest in opera. Her favorite tenor was Richard Crooks.

I also began my own late afternoon half-hour radio programs with Bobby Benson, Jack Armstrong, Buck Rogers and the Lone Ranger which also featured Rossini's great overture to *William Tell*, which well captures the sound of a galloping horse, and is for me one of the great opera overtures.

My reading during the Greenwich years progressed from the adventures of *The Hardy Boys, Tom Swift, and Ted Scott* to *Little Lord Fauntleroy* by Frances Burnett to the entrancing *Story of Dr. Doolittle* by Hugh Lofting with its marvelous menagerie of animals: Jup the dog, Polynesia the parrot, and the indescribable "PushMePullYou" and also featuring Mathew Mugg leaving his mark in jail; to *Winnie the Pooh* and *Alice in Wonderland, Gulliver's Travels, Robinson Crusoe*; and to the incomparable Kipling *The Jungle Books* and Jules Verne's *Twenty Thousand Leagues under the Sea* and *The Mysterious Island*, among the ones I now remember. Papa was a great admirer of Kipling and brought me *Kim* as well. I recently learned that Kipling spent several years in Vermont, there writing *The Jungle Books* among others.

Lindbergh's solo transatlantic flight to Paris in May 1927 is among my earliest memories of the outside world. A year later I had a tricycle of his plane the "Spirit of St Louis" without the wings as my favorite possession. Baba was teaching me to read "Peter Rabbit" and other stories and before my bedtime she read from Grimm's "Fairy Tales".

In September 1928 I began kindergarten at Rosemary Hall, a short distance from my house. Another boy, Dick Reilly, and I were in a class of about 10 girls. What we learned or did or who our teachers were for the two years I was there made no impression that I can recall beyond the sense of being outnumbered and perhaps outclassed by the girls none of whom I remember.

In September 1930 I was enrolled in the first grade at the Greenwich Country Day School which brother Mike had previously attended. This was a new school founded in 1926 by a near neighbor and friend of Mother's, Dorothy Baker, on beautiful spacious grounds in the countryside on Old Church Road, several miles from home. Alec would drive me there and back in the large maroon LaSalle sedan. I found several playmates in my class, among them "Poppy" (George Herbert Walker) Bush, David Close, Billy Gray, Sedgy Howard, and Ivan Ingalls, all their parents being friends of my parents and whose homes I often visited and they mine. Except for George Bush, I never saw any of them after we moved to New York in September 1933. I remained at this school through the third grade. Under the headmastership of John Minor, the teaching of the fundamentals of arithmetic, and reading and writing English was, as I recall, excellent. I was introduced to games and team play, football, soccer and hockey and our jerseys displayed the orange and black school colors. My brother Mike attended the School's 75th Anniversary in September 2001, about the time of "9/11". The School had invited its most distinguished alumnus, former President Bush, but he was not able to come and instead sent a gracious message.

Also in 1930 I had my tonsils removed in the Greenwich hospital, I believe by my pediatrician, Dr. Knapp. The ether then used as the anesthetic made me nauseous beyond the operation and the throat soreness persisted it seemed for many days. My only next hospital encounter, luckily, was not for about another 65 years when in the later 1990s I had to have a double hernia repaired from having foolishly struggled to lift an elderly friend into his hospital bed.

As I grew older the celebration of Christmas also waxed in importance for me. For three or four evenings before each Christmas eve, Papa would read aloud Dickens' *Christmas Carol* masterpiece to the family. After a Christmas eve service at Christ Church where we would listen to the story of The Nativity and sing the traditional carols, we would hang our Christmas stockings on the living room mantel for Santa Claus to fill during the night after descending the chimney from his reindeer-pulled sleigh. Mother and Papa would stuff them after everyone else had gone to bed, and Papa would add $10 and $20 gold pieces (this being before FDR took the country off the gold standard in 1933 and recalled all gold coins).

Occasionally we would have a white Christmas. Christmas morning we would open our stockings and then have a family breakfast, prolonging the suspense of opening the presents and heightening our anticipation. One year I had the great joy of receiving a Lionel electric train from FAO Schwartz which I had previously rapturously visited. Mike and I promptly set it up in the large third-floor playroom: tracks, tunnels, switches, signals, passenger and freight trains with steam locomotives, and transformers to control operations. This was to provide lasting pleasure and taught me something about the railroads.

I remember two weddings during these years. First, that of Alec to Antoinette. It was in a Greek Orthodox Church. We all held lighted candles for an interminable service. Sally began to laugh hysterically and trying to suppress it spilled candle grease on Papa's necktie. He was not amused. The bride and groom then lived in an attractive apartment above the garage until we moved to New York. Mother then arranged for them to work for and live in Greenwich with her friends Dorothy Walker Bush and Prescott Bush, the parents of my friend Poppy Bush. By then Antoinette had a daughter Marsella and soon Alec Jr.

I later learned from Sally that the Bushes paid for the college education of these children and that Antoinette remained as the personal maid and companion of Dorothy Bush for at least the next 50 years. Sally and Dottie Bush were lifelong friends and tennis partners. Sally attended her funeral at Christ Church in November 1992. She had died shortly after her son lost his reelection as president to Bill Clinton. President Bush spoke to Sally after the service: "Sally, we go back a long way."

In June 1931 my sister Louise, almost 23, married a young architect Henry Knowles Harding of Dedham, Massachusetts, called "Mooney" because of a roundish face. His parents, Charles Lewis Harding and Harriet Knowles Harding, had great textile-based wealth with lavish places in Dedham, Long Island, Maine, and Palm Beach. Mooney, the second of four sons, had graduated from Princeton in 1929 and started with an architectural firm in New York. They would live on Long Island.

The marriage ceremony was at the beautiful Episcopal church, Christ Church, in Greenwich followed by a lavish reception at the Round Hill Club. At age 6 I attended both events mostly impressed by the attractive boxes of wedding cakes at the reception. Mother regularly went to this church on Sundays as did I for Sunday School. Papa was brought up a Unitarian who after leaving Boston did not, so far as I know, attend Unitarian services. He would occasionally accompany Mother to the Sunday services at Christ Church and later Emanuel Church in New York.

Notwithstanding that Louise's wedding was during the depth of the 1929 Great Depression, that was not evident from the mass of costly wedding presents received at the house, necessitating the employment of a detective to guard them, nor from the scale of the wedding and the reception. On a beautiful summer day, the day before her wedding, my parents and siblings sat on terrace chairs in the garden for a family photograph. I was in the middle in front on the lawn with our black Cocker Spaniel, "Henry Topping" (Mrs. Topping having given him to Mother to replace the deceased white Terrier, "Billy," given us years before by the second Mrs. Close). (We never had cats as Mother was terrified by them.) My father wore a suit and tie, Pat his Groton blazer and tie, Mother and my sisters in summer dresses, and Mike a jacket, sports shirt and white duck trousers, and I short trousers and a sports shirt. The picture was framed and turned out very well.

During these summers Baba and I would visit Aunt Louise Coburn at her summer place in South Duxbury, near Plymouth, Massachusetts. It was called "Three Trees" after the elms that once stood in front. When her mother died of a stroke in her early 40s in 1905, her father and my grandfather, George Martin Coburn, said "Louise, you will now look after me." She did, and he lived until 1927 when she was in her late 40s. That cruelty condemned her to spinsterhood. They lived in an apartment in Jamaica Plain (near Boston) with summers in Duxbury.

The Duxbury property of some 40 acres had belonged to Martin Sampson who had built a two storey shingled Cape-Cod style house in the early 1800s, 3 or 4 miles inland from Plymouth Bay. His daughter Sarah Freeman, born in Duxbury in 1813, married my great grandfather

Jonas Coburn in the 1830s. Ownership of the property passed to them on the death of Martin Sampson, and one of their sons, George Martin Coburn, inherited the place from them. His three children, in turn, owned it equally. Papa and his sisters loved the place. Mother did not. My siblings and I and Aunt Dorothy (rarely her husband. my Uncle Sidney) and her daughters Dorothy ("Bunny") and Olivia ("Bugsie") Stone would visit Aunt Louise there over the many summers of our youths. The house had only two bedrooms and one bathroom above the kitchen. There were also two or three small bedrooms in the basement for servants. There was also a bedroom upstairs in the barn.

Aunt Louise, as I came to know and love her, was a very proper, old-fashioned Bostonian. Like Baba, mostly dressed in black, wearing a pince-nez and her black hair tied in a bun, she devoted her life to charitable causes in Boston and Duxbury. For many years she was president of the Fragment Society in Boston which collected clothing for the poor. Although strict and strait-laced, she had a generous, loving manner and was devoted to her seven nieces and nephews. For her there was "no such word as can't". John and Irene Cassidy looked after her in Duxbury. They lived in a cottage on the place, and John was the chauffeur of her vintage Chevrolets that in winter were placed on blocks in nearby Freeman's Garage.

Baba and I would stay in the little house on the place across the street from the main house and known as "the Weaver's Cottage" built in the 1630s. We had kerosene lamps and candles as well as a hand pump in the kitchen that she and I would prime by drawing water from the frog-filled nearby pond covered with lily pads. There was no bathroom. The stairs to the two tiny, low-ceiling bedrooms were vertical and narrow, and on sultry nights we longed for electric fans.

Some years later Aunt Louise sold this property and I would then stay in one of the upstairs bedrooms in the main house. Aunt Louise had the other one. During these later visits I grew especially fond of my cousin Bugsie Stone who two or three years my elder would also be visiting Aunt Louise. She later married Stacy Holmes, an executive at Filene's department store in Boston. Their daughter, the Rev. Olivia Holmes, a

Unitarian-Universal Church clergywoman, became and remains a close family friend. Many years later she presided beautifully at the second marriage of my nephew Lawrie Coburn (the second son of my brother Mike and his wife Joan) and at the funerals of my siblings Pat, Sally and Mike, and my brother-in-law Bob Fulton.

Aunt Louise had an old sailboat with a bay-bird rigging that she kept at the Duxbury Yacht Club. She was a competent sailor and loved sailing as did Papa and took me and any visiting Stone cousins on frequent sails in scenic Plymouth Bay. She taught me to sail close to and before the wind, to come about and to avoid jibing, and I came to love sailing that I would enjoy again in later summers in Wareham. In her Duxbury house there was a small room of sailing pennants and trophies form earlier sailing races.

She also took Baba and me on picnics to the Duxbury beach which was across an old wobbly wooden bridge. It was a lovely, wide beach on Plymouth Bay and she taught me to swim. There was little surf, although at times jelly fish to avoid. Baba did not swim or wear a bathing suit; and Aunt Louise's almost fully clothed her. On the way back to her house we would usually stop for cookies at her friend Miss Suzy Seaver. She had a lovely place on the water and her cook made mouth-melting cookies.

At Aunt Louise's we would play croquet. My brother Pat accused Grandfather Coburn of having cheated him, and would not speak well of him again. She also had an old-fashioned mounted jouncing board for jumping exercise as well as an old large see-saw or "tilt". There was also the daily ritual of raising and lowering the Stars and Stripes at the tall flagpole which I would perform when visiting. My parents and siblings always stayed in the barn which once housed cows and hay. It had a large upstairs bedroom with large windows and cooling winds. For Sunday suppers Aunt Louise would invariably serve Boston baked beans and brown bread which I slowly came to like. It was usually capped by her incomparable home-made fudge, the recipe for which did not survive her.

The Old Colony Railroad bordered the property, and the South Duxbury station was very near her driveway. There were about two trains each weekday, to and from the South Station in Boston. The sounds of the steam engines and their whistles became ingrained. One day Aunt Louise persuaded the locomotive engineer to let me ride with him to the next stop, Taunton, on the morning train to Boston. I must have been seven or eight and was thrilled watching him control the steam and the fireman stoke the furnace with coal. She met me at the Taunton station. This for me was a once in a lifetime experience from a vanished era from dear, dear Aunt Louise.

After the summer of 1932 my visits to Duxbury lessened: the 1933, 1934 and 1936 summers were at Camp Kieve in Nobleboro, Maine; 1935 with Louise in Palm Beach; 1937-1939 with Mother and siblings in Wareham, Mass.; 1940 with Mother in Seattle visiting her mother and sister; 1941 with Mother in Biddeford Pool, Maine; and 1942 at Harvard College. Over these years starting in 1937 I would see Aunt Louise mostly in Boston instead. During World War II, after the attack on Pearl Harbor, Aunt Louise served as a "gray lady" attending to the war wounded at one of the Boston hospitals and at the Plymouth hospital during the summer months.

After some 80 summers in Duxbury, Aunt Louise then in her 80s in the 1960s and increasingly infirm and arthritic could no longer live in Duxbury and repaired to a nursing home in Boston where she died a few years later. The family then sold the property, and it was a sad good-bye to years of happy memories of staying with her. There she was a pillar of the small community and to her many friends and several generations she was "Miss Duxbury". She, my parents, and my sisters are buried there in the family plot in the beautiful Mayflower Cemetery.

I would also from Greenwich and much later from Boston visit Papa's younger sister Aunt Dorothy and her husband James Sidney Stone, the parents of Bunny and Bugsie whom I first knew visiting Aunt Louise. Aunt Dorothy and Uncle Sidney lived in an old, charming farmhouse on a beautiful place in Wayland, some 25 miles west of Boston. I enjoyed their company. She was a gifted horticulturist and cultivated magnificent flower gardens. Their daughter Bugsie became a champion figure skater in Boston.

Uncle Sidney graduated from Harvard College in 1903 and from Harvard Law School in 1906. At the law school he was the president (then called "secretary") of the *Harvard Law Review*, as almost a century later was Barack Obama. After graduation Uncle Sidney joined the Boston law office of Louis Brandeis and remained there until President Wilson appointed Brandeis to the Supreme Court in 1916. He then established his own office in Boston for the practice of trust and estate law which he continued well into his 90s, commuting daily by train, and long after Aunt Dorothy's death. When I was at Harvard Law School in 1947-49 Uncle Sidney kindly and generously asked me to join his firm but my sights were then set on employment as a lawyer with the federal government.

During the Greenwich years Baba and I, and after 1932 until I went into the Army in February 1943, would periodically visit Mother's younger sister Florence ("Aunt Shonce") who in 1927 married Francis Goodwin Smith, a widower, becoming the stepmother to his three sons ages 12-16 and a daughter age 9. They had a lovely brick home on dead–end Northmoor Road off Albany Avenue and opposite a golf club in West Hartford. Uncle Goodwin came from old Hartford roots. His mother was a Goodwin and her mother and J.P. Morgan's mother were sisters, and Morgan himself grew up in Hartford. For several years Aunt Shonce's mother and my maternal grandmother, whom we called "Nana", lived in an adjoining house on Northmoor Road. When visiting the Smiths I would also often see Nana too. One April Fools' Day, the Smith boys detoured the night traffic from Albany Ave. into Northmoor Road creating pandemonium and anger of the fooled drivers who drove over the golf course fairways and greens trying to escape.

I became fond of all the Smiths. Aunt Shonce and Uncle Goodwin were affectionate and generous to me as were the Smith children, Robinson, Francis Jr., David, and Eleanor (called "Nuffie") who were closer to my siblings' ages than to mine. Later, in the 1960's when living in Washington, I would occasionally have lunch with Francis, Jr., ("Franny") at a downtown restaurant. He was a journalist with a Washington periodical. At college before World War II, he was the editor of *The Daily Princetonian* and after graduating became a writer for the left wing, short-lived newspaper *PM* started by Marshall Field. Despite a distinguished Army record during the war as a top aide to General Courtney Hodges commanding the First American Army in the invasion of Nazi-occupied France and of Germany itself, the CIA succumbing to the prevailing anti-Communist hysteria outrageously rejected his employment application because of the *PM* taint. He never fully recovered from this calumny that blighted his professional future. He died prematurely from cancer as did his father and siblings.

His sister Nuffie later married Hank Griffith and lived in Concord, MA. My brother Mike and his wife Joan living in Needham would see them occasionally until she too died prematurely from cancer. Franny's older brother, Robinson Smith, achieved renown as a producer and director of two or three plays on Broadway before World War II, notably *Richard II* staring Maurice Evans. After the war, my future partner Don Ellington met Robinson and his wife, the actress Betty Jencks, who lived and had a gift shop in St. Thomas, VI, when he would visit there for several years before I met him in 1959 until Robinson too died of cancer.

I continued to visit Aunt Shonce and Uncle Goodwin until I went into the Army in February 1943. Later that year the Supreme Court decided in a patent case that Uncle Goodwin's company, the Hartford Empire Company, with its monopoly of glass manufacturing machinery patents, violated the anti-trust laws and ordered divestiture. A few months later Aunt Shonce had a fatal stroke and early in 1944 Nana also died. Had that sequence been the other way round, Nana's surviving and then impecunious two daughters would each have received half of her estate instead of the one third which went to Uncle Goodwin who was independently well off.

Through the summer of 1933 my parents led an active social life in Greenwich over many years. Both were keen bridge players and bridge dinner parties at our or friends' houses were frequent, even during the week. My parents always dressed in evening clothes for dinner, even when they were alone. They gave my sisters lavish coming-out parties in New York hotels when they were 18, Louise's in 1926 at the Barclay and Sally's in 1930 at the Elysee. Neither sadly went to college as few of their contemporaries then did. Thereafter until they married each had a very full social life preoccupied with many attentive beaus. One of Louise's, Lyttleton Fox who later became a close friend, many years later told me when courting Louise and they were seated on a sofa in the living room, I hiding beneath was heard to say, "When are you going to kiss her?"

Yet during these years and thereafter Louise and Sally had a difficult relationship with each other. They were sibling opposites in looks, personalities and interests. Each was beautiful and bright in different ways: Louise, brunette, brown eyes, a graceful figure, above average height, good at games, a quiet come-hither personality, orderly intelligence; Sally, blond, blue eyes, an equally graceful figure and above average height, superb at games particularly field hockey and tennis, but a more confrontational, non-conformist, competitive, daring-to-be different personality and inscrutable intelligence. Their rivalrous relationship led to many quarrels and Mother wearied of adjudicating them. Sally, no pushover, not unfairly complained that Louise and Pat conspired to "put down her non-conforming ways" and that Mother usually sided with Louise who inherited Papa's calm and formidable brain which perhaps intimidated Mother. Unlike say the Stephen sisters, Vanessa and Virginia later known as Vanessa Bell and Virginia Woolf, Louise and Sally sadly never achieved a close loving sibling relationship later in their lives. This was also sadly true between Sally and my brothers. As I grew older my relationship with her was less troubled and at times affectionate.

During the fall of each of these Greenwich years Papa had season tickets to the Harvard football games. He was an ardent rooter of the Harvard team on which he had once played guard and would sing the Harvard songs in his off-key baritone. He and Mother would "motor" in his car on Saturdays to some of the away games at Philadelphia (Penn) and at Princeton and invariably to the Yale game whether at the Yale Bowl or the Harvard Stadium. Dressed in their coon-skin coats and fortified with picnic lunches and whiskey flasks against the chill of the game they and accompanying friends would sometimes be away for two days. Once I drove with them to the Yale Bowl and was glad to get home.

Papa loved to drive. I remember one early Sunday morning when I drove with him in his new black Cadillac roadster with bright yellow wheels as we proceeded along the newly completed Hutchinson River Parkway in Westchester County at high speed. Presently we were stopped by a motorcycle policeman, whereupon Papa succeeded in evading arrest by courteous talk expressing regret, pointing out that there was no traffic at this early hour, and explaining that he was demonstrating to his young son what this wonderful car could do, and to conclude the matter by offering the officer a $100 bill substantially above what the speeding fine would be. Somewhat mollified, the officer pocketed the cash, issued a warning and left. Papa was an excellent driver, through prone to speeding and setting new records on the driving time to the Harvard Stadium and to Duxbury.

My siblings each had a generous monthly allowance from Papa which rarely covered their personal extravagances. Each of them except Mike also had their own car. My sisters later in life had to learn the value of money, to be neat and to cook for their families. They would throw or leave their clothes on the floor and rarely put them away to everyone else's distress as I would then witness. My brothers too had to learn frugality. In 1933 Pat graduated from Harvard College and started at Harvard Law School as the family fortune declined. For Pat after 1933 and Mike after 1935, they mostly had paid tutoring jobs during the summers.

I gradually got to know them, particularly Mike. In Greenwich, instead of a car, Mike had a "motor wheel," a one-cylinder gas engine that he would attach to the rear wheel of his bicycle. It made an infernal noise and often broke down until restored by Alec who always said, "Me fix." This device gave Mike great pleasure and enabled him to visit his many friends, none of whom was also at Brooks.

In our Greenwich years the nearby Field Club on Lake Avenue toward the village was important for my siblings to play tennis on grass courts and for my brothers and Papa to play squash on the excellent squash courts. Papa was a nationally ranked squash player, also playing at the Racquet Club in New York and a championship player at the Field Club in the 1920s. I learned to skate and play hockey on the Field Club small pond, graduating from double runners to regular skates. In the winter of 1932 or '33 when Poppy Bush and I were playing ice hockey, when swinging his hockey stick at the puck Poppy accidentally hit my forehead with his stick. This required summoning a doctor and three stitches. The resulting scar visibly remains and I call it the "Bush Impression". When I saw him again in 1979 at a private gathering near Washington when he was running for the Republican presidential nomination I forgot to mention it.

For swimming we went either to Calves Island or the Manursing Island Club in Rye. We would be ferried in a passenger boat making regular 10-minute round-trip runs to Calves Island on Long Island Sound from the Greenwich Yacht Club. Although she did not swim Baba would take me there many times each summer sometimes with brother Mike who would teach me to swim. My parents and siblings preferred Manursing, also on Long Island Sound, which had an Olympic-size salt-water pool as well as a beach. There my sisters became excellent swimmers and divers, winning prizes for both. The club also served excellent lunches indoors or out which we would enjoy. Once Papa threw me into the deep end of the pool. Somehow I swam.

"Playland" was a nearby amusement park. There we would drive "dodgems" and slam into each other cushioned by rubber fenders. My sisters also loved to ride and hunt. They had a horse, "Miss Liberty", which they kept at the stables of Helen and Jack Wilshire, friends of my parents. Mr. Wilshire would later become a major investor in one of the first inventions of Sally's future husband, Bob Fulton.

During the summers when I was not away, we did not go to Christ Church, and I would instead join my parents for Sunday morning walks with their walking sticks, usually on Woodside Road, a dirt road that went on for miles up and down hills and inviting future development that I dare say by now makes this beautiful countryside blighted and unrecognizable. These walks for over an hour whet our appetites for the Sunday roast beef lunches that I have previously described.

During the Greenwich years we were greatly entertained by Charlie Chaplin's and other silent films (Laurel and Hardy and "Our Gang",

Mickey Mouse, etc.) that we were able to rent to show at home and at friends' houses with movie projectors and bed sheets for a movie screen. I also remember going to see *King Kong* with Poppy Bush at the Pickwick Arms movie theater in the spring of 1933 and being terrified.

In the fall of 1932 I became aware of two events of national importance. First, some 5 years after I was told about Lindbergh's historic solo flight across the Atlantic, I learned that Charles, Jr., the infant son of Charles and of his wife Anne Morrow Lindbergh, was kidnapped from their home in Lakehurst, New Jersey. This frightened many parents, including mine, who feared for their young children. Papa began locking all doors to the house and some of the windows at bedtime and having Alec for a few months check on the house once or twice during the night. Secondly and of far greater importance, the voters overwhelmingly elected Franklin Delano Roosevelt to be president of the United States. My parents and their friends had voted for the reelection of President Hoover. At school, the boys mispronounced FDR's name, stressing the "oos" and reflecting the dismay of their parents. To Papa's great annoyance, Pat in his first national election voted for FDR, then governor of New York, whom he met a few times at his Hyde Park home when visiting his Groton School classmate Eliot Roosevelt.

During these Greenwich years Papa was gradually becoming addicted to alcohol. Sadly this was not then recognized as a treatable disease but as a social disgrace. "Alcoholics Anonymous" did not exist. His addiction ultimately led to the loss of his job in 1934 and to his suicide in June 1937. During the week he and several friends would have drinks in the club car returning to Greenwich on the commuter train from Grand Central. Alec would meet the train and drive him home, sometimes intoxicated and often facing an evening bridge party, cocktails and more drinks. Even when dining alone, he and Mother would have martinis before dinner and a highball or two after. The law of Prohibition made no difference to the availability of bootlegged liquor. The next day Papa perhaps would have a "cold" and miss work.

This became a recurring anxiety and job-threatening. Mother thought if we were to move to New York this would eliminate drinking on the club car. Of this I was then oblivious. Mother with Papa's consent arranged to rent Louise Macy's spacious apartment at 1010 Fifth Avenue opposite the entrance to the Metropolitan Museum and furnished with beautiful French antiques. My parents rented the house to Dorothy Bush's brother and his wife, the Herbert Walkers who I believe bought it after Papa died; and, as I have written, the Bushes arranged to employ Alec and Antoinette. Baba had departed in the spring of 1932 to take care of Louise's daughter born April 8, 1932 and named Florence for her maternal grandmother. I do not know what became of the other servants. We rented our house to the Walkers unfurnished, and the Coburn furniture and assorted items were placed in storage in a Greenwich warehouse for the next several years.

We moved to New York in September 1933, and my parents enrolled me in Buckley School.

3. Summers at Camp Kieve 1933, -34, and -36.

But before recounting my life in New York I will write about my three summers at Camp Kieve[6] in Nobleboro, Maine, about 10 miles inland from the coast. My parents were friends with Emily and Julian Bishop. Her brother, Donald Kennedy, a teacher at Episcopal Academy in Merion, PA, had started this camp on a large fresh water lake, Lake Damariscotta, in 1926 for about 60-70 boys mostly from the Philadelphia's Main Line and other private schools. She told Mother about the

---

6   As the Kieve website informs us, " 'Kieve' is a Celtic verb which means to strive in emulation of—to work hard to acquire skills, knowledge, and attitudes from others so as to improve yourself."

camp. Mother decided I should go to be out of the way in preparing the move to New York.

Early in July 1933 Pat drove me there in his new Ford V-8 en route to a wedding in Camden. From Greenwich this was a long way, and I doubt if we drove there in one day. The roads all the way, mostly the Boston Post Road and U.S. 1, were one lane each way and the drivers were mostly slow-pokes and timid souls as in H.T Webster's then *New Yorker* cartoons. But the traffic was light and Pat, like Papa, was a fast driver and would frighten me in passing some of the cars.

When we arrived at Kieve, he dropped me off at the entrance and sped on. This was my first time alone away from home, and I knew no one. Don Kennedy, "Uncle Don" and his wife Harriet, were very warm in their welcome and made me feel almost at home. I was housed in the upstairs porch with several other boys in a dormitory with the Welsh name "South Glenayre" as the other principal buildings also had Welsh names. That night and for several more I was so homesick and nervous that when asleep I wet my bed only to have my bedfellows taunt me when morning came, "Look at the puddle, Timmy Coburn has wet his bed!" This was not an auspicious start.

We wore a uniform of gray shorts with gold vertical stripes on the sides and a sleeveless cotton shirt with a large gold "K" emblazoned on the front. Sundays for outdoor chapel we changed to dark blue shorts with the gold stripes. Meals were at "Pasquanny Hall", named for a similar boys' Maine summer camp that Uncle Don had attended as a boy and gave him the idea for creating "Kieve". The relationship of Pasquanny to Kieve was like that of Groton School to Brooks School. Papa sent cases of Post cereals for our breakfasts.

Camp was from early July through most of August. The daily routine began with making our beds and sweeping the dormitory floors after breakfast. In addition to Uncle Don, our activities were closely supervised and monitored by several counselors including two or three invaluable contemporaries of Uncle Don who started the camp with him and continued with him each summer, the others returning recent college graduates or undergraduates. In addition, there were several junior counselors who were about to be seniors at their prep schools. My brother Mike was one in 1934. Papa visited Mike and me there that summer.

The daily activities[7] included instruction by the counselors and junior counselors in swimming, canoeing, sailing, fishing, archery, handcrafts, tennis, .22-rifle marksmanship at a rifle range, soft-ball baseball, and camping in the woods. For the younger boys there would be one or two two-day camping trips. In my first summer we went to Moxie Cove on the ocean, and with my box Kodak I won a prize for a photograph of a lonely tree battling the elements in the rocks near the waters' edge.

One of the challenges each summer was to achieve the 600-yard swim to the island in the lake which I was able to do my first or second summer at Kieve. In the afternoons, we were organized into soft-ball teams rejoicing in names such as ""Kleptomaniacs", "Pixillated Pounders", "Wabanocki Wops", and "Wheaties", with each team playing each other team three or four times for the league championship. In the summer of 1934 junior counselors Mike Coburn and Eddie Collins, Jr., son of one of the great players of Connie Mack's $100,000 infield of the 1920s, competed vigorously for the homerun crown. I believe Mike won.

Most evenings there would be a campfire and Senior Counselor Jim Beighle, a founder of Kieve with Uncle Don, would lead us with his guitar in singing the traditional folk songs "Old Man River", "Home on the Range", "Polly Wolly Doodle", "Way Down in Tennessee", among many others which I remember. These would be accompanied on occasion by "Tree Talks" by the counselors on subjects important to character development. On Sundays Uncle Don would preach on similar subjects at the outdoor chapel services. We sang Episcopal hymns with one of the counselors playing a small organ with foot pedals to pump the air to the small array of pipes.

---

7   In what follows, my recollection is mostly refreshed by *The Kieve Annual 1936*, which records the principal events at Kieve for that, my last, summer there.

Thanks to *The Kieve Annual 1936*, I am able to report more fully on my activities of that July and August at Kieve. In addition to participating in many of the daily activities as above described, early in July ten other boys and I with counselors Andy Duer and Dave Scull and junior counselor Jack Lanahan set out in three canoes and a small sailboat, all towed by Uncle Don in the Camp utility boat *Lulu*, on a three-day camping trip to Muscongus Bay at a far end of Lake Damariscotta. There in the woods we learned to pitch tents with mosquito netting, collect firewood and make a fire without matches. Swimming and fishing in the afternoon and cleaning the fish some of us caught for our supper. Others went canoeing and sailing. After a supper of the fish, baked beans, hard tack and canned peaches, Jack Lanahan read us to sleep with a mystery story. The next morning, Dave Scull took me and another boy for a sail around the bay while the others went canoeing.

In the afternoon Duer, Scull and one of the boys hiked to Nobleboro to buy blueberry and apple pies and Hershey bars while the rest of us went swimming and hiking. The usual supper but with the tasty homemade pies and campfire and a bedtime story by Andy Duer. The third and final day, swimming and fishing in the morning. Uncle Don arrived at lunchtime with mail and the evening meal. In the chilly afternoon we explored a saw mill a half-hour canoeing away. Then more canoeing, some swimming and back to our campsite. The evening meal and campfire polished off the remaining pies. Dave Scull told a story and then we all voted for "best camper", "most helpful", and "water baby". To my surprise and delight, I was voted "best camper". The next morning, some of us canoed back to Kieve, and Uncle Don towed the others in the *Lulu*.

Upon my return, I rehearsed over three weeks the part of "Hands" in a dramatization of Stevenson's masterpiece *Treasure Island* superbly directed by counselor Jim Shellenberger, then a junior at Pennsylvania University who was to become a good friend. He writes that the performances on July 31 and August 1 received a "splendid reception".

The principal event for me that summer was the 6-day "Long Voyage" to the distant Rangeley Lakes near the 3000 ft. White Mountains in NW Maine bordering New Hampshire. We were 3 senior counselors, Jim Beighle, Dr. Ed Hagmann, M.D., and Franny DeLone, a Harvard College junior, and eleven boys ages 12-15. Riding our truck on August 6 loaded with two "war canoes" to accommodate seven of us in each, it took Fred driving on primitive roads over five hours to get us there. We arrived at Haines Landing on Deer Island at the upper end of the huge Lake Mooselukmaguntic late in the day and there pitched our tents, collected firewood and cooked supper. The next day with others who preferred climbing Deer Mt. to fishing, Dr. Hagmann led as far as the top of the commanding fire tower with a panoramic view and a friendly warden. For supper we feasted on the caught trout and baked beans, and Jim Beighle's telling stories and leading us in the familiar campfire songs. It all had a magic quality. The next day we were partly towed by the warden's boat and canoed the rest of the way to the Birches, another large island at the far lower end of the lake, stocked with beautiful white birch trees. There was a store at the nearby Upper Dam where we stocked up on pies, Hershey bars, chewing gum and other goodies. After a day of exploring this island we portaged struggling over two hundred yards over the dam into Richardson Lake, paddling downwind to Pine Island, our final destination and last night out. We slept soundly after making the campfire and heating canned salmon, corned beef hash, baked beans and hot cocoa and with desserts of blueberry and apple pies. The last morning we paddled to the village of South Arm about 20 miles south of Haines Landing where Fred and his truck were waiting for the long ride back to Kieve on August 12. We did not have the time to explore the other two Rangeley Lakes, Umbagog and Aziscohos. For me and the other boys it was a splendid adventure about learning to live in the woods with good companions.

The remaining weeks at Kieve passed swiftly. I wrote an essay, *Spending a Few Weeks with the Phoebe*, which with her chicks nested on our sleeping porch. It was published in the 1936 *Kieve Annual* for which I won the Natural History Essay Prize, to my astonishment. I qualified as a marksman on the rifle range with the .22 rifle, won the junior rowboat race, and, again to my surprise and delight, was tied with another boy for the "Junior General Excellence" award. Then it was time to go home and take the train to New York.

The three summers at Kieve were valuable formative and lasting experiences in my young life and taught me much about living away from home and with other boys and learning about nature and camping. All this was to facilitate my transition to Brooks School in the fall of 1936 and to the U.S. Army early in 1943.

There was a Coburn June wedding in Camden, Maine, about 2000. In driving there from Boston, Pat and I stopped at Camp Kieve which I had not visited since 1936. I reminded Pat how he had dropped me there in 1933, also on his way to Camden. Kieve was then run by Uncle Don's grandson, Henry Kennedy, who though we arrived unexpectedly greeted us warmly and showed pictures of my years in the dining hall. Camp had not yet begun. Although there were additional buildings the place looked much as I had remembered. We stayed about half an hour.

In 2006 Kieve merged with an adjacent girls' camp, "Wavus"[8], to form "Kieve-Wavus." Henry Kennedy is the director of both camps which maintain separate but adjoining facilities for each camp. Kieve-Wavus also runs a year-long educational program explained in its website. A few years ago I attended a Kieve gathering in Washington, DC, enjoyed meeting Henry Kennedy again, and was surprised to find an even older alumnus who had been at Kieve in the late 1920s. One of my brother Mike's grandsons, Timothy Gage Coburn, was a Kieve boy one summer in the 1990s. He too loved it.

---

8 "Wavus" is a revered legendary Indian chief whose people inhabited the shores of Lake Damariscotta aeons ago. The girls camp, some 4 miles north of Kieve on the lake, was formerly known as "Camp Wawanock, began in 1922 and continued until 1976. Later the property was purchased by the Wavus Foundation created by former alumnae to protect the property from commercial development. This led to the merger with Kieve in 2006. Like Kieve, Wavus is a camp for about 150 girls ages 8-16 through July and August at this separate facility..

4. New York 1933-36.

In September 1933 we moved to a spacious apartment at 1010 Fifth Avenue at the corner of 82d Street. The living room faced the entrance to the Metropolitan Museum of Art. In residence were Mother, Papa, Sally, and I. There was also a bedroom for Pat and Mike for their vacation visits. We had a German couple, Hilda and Kurt, to look after us, and there were servants' quarters for them. My parents rented this beautiful apartment from Louise Macy, a friend of Mother's, and because it was furnished with priceless French antiques I was admonished to be very mindful of not damaging them.

As noted above, I was enrolled in Buckley School, then at 120 East 74th Street, between Park and Lexington Avenues. Founded in 1913 by educator B. Lord Buckley, it was a day school for boys for the first through the ninth grade, ages 6-15, called Primary I-III, Junior I-III, and Senior I-III. The last 3 years before college were usually spent at one of the New England boarding schools. Mr. Buckley's vision, largely achieved, was a school offering a rigorous classical curriculum, and also stressing the importance of diligence, strength of character, leadership and compassion, all as subsumed in *Honor et Veritas*, which became the school's motto along with its colors of blue and white.

When Mr. Buckley died in 1932, he was succeeded by Mrs. Evelyn Adams who in turn was succeeded by one of my Buckley teachers, James Hubbell, in 1940. Mr. Hubbell served as the headmaster until 1972. The current headmaster, Greg O'Melia, was previously a teacher at Brooks School.

I began at Buckley in October 1933 in Junior II and continued until midway through Senior I in the winter of 1936 when Mother and I went to Palm Beach while she sued for a divorce from Papa in a Florida court which had a minimal residence requirement.

While many boys were driven by chauffeured limousines, Kurt walked me to Buckley each morning unless inclement weather necessitated a taxi. It irritated me that he invariably insisted on the same route going and returning. We had a dress code of coat and tie, short trousers for the younger boys and gray flannels for the older ones, and dark blue Buckley caps.

The first thing each morning all of the about 180 boys met in a morning assembly and recited the following uplifting lines written some 1,500 years ago attributed to Kalidasa, a poet of south India, and translated from the Sanskrit:

> Listen to the Exhortation of the Dawn!
> Look to this Day!
> For it is Life, the very Life of Life.
> In its brief course lie all the
> Verities and Realities of your Existence.
> The Bliss of Growth,
> The Glory of Action,
> The Splendor of Beauty;
> For Yesterday is but a Dream,
> And To-morrow is only a Vision;
> But To-day well lived makes
> Every Yesterday a Dream of Happiness,
> And every Tomorrow a Vision of Hope.
> Look well therefore to this Day!
> Such is the Salutation of the Dawn!

This was followed by the Pledge of Allegiance to the Flag, and then on to classes with 15-20 boys. The school was in a large tall building with five or six floors. My teachers were excellent. While I can no longer differentiate between my three years at Buckley, I recall the venerable Mr. Long who improved my penmanship and writing and got me started in English grammar as Mr. Gamble did in Latin grammar; and Chief Searfoss who was our long-time athletic director and taught us physical training in the gym. I recall our rides in an ancient Mack bus over the Hell Gate Bridge to playing fields in Flushing Meadows in Long Island most afternoons when the weather was good for football, ice hockey and baseball. We also had morning recess in good weather on the roof of the school where a frequent activity was "war", throwing rubber balls at each other. There were occasional games with our principal rival, The Allen-Stevenson School, who called us "Buckley Bums", and St. Bernard's School, both day schools like Buckley on the upper east side.

At Buckley I made some lasting friends that resumed when I was at Harvard: the late David Martin at Harvard Law School to become a godfather to David, Jr., a relationship with the son that continues to flourish; the late Guy Carey, Jr. and the late John Munroe, at Harvard College; and Bill Ziegler at Harvard College and Law School who had a distinguished career as a litigator with Sullivan and Cromwell and with whom I remain in touch.

While at Buckley I was also enrolled in The Knickerbocker Greys, a military drill organization of about 200 cadets ages 8-16 that met once or twice weekly in the late afternoons for about two hours at the Seventh Regiment Armory at Park Avenue at 66th Street. We wore gray uniforms, and older boys who were officers had caps with white plumes and wore swords. I soon tired of it. We practiced the fundamentals of close order drill which I was to repeat later at Brooks School and in infantry basic training in the Army beginning in February 1943.

In the fall of 1933 many of the Navy's ships visited New York and invited the public aboard. Papa arranged to take me to the battleship *Mississippi* built about 1912 which had recently undergone a major upgrade at the Brooklyn Navy Yard, replacing, for example, the tall cage masts with a modern bridge structure. She mounted at least 10 14" guns in two forward and two aft turrets. We met Captain Paulson, as I recall his name, who showed us his cabin and the bridge and arranged a private tour of the rest of the ship. I was impressed and excited by this tremendous 35,000-ton warship. I became a Navy fan and began to study the ships of our fleet as reported in the annual editions of the world's navies published in England by *Jane's Fighting Ships*. I remember treasuring my copy of the 1939 edition, the last I ever looked at. I wanted to go to the Naval Academy at Annapolis but, as I later learned, my eyesight was less than acceptable for the Navy.

In the fall of 1934 President Roosevelt invited his Harvard class-mates for a weekend gathering at the White House to celebrate the 30th anniversary of their graduation from Harvard College. My parents' plans to go were nixed by my coming down with chicken pox a day or two before their departure. Mother insisted on staying even though Hilda the cook or Sally could have looked after my minimal bedridden needs. I felt badly about this. There was never another opportunity.

I learned to roller skate and would spend happy times doing this extensively in the reaches of Central Park across the street from our apartment. One day three or four tough older boys stopped me and took my purse which had a quarter. I did not resist and was not hurt. I was frightened and did not roller skate again in the Park. Mother vainly tried to interest me in the treasures of the Metropolitan Museum, across the street from our apartment. I did have some appreciation of the Egyptian wing; but sadly at this stage of my life I remained a philistine to art.

I have written above about my summers at Camp Kieve in 1933, 1934, and 1936. I write here about my 1935 summer with Louise and Mooney in Palm Beach.

Their second daughter Harriet died of a strep infection early in 1935 when they were living in Long Island. Harriet was then about 18 months and penicillin which would have saved her was not yet available. Mooney's mother, Harriet Knowles Harding, then invited them and their surviving daughter Florence for an extended visit to her ocean villa in Palm Beach, "Chiora", to overcome their grief. They went, terminating Baba's employment as Florence's nurse and my further contact with her. While there, Marion Wyeth, a leading architect in Palm Beach, invited Mooney to join his firm, and so they stayed. Mrs. Harding had a very grand Spanish style house built in the 1920s and grounds on South Ocean Boulevard about a mile north of the Bath & Tennis Club opposite Mrs. Post's place that my parents and I had previously visited.

Louise and Mooney remained in his mother's house that summer. They would continue to live there until Mooney built their house on Orange Grove Road, a year or two later. Mrs. Harding would summer at her places in Sands Point, Long Island, and York Harbor, Maine. She and her husband, Charles Lewis Harding, led mostly separate lives with a succession of paramours once their four sons were on their own. He lived mostly on his yacht. One of hers, Joe Stevens, was the father of Pelham Stevens who married my cousin Dorothy ("Bunny") Stone then living and seeing us in New York. When the Hardings married in the early 1900s, Mr. Harding, as the heir to a textile fortune, was said to be the wealthiest man in Massachusetts. Their principal home, which I remember visiting with my parents, was called "Burntwood", a vast place in Dedham.

Thus it was arranged that I should spend the summer of 1935 with Louise and Mooney in Palm Beach. Louise had no intention of going to her sister's wedding. She and I would thereby miss the forthcoming wedding of Sally to Robert Edison Fulton, Jr. They had met before and again at the 1934 wedding of our cousin Rawn Brinkley to Frances Noble in Elmira, New York. Rawn and Bob Fulton were roommates at Harvard College in the Class of 1931, and he was one of Rawn's ushers at the wedding. Bob had returned by 1934 from his pioneering trip around the world on a motorcycle which he had filmed with a movie camera as he went. He was lecturing and writing a book, *One Man Caravan*, about his trip. Sally, having completed a typing class, undertook to type the manuscript. Bob was then living with his parents, Robert Edison Fulton and Hannah Travis Fulton in a spacious and grand Park Avenue apartment.

Bob's father was president of the Mack Truck Company, and each of his parents had a chauffeured Rolls-Royce town car. Bob nevertheless remained unspoiled and self-reliant despite all this privilege. Romance blossomed between them, and they planned to marry while I was away in Palm Beach. The reception was to be at our apartment. They would initially live in the apartment above our Greenwich garage. Bob soon was employed by Juan Trippe to film the maiden flight of the China Clipper to Hong Kong and Manila in 1936 for Pan American Airways. Sally accompanied him as far as Honolulu where she had a wonderful visit of several weeks with the Dillinghams.

At age eleven I travelled alone to Palm Beach in June by train, sleeping again in an upper berth which I had first experienced when returning from Camp Kieve. The Pennsylvania Railroad had recently electrified the line to Washington, as had the New Haven Railroad from New York to New Haven and Hartford. For the rest of the journey on the Atlantic Coast Line and the Florida East Coast railroads we had steam engines.

Staying with Louise and Mooney as paying guests was a young couple from Philadelphia, Joe and Eleanor Reeves, who were having their house built nearby on Middle Road. I spent a lot of time there with Joe helping him build a sailboat which taught me something about sailboat design and carpentry. We became friends.

I also came to know and appreciate Louise and Mooney. Their personalities were, however, increasingly incompatible and quite opposite: she outgoing and loving entertaining and parties; he very quiet, preferring to be at home to going out and entertaining. Both had superb creative minds: Louise for example at bridge, Mooney at designing houses. Both remained very saddened by the loss of the infant Harriet until their third daughter, Priscilla, named for her paternal grandmother's sister, Priscilla Knowles, arrived in October 1937. To replace Baba Louise found a splendid nurse for Florence, now called "Fifi", in Edith Mathis who remained with Louise and her daughters for many years.

There was a grand piano in the living room. Louise, to console her grief, over that summer learned to play well and from memory one of the most difficult and beautiful of Chopin's works, the scherzo in B minor. Achieving this after daily unremitting study and practice was a major triumph for Louise. Sadly she did not continue with this or with other great piano works.

The summer passed quickly and enjoyably despite the heat and high humidity and no air-conditioning. Most days Louise and I would go to the Sea Spray Club for lunch and salt-water swimming in the large pool and occasionally tennis. There was also wonderful swimming in the ocean from the wide beach across South Ocean Boulevard from Mrs. Harding's place. There was often substantial surf and one had to beware of Portuguese men-of-war and other jellyfish. There were no lifeguards, and I had to be careful.

I remained in Palm Beach through the September hurricane, one of the worst up to that time with winds exceeding 125 mph and tidal surges. I do not remember whether we stayed in the house or went to another building further from the ocean. But flooding from Lake Worth to the west of Palm Beach island was equally a threat so I imagine we stayed put. Shortly there was no electricity as the winds toppled palm trees and power lines. The storm noise was intense, and the darkness and driving rain persisted. We came through intact and without serious damage to the house but devastation to the trees and plantings. The brunt of the storm was south and west, particularly in the Florida keys at Marathon where the Florida East Coast railroad from Miami to Key West, which had been completed in 1912 as a tremendous 100-mile engineering achievement, was destroyed. The railroad then in bankruptcy was unable to restore service. In 1940 with the growing threat of Nazi Germany, President Roosevelt persuaded Congress to authorize and fund the construction of an "Overseas Highway" to Key West on the railroad roadbed. All the concrete bridges had survived the hurricane. The highway was completed in early 1942 and I drove it for the first time in June 1951.

In late September I returned to New York and Buckley School. It was a wonderful summer. By then Mother and Papa after Sally's wedding had moved to a smaller apartment on 73rd street between Lexington and Third Avenue as the family finances continued to dwindle. No servants, and Mother had to learn to cook. General Foods had terminated Papa's employment because of alcoholism with a generous $50,000 bonus at the end of 1934. He invested this sum with a stockbroker friend who proceeded promptly to lose or perhaps embezzle all of it. Papa had also invested extensively in a new process of bringing color photography to Hollywood film making, called "TrueColor". Sadly it lost the competition with "Technicolor", and that investment too was lost. Papa then borrowed increasingly against his substantial life insurance policy. In the fall of 1935 shortly after I returned from Palm Beach he contracted pneumonia and nearly died. It would have been a blessing for all of us if he had.

As it was, his job prospects were almost nil. His drinking continued unabated. Mother came under increasing pressure from Louise and Pat, Aunt Shonce and Uncle Goodwin, and Nana to divorce him. Aunt

Dorothy was strongly opposed, Aunt Louise less so. I never knew what Sally thought. I had no role in this. Papa when intoxicated was never abusive with Mother or me. He continued to adore her and become increasingly dependent on her. There was never anyone else, even after the divorce which he did not contest. It was all desperately sad.

In February or March 1936 Mother finally decided to seek a Florida divorce. She and I left Papa and I left Buckley for Palm Beach. I recall seeing Papa once again while visiting Aunt Louise after returning from Camp Kieve later that summer. We had a small apartment in Brazilian Court near Worth Avenue. What money Mother had for us to live on or who provided it I do not know. I was enrolled in a Palm Beach public school for three months. Having girl classmates and lady teachers as well was a new and pleasant experience beyond which I recall very little apart from making friends with one of the girls, Patricia Massey, whose mother was a friend of Louise's. At the end of June I returned to Camp Kieve for July and August about which I have already written. Mother remained until the divorce came through a month or two later.

So ended twenty-nine years of marriage. She returned to New York to live with her mother, my grandmother Nana, who had rented a small apartment for us on East 72nd street, and to which I returned for a few weeks before starting in the First Form at Brooks School in North Andover, Massachusetts, in September 1936, thanks to the generosity of a friend of Mother's, Mrs. Philip James of New York.

When I visited Aunt Louise after Camp Kieve, Papa had been staying in the Barn for an extended visit, an effort on her part to provide a home atmosphere for him with sailing and other recreational activities. Sadly that too failed; and she had to rescue him more than once from bars in Providence as previous attempts at his "drying out" in various sanatoria had also failed. That was to be the last time I would see him. He returned to New York and a lonely life.

At this point Pat, having graduated from Harvard Law School the previous June with an excellent academic record, having narrowly missed law review and having been admitted to the Massachusetts Bar, was beginning as an associate at the established Boston law firm of Herrick, Smith, Donald & Farley at an annual salary of $1,500. He had turned down an offer from Ropes & Gray, perhaps then and now Boston's preeminent law firm, because their salary offer was $300 less. He was living as a paying guest in the home of a friend, Ned Wheeler, on Beacon Hill. Mike was beginning the sophomore year at Harvard College, again thanks to the generosity of a family friend who paid his tuition.

5. Brooks School 1936-42.

I first visited Brooks School for about a week during my spring vacation at Buckley in 1934. Mike was then a fifth former. Papa probably drove me. I believe we first stopped briefly at Groton School in Groton, Massachusetts, where Papa had "entered" each of his sons shortly after their births and from which Pat had graduated in 1929. After a few days at Brooks I decided I greatly preferred Brooks to Groton even though the schools were essentially the same.

Endicott Peabody, an Episcopal clergyman and the founding headmaster of Groton School in 1884 (known as "the Rector"), also founded Brooks School in 1926, believing that there was a need for a similar small Episcopal boarding school like Groton as evidenced each year by the large numbers of qualified boys Groton had to turn down because it wanted to remain a small 6-year boarding school with no more than 150 boys. A wealthy friend, Richard B. Russell, gave about 250 acres of his farm land and buildings adjoining a large reservoir lake, Lake Cochichewick, in North Andover, Massachusetts. The Rector selected Frank Davis Ashburn, Yale 1925, a 1921 Groton graduate and Senior Prefect, and then a student at Columbia Law School, to be the first headmaster notwithstanding his refusal of the Rector's strong request that he become an Episcopal clergyman. He had recently married Phyllis Batchelder, a poised New York socialite whose mother was a friend of my mother.

The Rector named the school for Phillips Brooks, 1835-1893, an 1855 graduate of Harvard College. He had graduated next from the Virginia Theological Seminary in 1859 and was ordained an Episcopal clergyman. After several years at Holy Trinity Church in Philadelphia, he became Rector of Trinity Church, Copley Square, in Boston in 1869 until 1891. With the architect H. H. Richardson he created the magnificent new church there which was completed in 1877. A giant of six feet four inches and three hundred pounds, he became arguably the greatest preacher of Christianity of the 19th Century in the English-speaking world.[9] He was a founder of Groton School and was instrumental in selecting Endicott Peabody as its headmaster. In 1891 he became Bishop of Massachusetts. His home was in North Andover. By the time of his death two years later at 58 he had remained single. In recognition of his greatness, leading universities, Harvard and Oxford among them, awarded him honorary degrees.

He is remembered for the words of the Christmas carol, "O Little Town of Bethlehem". He also wrote the Groton School hymn[10] the music

---

9   See *The Consolations of God: Great Sermons of Phillips Brooks* edited by Ellen Wilbur, Wm. B. Erdmanns Publishing Co., Grand Rapids, MI (2003).

10   Father of all below, above,
Whose name is light, whose name is love,
Here be thy truth and goodness known,
And make these fields and halls thine own.

Thy Temple gates stand open wide;
O Christ, we enter at thy side,
With thee to consecrate our pow'rs,
And make our father's business ours.

For days of drought which yet shall be,
On untrod land, on unsail'd seas,
We kneel and fill our cup of youth,
At these fair fountains of thy truth.

for which was composed by Groton's long time organist and choirmaster, Twining Lynes. It became the hymn for Brooks too. Some 15,000 attended his funeral at Trinity Church.[11]

Brooks began in September 1927 with 14 boys in the first and second forms and two masters. More teachers and a form of about a dozen boys were added each year reaching the sixth form in 1931, the year my brother Mike began as a second former. The first graduating class was in 1932.

At the time of my 1934 visit the school had about 100 boys. I stayed in the Ashburns' house which had been the home of Mr. Russell's manager of the farm, a Mr. Delbert Arel, who continued in charge of the grounds and maintenance at Brooks. He was assisted by Jim Whitman as the school janitor, a giant of a man with the strength of a Sampson or Hercules and an honorary member of the Class of 1932. I got into trouble for accidentally falling into the lake from a rowboat. As it was a reservoir, swimming was forbidden. In any event I felt at home at Brooks and wanted to return as a first former in September 1936.

There were eight of us entering in that first form in September 1936: Charlie Allen from Haverford, Penn., whom I had known at Kieve; Dick

---

O world, all bright and brave and young,
With deeds unwrought and songs unsung,
For all the tasks thy strength will give
We greet thee, we, about to live.

Father, thy children bless the care
Which sheds thy sunlight ev'rywhere,
Shine on our school and let us be
Teachers and scholars taught by thee

The last line of the fourth verse, "We greet thee, we, about to live", was adopted in 1932 as the motto of Brooks School and incorporated in the Brooks shield, also adopted in 1932, as "Victuri te salutamus which also means "We about to conquer". The shield is a black cross superimposed on a white cross and centered on a field of emerald green. The motto is beneath the cross.

11   For more on Phillips Brooks, see Woolverton, John Frederick, *The Education of Phillips Brooks*, University of Illinois Press 1995.

Breck, Medfield, Mass.; John Grimes Butler, Pomfret, Conn.; myself; Jerry Dearborn of Lawrence, Mass., son of the school doctor; Mortimer Hall, Long Island; W.A. Hazard Leonard, Jericho, Long Island; and John ("Jack") Eliot Thayer III, Lancaster, Mass. All of us were to graduate in 1942 save for Butler, Dearborn and Hall who had left after the first two years. We lived in cubicles upstairs in "Old Whitney", the first school building donated by John Hay Whitney, a Yale friend of Frank Ashburn's and long time benefactor and trustee of Brooks.

Fessenden Wilder (1933-72) was the dormitory master and also the senior master. He would teach us English grammar our first year and English literature, particularly Shakespeare's *Hamlet*, *Lear*, *Macbeth*, and *Othello* later on. He would also read to us at bedtime. I remember his reading, for instance, John Buchan's *The Thirty-Nine Steps*, an exciting spy story of the Great War. Larry Morgan, a sixth former, was the dormitory prefect, and he frequently had to restore order amidst nocturnal pillow fights and blizzards of tooth powder sprayed from cubicle tops.

Among other subjects and teachers our first year was ancient history with Henry Bragdon (1930-45), a graduate of Harvard College, a very great teacher and one of the great teachers in my life. He instilled intellectual enthusiasm for whatever subject matter he put before one. He already was an authority on Woodrow Wilson, and would in 1967 publish the first volume of a biography, *Woodrow Wilson: The Academic Years*, which sadly he never completed. Later he and a colleague published what became the leading high school textbook throughout the country, *The Life of A Free People*. He was also in our early years the football coach and known as "Uncle Punt". One of his favorite expressions of surprise or alarm was "By Jeepers!"

That year Russell Morse (1928-42, 1953-65) taught us first-year Latin grammar with an emphasis on having us learn Latin mottos. One of the few I remember is "Haec olim meminisse iuvabit" ("Perhaps you will take pleasure in remembering even this"). One of Groton's great athletes and a graduate of Harvard College, he was an amiable man who would respond "How quaint" to a student bêtise. He became a dear friend to

Mike and later to me. My sister Sally years later vainly tried to launch a romance between him and her friend Eleanor Righter.

Our Math teacher was Bob Spock (1936-52), a member of the first Brooks 1932 graduating class and a 1936 Yale graduate. He was the younger brother of Dr. Benjamin Spock, the renowned pediatrician and author of books on infant care. We were Bob's first students, and we focused on decimals and fractions and perhaps began algebra. This was always to be my weakest subject.

Bob was a dormitory master and each year from the dormitory and beyond he would collect a small group of boys, who came to be derisively known as "Spock's chicks" with whom he had affectionate relationships both at school and during vacations. This created unfavorable gossip; and although I was not one of his "chicks" and strongly doubt he had sexual affairs with any of them while they were at Brooks, I believe he was a homosexual at a time when society was wrongfully wholly intolerant and criminally condemning of that innate sexual predisposition as I would later myself experience. Like racism, homophobia continues as I write in 2011 to linger in America as courts and legislatures grapple with a grow-ing entitlement to gay marriage.

Edward W. Flint was another faculty arrival in 1936 to be the organ-ist and choirmaster. He would later marry the sister of Eddie Norris who was a class ahead of me and a friend. Mr. Flint, a Harvard graduate, had the good fortune to have studied with Nadia Boulanger (1887-1979), the preeminent musicologist, composer, and conductor and above all teacher in Paris in the 1920s and later as did the luminaries of American music, Aaron Copeland, Roy Harris, Walter Piston, Virgil Thompson, and many others. Ned Rorem, the composer, said she was the greatest teacher since Socrates. Thanks to Mr. Flint, we were privileged to experience that great-ness as I shall presently relate. During my Brooks years I sang in the choir and learned to love not only some of the beautiful hymns from the 1940 Episcopal Hymnal but the great organ pieces of Bach Mr. Flint would play.

Life at Brooks's then followed well-trodden paths: meals were at appointed times in the dining room added as an extension of the Ashburn's house. About a dozen students from each form were assigned to a particular table each week and then a different selection from each form to a different table the following week and so forth throughout the school year, the assignments being posted weekly at the entrance to the dining room. In this way all boys would come to know each other and the faculty. The tables were hosted by a master and his wife or by single masters. The Ashburns had their own table to which every boy was rotated more than once in the course of the school year. Until 1942 and the demands of war work maids served the meals.

The dress code was always coat and tie, stiff collars for supper and blue suits and stiff collars for Sunday breakfast, chapel and lunch. Except for Sundays, chapel was every evening after supper. The Ashburns stood in a receiving line after supper to shake hands with and say "Good night" to every boy as he left the dining room to walk to chapel. Evening chapel was about 15 minutes: an opening and closing hymn, a sixth former reading a lesson from the King James Bible, and Mr. Ashburn leading us in two or three prayers from the 1927 edition of the English Book of Common Prayer. Sunday chapel lasted about an hour with the traditional Episcopal service, an anthem by the choir and a sermon by Mr. Ashburn. When conducting chapel services Mr. Ashburn wore a simple black cassock. His sermons were the most important and inspiring ones I ever heard.

Classes and study periods were mostly for about four hours in the morning with another hour of study period before and after athletics in the afternoon. Boys who had failed in their class recitations would be kept in detention in the afternoons until they overcame the particular failure to the master's satisfaction. The period after evening chapel and until bedtime was mostly for homework or research in the library. This induced preparation for class in order to avoid missing mostly mandatory participation in one of the afternoon's sports: football, soccer, hockey, basketball, baseball, crew, and tennis. I remember on several occasions Thayer and I in our first form year would sneak off to the library for an hour or two after midnight to write papers on assigned topics of ancient history for Mr. Bragdon.

Our ranks gradually grew, mostly over the next two years, to the twenty-six of us who graduated in 1942. As I write in 2011, we have shrunk to eight with at least two in failing health as the end approaches all of us. In WW II we lost Willie Frick, Fletcher Gill, and Hazard Leonard, all my good friends, the rest more gradually.

In the second form, I graduated from a cubicle to a more comfortable life in the farmhouse, one of the Russell Farm buildings opposite the headmaster's house. Kay and Henry Bragdon and their two young sons presided over the four or five of us second formers ensconced there and made us very welcome. For the third form year I resided in Peabody House, named for the Rector, which connected and consolidated two converted adjacent farm buildings known as "Limbo" and "the Ritz" into a two-storey dormitory presided over by Mr. Morse and located near the playing fields and some distance from the classrooms and the dining room.

For the fourth form and part of the fifth form year I was in Mr. Carr's dormitory in Gardner House, named for William Gardner, long time senior master at Groton under the Rector. There we had bedrooms and roommates. Mine were Hayden Shepley for the fourth form year and Danny Danforth for the fall term of the fifth. Shepley and I would confide our secret desires for the unrequited affections of two fifth formers who also resided there. For the winter and spring terms I returned as the dormitory prefect to the first and second formers in the cubicles of Old Whitney where I had begun four years before.

Starting with the fourth form boys could have radios and phonographs in their rooms. We were overwhelmed in the dormitories by the loud sounds of performances of the prevailing jazz and swing music by the bands of Tommy Dorsey, Benny Goodman, Glenn Miller, Artie Shaw and several others. I abstained. In my sixth-form year I had a table radio and in the evenings would listen to classical music broadcast by WMEX from Boston as well as occasionally to the broadcasts of the Metropolitan Opera superbly announced for many years by Milton Cross.

Mr. Carr (1935-44) came to Brooks having retired from a lifetime of teaching Latin at the Salisbury School in Salisbury, Connecticut, where he was revered as a legend, as I later learned. He was probably in his sixties when we were his students. He was far older than all the other masters except for Eric Starbuck (1934-43) who taught French and whom we believed to be a Communist because of his political beliefs and his touting the party line from *The Daily Worker* and listening to Moscow on his short-wave radio. One had better be prepared when called on by Mr. Carr to recite translations of passages from the texts of Cicero and Virgil Mr. Carr had assigned for that day or be prepared to spend the afternoon in detention until he got it right.

He was a demanding and exacting teacher and he would not tolerate slovenly work. As Henry Bragdon taught by intellectual enthusiasm, so Edmond Samuel Carr did by force and fear. Each in his different way was a great teacher, highly respected, loved or feared, and reaping his students' utmost performance. An eccentric, Mr. Carr always wore the same gray suit, and as a dormitory master he never invited students to his rooms. He had a singular, formal, old-fashioned way of speaking, much imitated by the boys whom he invariably called by their surnames. He had no faculty friends and society at Brooks. He would take long afternoon walks around Lake Cochichowick and so kept himself very trim and erect. He had an ancient automobile we called "the Bluebird" that reminded one of the car the timid soul drove in the H. T. Webster cartoons in *The New Yorker*. After WW II Danny Danforth and I drove to Salisbury to call on him in retirement. Then in his later 70s he was very gracious and seemed pleased to see us. He said he was weary of "pushing boys". We were glad to pay our respects and told him that he was one of our great teachers, as surely he was.

Most Wednesday and Saturday afternoons Mrs. Ashburn and the faculty wives——-Kay Bragdon, Ruth Holcombe, Janie Jackson, Jerry Kingsbury, Alica Waterston, and Merrill Wilder—hosted tea in their homes for about eight boys from the same form in accordance with a rotating schedule posted each week. This made us feel more at home, the better to know the Ashburns and the masters and their wives in a social setting.

Saturday nights we would have movies in the barn that had been converted to an auditorium with squash courts at one end and a locker room and showers at the other. We thus enjoyed the great films of the 1930s and early 40s. I remember Charlie Chaplin's *The Great Dictator*, a masterful spoof of Adolph Hitler. The other principal morale booster apart from sports was the mid-day arrival of the mail with hoped-for letters from home usually complaining of no letters from us.

We had daily delivery of *The Boston Herald*, *The New York Herald Tribune*, and *The New York Times* and *The Illustrated London News* and *Punch* each week, among others. Some of these were days or weeks late. The weekly arrival of *Life* and *Time* facilitated by our classmate Hank Luce added to our staying abreast of current events as Hitler pursued Lebensraum in Europe and Japan invaded China. With our second-form year the clouds of war were gathering.

To remind us of the horrors of war, Mr. Wilder in March of my first-form year directed a masterful performance of R. C. Sheriff's 1928 English tragedy, "Journey's End", as the school play starring Freddie Bradley as Captain Stanhope, the commanding officer of a British infantry company in trench warfare in north eastern France in 1918. Bradley, a sixth former, went on to a successful Broadway acting career.

While I was at Brooks the one or two annual school plays superbly directed by either Mr. Wilder or Mr. Waterston were first-class productions of great plays by Shakespeare, Thornton Wilder, Sean O'Casey, Bernard Shaw, Oscar Wilde, and others. I recall in my second or third-form years a riveting performance of T. S. Eliot's 1935 *Murder in the Cathedral* directed by Mr. Waterston and starring an English sixth former, Arthur Turner, as Thomas Becket, the Archbishop of Canterbury who was murdered in the 12th century on the orders of Henry II.

Each March was also "The Cabaret", a series of silly skits performed on a winter Saturday evening in the barn after much rehearsal. Mrs. Waterston prepared some of us for more than one of them. The high point was always the amusing, witty poem of that year's school life by Mr. Ashburn in which he somehow managed to include every boy and most of the faculty in his telling, rhyming, fun-poking verses.

In my fourth form year as Mr. Bragdon was teaching us modern European history, he invited me to be a "guinea pig" in a one-student "field course" to see if he could improve my written English. He would teach me to write in "Basic English", using only the 850 words developed in England in the 1920s by C. K. Ogden (1889-1957) and I. A. Richards (1893-1979), both leading literary critics. Their book, *Basic English: A General Introduction with Rules and Grammar* was published in 1930. It was supplemented by Ogden's *The General Basic English Dictionary* which translated some 20,000 English words into Basic English and which Mr. Bragdon gave to me.

The challenge was to translate masterpieces of English prose—for example, assigned texts by Carlyle, Emerson, Hazlitt, and Macaulay—into Basic English within the limits of the prescribed 850 words including only 18 verbs, called "operational words".[12] Under Mr. Bragdon's close supervision and corrections, I gradually overcame my faulty writing over several months. This basically changed how I would thereafter write English. Not surprisingly, my marks in classes graded on the basis of English composition went from a low pass to A's. As a result I was excused from taking the prescribed "English A" for Harvard freshman. For this I owe Mr. Bragdon a lifetime of gratitude. In September 1943, in the midst of WW II, when receiving an honorary degree from Harvard, Winston Churchill spoke of the importance of Basic English for those learning or wishing to improve their use of English. Likely present was Professor I. A. Richards, also the acclaimed co-author with C. K. Ogden of the seminal *The Meaning of Meaning: A Study of the Influence of Language upon Thought and of the Science of Symbolism* (1923 and subsequent editions) whom President Lowell had in the 1920s recruited for the Harvard faculty.

I was also blessed my fourth and fifth form years with field courses with perhaps the most brilliant and best-educated of the faculty masters, George Chychele Waterston (1932-59, 1962-71). An Oxford graduate, fluent in French and German, truly a polymath, he taught English and French, coached soccer, and directed the school plays along with

---

12 They are: come, get, give, go, keep, let, make, put, seem, take, be, do, have, say, see, send, may, and will. As necessary, they are also fully conjugated, e.g., "be".

Mr. Wilder. His wife, Alica Atkinson Waterston, an established artist, came to Brooks as the art teacher in 1935. Having retained his British citizenship, he joined the RAF in the summer of 1941 and became an interrogator of captured German fliers. I would later see him in London during the war.

I was as hopeless in Mrs. Waterston's art class as Hazard Leonard was to become proficient in clay modelling of horses. Thanks to her teaching some splendid paintings were created while I was Brooks, especially by Shirley Carter '37, John Henry Dick '38, and Richard DeMenocal '38. In the Manual Training class under Mr. Goodwin (1935-44) I did make a model of Stonehenge which remained on display for several years.

One of the single-student field courses I had with Mr. Waterston involved reading some French drama and poetry, the comedies *Le Mis-antrope* and *Tatuffe ou L'imposteur* by Moliere (1622-73) and the tragedy *Phedre* by Racine (1639-99) and poems by Alfred de Vigny (1797-1853), particularly *La Mort du Loup*.

The other field course with Mr. Waterston explored the new subject of linguistic semantics as developed by Messrs. Ogden and Richards in *The Meaning of Meaning* cited above as well as the new field of general semantics pioneered by Alfred Korzybski (1879-1950) in *Science and Sanity* (1933), both of which were rendered more understandable by S. I. Hayakawa's *Language in Action* first published in 1938. Mr. Waterston enlarged these seminal ideas in his magisterial magnum opus *Order and Counter-Order: Dualism in Western Culture* published in 1966 by the Philosophical Library in New York and based on the dissertation for his Ph. D from the Sorbonne.

Exploring these 17th century French literary masterpieces and the new 20th century difficult sciences of linguistic semantics and general semantics with Mr. Waterston was to experience the excitement and the wisdom of a great teacher. The Waterstons were to become among my great friends after WW II. They had two sons and two daughters, one the celebrated actor Sam Waterston, and one of the daughters, Ellie, my goddaughter.

The years at Brooks enriched my love of classical music. For this I primarily thank Mr. Flint, the organist and choirmaster. In 1938 he persuaded Mrs. Helen Danforth, a wealthy widow of Providence, Rhode Island, who had two sons at Brooks, my classmate Danny and his older brother Steve, to donate a pipe organ to replace the Hammond electric organ with which Mr. Flint had struggled in the chapel. Her insistence on the anonymity of her donation lasted only a few years. Mr. Flint arranged for the installation of an Aeolian- Skinner 1,444 pipe organ with three manuals and five pedals which closely matched the rich sound of the organs of Bach's day. The installation was closely supervised by G. Donald Harrison, the head of this South Boston firm that was then preeminent among church organ builders in the United States.

For the inaugural concert in the fall of 1938 Mr. Flint invited Carl Weinrich, the organist at Princeton, to play one of the Handel organ concertos with a small pick-up chamber orchestra as well as solo Bach pieces. The orchestra included a few Brooks students, Mr. Waterston, an accomplished cellist, and other instrumentalists mostly from the faculty at Phillips Andover Academy in Andover. The concert was a brilliant success and the organ a triumph that thereafter brought great music to the chapel.

A year or two later Mr. Flint rehearsed us in the choir in one of the Bach cantatas, BWV 150, "Nach Dir, Herr, Verlanget Mich, Mein Gott" (For thee, Lord, is my desire, My God") for a joint concert with Concord Academy while Miss Loring rehearsed the girls there with the performances to be at the Brooks and Concord chapels with organ accompaniment by Mr. Flint. The cantata was scored for soloists, chorus and small orchestra, and Nadia Boulanger would conduct the final rehearsal and the performances.

This was the first of our three experiences with Mlle. Boulanger. After the war began in Europe in 1939 she came to live in Cambridge and taught at the Longy School of Music. She dressed in black, wore a pince-nez and had her black hair tied in a bun. Short of stature and thin, she radiated authoritative force and commanded total attention and concentration on executing her musical directions. She always brought out the best in her performers and so it was on the three occasions we were privileged to perform for her.

The second occasion was performing a larger work for soloists, chorus and orchestra, the beautiful and stirring Bach "Magnificat" again with Concord Academy. At the rehearsal of one of the choruses, "Omnes, omnes generationes", Mlle. Boulanger instructed how to sing a full stop rest before a thundering return of "Omnes, omnes": "You are zeeing the Grand Canyon for the first time!" This made an indelible impression. Mr. Flint was the bass soloist, and Miss Loring provided the piano accompanist. I believe the performance mostly met Mlle. Boulanger's expectations.

The final experience we had with Mlle. Boulanger was in my sixth form year. Again with Concord we performed an abridged version of Henry Purcell's King Arthur, a semi-opera in five acts with a libretto by John Dryden, first performed in London in 1691. The beauty of Purcell's music captivated us and the choral parts were a joy to sing. Mlle. Boulanger was a dedicated and accomplished champion of this work which, sadly, is seldom performed.

In addition to Mr. Flint and Mlle. Boulanger, Mr. Waterston treated me to chamber music. As an accomplished cellist, he played in a string quartet with colleagues at Andover, and I was privileged to hear some of their performances of Haydn, Mozart and Beethoven quartets. I also heard him play one or more of the Bach solo cello suites. My growing exposure to great classical music was enhanced by the availability of 78 rpm recordings of the principal orchestral works of the masters that one could listen to in listening booths in one of the buildings as well as the Sunday evening two-hours of recordings Mr. Ashburn would play in his study for many of us. In this way I came to love some of the symphonies and concertos of Beethoven, Brahms, Hayden, Mozart, and Tchaikovsky. The greatness of Bach and Handel, of other choral and chamber music and of the principal opera composers would be revealed to me later on. But Brooks began for me this life-long love of much of the classical music repertoire.

Some thoughts about other important members of the faculty during my years at Brooks:

John Tower Thompson (1928-58, 1971-75). Tower Thompson lived to be a centenarian. A recent graduate of Williams College when he arrived as among the first faculty at Brooks, his field was English literature and he was my teacher of British poetry and prose from Chaucer onwards for at least two years. In his understated and gentle way he was an effective, dedicated teacher who created for many of us a lasting interest and love of the great English writers, particularly Shakespeare, Marlow, Milton, Addison, Goldsmith, Byron, Browning, George Eliot, and Tennyson. In 1958 he published *Thirty Years at Brooks*, a splendid history of the school almost from its beginnings. For many years he was the editor of *The Archbishop*, the school's quarterly magazine distributed to alumni and parents and always featuring the Headmaster's letter, news of the school, commissioned articles, and alumni notes. It was so named to distinguish it from *The Bishop*, the student quarterly. While I was at Brooks Mr. Thompson built an attractive residential house towards the lake for his own bachelor use which eventually reverted to the school. He became a Brooks institution and legend, retiring in 1975 to Sarasota, Florida, and returning to visit Brooks from time to time well into his 90s. He died in 2008 at 101.

Howard T. Kingsbury (1929-41, 1952-69), a Groton crew star in 1924, whence the nickname "Ox", came to Brooks to teach math and coach crew upon graduating from Yale. He excelled at both: he enabled me to enjoy math the year I was in his class; and he produced championship crews for most of his years at Brooks. He had a lovely wife Jerry who survived him by many years. I became very fond of both of them. He left in 1941 to serve in the military and did not return until about 10 years later.

Waldo H. Holcombe (1933-51), known as "Wok" Holcombe, a graduate of Harvard College and the son of Harvard's Professor Arthur Holcombe, a renowned teacher of government, came to Brooks to teach science and coach crew with Ox Kingsbury. He was not one of my teachers but I came to know and admire his gentle probing mind at faculty teas with his interesting wife Ruth who also taught math. He too was a great crew coach with championship crews with Ox and in the years after Ox left. In our sixth-form year, however, the first crew won only two races, St. Mark's and Noble's, and lost two very close races to St. George's and Exeter. Like Tower Thompson, the Holcombes also built a fine residential house toward the lake which eventually reverted to the school

Oscar M. Root (1933-69) taught biology and was also an esteemed ornithologist. In teaching us biology our third-form year there was no nonsense of his or our doubting the scientific validity of the facts of the evolution of species including man's descent from primates as has been suggested in recent years by some religious groups and school boards who disparage the work and the worth of Charles Darwin and his successors as contrary to holy writ as of course it necessarily and correctly is. Mr. Root was one of the great teachers at Brooks and strongly influenced many graduates to pursue careers in biology and ecology.[13] He was a pioneer environmentalist and in nature walks he interested many boys in the observable and beautiful species of birds, flora, fauna, and trees in the Brooks' environs.

Rogers Vaughan Scudder (1936-66) came to Brooks as a recent Harvard College graduate to teach English. He then went to Groton for about the next 40 years, also teaching Greek and Latin. While I was not one of his students I was well aware of "Doc" Scudder as we called him and of the affection in which his students and dormitory residents of "Hell's Corner" in lower Whitney held him. In later years while at Groton he came to two of our later class reunions where he was most welcome.

In our sixth-form English class, we had a new teacher, the poet Louis O. Coxe (1940-42), who introduced us to the more notable recent poets, via a magnificent new textbook, *Reading Poems: An Introduction to Critical Study* by two college professors, Wright Thomas, University of Wiscon-

---

13 A prominent example is Charles H. W. Foster, class of 1945, a Brooks trustee 1962-71, a 1994 winner of the Distinguished Brooksian Award, who has devoted his life to public service and teaching in the fields of environmental protection and ecology, as a Google of his website reveals.

sin, and Stuart Gerry Brown, Grinnell College, and published in 1941 in New York by the Oxford University Press. While the 301 poems were much of the great English poetry from the 16th century on, organized in seven parts (lyric, sonnets, narrative and dramatic, satirical, pastoral, serious wit and symbolism, and religious experience poems), Mr. Coxe focused mostly on how we should read the more recent poets Auden, Crane, Dickinson, Eliot, Frost, Hopkins, Jeffers, MacLeish, MacNeice, Pound, Spender, Stevens, and Yeats. Mr. Coxe was a gifted teacher and he made poetry a heady and lasting experience for us, particularly in trying to comprehend T. S. Eliot's *The Waste Land* published in 1923, perhaps the greatest 20th century poem in the English language. I have kept this book and continue to treasure it.

In sports, we had scheduled games on Saturday afternoons with several other school teams either at Brooks or at the other school. These included in one or more sports Andover Jayvees, Belmont Hill, our principal rival, Browne and Nichols, Governor Dummer, Exeter, Groton, Johnson High, Methuen High, Middlesex, Noble and Greenough, Pomfret, Rivers, St. George's, and St. Mark's.

I played one of the running guards on the football team my fifth and sixth-form years, perhaps responding to Papa's football prayerful exhortations to his youthful sons. I did not qualify in any other varsity sport. In football we had a new coach starting in 1940 with my fifth form year, Leo Cronin (1940-53). Leo had played guard on the Notre Dame football team under the legendary coach Knute Rockne (1888-1931) and he transmitted that excellence to the Brooks football teams: unremitting practice and preparation in the fundamentals of blocking and tackling and running perhaps half a dozen plays. "Give them that body shiver", he would exclaim and demonstrate. Leo truly was one of the great teachers of my life: cooperation, team play, sportsmanship, discipline, courage, determination to win, respect and tough but courteous treatment of your opponents, these were among the values he instilled in us. In 1941 we played against five schools. The Noble's team outplayed us by a wide margin; but thanks to Leo Cronin we won the other four games decisively, including the one against Belmont Hill, our principal rival.

Finally, we were sixth formers. The previous June Mr. Ashburn had appointed me to be the next Senior Prefect succeeding my friend Francis Parkman, Jr., as he had my brother Mike for his sixth form year in 1934-35. He also appointed four of my classmates as Prefects to assist me. To a large extent we had a student government to administer routine matters of school life and discipline with appointed officers in each of the lower forms. My functions were largely to plan and oversee the various activities, make announcements, preside at meetings, and resolve the more trouble-some disciplinary matters. One involved recommending to Mr. Ashburn the expulsion of a student who repeatedly had violated the no-smoking ban and flouted warnings; another the recommended expulsion of a boy for having sex with one of the maids.

In our fifth-form year, Mr. Ashburn, following the fall of France in 1940 and the growing Nazi and Japanese threats and the likelihood of American involvement in the war, established the Brooks Battalion to learn military discipline and close-order drill. The school was organized into three companies with appointed officers and lower ranks. We wore issued dark blue trousers, shirts and overseas caps and black shoes. Mr. Ashburn appointed me the battalion commander for our sixth-form year. After the Pearl Harbor attack and for Hitler his disastrous declaration of war against us shortly after in December 1941 that ensured his defeat, we all took the twice weekly afternoon drills seriously as most of us would soon join the military. We also manned a day and night observation post on nearby Cow Hill in case of enemy aircraft attack, although in hind-sight this was unrealistic and unnecessary. The battalion marched in the Memorial Day parade in North Andover along with veterans of the Span-ish-American War and WW I.

James D. Regan (1942-46), the retired long-serving senior master at Groton, came to Brooks during my sixth form year to teach French as a wartime service with the departures of Messrs. Waterston and Starbuck. He remembered fondly my brother Pat at Groton. I was sorry not to have had him as a teacher.

Our baseball prospects were brightened by the arrival of John P. McInnis (1942-46) as the coach. "Stuffy" McInnis had been a member of Connie Mack's celebrated $100,000 infield of the Philadelphia Athletics in the 1920s, then a record in professional baseball compensation. Despite his tireless efforts and the steady, outstanding pitching of classmate Dick Breck, the team won only four out of nine games. Success was ahead.

During my sixth-form year I and several classmates were confirmed as Episcopalians in a Sunday service at the chapel by Bishop Sherrill after extensive instruction by the Reverend Twombly, the rector of the North Andover Episcopal church. At that stage my belief and faith in God were inchoate. As I grew older and thought more about religion I gradually concluded that I had become at least agnostic about the existence of God while strongly supporting the teachings of Christ about the way one should live.

My best friends among my classmates at Brooks were Danny Danforth, Willy Frick, Peter Philip, and Jack Thayer. Peter Philip is the only one now living as I write this in 2011. Willy was the first to go, dying in an Army camp from a preexisting health condition that should have excluded him from military service. Then Jack Thayer, an advertising executive dying prematurely in Japan with a new Japanese wife who survives him in their Dedham home. Then Danny Danforth from cancer in middle age survived by his wife Sophie. I was privileged to be an usher at their wedding as I also was at Peter and Sabina Philip's.

At our graduation in June 1942, the Rector, Endicott Peabody, then recently retired as headmaster of Groton but chairman of the Brooks' trustees, handed us our diplomas and the various prizes. I received the Headmaster's Prize. My Mother and Aunt Louise were present, my brothers absent in military service. The Rector sat with us at lunch and fondly recalled Pat's years at Groton. I had been accepted as a freshman at Harvard College with a Harvard Club of Boston financial scholarship, probably on the strong recommendation of Mr. Ashburn; and because of the war classes would shortly begin.

I sum up my experience at Brooks by emphasizing the overriding, central, importance of Frank Davis Ashburn as the great teacher and molder of our lives. His aim was to prepare every boy at Brooks for life and he largely succeeded. As a preacher in the Sunday chapel services, he probably at least equalled Phillips Brooks in imparting the eternal values of a Christian life but forgiving of our failures if we would keep on trying.

FDA viewed his calling to be to empower the good in every boy in the life-long struggle within each of us between good and evil. This led him as headmaster to give many boys second and sometimes third chances to overcome their failings which distinguished and advantaged Brooks from other schools and often so enabled these boys to succeed. He was the master of the faculty at least during the years I was there. Highly educated and widely read, he planned the curriculum and selected the faculty. In 1944 he published the definitive biography of the Rector, *Peabody of Groton*. Contrary to a widespread impression that Louis Auchincloss's highly acclaimed novel, *The Rector of Justin* was based on the author's knowledge of the Rector from his years as a Groton boy, Auchincloss in his final book, *A View from Old New York*, written in his 90s in the last year of his life and published in 2011, wrote that Leonard Hand, the eminent federal judge, was the model for his fictional rector.

Mr. Ashburn also enabled me to complete six forms at Brooks by providing substantial financial scholarships. How the family managed to pay the remaining tuition and other fees I never knew as was also true of my freshman year at Harvard, to my regret.

I stayed in touch with the Ashburns for the rest of their lives. He appointed me president of the nascent alumni association for 1947 while I was at Harvard Law School. This renewed my contact with the Ashburns and with the faculty, particularly the Waterstons.

Phyllis Ashburn died of lung cancer about 1964. In complementing her husband's role, she had long established a high order of social decorum at Brooks and was a lifetime influence in improving the manners, the courteous behavior, and the attire of Brooks boys in all social settings. She was much loved and missed.

Jean Lang had been Mr. Ashburn's secretary for many years and they married a few years after Phyllis's death. After he retired in 1974 they lived in Plymouth near her family. In the 1990s my brother Mike arranged for them to live at Fox Hill, a retirement community in Westwood, Mass., to which Mike and his wife Joan had moved a few years earlier. When visiting them I would also stop and talk to the Ashburns. Personal relationships with him always remained formal and somewhat at arm's length. But they were always cordial. There was no small talk, and no equality of relationship despite the passage of time. His mind remained superb to the end. He died there in 1997 at 94. She survived him there for several more years.

Frank Ashburn was unquestionably one of the foremost educators and headmasters in secondary school education in the United States in the 20th century. I believe my brother Mike who knew him longer and better than I and who died in 2004 would endorse this appraisal.

6. Life Away from Brooks School 1936-42.

I will now write about my life for the years 1936-42 apart from Brooks. When I began at Brooks in September 1936, Mother was living in a small apartment in New York with Nana, her mother. A year later my brother Pat rented a new home for us on Pinckney Street on Beacon Hill in Boston. He had begun practicing law with Herrick, Smith, Donald & Farley in the fall of 1936. Mike was then a sophomore at Harvard; Papa was struggling on his own in New York. Mother would welcome this move to Boston to see more of her sons. New York and Greenwich friends and mothers of Pat's many friends provided introductions for her and she soon had a circle of friends and bridge-playing partners. I enjoyed Christmas and Easter vacations in Boston and being Aunt Louise's guest at the Friday afternoon concerts of the Boston Symphony Orchestra, then long conducted by Serge Koussevitzky.

For the 1937 summer Pat arranged to rent a cottage for us on the property of Mrs. Stephen Weld in Wareham, Mass., a summer resort on Buzzards Bay and adjoining the Cape Cod Canal. Pat was friends with her step granddaughters, the five beautiful, sophisticated Weld sisters, Mary, Rosie, the twins Adie and Kay, and Frotty, the first four of whom married his close friends at Harvard. Many years later, Kay and Benny Bacon's daughter Martha, married my godson, David Martin, Jr., as I will later recount.

Mrs. Weld's place in Indian Neck was not on the water, and the cottage we rented adjoined their private golf course and was near Long Beach for swimming. We had a 1934 Ford, and Pat helped Mother get a driver's license in Wareham as I was still too young. She was a very timid driver. This would be the first of three summers in Wareham.

The news of Papa's suicide in late June overwhelmed and devastated us. We were conflicted by his death as ending hope of his recovery and the further disgrace of suicide. He shot himself at age 55 in the bathtub while living alone in New York at the Murray Hill Hotel. He left notes for each of his children, and perhaps to Mother. Mine was: "This is the best I can do for you. Great love, Papa." The police notified Pat. Aunt Louise drove over from Duxbury to be with us. She arranged for him to be buried in the family plot in the beautiful Mayflower Cemetery in Duxbury as later she, Mother, and my sisters would be too. We all foregathered there for the burial and a fitting graveside service. This dampened the rest of the summer's activities. Mother eventually received the remains of his life insurance, about $50K, which Pat invested for her. Aunt Dorothy, Papa's younger sister, I later learned, would blame Mother for his death, having deserted her husband when he needed her most. Yet Mother surely could not have saved him, and I believe Aunt Dorothy's verdict to have been understandable but unjust. I also believe Papa had elements of greatness.

There was no money for Mike to continue at Harvard. That summer, thanks to the efforts of the father of a Brooks friend, Silas Howland, he and Si started working for the Chase Brass & Copper Co. in Waterbury, Conn., in a young executive sales training program. It was demanding physical and mental work. Mother decided to keep house for them so that in the fall of 1938 we moved to Waterbury, rented a house and furnished it with Mother's Greenwich furniture which had been in storage.

By 1939 Mike, who had started courting Joan Shaw the previous summer in Wareham on weekends, arranged after almost two years in the Waterbury mill to transfer to the company's Boston office as a salesman of their products. In the summer of 1939 we returned to Boston. Pat was now managing an apartment building for his law firm at 1056 East Beacon Street, almost in Brookline. Mother, he, Mike, and I were able to live there in a spacious apartment free of rent. The furniture was duly moved from Waterbury. Si Howland married a Waterbury girl, Beebee Philips, whom I would come to know as a widow and cherished friend many years later in the magnificent Howland home in Vineyard Haven on Martha's Vineyard.

Our second summer in Wareham in 1938 was in the larger Mrs. Nye's house, also on the Weld property. My sister Louise joined us from Palm Beach with her two daughters, Fifi now 6 and baby Priscilla born the previous October. Pat and Mike would be with us on weekends, Pat from Boston and Mike in his radiator-overheating Buick from Waterbury.

That summer we came to know the Shaw family from Needham who had a turn-of-the-century summer place at Cedar Point on Buzzards Bay next to the Cape Cod Canal acquired and built by their maternal grandfather Howard Stockton, the founder of AT&T. Like the daughters of the Weld family, there were four very attractive, sophisticated, bright Shaw daughters, Eleanor, Rosie, Joan, and Gertrude. There were also two sons, Samuel Parkman Shaw, Jr., a Groton graduate and classmate of Mike's at Harvard, and Howard Stockton Shaw the youngest member of the family. Mike's best friend and classmate from Brooks and Harvard, Baty Blake, was courting Rosie Shaw whom he married in 1939. Through Baty, Mike had met and started seeing Joan Shaw, commuting from Waterbury on the weekends.

Howard, "Howie", and I became best friends. We were the same age. He was at Groton, and we became almost daily companions that summer and the next one. He had a Nathanael Herreshoff 12' sailboat, and I would crew for him in the Saturday afternoon races of the Kittansett Yacht Club off Marion as well as other sailing outings. I don't recall winning but we had a lot of fun and I learned more about sailing in those beautiful waters.

We also played tennis singles and doubles with his sisters on the family tennis court; swam from their beach and hiked the two mile long dike built by the Army Corps of Engineers to protect the canal. He took me that summer and the next to the national men's and women's tennis doubles at the Longwood Cricket Club in Brookline where we watched the great of those days—Don Budge, the Australians Bromwich and Turnquist, Alice Marble, Helen Wills Moody, and Sarah Palfrey, among the other greats I no longer remember. I became fond of his parents and siblings and virtually became a member of the Shaw family.

There was a severe hurricane in September 1938 that badly damaged coastal New England and some interior areas as well. Mother and Sally narrowly escaped flooding as they drove through Providence en route to a social engagement. I was back at Brooks and there we lost some magnificent trees and were without power for several days.

For the 1939 summer in Wareham we rented a Mrs. Parker's house which was much nearer to the Shaw's place. Now in Boston Mike intensified courting Joan and they became engaged before year's end with a planned June 1940 wedding. The European war began early in September and the country became divided between the interventionists quietly encouraged by FDR and the "America First" isolationists led by Charles Lindbergh. Congress, mostly isolationist, at FDR's request revised the Neutrality Act to end an harms embargo but required any supplying of munitions to England and France to be on a "cash and carry" basis in foreign bottoms.

In the spring of 1940, during the Easter vacation from Brooks, I was treated to a Metropolitan Opera performance in New York of Wagner's "Tristan und Isolde" starring Kirsten Flagstadt and Lauritz Melchoir as the principals. Her performance, especially of the "Liebestodt" or "love death", was one of the great musical experiences of my life. This was for me the beginning of a new appreciation of the greatness of some operas as at the summit of man's artistic creativity.

We did not return to Wareham for the summer of 1940. Mike and Joan married in June in Needham and began living in the house her parents had built for them on their place on South Street in Needham that would remain their home for the next 50 years when they would sell it and move to the newly built retirement community, "Fox Hill Village", in nearby Westwood. Their first child, a son, John, Jr., was born on August 1, 1941.

After the wedding Mother and I departed for Seattle to spend several weeks with her mother (Nana) and sister (Aunt Elizabeth Brinkley) on Bainbridge Island, a ferry ride across Eliott Bay and Puget Sound from Seattle. On the way we stopped to visit the New York World's Fair at Flushing Meadows, later the site of LaGuardia Airport. It had opened the year before as the war in Europe began. Our hosts were Betty and Carl Elhermann. He was an eminent lawyer, a friend of Papa's and one of my godfathers (Pat being the other). I liked and respected Uncle Carl but did not know him well. He was an authority on the Bible, and I remember from Greenwich and New York days his occasional visits and his unavailing efforts to interest me in the Bible. Mother said he was also a superb bridge player. After some sightseeing at the Fair we dined as their guests at the lovely French Restaurant. Later that evening they put us on the train to Chicago. I never saw them again. Nana, my grandmother, had arranged that we should travel in grand style in a drawing room accommodation for the four-day journey, changing to the Great Northern line in Chicago the next day.

By then Hitler's army had swiftly overrun France and the Luftwaffe was bombing the airfields and aircraft factories in England preparatory to landing German troops. It was a grim, fearful time. With the fall of

France and the German occupation of the Low Countries the Japanese were advancing on Indochina and the Dutch East Indies. President Roosevelt persuaded a reluctant Congress to enact a draft law for the U.S. Army and to fund large-scale rearmament including a two-ocean Navy. We were heading towards war although in our innocent ignorance these bad tidings did not intrude on our summer.

I had a marvellous several weeks with family and new friends on Bainbridge Island. At sixteen, I had recently acquired a Massachusetts driver's license, and I had the use of a car while I was there. We had a house near the country club and lovely homes overlooking a golf course and breathtaking views of snow-capped Mt. Rainier (14,440 ft.) to the south and the Cascade mountains to the east of Seattle and the Olympics to the west. My cousin Betty Brinkley Nickum and her husband, the naval architect George Nickum, had a nearby summer house with very young children and I grew fond of Betty and George who were about the ages of Sally and Pat.

Sally had visited there in the summer of 1931, still much remembered by Nana, Aunt Elizabeth and Betty not entirely in a complimentary way. Sally then was provocatively beautiful and her somewhat forward manner provoked comment. Also Nana and Aunt Elizabeth had hoped Betty would marry Bob Fulton, her brother Rawn's college roommate, and accused Sally of stealing Bob from Betty, a charge Betty stoutly denied.

I made some lasting friends. One was Catherine Baillargeon, then about my age whose formidable mother had one of the grand places near the country club and would receive friends of her children on her porch but not inside the house. Catherine and I would enjoy the weekly dances at the club, including Scottish reels, as well as other activities. She would elope later to a young naval officer, Dermott Noonan; and some 30 years later she and I would meet again in Seattle while I was there for extended litigation for the Lockheed Shipbuilding and Construction Company.

On returning to Boston early in August Mother and I went for a few weeks to "The Inn" at Biddeford Pool on the Maine coast just above Kennebunkport and below Portland, where Mrs. James and other friends of

Mother's had summer places. She would return there for the next several summers for lots of bridge and walking on the golf course by the sea. The ocean temperature was rarely above the low 60s which discouraged swimming as did the rocky beach. The Thursday night lobster dinners at The Inn I still remember as great treats.

While I was there Aunt Shonce invited me to be the guest of Uncle Goodwin's relative, Gertrude Robinson Smith, over an August weekend for performances of the Boston Symphony at Tanglewood in Stockbridge, Massachusetts. This was to be a far bigger treat. Of course I went and was thrilled. Miss Smith, then at least Mother's age, had given the land for this summer classical music school and festival to the Boston Symphony a few years before; and this summer was perhaps the first with performances in the newly completed concert shed. She of course had the best seats and I was honored to be among her guests and meet the legendary conductor, Serge Koussevitzky (1874-1951), after one of the two concerts I attended. I don't remember what was played other than that the sound was glorious.

I returned in August 1941, again as her guest, to hear memorable performances of Mozart's Symphony No. 29 in A, Mendelssohn's "Italian" Symphony, and above all a compelling, masterful Koussevitzky reading of the recent Shostakovich Fifth Symphony as the Germans were approaching Moscow. One just knew from the dynamic last movement of this work that they would fail to take that city as we would later learn they had.

In October 1940, Pat was called to active duty in the Navy. While at Harvard he had enrolled in the Navy ROTC and on graduation was commissioned an ensign in the naval reserve. Thereafter, for modest pay, he maintained his active status by attending periodic drills at the Boston Navy Yard and two-week summer cruises on Navy ships to the Virgin Islands and similar destinations. That month, FDR ordered the Navy to start convoying ships going from East coast and Canadian ports to England as far as Iceland to relieve the overtaxed burdens of the Royal Navy in combating German submarines which had been sinking alarming and growing numbers of British and Allied ships. This led to his call to active duty, and by then he had been promoted to lieutenant junior grade. He was placed in command of a small mine clearing ship in Boston Harbor and points northeast. Within a year he was promoted to lieutenant and began training in antisubmarine warfare.

For the summer of 1941 there were two principal events in addition to visiting Mother again in Biddeford Pool. I have already described returning to Tanglewood. Before that, Mr. Ashburn had suggested that I spend about four weeks earlier that summer as an unpaid counsellor with free room and board to underprivileged boys from the Boston slums at a summer camp near Brooks in Boxford. Brooks had supplied two counsellors for several previous summers. The camp was run by the North Bennett Street Industrial School in Boston.

A Brooks classmate, John Dexter, and I reported to the school near the North Station to meet the boys and ride by bus with about twenty-five of them, ages 10-15, to the camp for one week. This would be repeated with a different group for each of the following three weeks. The boys had mostly Italian parents and many had never left the city before, much less had had a camping experience. For me, the prior Kieve experience was invaluable in having prepared me to organize and supervise the daily activities of softball, swimming, fishing, hiking, and overnight camping in the beautiful countryside. A few of the boys were belligerent, at first resisting doing what John Dexter or I asked them to do, sometimes threatening to have an older brother or dad come and beat us up. That never happened, but it was inwardly intimidating. In all, that summer camp was a great experience for them and for John and me.

The second event was Pat's marriage that August to Martha Means Davons of Boston. Their courtship of the preceding two years had been interrupted by Pat's Navy service. Her prior brief marriage to Lithgow Davons had terminated several years before. She was a year or two younger than Pat, now 31. It was time for each to marry the other after unsuccessful efforts by each to find the lifetime mate.

Marty, attractive. educated and well read in English literature, particularly Trollope, was the youngest of the three daughters of Marjorie

Rice Means and Gordon Means. Her sisters, then married, were Cynthia married to Zenas Colt, an executive with the Crane Paper Co., and Nancy married to Robert Hallowell with a family business. Her parents had divorced: her mother also living in Boston and her father having remarried on the North Shore of Boston. The wedding was at the lovely place of Cynthia Colt and Zenas Colt in Dalton, near Pittsfield in western Massachusetts. Pat got leave from the Navy and was married resplendent in his lieutenant's dress whites. I enjoyed meeting Marty's sisters and the almost grown up Colt children.

Pat's leave was brief. In early 1942 he would be transferred to the Navy submarine warfare school in Key West and Marty was able to live with him there while expecting their first of four sons, Peter Durant, who arrived that November 17 in a Miami hospital. I was asked to be one of his godfathers, a rewarding and affectionate relationship for me that has continued.

7. Freshman at Harvard College.

Shortly after graduating from Brooks, I became a freshman at Harvard. Because of the war Harvard and other colleges accelerated their academic programs to enable undergraduates to complete more of their education before reporting for military service. On this basis we would complete the freshman year early in 1943 instead of the usual June.

For the freshman year I lived in Kirkland House with Brooks classmates Bingo Carroll and Jack Thayer as roommates. Freshmen traditionally lived in the Harvard Yard. Because of the war the dormitories in the Yard were occupied by ROTC students. Kirkland House was one of the several houses built in the 1930s near the Charles River for the upper classmen.

Having been awarded a financial scholarship, I also was able to reduce the cost of room and board by waiting on tables for either the lunch or evening meals in the Kirkland House dining room. Learning to carry the heavy trays held high with one hand and serve the food was a challenge that was good for me; and I made friends with some of my fellow waiters one or two of whom later became my classmates at Harvard Law School after the war.

The freshmen courses were mostly lectures by the professors to large numbers of students followed up by smaller classes with so-called "section leaders" who were graduate students. In the lectures one sat there passively taking notes. There was no dialogue with the professor. So it was with History 1, lectures on modern European history by Professor Roger "Frisky" Merriman recalled from retirement as a war service as younger faculty joined the military; with Music 1, lectures on a survey of the history of music by Professor Archibald Davidson; with lectures on Jonathon Edwards and his influence by Professor Ralph Barton Perry; and lectures on government by a Professor Eliot as I remember. All this compared unfavorably with the interactive teaching at Brooks. There was, I believed then and now, over-emphasis on fact memorization at the expense of the meaning and a deeper understanding of the subject matter. I comfortably passed these courses but did not achieve distinction in any of them. There was no spark of inspiration.

That summer I sang in the Harvard Glee Club under its splendid director G. Wallace Woodworth, long an assistant and recently the successor to Professor Davidson as its director. We rehearsed four choruses from the Brahms's Requiem and performed them with the Boston Pops at the shell on the Esplanade along the Charles River. It was another wonderful experience with great music which I renewed when I returned to Harvard after the war.

That fall, again because of the war, election to the various social clubs was moved up from the fall of the sophomore year. As a legacy with brothers Pat and Mike having become members, I was elected to the Fly Club while my roommates Bingo Carroll joined the Porcellian and Jack Thayer the A.D. Club, each as a legacy. The Fly had an attractive and comfortable clubhouse at 2 Holyoke Place off Mt. Auburn Street next to the entrance to Lowell House and was superbly run by the long-serving steward James Corcoran. There I was pleased to find Francis Parkman and Larry White who had graduated from Brooks the year before I did. Also elected when I was were two Buckley classmates, John Munroe and Bill Ziegler. I increasingly spent my spare time at the club with these friends and making new ones. Most days the club served lunch and dinner which I also enjoyed whenever I could.

Soon it was final exam time in late December or early January. In November I enlisted in the Army Reserve Corps with a scheduled active duty reporting date of February 15, 1943. I would have preferred the Navy but I could not meet their 20-20 uncorrected vision requirements. Needing glasses did not disqualify one from serving in the Army. Having learned later in January that I had satisfactorily completed the freshman year and would be eligible to return as a sophomore after the war, I now faced life in the Army which I will relate in Part Two of this autobiography.

I now conclude Part One of this enriching first eighteen years of my beginnings.

Part Two Army Life 1943-46

1. USA 1943-44.

I reported for duty to Camp Devens on February 15, 1943, as previously arranged. Camp Devens, a reactivated World War I training camp, is near Ayer, Massachusetts, and the Boston & Maine railroad then provided direct service from the North Station in Boston. It was bitter cold when I arrived in the early afternoon, and the temperatures at night went down at least to twenty-five below zero Fahrenheit. In the initial processing, I was examined by a doctor and determined to be fit for duty, issued a uniform, an overcoat, boots, other clothing, a steel helmet, miscellaneous items and toiletries, a Gideon Society bible, and a barracks bag to store my few possessions. I was assigned and thereafter identified by serial no. 11121877 and engraved on dog tags I was told to wear around my neck at all times. I was now a private in the U.S. Army.

After being shown the barracks and a bed, I went on KP (kitchen police) duty for at least the next six hours washing pots and pans in the huge mess hall kitchen. The hot water was mostly steam and it was difficult to avoid burning my hands. Someone provided rubber gloves and that helped.

I remained at Camp Devens about a week. About half the time was spent on KP. Finally I was assigned to a group being sent for thirteen weeks of infantry basic training at Camp Wheeler near Macon, Georgia.

We travelled there later in February for about 30 hours in ancient Boston & Maine passenger cars with wooden benches. One of my companions was so depressed that he got off the train at Washington and stated walking back on the tracks toward Baltimore. He was soon apprehended.

As at Camp Devens the train took us into Camp Wheeler. We were assigned to a new company which with two other companies would form a new battalion for this basic infantry training. My company was commanded by a Captain Murrah, a West Point graduate recently returned from the North African campaign to liberate Tunisia and adjacent areas from German occupation. He was as splendid a leader and teacher of infantry combat as Leo Cronin had been at football as my coach. He was assisted by a Lieutenant Doheny who was at best adequate and by First Sergeant Koch, another giant like Phillip Brooks. When we did not meet either Captain Murrah's or Sergeant Koch's demands, the Sergeant would give us "the growl", as a warning of worse to come if we did not shape up immediately.

As at Camp Devens my company lived in a barracks with perhaps about 75 beds on each of two floors. Heat was provided for the first several weeks of cold weather by a pot belly coal stove which mostly burned dirty brown coal from which the fumes were pervasive. We each had an assigned bed and blanket and pillow. There were no sheets. There were a foot locker at the foot of the bed and a shelf above the bed for personal items. There was a latrine at one end of the barracks with showers, toilets, and a trough urinal.

Recently built, Camp Wheeler occupied an enormous area of undeveloped land, mostly woods, somewhat hilly, trails, and red-clay earth. The camp hosted thousands of troops in various stages of infantry training. There were some amenities: chapels, post exchanges, movie theatres, and libraries for the rare occasions the daily routine would permit us to partake of them.

Each member of our company was assigned to a particular squad and platoon. Those assigned to my squad and platoon were mostly farm boys from the hills of Tennessee with little schooling. One not from Tennessee had been a "yell leader" at Indiana University. He and I competed for squad leader; he was chosen after I, as the acting leader got the squad lost in a beginning training exercise when I misplaced my glasses.

For the Southerners who comprised most of our company, the Civil War or the "War Between the States" as they called it, lived in their minds and Yankees were still presumptively to be damned. It was hard at first to make friends. Telling them I had been to Harvard would have put me at a serious disadvantage. I did meet another boy in a different company from Harvard who had made that mistake and became an object of derision. He also frequently went on "sick call" and that added to his unpopularity. There was no benefit in his company.

There were no blacks in infantry training at Camp Wheeler or in my other Army assignments as the Army, like the other services, shamefully perpetuated the total segregation of black and white servicemen until President Truman ordered the integration of all the armed forces in 1948.

Most days there was reveille at 6:00 a.m., followed by falling in to a prescribed formation of the company by squad and platoon for roll call about 15 minutes later. Sergeant Koch presided at roll call, and those inexcusably not present or late were subject to punishment such as extra push-ups or guard duty. He then would march us to the mess hall for breakfast of cereal, milk, powdered eggs, sausage or bacon and coffee which we received in our issued mess kits in a chow line dispensed by other soldiers assigned to KP duties which would also be our turn in due course. After breakfast we returned to our barracks to make our beds for inspection so that a 50-cent piece would bounce off the tightness of the blanket. The daily training would shortly commence.

We had been issued the Garand M-1 rifle to replace the Springfield 1904 rifle used in World War I. We had to learn how to shoot the M-1 and how to maintain it. There was daily target practice at a rifle range with live .30 caliber ammunition until each of us achieved a minimum level of competence in rapid loading and accurate firing. Maintenance was also challenging as it required learning to assemble and disassemble and clean the rifle and its component parts and eventually be able to do this blindfolded as knowing how to do so at night and without light would be requisite in combat. Many thought the Springfield 1904 had greater accuracy; but it had the disadvantage of having to reload after each shot whereas the M-1 would fire up to about eight shots in rapid succession before reloading the cartridge. All this was supervised by Captain Murrah. The officers were issued carbines, a light automatic rifle.

Most mornings we had physical training to prepare us for the increasingly long hikes with increasingly heavy loads in our back packs. This included push-ups, sit-ups, stretching, and other calisthenics, all of which after a few weeks made us physically fit for the marches to come. There was also daily close-order drill and practice of the manual of arms which was learning to position the M-1 correctly in response to commands such as "right shoulder arms," "port arms," "present arms," and "order arms" and in unison. There was also a weekly inspection of each of us and our beds by Captain Murrah.

At first, the hikes were after lunch in the mess hall to which the company was marched. In the chow line we had meat, potatoes, gravy, a vegetable and canned fruit dispensed into mess kits to eat from tables and benches in about fifteen minutes. Then perhaps another fifteen minutes to receive mail in the barracks before falling in for the next roll call.

Receiving mail was most important to morale, including mine. I had weekly letters from Mother and occasionally from my siblings and Aunt Louise. Henry Foster, a friend still at Brooks, and I started writing to each other with increasing frequency and this continued importantly throughout my Army service. His friendship and letters meant a great deal to me then and long thereafter. When I later was sent to England, France and Germany in 1944 we wrote and received letters by "V-mail", a then recent means of electronic transmission which greatly speeded delivery but limited length to less than two sheets.

We also had some personal time in the barracks after supper to read and write letters in the dim light before lights out at 10pm.

As the weeks went by the training and marches led by Captain Murrah increased in intensity and duration. We were introduced to firing machine guns and mortars, digging fox holes, crawling beneath barbed wire with live machine gun fire overhead, and rope climbing vertical obstacle courses over fifteen feet high within a prescribed time limit. The marches grew longer and the field packs full of what we would carry in combat plus other items such as parts of machine guns and mortars. Many developed blisters on their heels from ill fitting boots or had other physical problems that prevented their completing that day's march. Eventually these marches would last all day, with 10-minute breaks and short additional periods for eating the C and K rations we carried at meal times.

Gradually the weather gave way from a cold winter when we arrived to the beginnings of spring as March progressed. By April many days turned hot and humid which made the marches more taxing. There was no doubt in our minds that the increasingly realistic training was preparing us for forthcoming infantry combat in which our casualties would likely be high. So it behooved us to learn all we could. There was not, as I recall, in the time available, training in infantry tactics of attacking or defending different kinds of objectives in varying terrain conditions. Perhaps the thought was that that essential training would come once we were assigned to a combat unit and perhaps even under battle conditions. I would not find out.

In the summer of 1942 a delegation of college presidents called on General George Marshall, the Army chief of staff, in Washington. They told him that the Army was taking most of their students with the result that the colleges could not survive financially. General Marshall said he would think about it and let them know his decision. He was then beset by demands for ever more troops for the forthcoming North African campaign, to be followed by the invasions of Sicily and Italy, and reinforcing General MacArthur in fighting the Japanese.

Having obtained the enthusiastic approval of Secretary of War Stimson, General Marshall notified the college presidents that he would make 100,000 troops available to them starting in June 1943 when they completed infantry training. For about nine months they would study specified engineering subjects or various language courses among them German, Japanese, French and Italian. In the language courses, the students would be expected to be proficient in reading, writing and speaking the particular language. That spring the Army would conduct a special intelligence-quotient test at the training camps to determine the student selection. Thus Secretary Stimson and General Marshall created what became known as "the Army Specialist Training Program" or "ASTP". I took the IQ test and was among the fortunate to be selected. The rest of my company was sent to Sicily as infantry replacements. I later learned that few survived.

Before I departed Camp Wheeler, Mother travelled from Boston to Macon, Georgia, early in May for a weekend visit that we had arranged. She stayed at the Dempsey Hotel and I got leave to be with her. She went next to Washington to be with Sally who on May 6 bore her second son, Travis Fulton. Mike and Joan's second son, Lawrence Stockton Coburn, would arrive on July 11.

I left Camp Wheeler in late May or early June 1943 and was sent to a small college in Auburn, Alabama, for processing and assignment into the ASTP program. I was given a choice of language preference and selected German. A week or so later I was told I was being sent to Lehigh University in Bethlehem, Pennsylvania, to learn German. I arrived there in late June. Lehigh was primarily an engineering college started in 1865 by the Bethlehem Steel Co. By 1943 it was long well established as a leading engineering school in metallurgy and cognate subjects, and many of its graduates worked for Bethlehem and other steel companies. It also had a strong German department.

For the next nine months I led essentially a college-student life at Lehigh. About the only connection with the Army was the daily wearing of the uniform. There were about twenty-five of us in the German program from various Army training camps. Most had had some college. We lived in Taylor Hall, one of the college gothic stone dormitories in the Quad on a steep hill. There were also other ASTP students there studying French and Engineering. The classes began almost immediately: grammar in the morning and conversation in the afternoons with native German speakers. We were taught "high German" or "hoch Deutsch" as distinguished from the several German dialects throughout the country. Increasingly the classes were conducted in German. Our grammar teacher, a Mr. Bull, was very thorough and exacting, making us recite daily in German what he was imparting to us. Those of us who had studied Latin grammar had an easier time because of the strong influence of Latin grammar on German grammar, far more so than it had on English grammar which unlike German is highly irregular and disorderly. In addition, because German is essentially phonetic the conversation classes facilitated reading and writing German as well. Each week we made measurable progress and soon began conversing with each other "auf Deutsch".

Once the grammar instruction was completed after several months and we passed the qualifying grammar exam, we also studied German government with Professor Schulz and Economics with Professor Carothers. Professor Schulz had us study the German constitution of 1936. We wondered why since it was obvious to us if not to Professor Schulz that it did not constrain Hitler or his gang of Nazi thugs. Professor Caruther's lectures mostly harangued us about the New Deal's excessive regulation of business and how it was strangling free enterprise, also further wasting our time with nonsense.

Surprisingly, I had an enjoyable social life at Lehigh. Early on at a social event that summer I met Ellen Williams, a young lady who had completed the first year at Swarthmore, a college near Philadelphia founded by Quakers. I soon met her older sister, also a Swarthmore student whom another ASTP student was seeing. The four of us began double dating. Until the sisters returned to college in the fall, we were their frequent guests for meals in the lovely home of their parents, President and Mrs. C.C. Williams, and then again when they returned home for the Christmas vacation. This gave us a welcome home-like refuge from dormitory life. I liked the parents very much and they were very hospitable and kind to me. President Williams told me how important the ASTP program was for Lehigh and other private colleges and how much he admired General Marshall for creating it.

That summer or fall I developed two impacted lower wisdom teeth, teeth that were painfully growing horizontally instead of vertically in my lower jawbone. Luckily I was able to persuade the Army to enable me to go to a civilian dentist in Easton, some twenty miles distant, whom Mrs. Williams recommended as the best available. Luckily there was no available Army dentist nearby. One day I took a street car there from Bethlehem. I do not remember the dentist's name but he was first-class. After administering the anesthetic novocaine (procaine) he proceeded with a hammer and chisel to extricate one of these teeth. I held an icepack next to my jaw on the trolley ride back to Bethlehem, and thankfully the pain and swelling were short lived. I repeated this about a week later for the second tooth, and that too went well.

I also sang in the choir in the beautiful Lehigh gothic-stone Packard Memorial Church. A highlight that Christmas was rehearsing and performing with a local orchestra Handel's *Messiah*, most of which I was learning for the first time. Surely it is one of the supreme works of choral music for performance at Christmas and Easter.

In December or January as we approached completing our time at Lehigh, each of us was interviewed and our records reviewed by a member of a small team from Camp Ritchie, the German prisoner-of-war-interrogation-training center in Maryland. They were recruiting for the next training class of about three months that would begin shortly after we finished at Lehigh. Those not selected would probably return to the Army and to whatever they had previously been trained for, in my case as an infantry replacement. I expressed a strong interest in the interrogation training to my interviewer and we seemed to connect on a personal level as well. I was selected for Camp Ritchie, to my great benefit.

In January before leaving Lehigh in mid-February for Camp Ritchie, I received word that Nana, my grandmother, had died in Boston. She and Mother had been living at the Vendome Hotel on Commonwealth Avenue near Dartmouth Street in Boston at some point after October 1940 when Pat was called to active Naval duty. I had visited Mother and Nana when I had a few days of leave over the Christmas holidays and her health then seemed as ever. She apparently contracted pneumonia early in

January and that was it. I was given compassionate leave for her funeral. Few family members were present.

My siblings were then unable to be there. Louise was caring for her two daughters in Palm Beach and was about to give birth to her third, Katherine on February 17, who was named for Mother. Her husband Mooney was a Naval officer stationed in Norman, Oklahoma. Pat, recently promoted to Lieutenant Commander, then had or was about to be given command of a newly commissioned destroyer-escort, the USS Emory, DE 28, at Mare Island, California, for convoy and antisubmarine service in the southwest Pacific. Mother and Marty travelled to the commissioning ceremony. Sally was living in Washington with Bob and her two young sons, Robert, Jr. ("Robin") and Travis, while Bob was producing the "Fulton GunAirstructor" for the Navy, a device he developed to teach Navy pilots to fly and to become proficient at aerial gunnery while seated in a mock cockpit facing a movie screen which responded to the controls manipulated in the cockpit. Mike and Joan and their two young sons, John Jr., and Lawrence Stockton, were living in Boise, Idaho, where Mike was a communications officer assigned to the Army Air Corps B-29 bomber aircraft training center there.

Only my sister-in-law Marty and I were there with Mother, Aunt Shonce, Uncle Goodwin, and Aunt Louise for the funeral service, as I remember. We now had to find Mother a place to live since she could not afford to remain at the Vendome. The Vendome was an old-fashioned residential hotel with a French cuisine that I had enjoyed visiting and dining on vacations from Brooks and Harvard. In the hotel's French dining room a piano trio would often play Haydn trios during dinner to my great enjoyment that began for me a lifetime of affection and appreciation for most of his music: his symphonies, chamber music, piano sonatas, choral music and some of his operas. For me he was one of the top ten composers of classical music.

Marty suggested I visit the Hunneman real estate office at 5 Arlington Street in Boston where she knew Ted Francis, one of the agents. I promptly did and explained Mother's need to Mr. Francis. Perhaps because Marty was his friend and I was in my Army private's uniform, he said "you and your mother are in great luck. An apartment in this building, a converted town house, has just become available. You may now see it, but we need an immediate decision." He showed it to me. It was on the third floor and the large living room faced the Public Gardens on Arlington Street. It had a small dining area and kitchen and one medium size bedroom and a bathroom. The monthly rent was $100. I told Mr. Francis that Mother, whom I did not have time to consult, much less let her see it, would take it. She was delighted, and this was her attractive home with her furniture and piano for perhaps the next fifteen plus years until the Katherine Gibbs secretarial school bought the building.

The next few weeks at Lehigh passed quickly. On one of the last weekends in January I travelled by train to Swarthmore in Media some dozen miles southwest from Philadelphia with the sister's beau. I enjoyed seeing Ellen and liked Swarthmore. I did not see her again, nor did I write to her. So ended my friendship with the Williams family that greatly contributed to the enjoyment of my time at Lehigh. The German instruction was first-rate, and also thanks to the training of my musical ear in the correct sound of spoken German by my nurse Baba many years before, I was then able to speak fairly fluent German correctly although with a still limited vocabulary that was aided by the use of my "Brockhaus", the German equivalent of our Webster's dictionary.

I arrived at Camp Ritchie about the middle of February 1944, the beginning of my second year in the Army. Camp Ritchie was located at Blue Ridge Summit, Maryland, about 10 miles northwest of Thurmont, Maryland, the property bordering the Mason-Dixon line separating Maryland and Pennsylvania, and about a dozen miles southwest of Gettysburg. Baltimore was about 50 miles to the southeast. The camp was on a 650-acre tract that the Army had acquired about 10 years before. It adjoined what we now know as Camp David and what FDR then called "Shangrila".

New arrivals were welcomed by Man Mountain Dean, the professional wrestler, now in an Army uniform. No one else among the cadre was. Instead, they all wore German Army uniforms of varying ranks and spoke to you only in German. The idea was to immerse the trainees in the order of battle and captured equipment of the German Army, weapons and equipment of every type. Classes began the next day, and I was enrolled in the eighteenth class of instruction of interrogation of German prisoners of war and civilians and in the order of battle of the German Army which meant memorizing the organization of the German Army and its various components. Classes were in the mornings and mock interrogations outside in the afternoons. Both conducted in German. The instructors were mostly academics fluent in German and expert in German Army weaponry and tactics. At the end of most classes each day there written tests, and one had to maintain high grades to remain in the program. I survived.

My 50-75 classmates included many German-speaking refugees from Germany and other countries in Europe. One who lived in the same barracks with me but in a different class was Heinz Kissinger who was about my age. He was then as insufferably arrogant, bright and knowledgeable as I found Henry Kissinger to be as he was later known.

Each morning the early reveille began with the playing of military marches over the scratchy public address system throughout the camp. One got to know them all, with some German ones and also a few by Haydn and Mozart. Every eighth day was a day off, called "Banfield Day", the name of the commanding brigadier general. One could take a train to Baltimore or Washington from Thurmont for a change of scene for a few hours. The fairly large town of Hagerstown was also quite near and accessible.

Sally and Bob were living in Washington. Bob had his own plane and he flew early to an airport near Camp Ritchie where I met him for the short flight to National Airport in Washington. In the late afternoon he flew me back. He did this twice while I was at Camp Ritchie. This interrupted his important wartime work which he would immediately resume between the flights. As I have written in Part Six on the occasion of his 90th birthday on April 15, 1999, he was producing a few hundred "Fulton GunAirstructors" for successfully training the Navy carrier pilots to defeat the Japanese carrier pilots in aerial combat. Sally, with the help of a newly found English nanny Kathleen, was raising sons Robin and Travis then about ages five and almost one, respectively. They lived in a small row house on O Street in Georgetown about 28th Street opposite tennis courts that Sally welcomed. These visits boosted my morale with the added benefits of knowing Sally and Bob better.

The training at Camp Ritchie concluded in early June with a full-time three or four-day field exercise of simulated combat situations. This was a final exam, requiring each student to demonstrate proficiency as an interrogator with knowledge of the order of battle of the German Army in relation to each different tactical situation. The class was organized into separate teams of several students headed by a military instructor to address different and rapidly changing tactical situations throughout each day and night with repeated interrogations of other instructors posing as prisoners of war and doing their best to confuse and confound their interrogators. Each would grade our performance and the team instructor would grade our overall performance including our effectiveness in conducting nighttime interrogations in changing locations with little or no sleep.

This was a severely challenging, mentally and physically exhausting, series of tests and extremely combat realistic involving the use of the captured German army equipment and weapons. I enjoyed it and I passed. At the graduation a few days later I was promoted from private first-class, the rank I had achieved after completing the program at Lehigh, to Technician Third Grade (T-3), equivalent to a staff sergeant rank for pay purposes. I thus now wore a staff sergeant's stripes with a T-3 between the lower stripe and the upper ones. I would remain a T-3 for the duration of my military service.

Camp Ritchie was the most intensive and challenging combined physical and mental experience of my life. The training was superb in every way and benefitted us from imparting thorough and current knowledge of the German Army, its organization, its equipment and weapons, its tactics. For this the Army merits high praise.

2. England, France and Germany 1944-45.

After several days leave visiting Mother now comfortably settled in her apartment at 5 Arlington Street in Boston, I returned to Camp Ritchie for my next assignment. With a group of other graduates I was sent to Bayonne, New Jersey, in mid-June to sail to England on the SS Brazil, a passenger liner to South American ports and now converted to a troopship. My group was pleasantly quartered in cabins on the main deck along with thousands of soldiers below en route to Normandy to reinforce General Eisenhower's recently launched Allied invasion of France. The ship cruised at about fifteen knots, a speed sufficient to avoid German U-boats by convoying or zigzagging. For the week's crossing the Atlantic was like a millpond. We landed at Glasgow in Scotland and boarded a troop train for London. We reached London late that evening as German flying bombs[14] were beginning their renewed battering of the city. None fell near us then or near the top floor of the row house at Cadogan Place where a few of us were billeted.

With a few of my classmates from Camp Ritchie I was assigned to an aerial photographic intelligence analysis office on the Kensington High Road near the Albert Hall, a bus ride from Cadogan Place. RAF Squadron Leader Jones was in charge of the daily interpretation of ongoing aerial photography by the RAF and American reconnaissance aircraft of German deployments opposing the Allied advance in Normandy and beyond. We were not told why we were so assigned, but it was probably because of our knowledge of the German Army, its equipment and weaponry drummed into us at Camp Ritchie that would enhance the evaluation of these aerial photographs. Nor do I know where most of my classmates were assigned, perhaps as interrogators in front-line combat units, as I would later be.

---

14   This was one of Hitler's two "vengeance" weapons, the V-1, and the later V-2 super-sonic space rocket bomb. *Wikipedia* on Google has an excellent account of each of these weapons and the harm they did.

Two aerial photographs of each location were taken a few seconds apart so that they could be examined side by side by looking through a stereoscope to create a three-dimensional image of what was depicted. With knowledge of the altitude at which the aerial photographs were taken, one would measure heights by the length of shadows made by sunlight. In this way we were able to acquire a real-time awareness of the German army deployments from day to day that were immediately communicated to the Army and Air Force commanders concerned and to General Eisenhower's headquarters. We were one of several such units responsible at any one time for a particular geographic area. The work was challenging, exciting, non-stop, exhausting, and enjoyable. Cloudy or stormy weather precluding aerial photography would give us frequent respites from the demands of this work. The flying bomb attacks persisted and we had some close calls at work and at Cadogan Place. Some nights when the bombs were falling in our neighborhood we took shelter in the deep Underground subway station near us at Sloane Square with hundreds of residents where cots and blankets were usually available.

RAF Squadron Leader Jones ran a very efficient and effective operation. But almost without regard to urgency, we stopped for about half an hour for tea and conversation in the late afternoon as the British military traditionally did. These were pleasant interludes. We would usually repair for lunch at a nearby Lyons Corner House. Breakfast and dinner were at an Army mess hall manned by black soldiers near Sloane Square. In addition, weekends were ordinarily free. There were two or three handsome young men in the office, and it became apparent that Squadron Leader Jones was trying to develop a personal and probably sexual relationship with one or more of them. I doubt he succeeded. This was my first encounter with a gay commanding officer. My relationship with him was correct and impersonal.

After a week or so in London I was invited to visit the Bevans at their country home in Midhurst, Sussex, for the coming weekend. I had met Colonel John Bevan and his three children, Jennifer then about 13, Julian, 10, and Marion, 6, while visiting Henry Foster and his family over the Christmas holidays in 1941. The Fosters lived in a beautiful house and place in Charles River, a suburb of Boston. Their eldest son,

Adam, a class ahead of me at Brooks and now at Harvard, was also a friend. Their mother, Frances Hoar Foster, and I established an affectionate relationship and I became an honorary nephew to "Aunt Fran" as I would henceforth call her. The Fosters and Bevans had been close neighbors and friends for several years in London before the war. After the war began and it looked like London would be bombed many well-to-do families sent their children to live with friends in America and Canada. The Bevan children thus came to live with the Fosters in Charles River in the summer of 1940, just ahead of the blitz on London, and were enrolled in private schools. They returned to England in the summer of 1943.

John Bevan, a graduate of Eton and Oxford, "Pops"[15], a stockbroker, now a Colonel of the Imperial General Staff, was married to the Lady Barbara Bevan, eldest daughter of the Earl and Countess of Lucan. She had been a lady-in-waiting to the Princess Royal, the sister of the sons of George V and Queen Mary, including the then Prince of Wales, later briefly Edward VIII and after abdicating in 1937 the Duke of Windsor, and his younger brother George who succeeded his brother as George VI. During the war, Colonel Bevan worked directly for Churchill's military chief of staff, General Sir Hastings ("Pug") Ismay,[16] in increasingly important assignments. In much of 1944, for instance, he was responsible for the successful "disinformation" campaign that convinced Hitler that the forthcoming Allied invasion would be at the Pas de Calais, opposite Dover at the narrowest crossing of the English Channel, rather than far to the south at Normandy, with the resulting fatal northerly disposition of German forces that might otherwise have repulsed the Normandy landings.

Thanks to Aunt Fran, Lady Barbara soon contacted me in London with a resulting weekend invitation. The Bevans welcomed me warmly at their country home, "Guillard's Oak", in Midhurst, Sussex, to which I travelled by train from Victoria Station, changing for Midhurst at

---

15   A top social club at Oxford akin to the top final clubs at Harvard.

16   In Churchill's capacity as Minister of Defence in addition to being Prime Minister. *See The Memoirs of General the Lord Ismay*, Heinemann, 1960, "Part Two. The Crucial Years", for a splendidly written account of this critical period of British history by this remarkable Army career officer.

Hazelmere. Jennifer was now about 16 and attractive, still a student at "the Monkey Club"; Julian was at Eton College. For that and the ensuing frequent weekends we mostly tended the vegetable garden, collecting what was ready and removing weeds, and walked on the beautiful South Down stretching towards the English Channel. One weekend we visited their son Julian at Eton, founded in 1440. The war notwithstanding, the boys were as usual formally attired in their black morning coats, waist-coats, pin-stripe trousers, white ties, and top hats. Near Windsor Castle, Eton, with its ancient buildings and traditions of scholarship and games and beautiful grounds, incubates this greatness in its students to surpass it in their lives. With his father's example before him, Julian was meeting expectations.

On another occasion we went to see Winchester Cathedral, one of the largest in England. Building it began in the 11th century and took hundreds of years. Its soaring majesty and long nave are breathtaking. We went on to Winchester College, started by William of Wykeham in 1382, which along with Eton and Harrow are the principal great English public schools. A close friend of Julian's, Noel McClellan, was a student there and he showed us about. The famous motto of the school from Wykeham is "Manners makyth man." I was greatly impressed by these manifestations of English achievement.

The Bevans became family to me and made a great positive difference to the enjoyment of my life in England. Lady Barbara and Colonel Bevan were highly educated and cultivated with superb manners and I dare say nothing worthier in English society. During the week Colonel Bevan stayed in London and he occasionally invited me for dinner at his club, Brooks's on St. James Street. Their country home, a lovely stucco stone house that seemed to have grown out of the ground amidst the beauti-fully surrounding oak trees, was a home for me too away from the war.

Lady Barbara's parents, Lord and Lady Lucan, had an attractive, spa-cious flat in Portman Square in London. Then in their 80s and seemingly in robust health, they invited me to a cocktail party to introduce me to some of their "younger" friends, mostly officers and their wives about the ages of the Bevans. They were apologetic that they had no guests closer to my then age of twenty. I assured them how much I appreciated and welcomed their kindness to me. I liked them. They were "the Establishment". The family name of Bingham had a long history in British wars including the Crimean war.[17] Lord Lucan, then a sitting member of the House of Lords, showed me both Houses of Parliament with most interesting commentary which was a rare privilege for me.

Two other social events further brightened my London life. When we lived in Greenwich, the English couple Charles and Marjory Walker also lived there and had become good friends of my parents. He was working for an English firm in New York. From Mother I knew who they were. They had long ago returned to England and were living in Wiltshire when I was London. Mother arranged for them to contact me and invite me for a weekend. It was a lovely visit. They were my parents' ages and had no children. They lived in a beautiful ancient ivy-covered stone house not far from Stonehenge which we visited. I greatly enjoyed their warm welcoming company. Mrs. Walker had one of the loveliest complexions I ever saw—rose-like and so healthy. She and her husband were dear. Sadly, that one visit was the entirety of our relationship.

The other was a reunion with Chych Waterston, one of my most important Brooks mentors, now an officer and German interrogator in the RAF since 1941. He was living with his mother and sister in the London suburb of Putney. We got in touch and I visited them there for stimulating talk and an excellent meal. Much, much later when I was visiting Chych in his last years the sister was there too.

Early In September some of us were transferred to the headquarters of the First Allied Airborne Army at Ascot, near Windsor, under the command of Lt. General Lewis H. Brereton. We were ensconced in "Nissan huts" on a grand private estate, "Sunningdale", which had been requisitioned for the war effort. The work at first was much the same as in London.

---

17 *See Earl of Lucan* in WikipediA on Google for a history of this family. Lord Lucan (1860-1949) who befriended me was the fifth earl.

The British Lt. General Frederick "Boy" Browning, the husband of the renowned writer Daphne du Maurier, was the deputy commander and the commanding officer of the First Airborne Corps that was about to be heavily engaged in operation "Market Garden", as were the American 82nd and 101st airborne divisions. This was an attempt by Allied airborne and ground forces under General Montgomery to leapfrog into Holland to seize Rhine river crossings, particularly at Arnhem, to outflank the Germans and occupy the Ruhr in the industrial heart of Germany. It failed with a heavy loss of life and much recrimination by the American airborne commanders of Montgomery and Browning, among others, for faulty command and ignoring photographic intelligence of the presence of considerable German forces at Arnhem and elsewhere, among other failings. The British "Red Devils" division (First Airborne Division) was decimated at Arnhem, a "bridge too far",[18] and never fought again. I soon became friends with Private Bob Hardcastle, one of the survivors.

That fall I was assigned to be an interrogator of German prisoners for the 13th Airborne Division. While remaining at Ascot I began several weeks of glider training which was a principal means of transporting units of the division to combat, the other being landing by parachute. The gliders were towed by twin-engine Douglas transport aircraft, commercially known as DC-3, with the Army designation of C-47. They also separately transported the parachute troops. The gliders, made of plywood and other light materials, would seat about twenty-five troops fully equipped or far fewer if a jeep was also aboard. As the tow plane and glider approached a designated landing zone, the tow plane would release the glider causing a sudden and jolting deceleration of the glider as it flew on its own and the pilot maneuvered to land. One day at a training exercise we could choose flying in a British or American glider. We chose the American one and waiting our turn watched the British one as it approached release from the tow plane. Upon release at about 1,500 feet, suddenly to our horror it broke in half, some 25 occupants tumbling out to their instant deaths. I did not know any of them. Further training that day was cancelled.

---

18   For a detailed account, *see Battle of Arnhem* in WikipediA on Google.

My qualification as a glider trooper resulted in a pay raise of $50 a month which given the increased risks of flying, landing and enemy fire was warranted.

After a few weeks at Ascot, Lady Barbara's sister, Lady Margaret Bingham Alexander, married to Field Marshall Sir Harold Alexander, the Allied Commander in the Mediterranean, invited me to her home. She lived nearby. So began another round of welcome if occasional visits while I remained at Ascot. While I liked her and she was very kind and hospitable to me and a companion she would ask me to bring, she lacked some of the abundance of charm and zest of Lady Barbara. I did not meet her husband, and when I did visit there were often other guests present.

The last important social event of 1944 for me was the 21st birthday dinner the Bevans gave for me at the Savoy Hotel in London on December 15. Lady Barbara said bring two friends to join them and Jennifer. I invited Sergeant George Milner from Oklahoma and Private Robert Hardcastle, a survivor of the Arnhem massacre. It was a grand occasion. The Bevans could not have been more charming and forthcoming. Milner took it in stride and enjoyed the evening. Hardcastle froze and was mostly speechless. Coming from an entirely different social background, he had never met anyone like the Bevans, and Colonel Bevan's imposing uniform intimidated him further. Jennifer and Lady Barbara, despite every effort, were unable to put him at ease. I would later visit Bob in Bristol where his family lived above their dry goods shop. Plain hard-working English folk, they were immensely proud of their son.

In December, the Germans, in a last roll of the dice, launched their final campaign in the west to gain Antwerp. So began the Battle of the Bulge. Persistent clouds prevented Allied planes from bombing the advancing Germans who made impressive gains, disrupted Allied plans, and created much anxiety. By late January the status quo ante had been restored and German defeat assured. Nevertheless, this resulted in my transfer to Maison Lafitte, a suburb of Paris on the Seine River, early in January 1945. There, another inactive race course town like Ascot, the work remained much the same as in Ascot, still primarily the interpretation of aerial photographs of the deployment of German forces opposing tentatively planned operations of the 13th airborne division to which I was still attached. I was quartered in a concrete building, previously a German barracks.

One Saturday shortly after arriving, in visiting a local bookshop I began conversing in my limited French with a young Frenchman, Hubert Wenger, about seventeen or eighteen. He said his mother had spoken English in the last war to the Canadians and would like to meet an American. He invited me for tea at their apartment the following Saturday. Monsieur and Madame Wenger had a lovely, large apartment with several bedrooms. They had moved to Maison Lafitte from Paris early in the war to shelter their then young children from the German occupation. Their daughter, Edith, was a year or two older than Hubert. They were a cultivated, educated family. M. Wenger, an Alsatian with whom I spoke German, had a perfume manufacturing business and a farm in Normandy which provided much of their food brought weekly by an old Ford truck that ran on charbon (charcoal). After a few visits, Madame Wenger asked me to live with them, an invitation I gladly accepted. This idyllic home life lasted about three months until in mid-April 1945 I was ordered to report to the 13th airborne division headquarters in Nancy, in eastern France, in preparation for a Rhine crossing in support of General Patton's Third Army. Shortly afterwards President Roosevelt died, and we had no idea who his successor, Harry Truman, was.

Living with the Wengers was an important experience. Evenings and weekends at their home brimmed with creative cultural pursuits in the leisure hours of that family. Each member played a musical instrument: Madame Wenger the piano; her husband the cello; Hubert the violin; Edith with a beautiful mezzo voice mostly sang but also played the viola. We often had musical evenings with chamber and vocal music of Bach, Haydn, Mozart and French opera composers. When I explained to Madame Wenger that perhaps I could sing some Stephen Foster folk songs she produced the music for me and I did. This somewhat mitigated my embarrassment at being unable to perform musically at their level.

We also read aloud plays of Moliere, Racine and others, of which they had several copies enabling each of us to take a separate part. This was another example of the superiority of their cultural attainments to what I had experienced at home. All this did wonders for my further cultural education and for improving my speaking and understanding French when beautifully spoken as the Wengers did. Thus they, like the Bevans, became a second family to me. I was able to reciprocate somewhat by providing many items from the PX which they had not had since 1940.

In Nancy we lived in tents amidst much rain and mud preparing for the airborne operation and becoming familiar through maps and aerial photographs with the terrain of the landing zones and adjacent areas. After about ten days of this and on the eve of departure, we were told that Patton's tanks had crossed the Rhine ahead of schedule and therefore our operation was cancelled. I was delighted.

I rejoined the Wengers for a few days and on the day before VE-Day I was able to fly to London. Colonel Bevan invited me to dine again at Brooks's, his club. After a splendid dinner served as always by elderly retainers in full dress we all repaired upstairs to the library to hear the 9 pm BBC news. This was the first public announcement of the German surrender and that the next day, May 6, would be a national holiday and celebrated as "VE-Day". To a roomful of high ranking British and American officers there were low murmurings of "hear, hear".

I would not see Colonel Bevan or Lady Barbara again. I would see Jennifer in Boston later.

Several days later after returning to Paris I made my first trip to Germany. Having a few days of leave, I drove with two friends into Germany who had the use of an Army jeep. Driving on the autobahns which mostly were passable, we went first to see the medieval walled town of Rothenberg on the Tauber, a few miles east of Nuremberg in Bavaria. Driving about this beautiful, historic place with a functioning clock tower in the central market place, we were delighted to see it had survived the war largely intact and without bomb damage. Then we briefly drove through heavily damaged Nuremberg which would hold the forthcoming war crime trials of the captured Nazi leaders. We continued on, going north and east to Leipzig and Halle.

On the way we stopped at Buchenwald, the notorious concentration camp near Weimar in east central Germany where the Nazis had exterminated many thousands. American troops had captured it only a few weeks previously. Scores of survivors remained, walking skeletons in their striped clothing awaiting medical treatment and resettlement. The smell of burned bodies from the ovens lingered and there were many mass graves still exposed. This and the other similar camps were the ultimate horror and nadir of human depravity. Despairing, we hastened to depart for Leipzig and Halle.

These historic cities would presently become part of the Russian zone of occupation when the American forces would withdraw. They in contrast to Rothenberg were mostly in ruins from Allied bombing them as important industrial centers of war production. In Leipzig, the St. Thomas church, the site and home of where J. S. Bach's most important choral music was first performed, had largely survived. The home of his contemporary, George Frederick Handel, in nearby Halle had not along with much of the rest of the city. We wondered how the people we saw on the streets could live amidst this devastation. It could easily result in starvation, disease, and the breakdown of society. We were glad to return to Paris for our assignments in the American zone in west Germany.

Later in May, I with a group of other German interrogators was driven in Army trucks from Paris to Bad Schwallbach, a spa some 15 miles northwest of Wiesbaden on the Rhine. At this resort we were organized into teams of two officers and four T-3s to be sent to various locations to screen Germans for local government jobs and to arrest designated Nazis and others wanted as war criminals. In doing this we would be assigned to the Army Counter Intelligence Corps (CIC), and each of us for our protection and effectiveness would wear no indication of rank on our uniforms. While this was being sorted out we had time to enjoy the warm soothing mineral baths of the spa which had long made the spa an important resort for European royalty.

Several days later I was assigned to a CIC team, along with several other teams, for a week's training in doing this screening and arresting in the city of Wiesbaden. I was billeted with a family named Mueller in a suburb that had not been bombed. The parents had been in war production work and were now unemployed. Their son Erich, about 17, had joined the local defense force at age 15 and had escaped injury and capture. He was hoping to return to school. Food was very limited and they were hungry. I helped with some Army rations and they were extremely grateful. I liked them and stayed about a week. The training gave us a good idea of the work before us at other locations.

Over the next five months my team worked in three or four different small to medium size villages which had largely escaped war damage. I shall report on two of them, Schwaebisch Hall and Geislingen an der Steige.

Schwaebisch Hall on the river Kocher was another medieval town in Baden-Wuerttemberg about 50 miles northeast of Stuttgart. It had a beautiful, ancient Lutheran church, St. Michael's (1526), in the town square. The population was at least 15,000, swollen by swarms of displaced persons from much of Europe whom the Nazis had impressed as slave labor seeking food and shelter. We were there for several weeks and comfortably billeted in a house on the outskirts. We had offices in the Rathaus or city hall in which to screen applicants for local government jobs with the assistance of a few Army military government officers who temporarily were in charge of the local government until we could find and install their civilian replacements for the top positions which Nazis mostly had held.

We had each applicant complete a detailed lengthy questionnaire that we drafted to learn about his past, politically and militarily, and about his education, experience and qualifications for the position sought. We would follow up with interviewing applicants that appeared acceptable. Because of the high volume of this work, most of our work was done individually by the team members. When one of us recommended a particular applicant for a position, at least two other members of the team would participate in a combined interview. If the applicant did well we would tell him that we would soon decide on his appointment depending on his comparative evaluation with any other qualified candidates. We would also interview references the applicant had given us before making appointments. In doing this work we were amazed at the frequency of denunciation of applicants by their fellow citizens, charging that they were concealing their Nazi past and crimes. Our investigations of these allegations, many of them spurious and self serving, seriously delayed some important appointments.

We also had a responsibility to hunt for Nazis wanted as war criminals believed to reside in the vicinity of our work. For this purpose each of us had the authority to arrest and incarcerate anyone whom we suspected of war crimes. There was no requirement for obtaining a warrant or prior approval from higher authority. This was a frightening, potentially corrupting power which I exercised sparingly, once arresting a high ranking SS officer when loot was dug up in his garden leading to his confession. More often I and other members of the team used this authority to release persons whom we thought to have been needlessly arrested by the Army in the early days of the occupation.

While so engaged we found that this SS officer had a beautiful Mercedes touring car mounted on blocks in his barn. It was in mint condition. The hood was falsely painted with the Red Cross symbol. We found the hidden wheels and "liberated" the car. Of course this was theft but then wrongly viewed as the spoils of war. After we drove it for a few weeks, it moved up the chain of command, no questions of title asked. A month letter it displayed three stars and flags.

In our discussions with applicants and others here and elsewhere we found that most of them blamed Hitler for losing the war, not for starting it, not for the atrocities or for the holocaust for which he was responsible and of which they falsely denied any knowledge. Those who admitted being Nazis usually said self-servingly they were "compelled" to join the party. Most Germans told us of the extraordinary mesmerizing appeal Hitler had on them personally from early on until almost the end through his broadcast speeches and appearances on film, which probably explains the strong, widespread public support of him for most of the war. Yet we also found a strong determination to renounce war, to reject Nazism and Communism or other totalitarian form of government, and to rebuild a new democratic society. On the whole the educational level of the applicants we interviewed was quite high and most had at least finished the equivalent of high school. Restoration of the largely destroyed economy was widely recognized as the first priority demanding unremitting effort.

We finally completed our work in Schwaebisch Hall, and in late September we moved south to my last assignment in Geislingen an der Steige also in Baden-Wuerttemberg near Ulm. It was another medieval town, smaller than Schwabisch Hall but very similar in its architecture and Swiss chalet style of houses. Again we were billeted in a comfortable house.

The work was mostly the same as before but less intensive with fewer government positions to fill. We also had an efficient staff of two trustworthy Germans who managed the office in the town hall and kept track of our records. While there I and the members of my team had the use of a German passenger car, an Opel Olympia, in addition to one or two jeeps. The car came with a driver, a young Austrian named Fritz Zaloudek who also lived in the house. We became friends. He was an accomplished pianist of classical music which he often played in the evenings on the adequate piano in the living room. He was also our excellent cook.

Many Germans in the despair of their lives sought consolation in the churches, particularly in the church music of Bach that was performed at Sunday services in the Lutheran churches both in Schwaebisch Hall and Geislingen. One Sunday a German family I had met in church invited me to their house for a meal. It consisted of potato soup, and every other imaginable serving of potatoes. That is all they like most others had to eat.

The weeks passed quickly. With the Japanese surrender and the end of the war in August I had enough points for release. I declined requests to stay on for another 6-12 months. In early December I started the long journey home and to resuming civilian life.

The experience in Germany was invaluable for me in acquiring language proficiency and, more importantly, some understanding of the

Germans I interviewed, of the governance of villages of varying sizes and of the German public in resolutely responding to these circumstances of severe deprivation and despair brought on by their leaders. I had few social activities.

Apart from work, letter writing and reading, I saw little of my teammates or anyone else. Not that there were not temptations for physical intimacy, particularly in Bad Schwallbach and Wiesbaden. In the former, Inge, a voluptuous and beautiful young lady, made unmistakable advances in the hope of food and cigarettes as so did Eddy, a beautiful teenager, who went so far as to say he and I "belonged to each other." In the Mueller home in Wiesbaden, the son, Erich, was so hopeful too. I somehow, thankfully, summoned the fortitude to reject the temptations of these fleeting relationships. I made sure they did not recur for the remainder of my stay in Germany. I did succumb to cigarettes, finding that offering them to the people I interviewed facilitated obtaining information. While not becoming a heavy smoker I did not finally quit until 1974.

On a cold winter day a group of us boarded the back of an open Army truck with a canvas top and sides for the long drive to Marseille where we would board a ship for home. We kept warm by drinking brandy out of our canteens in this non-stop trip. I developed a painful toothache which killed one of my lower rear teeth. A 10,000 ton Liberty ship, the SS John Jay, awaited us to be jammed in with other troops in the forward two cargo holds which had been converted to accommodations with about 6 hammocks stacked vertically throughout much of the hold from floor to ceiling. I was put in the No. 2 hold which also had the mess hall. The rear holds were empty and the ship had no ballast.

We immediately encountered a very rough Mediterranean and most of us were severely sick. After a miserable couple of days I found that by forcing myself to eat I overcame this and thereafter felt fine for the rest of the voyage despite an even rougher Atlantic Ocean most of the way. The Captain later told us it was the roughest crossing he had experienced in 25 years. Our top speed of 10 knots was rarely reached because without ballast the high waves frequently raised the propeller out of the water which created difficulties in controlling the propeller.

Some days with strong head winds as well we seemed to make almost no headway. We were also fearful that this riveted ship, perhaps hastily built, might break in two from the strong waves which had happened to a few similar ships. Much of the time we could not go on deck lest we be swept overboard. As it was, it took the ship most of December, including my twenty-second birthday and Christmas, to reach Norfolk for which we gave hearty thanks. I returned by train to Camp Devens, where I had started almost three years before, at the end of December. I was honorably discharged from the Army there on January 3, 1946, refusing all requests to reenlist or join the reserves.

I had an exceptionally lucky and rewarding life in the Army: an enriching experience in education, in military training, discipline and work, in living with all sorts and conditions of men, in making lovely civilian friends in England and France, in participating in the first several months of the American occupation of part of war-ravaged Germany, in growing up and in coming home in splendid health.

This concludes Part Two of my enriching life.

Part Three Harvard College and Harvard Law School 1946-1949

1. College 1946-47.

I returned to Harvard College in February 1946. In 1944, Congress enacted the GI Bill of Rights (GI bill) that enabled millions of veterans to go to college and beyond by paying their tuition and a monthly stipend towards room and board, in my case $50, double that for married couples. This enabled me to resume my education. Living with Mother in her Boston apartment at 5 Arlington Street, although crowding her since I would sleep on a day bed in the small dining area between her bedroom and the living room, I would further reduce expenses and she graciously consented. Commuting to Harvard Square was the good exercise of a ten-minute brisk walk to the Charles Street subway at the Pepper-Pot Bridge over the Charles River and another fifteen-minute subway ride with frequent service.

Harvard had to decide what academic credit I would receive for my Army experience. Since I was one of the first to return with the intensive German language training at Lehigh and the concentrated German prisoner-of-war interrogation training of Camp Ritchie and the further experience of the active participation in restoring local government in several German villages, Dean Bender decided I was to be given full academic credit for the sophomore year and for half of the junior year. Thus I would return for the second half of the junior year and for the senior year, all to be completed within the next twelve months. I was told I could not take any German course for academic credit. I had to select a subject as my "major" and I chose American history. To accommodate the returning veterans, the college continued the academic year on an accelerated basis throughout the calendar year, a practice begun in the summer of 1942. Classes for me began in early February. I would complete the sophomore year in June and a week later start the senior year with graduation in January 1947, some seven months after I would have done had there been no war and financially had I been able to go. I remained in the Class of 1946.

I found Mother, then in her early 60s, to be in good health and spirits. She was leading an active social life, seeing interesting friends for lunch and bridge which she played well. She did the daily crossword puzzle in the *New York Herald Tribune* and kept up with current events listening to Raymond Gram Swing on the evening news. Her friends were mostly widows. Among the ones I remember were a Mrs. Bradley whose son I had known at Brooks, Beth Hubbard, Beatrice deMenocal, Ann Olney who also lived in an apartment at 5 Arlington Street, Laura Stackpole, and Lucille Swift. There were also the Charlie Boydens for bridge and music. He was a competent flutist. With Mother at her piano and one or two others they as amateurs and with great enjoyment would play classical music featuring the flute or piano trios with the flute playing the part of the first violin. Shades of my similar experiences with the Wengers in Maison Lafitte in the winter of 1944!

Mother would also see Aunt Louise and Marty's mother, Mrs. Marjorie Means who had an apartment in Boston. Although not a member Mother played a lot of bridge at the Chilton Club and she was a frequent lunch guest of Mrs. Swift at the Ritz Hotel which was conveniently near her apartment.

My brothers had come home too. Pat was released from the Navy late in 1945, in time for the November 20 birth of his second son Richard

Gage Coburn. Pat found his salary when he returned as an associate at the Herrick, Smith law firm insufficient to support his family. Presently he found a job as a lawyer with the entrepreneur Royal Little at his new venture, Textron, in Providence, Rhode Island, a manageable commute from his house in Dover near Boston. Pat and Marty would have two more sons: Gordon Means Coburn, December 3, 1947, and David McGregor Coburn, April 7, 1949. During the years they lived in Dover, Pat and Marty would occasionally invite Mother and me and sometimes Mike and Joan too for Sunday lunch and Pat would collect us in town and bring us home, all to our great enjoyment.

Mike and Joan with their two young sons, John, Jr. (August 1, 1941), and Lawrence Stockton ("Lawrie") (July 11, 1943), were back in their Needham home from the Army Air Corps in Boise by late 1945. Mike returned to his prior job with the Chase Brass & Copper sales office in Boston. But soon he decided that with the availability of the GI bill he needed to complete his college education at Harvard as a member of the Class of 1939. This would take about a year. He also wanted at least a year at the Harvard Business School as well. All this he accomplished before I finished law school. This led to a better marketing job for him with a company called Fabrika Products in Boston, a manufacturer of industrial cushioning materials. Their daughter Joan arrived on November 12, 1948. While I was at college and law school, Mike and Joan would also invite Mother and me to Sunday lunch, and would drive in for us and take us back, about twenty minutes each way. This too was very agreeable to be with another lovely Coburn family.

My sisters' husbands had returned to peacetime pursuits as well: Mooney Harding to architecture in Palm Beach and Bob Fulton to a new venture of developing a flying automobile, the "Fulton Airphibian",[19] in a rented facility near the airport in Danbury, Connecticut, and living with Sally and two young sons Robert III and Travis in their new home, "Flying Ridge", with an airstrip in Newtown, Connecticut. Their third son, Rawn Coburn Fulton, would arrive on June 23, 1946.

---

19   I discuss this in my tribute to Bob on his 90th birthday in Part Six.

My sister Louise, living in Palm Beach, had persuaded Mooney to send their eldest daughter Florence, then about 15 and called "Fifi", to Farmington where Louise and Sally had also gone. Priscilla, about 9, was at home. I saw all of them in the summer of 1946 in Edgartown on Martha's Vineyard, where Louise and Natalie Brown had rented a house. In 1947 Louise had her fifth daughter, Susan Appleton Harding. By then, tragically, Louise, like Papa, had become an alcoholic with the result that Susan, we later learned, was born retarded and eventually had to be institutionalized. Yet Susan seemed cheerful as she grew older. She died in her fifties.

Thus with Mother now having fourteen grandchildren, seven Coburns, four Hardings, and three Fultons, there was no felt need for me, still single, to increase this number. I never did.

The principal teachers I had in my remaining calendar year at Harvard College were Professor Arthur M. Schlesinger, Sr., in American History, Professor David Owen in English History, and Professor Benjamin F. Wright in American Constitutional Law. Professor Schlesinger, a renowned scholar and author of books on American history, was a dull speaker which detracted from the importance of what he said in his lectures.

We had to learn primarily from the assigned reading than from our lecture notes. Professors Owen and Wright, by contrast, were both engaging teachers and established scholars in their fields. In their lectures they made their subjects interesting and at times exciting.

I have concluded that to be an effective teacher one must communicate interactively and intensively with the students. Since this is mostly impossible in large classes, it is all the more necessary that lectures be delivered dynamically and dramatically. Professors Owen and Wright had this gift; Professor Schlesinger's modesty and aversion to showmanship precluded it. In 1949 Professor Wright who also had a principal role in the 1946 reform of the college curriculum became President of Smith College for the next decade.

I enjoyed studying these subjects. In American history I was helped by the solid grounding in Henry Bragdon's teaching of it at Brooks School some five or six years earlier. The assigned textbooks in American history by Professors Morrison and Commager, *The Growth of the American Republic*, and Professor Wright's *The Growth of American Constitutional Law*, well and engagingly recounted our political and constitutional history without whitewashing, particularly in the despicable treatment of Native Americans in stealing their land and destroying their way of life[20]; and of Blacks, first enslaving them and after emancipation then segregating them and denying them equal opportunity in life.

I learned we have much to be ashamed about in our history; but also much to celebrate: the steady if uneven progress of the rule of law, of acceptance of Constitutional Law as proclaimed by the U.S. Supreme Court, of political stability and widespread suffrage, of public education and economic growth, of providing benefits for the poor and disadvantaged, and of civil rights and equal protection of the law for women and minorities, among other things.

Professor Owen's classes and assigned readings in English history were equally unsparing, emphasizing the long perpetuation of the patriarchy of male class and land ownership and suffrage to the political and economic disadvantage of the majority of the population, the denial of religious freedom, and the slow transition from absolute monarchy to popular sovereignty and the rule of law; but also equally emphasizing the growth of the common law, the spirit of liberty, freedom of speech and the press, the abolition of slavery, the gradual emancipation of women, the recognition of the Monroe Doctrine in protection of Latin America against European encroachment by the Royal Navy, the non-recognition of the Confederate States by the British Government during our civil war despite enormous economic pressure, and twice in this century defeating German aggression, among other achievements.

Studying these subjects I mostly did between classes and in the afternoons in the Reading Room at the Widener Library, occasionally at the

---

20 "When the Pilgrims landed, they fell upon their knees, and then fell upon the Aborigines."

Fly Club when I would have lunch or dinner there and if uninterrupted study was possible, and at home. I was usually home in time for dinner which Mother had learned how to prepare very well.

Yet my college education was in many respects incomplete. The benefits of the academic credit for my military service were offset by the lack of opportunity to take courses in Greek and Roman civilization, in Shakespeare and other areas of English and American literature and poetry, in European history, in political science, in philosophy, and perhaps in other fields of knowledge. There was also no opportunity to develop intellectual interaction with any of the professors such as I had with some of the masters at Brooks School. By living at home I forewent the experience of the college "House" life for students for their last three years with social and cultural interactions with other residents including graduate students and professors.

I did enjoy seeing and making friends at the Fly Club. These included John Munroe and Bill Ziegler from St. Mark's whom I had known at Buckley, and Larry White who had been a class ahead of me at Brooks. The new friends included Casie deRham also from St. Mark's, Harry Cobb from Milton, Hamilton Coolidge and John Motley from Groton, Fritz Drayton from St. Paul's, and Franklin ("Connie") Tyng from St. George's, all veterans of military service and determined to press on with their education. They were all splendid company for me. I was honored to be in Fritz Drayton's and Larry White's weddings. Fritz left college after finishing the junior year and tragically died of some apparently incurable malady within the following year after a brief marriage to the lovely Edith Bettle who fortunately remarried a year or two later.

I note that in my time there were no public school members of the club or Blacks or Jews. That slowly changed and also foreign students were elected as well. Whether the Fly and the other final clubs will eventually admit female students, as I believe they should, remains unresolved notwithstanding that Radcliffe College merged into Harvard College many years ago and lost its separate undergraduate status.

Rejoining the Harvard Glee Club which I continued partly through the first year of law school again provided first-class immersion in some of the great choral masterpieces. I well remember the hard work of learning the first bass choral part in the towering Bach B-Minor Mass, one of the supreme works of the choral literature. The intensive, detailed uncompromising rehearsing of the several choruses of this work by our masterful director G. Wallace Woodworth, known to all as "Woody", gradually gave us an awareness of the majesty of the piece. Serge Koussevitzky would conduct the performance with the Boston Symphony at Harvard's Sanders Theater. At the one rehearsal with him, but without the orchestra, standing at the podium, he silently mouthed words to create total silence and our undivided attention. Showman that he was, I thought his conducting and interpretation of the work were inferior to Woody's. It was nevertheless a thrilling experience with that incomparable orchestra. Koussie excelled in the music of 19th and 20th Century composers, not in Bach, Handel, Haydn or Mozart.

Shortly after returning to Harvard, I joined the student German club. Presently I was invited to speak one evening about my experiences in Germany before an audience of perhaps 25 students and some members of the faculty of the German department. My prepared talk and the ensuing colloquy were in German. I pointed out how strong Hitler's public support remained until the end, probably due to his mesmerizing appeal; and how few blamed him for starting the war, most for losing it.

In the discussion there were questions about how close Hitler came to winning. My answer, then and now, was how lucky the British and we were that he lost the war several times: first, when he failed to capture the British and French troops who escaped at Dunkerque; next when he diverted the Luftwaffe from attacking the British airfields and aircraft factories after Churchill shrewdly ordered a small, token bombing attack on Berlin, to retaliate with the blitz against London and other cities, thereby losing the destruction of the RAF and preventing the invasion of Britain; next by attacking Russia before defeating Britain and by failing to concentrate his armies to capture Moscow; and finally and fatally by declaring war on the United States. Probably he would have won had he avoided any of these blunders. There was also no doubt that the German

Army was primarily defeated by the Russian Army at tremendous cost. This was a remarkably interesting evening, good questions and a receptive audience.

I did not say what I have since learned from General Ismay's Memoirs[21] is that the failure of Hitler and his Italian and Japanese allies to concert their strategies also cost them the war. For example, he writes, had Hitler postponed the attack on Russia and concentrated on defeating the British and had the Japanese postponed the attack on Pearl Harbor and gone after the British possessions in the Far East and then on to India instead, it is very doubtful that Britain could have survived and that our isolationist Congress would have declared war on either Germany or Japan unless the U. S. was directly attacked despite FDR's best efforts to do so. With Hitler the master of Europe and Russia and Japan of much of Asia, our future and that of Latin America would have been gravely imperilled.

My use of German continued with occasional meetings with students at the German Club and reading a weekly newspaper published in New York, "Der Aufbau", "The Rebuilding". Once in law school I had no more time for this, and I gradually lost fluency and vocabulary.

After the examination results of the second half of the junior year became available in July or August 1946, I applied to Harvard Law School for admission in February 1947 following graduation from college in January. I had decided on law school while in Germany as it seemed the best route to realizing my preference for a career in government service rather than one in business. In due course my application was accepted. Again I was very lucky since my college grades were acceptable but not outstanding. I graduated from college in January but did not receive the A. B. diploma from President Conant until the usual graduation ceremony in June 1947.

---

21 *The Memoirs of General the Lord Ismay* at 280-81, Heinemann (1960).

2. Harvard Law School 1947-49.

I had little idea of what studying or practicing law involved. It was all somewhat mysterious. Our class was over 500 male students from many colleges, almost all veterans of different ages depending how long the war had delayed their college graduations. Beginning in February 1947, we constituted the second half of the Class of 1949, the first having started the previous September and who would graduate in February 1949, the second half the following May. The law school did not begin admitting women until 1950. Erwin Griswold, principally a teacher of federal tax law and a 1927 graduate of the law school, had been appointed Dean in June 1946 succeeding James Landis who in turn had followed the legendary Roscoe Pound who was Dean from 1916 to 1936 and who was still teaching at the law school.

Among my classmates were Messrs. deRahm and Ziegler from college and David Martin from Buckley and Yale, and I soon would make other friends as well including my contemporary John Carey from Yale and John Ferry whose graduation from Harvard was delayed for several years. More would follow. I continued to live with Mother in Boston, commuting to Cambridge for classes and study.

For the first of our two-semester first year on an accelerated schedule which would end in September 1947, we had courses on contracts, criminal law, personal property, torts, and judicial remedies for these and other areas of the law. These were courses on the "common law" among Englishmen of these subjects as developed by judges of the English courts over many centuries and transplanted to the thirteen American colonies and from them after the American Revolution to the thirteen states and ultimately to the United States with the ratification of the Constitution in 1788.[22] These courses were to be distinguished from courses based on

---

22 For a magisterial account of this history, *see* Holmes, *The Common Law* (1881), based on a series of a dozen lectures delivered at the Boston Public Library by Oliver Wendell Holmes, Jr., appointed by the first President Roosevelt to the Supreme Court in 1902 after having served as a justice of the Massachusetts Supreme Judicial Court

statutory law such as taxation and government regulation of business and some of criminal law and judicial remedies. All these courses continued in the second semester as well except for criminal law which was replaced by a half-year course on the relationship between principal and agent, employer and employee, and master and servant, and known as the law of "agency".

Because of the large size of our class, for the first and second year courses we were divided into two and sometimes three sections with different professors for each. For the third year the division into sections depended on the class choices of the elective courses. Even so, until the third year there were usually more than 150 students in each course class that limited direct interaction with the professor. The classes were held in the two then principal buildings of the law school: Austin Hall, a Romanesque structure designed by H. H. Richardson, also the architect of Trinity Church in Boston for Philips Brooks, in the 1880s, and Langdell Hall, a larger classical Greek building completed in the 1920s, each with large lecture-size class rooms.

The method of instruction, pioneered by Dean Christopher Columbus Langdell in the 1870s, was the study of appellate court decisions organized by subject matter into casebooks mostly compiled by the faculty, for example, on contracts, torts, etc. We would make digests of the assigned cases for each class and be prepared to be called on by the professor looking at a chart of assigned seats.

For a particular case, a student would be asked to summarize the essential facts, the questions presented, the applicable legal principles for the court's decision and its supporting reasons. The professor would often intensively interrogate the student with hypothetical changes in the facts to ascertain whether that would create a different result; or he would ask whether the decision really followed or overruled established precedent or why a different legal principle should not govern; or he would ask the student to state the grounds for a dissent; or he would call on a different student or students to answer these and similar questions, particularly if

---

and briefly as its chief justice since 1882. His book's opening has the famous passage "The life of the law has not been logic: it has been experience. " *Id. at* 1.

a student was insufficiently prepared or incoherent. The professor would rarely suggest or even intimate a correct answer. This was the essence of the "Socratic" method of teaching, namely, each student learning by thinking out for himself the better reasoning as to which facts were crucial and which legal principle to apply to the particular facts as distinct from learning legal rules by rote.

This was an entirely different method of instruction and learning from what we had experienced in school and college. The focus was on analysis of the facts and the law applicable to them, not on memorization of legal rules. This method of teaching spread to most American law schools

The professors were mostly first rate in this method of teaching: Robert Braucher, a wartime hero in the Army Air Corps who later served as the principal reporter for the second restatement of contract law and as an associate justice of the Massachusetts Supreme Judicial Court, for contracts; Sheldon Glueck, a noted criminologist, for criminal law; Ernest Brown, a versatile teacher of most legal subjects with a particular focus on the facts of cases, for personal property in the first semester; Bob Amory, fresh from having swiftly risen to high Army rank, for real property in the second; Judge Calvert Magruder of the First Federal Circuit Court of Appeals, for torts; Livingston Hall, the vice dean of the law school, for agency in the second semester; and Dick Field, an experienced trial lawyer, for judicial remedies which addressed the jurisdictional and procedural rules of the courts for bringing cases to court.

Most importantly, these subjects were at the heart of the rule of law affecting everyone's daily activities. The law of contracts fundamentally controls much of what we do, so as law students we had to learn what words constitute a promise, what words or acts of the other party to a contract make the promises enforceable by a court in awarding money damages for non-performance by either party, what acts by either party may excuse non-performance, the various rules for measuring damages, in some cases ordering specific performance of the broken promise, and the requirements of proof to establish the contract and its performance or non-performance.

Criminal law and tort law address individual and corporate liability for behavior that harms others necessitating that we learn the types and elements of the wrongful acts or omissions for which the law provides either criminal penalties or civil remedies, including tort law damages for negligence or liability without fault in some cases. The law of personal and real property is equally endemic and pervasive in our society requiring thorough study of the history of English law in the development of interests in land, in estate planning, and in personal property that we have inherited and further developed.

The course on judicial remedies first covered the complex and highly technical forms of action usually using Latin terms depending on the type of claim that governed the bringing of lawsuits under the English common law and that we inherited in the procedures applicable to our state and federal courts. This began to change in 1938 when the Supreme Court, acting on an earlier Congressional authorization, first promulgated the Federal Rules of Civil Procedure applicable thereafter to all suits in the U. S. district courts. Most states eventually revised their trial procedures along the lines of the Federal rules which greatly streamlined and simplified those that had previously prevailed in both court systems. The Federal Rules have been revised and upgraded repeatedly since 1938 to take account of changing conditions and the lessons of experience.

The course also focused on the sources of the jurisdiction, that is, the authority of the state and federal courts to adjudicate various kinds of cases. Jurisdiction is ordinarily conferred on courts by the statutes that create them. We therefore studied cases that presented jurisdictional questions that the courts had to resolve at the outset and usually before reaching the issues on the merits of the particular suit. I would study this further in Professor Hart's course on the jurisdiction of the federal courts in my third year.

Daily concentration on these cases in preparation for the next class and on reviewing and revising one's notes of the discussions of the cases in the last class were essential steps in the learning process. For this purpose many students formed small daily study groups to hammer out better understandings of what was said in class. I did this in my last year with considerable benefit. Doing this studying faithfully for each course consumed most of the non-class time each day and evening and weekends and left little time for other activities. In my first year I should have done a lot more if I were to earn the "A" grades on the first-year exams needed to be invited to join the law review. While I comfortably passed all of the first-year courses I received no "A"s.

Early in June 1947 at the Commencement Exercises in the Harvard Yard I received with other members of the Class of 1946 my undergraduate A.B. degree from President Conant. That afternoon Secretary of State George Marshall, the recipient of an honorary degree for his wartime military leadership, gave the famous speech that launched the "Marshall Plan" inviting the countries of Europe, individually and collectively, to formulate plans for urgent economic recovery from the prevailing chaos of wartime devastation and indicating that the United States Government would provide requested and necessary planning and financial assistance over several years.[23] The implementation of the Marshall Plan would have a transforming effect on the recovery of Western Europe and probably prevented its economic collapse and succumbing to Communism. This was a great occasion in the Harvard Yard that I was privileged to attend.

The second-year courses starting in September were administrative law with visiting Professor Kenneth Culp Davis from Minnesota Law School, later the author of the acclaimed multi-volume treatise on that subject first published in 1951; equity (first semester course) with renowned Professor Zachariah Chafee; evidence with Professor Maguire; future interests in real property with Professor James Casner; legal accounting (second semester course) with Professor Robert Amory; negotiable instruments (first semester) with Professor Braucher; and sales (second semester) with visiting Professor Soia Mentschikoff later at Chicago Law School; and trusts with Professor Austin Scott. All the courses were prescribed except I elected administrative law over admiralty and legal history.

Administrative law was a new and growing field of federal law largely created during FDR's first term in the 1930s concerned with judicial

---

23   For an authoritative account of the speech and its origins, *see* Pogue, *George Marshall: Statesman 1945-1959*, Chapter XIII, *The Harvard Speech*.

review of the decisions of the administrative agencies of the federal government in the regulation of business, with the agency procedures of promulgating substantive and procedural rules in implementation of the agency's statutory mandate, and with the agency procedures for the administrative adjudication of disputes with the regulated entities. Congress had recently regulated this relationship with the enactment of the Administrative Procedure Act of 1946, 5 U.S. Code Chapters 5 and 7. The statute also provided some public access to agency records, later expanded as the Freedom of Information Act and codified at 5 U.S. Code § 552. All this supplemented the Federal Register Act of 1935 in which Congress initially required most federal agencies to publish their rules affecting the public in the daily Federal Register which would be codified annually by agency in the Code of Federal Regulations.

Since in 1947 there were few appellate decisions interpreting the recent Administrative Procedure Act, Professor Davis had us study mimeographed copies of earlier Supreme Court decisions reviewing challenges to agency actions and addressing the availability of judicial review of them, the fairness of agency adjudication procedures, and the extent of finality of agency factual determinations, among other issues. While administrative law was a stimulating course, Professor Davis had more the zeal of a committed preacher than a practitioner of the Socratic method of teaching.

The course on equity with Professor Chafee, the acclaimed champion of freedom of speech, was in part a survey of the case law on the historical development of equity in England from the 16th Century as an appeal to the King's conscience to mitigate in particular the severity of the common-law judgments of the law courts. The King later delegated this function to the Lord Chancellor which in turn led to the establishment of the Court of Chancery which began to issue its own decisions and establish precedents of the cases in which relief from the decision of a law court would be available. A typical example would be a decree denying execution of a damages award for breach of contract upon a showing of a mutual mistake of the parties establishing that the contract as written did not express their intention.

The course also focused on cases on the differences in remedies between the law and equity courts. Except for a few common-law writs the law courts granted only money damages usually after a jury trial, not specific relief such as injunctions ordering one of the parties to perform or to cease performing a particular act which was only available in the Court of Chancery with no right to a jury trial.

In England this separation of the law and equity courts continued until a late 19th century act of Parliament combined them and in the United States for the federal courts until the adoption of the Federal Rules of Civil Procedure in 1938 and gradually thereafter in most state courts. However, we also learned that the common-law right to a jury trial incorporated into the Seventh Amendment to the U.S. Constitution does not extend to suits in equity. There can be no doubt of the continuing importance in today's legal world of the potential availability of evolving equitable relief in the American courts from harmful, unconscionable behavior for which there is no adequate legal remedy. Professor Chafee was a gifted, inspiring teacher.

The law of evidence with Professor Maguire was concerned with the proof of facts in civil and criminal cases deriving from a long history of English law on the admissibility of evidence in jury trials. Understanding this complex subject is fundamental to most areas of administrative and court litigation. Although a competent but boring teacher, Professor Maguire did immerse us in this subject aided by a superb casebook he and his colleague Professor Morgan, a leading national authority on evidence law, had compiled.

Future interests in the ownership of real property with Professor Casner again had us examine English case law for its development over many centuries before being transplanted to our courts. We studied the variety of the forms of these future interests, called "remainders", some vested, others contingent, that reflected the creative ingenuity of English lawyers in attempting to perpetuate the ownership of land indefinitely. We learned about the judicial and later statutory reaction known as the rule against perpetuities which generally proscribed creating future interests in land beyond designated lives in being plus twenty-one years. Unlike the others, Professor Casner's method of teaching was primarily by lecturing or "laying out" for us the property rules we should know to apply, for example, to various types of estate planning. In some ways it was an effective alternative to Socratic questioning.

Professor Amory's one semester course on legal accounting, or what lawyers should know about public accounting, was concerned with teaching us to read financial statements, to have some understanding of the fundamentals of costs, accrued and incurred, direct and indirect, and the public accounting rules for how and when they are to be recorded. This knowledge would be fundamental to the practice of corporate and tax law. He taught it well and it helped me later on in the practice of public contract law.

Negotiable instruments was an important, brief course in teaching us the every-day legal world of documents creating obligations to pay money, and the rights of those who receive them, a subject later covered by the enactment of Article Three of the Uniform Commercial Code by all the states for obligations other than those of the U. S. Government. An issued check is the most common example of a negotiable instrument; a promissory note is another. We were well taught by Professor Braucher..

In the second semester Visiting Professor Mentschikoff taught us sales and the Uniform Sales Act, also enacted by the states. It applied to sales of goods only, not to sales of land or services. Her teaching was particularly valuable because she was then deeply involved in drafting the provisions of the Uniform Commercial Code that would replace the Sales Act mostly drafted many years before by Harvard Law School Professor Samuel Williston, the author of the magisterial treatise on contract law. A splendid teacher, she had us study the significant differences between them and apply them to varying facts.

Professor Austin Scott, then probably the leading authority on the law of trusts, we were privileged to have as our teacher of the fundamentals of that subject. It addressed the ways in which the ownership of property could be separated between legal and equitable ownership so as to create an obligation of "trust" in the legal owner to administer the trust for the benefit of the owner(s) of the equitable interest(s). The scope of that obligation, the rights of beneficiaries and others, how trusts differed from other property relationships such as a bailment were large subjects with a library of English and American case law for us to grapple with in his casebook. Professor Scott had a singular way of beginning each class by saying, for example, emphatically, "Last time we were considering the distinction between a trust and a bailment, which is namely, what Mr._____?" Whereupon probably due to nearsightedness he would invariably call on the same student each time in the front row, my friend John Ferry who would manage a responsive reply. Somewhat a ham actor who had been teaching this course for about 40 years in our day and become somewhat entrenched in his opinions, Professor Scott was an unforgettable teacher.

During our second year we all participated in the Ames Moot Court Competition. This was participating in briefing and orally arguing before the fictitious Supreme Court of the Commonwealth of Ames the appeal of a hypothetical set of facts and judgment below prepared by the third-year students whose first and second-year grades rewarded them with that honor, one notch below the law review, and a faculty advisor. Members of the class were assigned to various teams within moot court clubs, mine being the Scott Club named for Professor Scott.

This was an intensive exercise without academic credit in learning how to look up law and draft legal arguments on whichever side of the argument the team was assigned, and for some the opportunity to argue the case orally before a panel of third-year student members. Those teams scoring well would advance to the next round of the competition. Ultimately two teams as the Ames finalists in their third year would brief and argue a case to the Ames Supreme Court before a panel of federal and state judges, usually including a member of the Supreme Court, to determine the winner of the competition. This was splendid learning experience in the teamwork of brief writing and of looking up law in the Langdell Law Library. My team did not progress beyond the second round.

Our third year began in September 1948. That summer Mother sublet her apartment to return to Biddeford Pool in Maine. John Carey invited me to join two other friends from Yale, Willim Butts Macomber and Ross Traphagen, to stay in his mother's apartment on Beacon Street as she too was away. For me it was a wonderful, companionable arrangement. By then I had an old Ford in which we would all commute to the law school early each morning and return for supper and study in the evenings to the accompaniment of the great artistry of Wanda Landowska on the harpsichord playing Bach's Goldberg Variations on 78 rpm records.

Butts Macomber would have a distinguished career in the foreign service, as an ambassador to Turkey, and finally as president of the Metropolitan Museum of Art. Ross Traphagen after many years of law practice would become the chief executive officer of Trans World Airways. John Carey, an exceptionally first-class lawyer, would become a senior partner in the long established international law firm of Coudert Brothers. This was confirmed to me many years later by Ferdinand Coudert an older lawyer who for many years had been one of the principals of the firm and had in retirement become one of my friends.

For the third year we could choose some of our courses. I took constitutional law with Professor Brown (first semester) and Professor Paul Freund (second semester), corporations with Professor Merrick Dodd (first semester) and Professor Ralph Baker (second semester), federal jurisdiction with Professor Henry Hart, federal taxation with Professor Brown, and jurisprudence with Visiting Professor Karl Llewellyn from Columbia Law School. Because of the variety of elective courses, the sizes of some of my third-year courses were noticeably smaller than those for the first and second years. This enabled greater individual student participation.

In constitutional law, we began with the 1803 Supreme Court decision in *Marbury v. Madison*, 5 U. S. (1 Cranch) 137, that an act of Congress that violates a provision of the constitution is void, in this case a provision of the Judiciary Act of 1789 found impermissibly to enlarge the Court's original jurisdiction under Article III of the Constitution. This landmark decision under the leadership of and written by Chief Justice John Marshall, only recently appointed by President John Adams, rightly created the authority of the Court to declare statutes unconstitutional notwithstanding the silence of the Constitution on that issue.

Although judicially established, the exercise of this authority remains politically controversial. In our class discussion, there was little dissent and general recognition of the indispensability of that authority for the Supreme Court to have finality on litigated constitutional questions.

This course for both semesters brilliantly led first by Professor Brown and then by Professor Freund was also challenging and instructive in assessing the controversial turbulence on many other issues in the Court's history, for examples, the uproar over the decision in the *Dred Scott* case (*Scott v. Sanford*, 60 U. S. 393 (1857)), in which the Court decided in an opinion by Chief Justice Roger Taney that slaves were the personal property of the slave owner and ineligible for U. S. citizenship; in the Court's decision in *Plessy v. Ferguson*, 163 U.S. 537 (1896), holding that the 14th Amendment did not entitle blacks to violate a state law requiring separate but equal seating in railroad cars over the strong, solitary dissent of Justice Harlan; and in the "stitch in time saves nine" decision of the Court in *West Coast Hotel v. Parrish*, 300 U. S. 379 (1937), in which Justice Roberts switched sides to make a 5-4 majority to uphold a Washington State minimum wage law, thereby forestalling President Roosevelt's plan to enlarge the membership of the Court to end the Court's striking down much New Deal legislation.

In our day, the Court had yet to confront its entrenched "separate but equal" precedent although it was then evident that the majority of the members of the Court appointed by President Roosevelt, including former Harvard Law School Professor Felix Frankfurter, would likely eventually overrule it which it did unanimously in 1954 in *Brown v. Board of Education*, 347 U.S. 483 (1954), holding that separate schools for black students are "inherently unequal".

We had no doubt even then that most all the strongly contested issues of life and death in our society would eventually become the subject of Supreme Court jurisprudence as they have in such disparate areas such as abortion, homosexual acts between consenting adults, prayer in public schools, freedom of speech and of the press, and separation of church and state, to name a few in this cutting-edge field of constitutional law.

The well-attended two-semester course on corporations and other business associations conducted by Professors Dodd and Baker, respectively, had us study these organizations in the context of their common-law origins, their formation, their governance, the extent of federal and state regulation of their activities, the extent of the liability of directors and shareholders and of corporations to shareholders and third persons for wrongful corporate acts, as well as many other facets of their operations. The teaching of this foundational course on business life from the Baker and Dodd casebook was entirely excellent.

Professor Henry Hart was the teacher of the course on the jurisdiction of the federal courts. Professor Hart was the most stimulating teacher I experienced at the law school. The size of the class permitted widespread student participation in the case discussions he incubated. The subject matter was complex and rooted in Article III of the Constitution creating the judicial branch of the federal government. Professor Hart was then creating what would become the leading casebook on this subject and we worked from mimeographed materials of cases and notes that he distributed in advance of each class. We studied, for example, the Article III limitations on jurisdiction of the federal courts arising from the words "Cases" and "Controversies" so as to preclude advisory opinions and to require a plaintiff to show injury in fact from the acts of the defendant for which redress is sought. This too was a necessary course for students intent on becoming litigators. It was the only course in which I received a grade as high as an "A minus".

Professor Karl Llewellyn was our teacher in the half-semester course on jurisprudence or the philosophy of law. He too was a dynamic, forceful teacher who provoked much class discussion of the cases and materials he assigned us. A proponent along with Justice Holmes and Dean Pound of the "legal realism" school of jurisprudence, Professor Llewellyn argued that law is best understood as shaped by the factual context, not always evident, in which cases arise and are decided as distinguished from the deductive application of settled rules. He also had us study the dispute-resolution practices of the Cheyenne Indians which he had written about in his 1941 book *The Cheyenne Way*. He once wisely cautioned me "Don't be too dogmatic!" in commenting on a response I had made during a class discussion. With his wife Professor Soia Mentschikoff, he was a principal draftsman of the Uniform Commercial Code. He was a brilliant teacher.

The third year classes and exams were concluded in May 1949 and we received our LL.B. degrees at the Commencement Exercises in the Harvard Yard early in June from President Conant.

There is no question of the great importance and the value for me of the educational experience provided by Harvard Law School under the leadership of Dean Griswold. It equipped its graduates to practice law with the ability to analyze problems arising from personal and business or organizational activities in depth and craft solutions through counselling and litigation when necessary, always based on thoroughly performing and knowing the underlying research of the relevant law in whatever field. While there was no instruction in the economics of law practice, we learned that law was to be practiced primarily as a profession and not as a business, and there would be no advertising or soliciting of our services or accomplishments. Sadly, in my lifetime, much of the practice of law in the United States has become indistinguishable from conducting a business with an over emphasis on advertising, soliciting clients, and making money and with the resulting loss of professionalism.

Next studying for the bar exam for admission to practice law in a particular state or in the District of Columbia would follow. I chose Massachusetts and enrolled in an intensive six-week course in Massachusetts law given in Boston by lawyers employed by a commercial firm and paid for by the GI bill. The law school did not prepare students for state bar exams. The bar exam given in July in Boston took all day and consisted of eight essay questions. Our study of prior exams and the course materials prepared us quite well, and as with most I passed. I and some others were summoned for an oral interview by the examiners. I was asked two questions: an ethics question I no longer remember and a question to explain the difference between a bilateral and unilateral contract. The easy answer was the difference between a bilateral exchange of promises of performance and a unilateral promise for the performance of an act—"I promise to pay you $10 if you cut my grass". My answers sufficed, and I was later notified that I would be admitted early in November.

While awaiting the exam results I and a couple of classmates started looking for a job as a government lawyer in Washington. Few agencies were hiring recent law graduates except for the Justice Department for its honors program which was limited to the top graduates of the principal law schools and for which my grades were insufficient. My sister Louise, then in Dark Harbor, Maine, for the summer with her children and Mother, Louise put me in touch with Lyttleton Fox[24], a former beau and now a civilian lawyer with the Navy. He could not have been more helpful and we began what would become a close friendship.

This was a difficult time for Lyttleton as he was unhappily in the throes of being divorced to his great dismay. He nevertheless arranged interviews for me with the appropriate lawyers in his office including one with Harold Gross, the General Counsel of the Navy Department. A month or two later Mr. Gross offered me a job to fill a newly created position for a second lawyer in a Navy purchasing office in Philadelphia contingent on my admission to the bar. There being no prospect of any other appropriate government job, I gladly accepted.

After the interviews in Washington and before receiving the offer from Mr. Gross or knowing the bar exam results, I joined Mother and Louise in Dark Harbor for a marvellous vacation of several weeks in late July and August. Louise's eldest daughter Fifi was now 17 with one more year at Farmington; Priscilla was 12, Katherine 7, and Susan 2, and all except for Susan with days and evenings filled with friends and activities. Edith Mathews looked after the younger ones. Louise and Mother too had lots of bridge and parties in the beautiful setting of Dark Harbor at the southern tip of Islesboro Island facing Penobscot's Bay and across from Camden on the coast and accessible by ferry from Camden. Mooney came for about a week toward the end of their stay.

---

24 A 1934 graduate of Harvard Law School, Fox as a second-year student wrote an article for the long gone Forum magazine entitled "Harvard Law School: The Incubator of Greatness". It was later republished in a now out-of-print *College Book of Essays* along with passages from Plato and Aristotle. Many years later Lyttleton encountered his former teacher, now Mr. Justice Frankfurter, who said to him with characteristic hyperbole, "Fox, you have fouled your nest."

The grand dame of Dark Harbor was Irene Langhorne Gibson, the original "Gibson girl" drawings of the early 1900s and since 1944 the widow of her husband, the artist Charles Dana Gibson.[25] Mrs. Gibson was the eldest of the celebrated five Langhorne sisters from Virginia. One of them was Nancy, later Lady Astor and the first female member of Parliament. Another was Phyllis who married an Englishman, Robert Brand, and was the mother of Dinah Brand the future wife of Lyttleton Fox and now divorcing him and returning to England with their two young children, Phyllis and James Fox whom I would later know.

Mrs. Gibson spent her summers on 700 Acre Island off Dark Harbor which her husband had acquired many years before. Her launch made the continuous short trips back and forth from Dark Harbor. With her that summer from Cincinnati was her daughter Irene ("Babs"), her husband John Emory and their daughters Irene ("Renee"), Leila, already engaged, Melissa, and a younger brother Ethan. Louise introduced me to all of them, and I became a frequent almost daily guest in a variety of activities indoors and out, principally as the guest of Melissa, 16, with another year at Foxcroft. I liked all of them. Renee had a heavy beau, David Clark, an aspiring artist and recent Harvard graduate. The Emory parents and Mrs. Gibson were particularly nice to me, redolent of my relationships with the Bevans in England and the Wengers in France. All this was a wonderful episode for me after the rigors of law school thanks to the kindness of Louise and Mooney.

Early in September Mother and I returned to Boston in the new Ford she had purchased for me earlier that summer. I would start the Navy job on November 10 in Philadelphia shortly after my admission to the Massachusetts Bar which along with many other successful candidates took place at an appropriate ceremony before the Supreme Judicial Court early in November. I was now a lawyer admitted to practice in Massachusetts, but with no intention to practice law there.

This concludes Part Three of my enriching life.

---

25 *See Five Sisters: The Langhornes of Virginia* by James Fox, the son of Lyttleton Fox and a grandson of Phyllis Langhorne Brand, published in 2001.

Part Four Navy Public Contract Lawyer 1949-62

1. Assistant Counsel, the Aviation Supply Office 1949-51.

On November 10, 1949, at age 25, I began my first job as a lawyer. As a fledgling member of the Navy's Office of the General Counsel (OGC), I was hired as the assistant counsel at the Navy's Aviation Supply Office (ASO) in northeast Philadelphia. The counsel was Robert B. Garnett, an experienced corporate lawyer trained at the Wall Street firm of Reid & Priest. Bob and I soon established a harmonious working relationship, and a personal one with him and his wife Mary Elizabeth as well. He was a splendid, thorough, hands-on teacher that enabled me do the work from day one. We shared an excellent secretary, Helen Sanders of indeterminate age whom we always called "Miss Sanders". Her salary was $3,500, mine $3,100, and I had no complaint. I lived across the street from ASO as a boarder in a row house with an accommodating family.

ASO, established in 1942, consisted of a sizeable new brick office building and a large complex of warehouses occupying several acres. ASO had the enormous responsibility for the procurement of replacement parts for all the Navy's aircraft. For this purpose even then it annually awarded contracts to the aircraft airframe and engine manufacturers at prices aggregating $1 billion in the context of a total national defense budget of about $12 billion. In addition, ASO was the Navy's purchasing office for the procurement of general-purpose supplies ("stores" in Navy terminology), except clothing and food, needed for the Navy's operation afloat and ashore, another large responsibility. That function on a government-wide basis would later become the responsibility of the General Services Administration created by Congress in 1949. Anticipating the Navy's requirements for each fiscal year for all these items and timely procuring them were major management challenges. Large computers from IBM were then beginning to be used for this purpose.

These procurements obviously would raise a host of ongoing needs for legal services. The office of counsel at ASO was created during the war and was then staffed by three or four very able lawyers from Wall Street to draft the contracts and advise on the legal questions arising from wartime contracting to meet the far greater requirements for these items. Bob arrived in 1947 or 1948, by then the sole lawyer at ASO with still a considerable backlog in resolving claims from the termination of wartime contracts. The increasing workload was too much for one lawyer and Bob finally persuaded his superiors in Washington to approve hiring a second attorney for ASO. I was that second attorney.

The contracting function at ASO was staffed by Navy Supply Corps officers and by career civil servants. The Supply Corps officers, usually graduates of the leading business schools, were mostly highly competent professionals versed in the varied aspects of supply management including contracting. The civil servants tended to specialize in particular procurement functions such as commodity buying, the conduct of competitive bidding for the procurement of the general-purpose supplies, and the related production-line preparation of thousands of contract documents each year.

Prior to World War II procurement contracts of the federal government with exceptions for small purchases up to $500 and few others were made by competitive bidding, called "formal advertising for bids", under the authority of Section 3709 of the Revised Statutes enacted in the 1870s. This method still prevailed for the general stores purchases at ASO while I was there but under a successor statute, the Armed Services Procurement Act of 1947 which took effect on May 18, 1948.

Military procurement during World War II largely dispensed with formal advertising for bids as too cumbersome, inflexible and slow. Instead by the First War Powers Act of 1941, enacted promptly after the attack on Pearl Harbor, Congress authorized the President with power of delegation to make and modify contracts for the war effort without regard to any other applicable law whenever that action would facilitate the prosecution of the war. The President promptly delegated his authority to the Secretaries of War and the Navy with powers of redelegation. As a result, most government wartime contracts were made by negotiation of the prices and other terms with individual contractors. This authority continued until the above effective date of the new procurement law and under which formal advertising for bids was still generally required.

Formal advertising involved several time-consuming steps. First, was the preparation of a formal invitation for bids (IFB) on standard IFB and bid forms now newly prescribed by GSA, altogether a lengthy document of up to 50 pages inviting bids to be submitted in duplicate and which described the required supplies or services, the detailed specifications of the items to be made or performed, the required time and place of delivery or for performance, all the terms and conditions on another GSA prescribed form of "General Provisions" of standard contract clauses prescribed by statute, executive order, and GSA that would apply to any bid and resulting contract[26], the exact time and place for the receipt and public opening of bids which ordinarily would be 45 days from the estimated date of receipt of the invitation, the statement that each bid may not be revoked for a period of 60 days from the date of opening, and the announcement that any late bid or any bid taking material exception to

---

26 Some of the clauses prescribed by statute or executive order were socio-economic on the application of the Buy American Act, labor laws, non-discrimination in employment, and preferences for awarding subcontracts to small business firms. Others addressed the covenant contingent fees, officials not to benefit, assignment of claims, and the recovery of excessive profits.

the IFB would be rejected. The second step was the public posting of the IFB at ASO and mailing it to firms on the ASO bidders' list for the particular class of items. Although ASO had authority to advertise IFBs in the commercial press it rarely did so.

The third step was the public opening and reading aloud to attending bidders and commercial services in a designated public bid-opening room, and the public posting, of the bid prices received and the availability of duplicate copies of the bids for public inspection in the bid-opening room at ASO. The fourth step was the detailed evaluation of bids that appeared eligible for the contract award, usually to the lowest priced bidder from a responsible bidder whose bid was responsive to the IFB in all material respects. The fifth and final step was making the contract award, preparing the award document on another prescribed GSA form, having it signed by an authorized contracting officer depending on the dollar amount, and timely mailing the award document to the successful bidder before the expiration of that bid, and the public posting of that award document in the bid room.

All these steps with at least one or more weekly bid openings bristled with the potential for simple to knotty legal questions which had to be resolved very promptly and frequently on the spot in the context of ongoing procurement. I was on that firing line from day one of arrival. Our law library was limited: the published decisions of the Comptroller General[27]; Williston on Contracts; the excellent monograph "Navy Contract Law" published in 1949 by the Navy OGC and written by several of its lawyers; the Navy Procurement Directives; and the Commerce Clearing

---

27   The Comptroller General was head of the General Accounting Office (GAO) created by the Budget and Accounting Act of 1921 over President Harding's veto. The veto was based on the violation of the Constitutional separation of powers between the legislative and executive branches of the federal government on the ground that the GAO located in the legislative branch had the authority to audit the accounts of government agencies and to disallow any expenditure paid by a disbursing officer that the Comptroller General determined to violate an applicable provision of law. This authority, now codified at 31 U.S.C. § 3526, was particularly relevant to the obligation and expenditure of contract funds which GAO auditors routinely examined as well as the related contracts and modifications copies of which were furnished to GAO as they were executed.

House Government Contracts Reporter which with monthly updates provided the text of the statutes applicable to government contracts, the text of decisions of the federal courts, primarily the U.S. Court of Claims, on government contract disputes, and digests of the decisions of the Armed Services Board of Contract Appeals and the predecessor boards on these disputes, and digests of the decisions of the U.S. Comptroller General (GAO) on protests of IFBs and contract awards by aggrieved and unsuccessful bidders. Particularly valuable were file copies of well-written memoranda of law written during the war by the OGC lawyers at ASO which continued to have relevance.

The contracts for aircraft replacement parts, however, were negotiated, usually solely with the manufacturer of the item. These contracts while far fewer numerically than those awarded after formal advertising generally accounted for about two-thirds of the procurement dollars in the awarded contracts each year at ASO. Under the new Armed Services Procurement Act of 1947, the military departments were authorized to procure supplies and services for which funds had been appropriated by negotiation instead of by formal advertising if any one of sixteen circumstances was present. Of these only two were apparently available to contracting officers at ASO: (1) when the contract did not exceed $2,500; and (2) when it was impracticable to obtain competition when supported by a written justification of the facts supporting that conclusion signed by the contracting officer and sent to the General Accounting Office. The other exceptions to the use of procurement by formal advertising either did not apply to ASO procurements or required the advance approval of the Secretary of the Navy. With the Presidential declaration of a national emergency in December 1951 eighteen months after the outbreak of the Korean War, the authority to negotiate procurement contracts during periods of war or national emergency was primarily used at ASO for the duration of that conflict. By then I had been transferred to the office of counsel of the Navy Bureau of Supplies and Accounts in Washington.

Bob Garnett or I had to approve, and in many cases draft, the factual justifications for finding that it was impracticable to obtain competition. Such would be the case, for example, if there was only one supplier, usually the manufacturer of the item or its subcontractor but subject to the strict quality control of the manufacturing process, or the design of the item was controlled by patents or trade secrets, as was frequently the case for aircraft parts. While I was at ASO these justifications were never questioned by or protested to the GAO. Nevertheless, the preparation of them required our due diligence.

ASO negotiated annual contracts with the principal manufacturers of the aircraft industry, procuring the air engine parts directly from the engine manufacturers, primarily Pratt & Whitney and Hamilton Standard divisions of United Aircraft for jet and reciprocating engine parts and propellers, respectively; Curtis Wright for jet and reciprocating engine parts; Westinghouse for jet engine parts; and from the airframe manufactures such as Douglas, Glen Martin, Grumman, Lockheed, and others for airframe parts. These contracts, known as "master indefinite-quantity contracts", established the terms and conditions that would apply to parts ordered by ASO during the period of the contract and the procedures for ordering.

Because ASO did not promise in these master contracts to order any minimum quantity or dollar value of parts, the contractors would not be bound to accept any order and the parties would therefore negotiate the price, quantity and delivery terms for the particular items depending on the quantities ordered and other relevant price factors. The individual orders then were the contracts which incorporated by reference the terms of the master contracts. Bob and I also had to draft with care the factual justifications for each of these orders why it was impracticable to obtain competition for signature by a contracting officer to submit with the order to the General Accounting Office. Because these were sole-source contracts without price or product competition, we never knew whether the prices were reasonable or excessive. The regulatory requirements for detailed disclosure and analysis of contractors' estimated direct and indirect costs and profits prior to awarding non-competitive contracts of large dollar amounts were not in place for another decade.

Yet the experience Bob Garnett and I had in participating in the negotiation and drafting of particular clauses for these master contracts with counsel for the contractors was especially stimulating and enriching.

The lawyers representing Pratt & Whitney and Hamilton Standard were highly competent and professional, and it was a pleasure to deal with them.

Prior to award of the larger contracts, the head of the ASO contracts division, a Supply Corps Commander Otis Stafford when I was at ASO, would convene a review board of senior procurement officials to question and challenge the contracting officer's bases for proposing the particular contract award above a dollar threshold or presenting novel issues. The review board also focused on any protests to the GAO, actual or potential, that the award might engender. Bob Garnett and I found that participating in these frequent reviews forestalled trouble later on. Again the professionalism of the participants was admirable.

Time passed quickly and very busily. We had periodic visits from our superiors in Washington, first, Meritt Steger, then counsel to the Navy Bureau of Supplies & Accounts which had management oversight of ASO's procurement functions, and then his successor William Sellman, after Merritt was promoted to be the OGC deputy general counsel for procurement law in 1950. This was a good opportunity for them to appraise my worth and for me to know that they were highly competent lawyers.

By late June 1950 Bob Garnett was on vacation for a couple of weeks apparently satisfied that I could "mind the store" in his absence. On June 25, North Korea suddenly invaded South Korea, quickly taking Seoul and moving rapidly south. President Truman promptly obtained a UN Security Council resolution, the Soviet Union member being fortuitously absent, authorizing the use of international military force to defend South Korea. President Truman ordered General MacArthur in Japan to dispatch troops and air and naval forces to halt the North Korean advance which appeared likely to overrun all of South Korea.

Several days later Rear Admiral McCartney, the Supply Corps officer in command of ASO, telephoned me. He said the Navy carrier pilots desperately needed a large quantity of World War II surplus aircraft gasoline drop tanks that extended the combat range of carrier aircraft and would be dropped when the fuel was exhausted. They could now be filled with napalm and then dropped on the advancing North Koreans with devastating results. His staff had located the needed quantities at a number of dealers in surplus war materials around the country. Obtaining them by the usual procedures of advertising for bids was unacceptably slow; they could not be obtained in time that way. Was there any alternative, he wanted to know. I said I would promptly get back to him.

I carefully looked at the list of exceptions to the use of procurement by formal advertising in the Armed Services Procurement Act. One of them authorized negotiated procurement when "the public exigency will not permit the delay incident to advertising." The statute did not define "public exigency" and was silent at what level this authority could be exercised. The Navy Procurement Directives were no help; the OGC monograph on "Navy Contract Law" gave some helpful examples of what might be a public exigency. I quickly concluded, without checking with Bob Garnett or Washington knowing that a prompt response was highly unlikely, that Admiral McCartney could now proceed to acquire the drop tanks under this authority and so orally advised him. I promptly followed up with a memorandum confirming this advice and suggesting that the drop tanks could be ordered by telephone with a confirming purchase order document and the Navy would arrange for pickup at the dealers' place of business for immediate air shipment to designated locations. I also prepared a detailed justification of the use of this authority and the methods of obtaining them for the Admiral's signature and attachment to a copy of each purchase order to be sent to the GAO. The drop tanks arrived in time to help halt the North Korean advance on the Pusan perimeter; and the purchases were never questioned by my superiors or by the GAO. Bob Garnett was very complimentary.

That summer I had a welcome weekend visit from Henry Foster and a renewal of our friendship. He had finished his college education and was now in a graduate program studying ecology which would become his life work in public service and academia. I was privileged to have him as a friend. That summer with help from Mother I purchased a 1950 Ford sedan, the last Ford I would have.

The Korean War accelerated the tempo and quantity of our work to meet the increasing demands for the items ASO procured. Congress greatly increased its appropriations for national defense. American rearmament approaching the scale of that in 1940 and 1941 prior to Pearl Harbor was now underway, and also to counter the Soviet threat to Western Europe as it was widely understood that Stalin had encouraged, if not instigated, the North Korean attack. The Soviet attempt to drive us from Berlin in 1948 reminded us of a continuing military threat. Our European allies and the U. S. Government therefore increased their military commitment to the 1949 North Atlantic Treaty Organization (NATO); and President Truman recalled General Eisenhower to active duty to be the Supreme Allied Commander of the NATO forces.

I spent several days over Christmas and New Year's with Mother in Boston. We undoubtedly were with Mike and Joan on one or the other of these holidays. Pat, now a captain in the naval reserve, was continuing his reserve duties of weekly meetings at the Brooklyn Navy Yard and two-week summer cruises. He and Marty and their three sons had moved to Banksville in Westchester County, New York, in 1948 to begin a new job in New York with the business brokerage firm of Hubbard, Westerfelt & Motley. There was some risk that he might be recalled to active duty during the Korean War. Luckily for him and his family, he was not.

The production of contract documents at ASO was impeccably ruled by a Miss Greenstein, a formidable battle-axe who also had a great love of opera. She and I became friends. I was her guest at two or three performances of the Metropolitan Opera which in those days came weekly during the opera season to Philadelphia's venerable Academy of Music, home of the Philadelphia Orchestra but built as an opera house in the 1850s. Miss Greenstein had center seats in the top balcony from which without opera glasses the singers looked like midgets while the sound was always glorious and full throated. She also would bring the full score of each opera which she seemed to know by heart and would discuss with much learning. She added much to my appreciation of opera.

The work at ASO during 1951 continued to increase at a more intensive pace as the rearmament program gained momentum. Bob Garnett and

I finally convinced our superiors of the need for a third attorney to cope with the growing workload of legal services. By late summer we hired Peter Hanke, a recent law-school graduate already admitted to the bar, to join us. By then, my transfer to Washington in the fall was looming, and a replacement attorney would be recruited by the time of my departure..

In February, one of my friends at ASO, Lt. Jim McGarry and his wife-to-be, Lloyd Wolfe, invited me to join them one Saturday evening to attend a small party at the home of a friend of hers in Merion, a suburb west of Philadelphia on the "main line" of the Pennsylvania Railroad's commuter train service from Philadelphia to Paoli. Lloyd had grown up in that vicinity, and our host for the evening, John Shollenberger, was a long-time friend of hers. John, a recent graduate of Rollins College in Winter Park, Florida, was a young artist in his early twenties studying both at the Philadelphia Academy of the Fine Arts and at the Barnes Foundation[28] in Merion. He lived with his parents in "Welcomestone", a large three-storied stone house built in 1888 to the Romanesque design of the then celebrated Philadelphia architect Frank Furness which they acquired in 1937. The house situated on about an acre of land with beautiful large different trees was on a quiet residential street, South Highland Ave., near the Merion commuter railroad station. His parents were then having a month's vacation in Key West from his father's busy surgical practice at the Crozier Hospital in Chester, Pennsylvania.

John had invited a few other friends in addition to the Lloyd and Jim who asked if they could bring me. John and I established an instant

---

28 It was established in the 1920s by Dr. Albert Barnes as a small, selective, art school for the underprivileged for the study of his world-class collection of mostly impressionist paintings by Cezanne, Gaugain, Matisse, Modigliani, Picasso, Renoir, Seurat, Soutine, Van Gogh, and others that he amassed from his fortune from the invention and sales of the patent medicine Argyrol. The 800 some paintings of the collection now have an estimated worth of $25 billion. The teaching at the Barnes Foundation by Dr. Barnes, John Dewey, and Bertrand Russell in the early years and later by Violetta de Mazia who co-authored several books with Dr. Barnes on painting, was wholly at odds with the traditional art teaching at the Philadelphia Academy. Wikipedia on the Barnes Foundation on Google provides an account of its history, its planned relocation to central Philadelphia in 2012, and photographs of some of the important paintings. I would twice visit this collection with John.

rapport. I was impressed by his knowledge and love of art and opera, about which I knew too little and welcomed his willingness to increase my appreciation of each. He suggested we continue the discussion at his house the next day, to which I gladly assented. During that visit he invited me to live in his house, not as a lodger but as a dear friend and which he was confident his parents would approve. Merion was about a 20-30 minute drive from ASO, and I was glad to return to the family life I had experienced during the war and with Mother. He would soon do my portrait attired in a business suit and a second, informal one a few years later.

John had deformed hips either since birth or the result of a severe illness in infancy which made one leg longer than the other. An operation to correct this in 1949 did not succeed and indeed worsened his walking and mobility. This condition would require hip replacement decades later. His calm fortitude in cheerful acceptance of his physical disability throughout his life inspires great admiration for his inner strengths.

I moved in within a few days. John and I began a loving, gay relationship, a first for me but in accord with the principal tendency of my genetic sexual orientation. When I moved to Washington in October there was no question of our continuing to live together. His life and future were rooted where he had always lived; and for my future as a government lawyer in Washington in the prevailing government and public homophobia of gays as security risks, we could not risk our living together there. As it was, I would try to visit every other weekend and did for the next several years. Gradually our relationship evolved into a close, intimate and lifetime friendship which has flourished for more than 60 years until his death in his 85th year on January 30, 2012.

I also became devoted to his parents, and I liked his twin sisters, Jean and Priscilla, five years older than John, married with young children respectively to Don Noble and Fred Schimpf, each a graduate engineer who had been roommates at Penn State, and then living nearby. John's mother, Gladys Swortley Shollenberger, raised in Philadelphia and a 1916 Cornell graduate and former teacher in the Philadelphia schools, was highly educated and intellectually challenging and with a heart of gold that made me feel entirely a member of the family. Her husband, Dr. Clarence Lewars Shollenberger, born in the 1890s, raised in Auburn, New Jersey, and a graduate of Dickinson College and in 1921 of Hahnemann Hospital Medical School in Philadelphia, presented a calm, gentle, kind manner that invited the trust and confidence of patients and friends alike. He too welcomed me as a second son.

They returned from Key West two or three weeks after I moved in, and all was immediately well from their pleasure seeing John's delight in my company. They told us that they had purchased a double lot of property in Key West near the ocean and had engaged a contractor to build a two-bedroom house on one floor there. It should be finished by June. John and I would then drive to Key West to open it. I was able to get leave for two weeks.

We had a very long two-and-a-half-day 1,200 mile drive to Key West. In June 1951 there were no interstate highways. The two-lane route was U. S. Highway 1 to Wilmington, U.S. 40 to Baltimore, U. S. 301 to Virginia and connecting shortly with U. S. 17 to Jacksonville, and then finally U. S. 1 to the Florida keys and over the magnificent 100 miles of the "Overseas Highway" completed in 1942 on the roadbed and bridges of the Florida East Coast Railroad to Key West.

We were thrilled by the house awaiting us at 915 Johnson Street: pink cinder-block construction, terrazzo flooring throughout, sitting room, dining area, two bedrooms and bath, and a carport; lovely grounds with beautiful trees and plantings already in place. John's mother had arranged for the installation of an electric stove and a refrigerator, a telephone, two beds and bedding for one of the bedrooms, dishes, cutlery and cooking utensils, lamps, a card table and folding chairs, towels, indeed enough for us to get by comfortably. But no shades or blinds! We found a food store and stocked up. John prepared our first dinner. Exhausted, we were early to bed.

The house was ideally located in Key West. A beach and pier for ideal swimming in the Atlantic Ocean were two blocks away and which we enjoyed daily. A distant barrier coral reef kept the waters mostly calm and the sharks away. The Casa Marina luxury resort hotel built by Flagler in 1918 was a block away. Occupied by the Navy during the war it remained closed despite the growing tourism due to President Truman's annual vacations at the Key West naval base. Flagler had built the hotel as a way stop to and from Havana, the ultimate destination of the railroad between Miami and Key West, a major engineering achievement over 100 miles of ocean that was finally completed in 1912 and opened by President Taft. Boat trains traversed the ninety miles of ocean between Key West and Havana. The lure of Havana was primarily for gambling and other vices during the era of Prohibition.

For much of the 19th and early years of the 20th centuries, Key West was the largest city in Florida accessible only by sea until Flagler built the railroad there from Miami. The hurricane of 1935 washed away much of the roadbed in the area of Marathon Key. The Florida East Coast Railroad, then in bankruptcy, was unable to finance the restoration of service. Commercial air service to Key West and to Havana from Miami and Key West on the newly created Pan American Airways began about that time.

There was much of beauty, charm and interest to see and admire in Key West: wonderfully restored 19th century New Bedford style ship-captains' wooden houses with widows' walks when the salvage of ships stranded on the Key West reefs was big business; semi-tropical flowers, plants and trees; pelicans, and other sea birds; the dazzling and varying colors of the ocean; magnificent ocean sunrises and sunsets on the Gulf of Mexico side of the island; and an abundance of delightful places to eat native seafood. There were crumbling brick Civil War forts, one, Fort Zachary Taylor at the southern end of the island and then part of the Navy base, another facing the ocean near Johnson street and now the site of the Key West Garden Club, and the third at the northern end by the airport and now an art gallery.

The Navy was still the primary land occupier with perhaps a third of the island and most of the harbor and docking areas. There was a continuous presence of Navy ships and sailors with shore leave in addition to the numerous naval personnel stationed in Key West and at the nearby Naval Air Station on Stock Island.

During our visit the days were mostly hot and humid, usually mitigated by ocean breezes, and the nights somewhat cooler. We had no air
conditioning. We met and liked our immediate neighbors, particularly
Doris and Frank Johnson. He worked in his father's jewelry store; and she
was raising their young children. We also met Fred Johnston and his sister Dorothy. They had the same contractor, Roy Edwards, building their
vacation house at the same time as the one for John's parents. Fred was
an antiques dealer in early American furniture in Kingston, New York,
and a former curator at Winterthur, the magnificent home and estate of
Henry Francis Dupont and museum of Americana at Brandywine Creek
in Delaware. We later learned that Edwards had double billed each of
these clients for some of the work performed for the other one. Neither
sought redress.

After several days I drove to Palm Beach for a brief visit to Louise as John preferred to stay instead of our stopping there on our return
north. She and Mooney had divorced the year before, he to remarry and
finally to have a son and namesake after five daughters. Louise remained
in their Orange Grove Road house. She seemed to be in good spirits, and
the three younger daughters were with her. Fifi, the eldest and at her
request now called by her middle name Rawn, was then acting in summer stock theater after studying at the Neighborhood Playhouse School
of the Theater in New York. She had recently starred in the school play
at Farmington, and she was hopeful of having an acting career. I had an
enjoyable if brief visit with Louise and returned to Key West, a distance
of about 230 miles.

John and I drove back to Merion a few days later and reported to
John's parents about their Key West home with great enthusiasm. I
would return to Key West with John for several days for several winters thereafter when his parents were there until a decline in his father's
heath compelled them to sell the house at less than they paid for it. It
would later be modestly enlarged and resold at ever higher prices finally
approaching $1 million.

That summer I began a long friendship with Ann and Graydon Upton
who were then living in Wawa on the Main Line. Graydon, a Philadelphia

banker, was the eldest son of Lorna Graydon Upton and George Upton of Boston who had introduced my parents to each other at the Graydon-Upton wedding in Cincinnati in 1906. Ann and Graydon would move to and remain in Washington when President Eisenhower appointed Graydon in 1953 to be an assistant secretary of the Treasury and President Johnson later appointed him to be president of the Inter-American Development Bank. Graydon, born in 1908 and growing to a towering six and one-half feet, had married the belle of Savannah, Annie Nash, during World War II. They were delightful, witty company whom I would continue to see and savor in Washington for many years.

The remaining several weeks at ASO passed quickly. I was eager to move to Washington for which the ASO experience had me quite well grounded in the fundamentals of the practice of government contract law from the wide range of issues Bob Garnett and I had to address at times daily and often that day. I am grateful to Bob for the wisdom of his training and the exemplary conscientiousness and thoroughness of his work habits.

2. Assistant Counsel at the Bureau of Supplies & Accounts 1951-54.

In October 1951 I began as an assistant counsel in the office of counsel of the Navy's Bureau of Supplies & Accounts (BuSandA) in the old World War I "temporary" concrete office building at 17th and Constitution Avenue Northwest serving as the main Navy building under the direction of the assistant secretary of the Navy for procurement and supply management. The secretary of the Navy and the office of the chief of naval operations were located in the Pentagon.

Bill Sellman was the counsel for BuSandA and there were almost a dozen other attorneys, most of them older and more experienced than I. Bill reported to the Navy General Counsel, Harold Gross, who had hired me two years previously. BuSandA was one of the principal bureaus of the Navy, each commanded by a rear admiral, which under the direction of the Chief of Navy Material, a vice admiral, supported the command and operational functions of the Navy headed by the Chief of Naval Operations by providing the required personnel, ships, aircraft, weapons, facilities, and supplies authorized and appropriated for annually by Congress. BuSandA had procurement and supply management responsibility for all supplies and services required for naval operations not assigned to another bureau such as the foregoing other than supplies. It also was responsible for auditing naval activities and contractors performing cost-reimbursement contracts and for supervising all procurements by some 50 field activities such as ASO. These were vast responsibilities now enlarged by the demands of the Korean War and the Cold War.

To guide BuSandA and the Navy's field activities in the performance of their various supply and procurement functions, BuSandA had long published and maintained a multi-volume manual. The volume on purchasing, last revised at the outset of World War II, was hopelessly out of date. There was an urgent need for a complete revision. Bill Sellman was asked to assign an attorney to work on this substantially full time with a Supply Corps officer, Lt. Skip McMorries. Bill selected me. For the next six months I did little else. McMorries was a highly intelligent, educated young supply corps officer with whom I established an excellent working relationship. He many years later was promoted to Rear Admiral and was the Contracting Officer for the Naval Air Systems Command (formerly the Bureau of Aeronautics) when Secretary of Defense Cheney in 1991 directed that the Navy terminate the contract for the development and production of the A-12 fighter aircraft because of cost overruns. As discussed in Note 158 in Part Five, the litigation over that dispute now awaits the results of a Supreme Court decision in 2011 remanding the issue of whether the Justice Department could invoke the "states secrets" doctrine to bar the introduction of any classified information necessary to proof of the contractors' claims to the Federal Court of Appeals for the Federal Circuit, the successor to the U.S. Court of Claims.

The issuance of procurement regulations in 1951 was in transition from instruction at the bureau level to the Navy Department level, and gradually to the Department of Defense level through the issuance and growing coverage of the Armed Services Procurement Regulation (ASPR). This trend would culminate beginning in the later 1970s during the Carter Administration with the gradual emergence of the government-wide Federal Acquisition Regulation (FAR). But as Skip and I worked on this we found that much of the needed guidance had not yet been addressed either in the Navy Procurement Directives (NPDs) or the nascent ASPR. There was also the question of whether to repeat the coverage of those documents or to reference them. There was much to be said for all the needed guidance to be in a single publication rather that in the necessity to be conversant with three publications. Our solution was a pragmatic one: what was important we would repeat in the purchasing manual; the rest we would cross reference.

Collaboratively writing this purchasing manual with Skip McMorries was first drafting an outline of what subject matter we would cover and then dividing between us the initial research and drafting of each topic whereupon each would review and critique the other's work product. This worked well and each improved the other's work. We completed the text in about six months and after a cursory review by our superiors it was published as Volume 6, "Purchasing" of the BuSandA Manual. My ASO experience was indispensable, yet I learned a great deal more about making and performing government contracts.

One of Bill Sellman's responsibilities as counsel to BuSandA was to provide legal services to the Navy Purchasing Office (NPO), Washington, D.C., a field activity of BuSandA and located in our building. Bill assigned me along with one or two other attorneys to this task. It was quite similar to the ASO experience but with a greater emphasis on contracting for a wide variety of services and on the use of cost-reimbursement contracts. Some of the services contracts would raise questions of whether the work if usually performed by government employees could be contracted out. These were mostly logistics type support services such as ship provisioning and resupply, inventory control functions, and some equipment overhaul and repair work usually performed at government facilities. It was important to draft work statements that fully described the services to be performed and how the concerned naval activity would supervise the contractor's performance. We were mindful of decisions by the Comptroller General that such services were considered to be government-supervised "personal services" to be performed only by government employees with limited exceptions not to exceed one year and approved by the agency head.

The increased workload from the Korean War necessitated these contracts because the available government work force, for which Congress had yet to authorize additional hiring, was inadequate to meet the demands for these services. I prepared detailed factual justifications for each of these usually negotiated awards which were filed with the General Accounting Office with a copy of the related contract. None was ever questioned.

Some of these services contracts were negotiated as cost-reimbursement type contracts because of the difficulties of estimating the quantities of the services to be performed during the period of the contracts which ordinarily were for one year with renewal options. In these circumstances the cost-reimbursement contract provided the flexibility to adjust the performance to rapidly changing circumstances. The contract would establish an estimated maximum cost subject to unilateral upward adjustment by the contracting officer, and the contractor would promise to use "its best efforts" to perform the contract within that estimated maximum costs, with no obligation to continue performance when its costs reached that limit regardless of the status of completion of the work.

This fundamentally distinguished it from a fixed-type contract under which the contractor would have an unconditional performance obligation, subject only to non-performance due to causes beyond its control and without its fault or negligence. The contractor would be reimbursed each month its allowable and allocable costs as determined in accordance with a prescribed BuSandA regulation of allowable costs and as finally audited and determined by the BuSandA Navy Cost Inspection Service and by the contracting officer if the contractor disputed any cost disallowance. The contractor could appeal the contracting officer's decision to the Armed Services Board of Contract Appeals (ASBCA) and obtain limited judicial review of an adverse ASBCA decision in the U.S. Court of Claims.

In addition to the counselling and drafting work for NPO, I also assisted contracts personnel in BuSandA in processing bid protests to field activity solicitations and awards to the GAO. GAO had long exercised authority through its office of general counsel to review these protests to see if the challenged agency action was in violation of applicable procurement law; if so the protest would be sustained and the agency would usually have to start over. Our role was to review the merits of the protest and the justification of the contracting officer of the purchasing activity in accordance with the extensive published GAO decisional law. If we found the protest meritorious, we would direct the contracting officer to take appropriate action and so notify GAO which would usually dismiss the protest as moot. If we thought the protested action of the contracting officer was correct we would so advise GAO and await its decision. With the increasing Korean War workload there was a corresponding increase in the volume of protests.

In performing the foregoing tasks, I was one of several of Bill Sellman's attorneys engaged in this work. I came to have great respect and admiration for Bill's deputy, John Phelan, an exceptionally bright and able lawyer, who had started law practice with the esteemed Boston firm of Ropes & Gray, later became chairman of the Navy panel of the ASBCA, and then Navy deputy general counsel succeeding Merritt Steger when Merritt became general counsel in 1960 suceeding Trow vom Baur. Eugene Maher was another highly imaginative, first-class lawyer in Bill's office. Bill too I respected as an able attorney who ran a very efficient and effective office. Other lawyers in Bill's office focused on litigating appeals before the Navy panel of the ASBCA arising from contractor appeals from contracting officer decisions on contracts of the various BuSandA numerous field activities such as ASO and NPO Washington.

Other assignments from Bill included giving some lectures on various aspects of government procurement law to contracting personnel at the NPO Washington and serving as the Navy's legal member of the ASPR contract forms committee. This was my first encounter with attorneys from the Army and Air Force. Our immediate assignment was to develop a purchase order form for DoD-wide use to procure supplies and services up to $2,500 which the recently enacted Armed Services Procurement Act had authorized to be purchased without formal advertising for bids. We decided on a form of a unilateral contract describing the supplies or services and applicable specifications, stating the price and delivery or performance terms, and the general provisions required by law or regulation and printed on the back of the form. It would be signed only by the contracting officer. The recipient of the purchase order would not be contractually bound since the purchase order by its terms did not accept any offer from the recipient. Rather it was a written offer of a contract by a contracting officer, usually following receipt of a solicited quotation, a promise to pay the recipient the stated price if the recipient timely delivered or performed the specified supplies or services. As such the contracting officer could revoke the offer at any time prior to acceptance of the offer by evidence of the contractor's having commenced substantial performance. Working out the details of the design and terms of this form over several months was challenging, interesting, highly collaborative and successful. I believe the form is still in use, but revised to reflect later developments. The highly competent Army lawyer, a Major Phil Rizik, later became one of the administrative judges of the ASBCA.

During my first few years in Washington I lived in a bachelor household in a townhouse near 22nd and Que Streets in NW Washington about half an hour's walk to work or a ten- minute bus ride. While I still had my car there was no place to park at the Navy Department. A law school classmate, Bill Barton, invited me to join the group. My housemates included Ted Stevens, HLS Class of 1950, who would become the Republican senator from Alaska for many years, and David Westfall, also HLS 1950, who after completing his military service would become a distinguished professor of property law at the law school. David also bought my car when I moved to the University Club a few years later and because of parking difficulties there I had to give it up. I would not purchase a car until 1962.

Life in this bachelor household was congenial. We hired a woman to do the marketing and cook dinner for us week nights and for which we paid her in advance each week. We took turns each month acting as treasurer to collect the rent and other expenses and pay them. The dinner table talk was usually stimulating and occasionally with interesting guests. We were on our own weekends since most would be away or out. I made a few trips to Foxcroft School in Middleburg, Virginia, to see Melissa Emery, then in her final year, after persuading the long-serving, formidable headmistress, Miss Charlotte Noland, that Melissa would be safe and sound in my company. Melissa invited me to attend her sister Leila's wedding in Cincinnati in June 1952 which I enjoyably did and had a pleasant reunion with their sister Renee and their parents. After Melissa graduated from Foxcroft we lost touch. I later learned she had married and was living in Buffalo.

For exercise, I joined the University Club, then a men's club at 16th Street near L Street NW, to play squash on their excellent courts. I had played at Brooks and at Harvard. About 1953 when our bachelor household broke up as members moved away from Washington or got married, I moved to the Club and into a small bedroom and bath on one of the upper floors. Living there comfortably provided most of the services of a hotel, including a restaurant, gym, locker room, maid services, barber shop, laundry, etc., plus a good library with the principal newspapers and leading magazines. The costs were then very reasonable. I made friends with some of the residents. One was Senator Theodore Francis Green (1867-1966), the senior senator from Rhode Island and chairman of the foreign affairs committee. I would see him early most mornings in the large swimming pool in the basement where I too would have a morning swim. Occasionally we would breakfast together before his usual walk to the Capitol. Then well into his 80s and seemingly vigorously healthy, old fashioned and courtly with a pince-nez, he was delightful company. Highly educated with degrees from Brown and Harvard, and a Ph. D. from a German university in philology in the 1890s, successful in business, a former governor, an early supporter of FDR, and a long-time senator, he personified what is most admirable in public life.

In the late fall of 1951, my niece Rawn Harding, now 19 and living in New York, was among several young ladies being introduced to society at a debutante ball at the Mayflower Hotel in Washington. I was one of her escorts attired in white-tie and tails for this gala. As I remember, both of her divorced parents were there, and I enjoyed seeing each of them. Sometime after that Rawn introduced me to Jacqueline Bouvier, a school friend from Farmington. Jackie and I went out together a couple of times. She was an "inquiring photographer" for the *Washington Star* newspaper. While I liked her well enough, she evidenced little of the glamour and sophistication she radiated after she married Jack Kennedy and became First Lady. I liked her mother, Janet Lee Bouvier, a friend of Louise's, who was then married to Hugh D. Auchincloss and lived in a lovely place on the Potomac across from Washington in Virginia. Janet and Hugh's son, Jamie Auchincloss, would later become a good friend through Brooks School.

General Counsel Harold Gross resigned later in 1951 to accept a job in private industry. The Secretary of the Navy appointed Bob Paisley, the other deputy general counsel with Meritt Steger, as the acting general counsel. Since 1952 would be a presidential election year, the appointment of the next general counsel should be left to the Secretary of the Navy in the incoming administration. As a result Secretary Robert Anderson, in 1953 appointed Francis Trowbridge vom Baur, HLS 1931. Bob Paisley, a first-class legal scholar, then accepted a teaching position at Cornell Law School which he filled with distinction and during which he taught among other subjects government contract law and produced the first casebook on that subject. Albert H. Stein, HLS 1940, formerly counsel for the Bureau of Ships, had replaced Bob Paisley as deputy general counsel and would ably serve in that position until his premature death in the 1970s.

Trow vom Baur had practiced law as a trial lawyer with the Wall Street firm of Milbank, Tweed, Hope & Webb before the war and while there wrote the first textbook on *Federal Administrative Law*, published in 1942 and revised in 1947 to take account of the Administrative Procedure

Act. A childhood eye injury rendered him ineligible for military service. Instead, he worked for Nelson Rockefeller and kept track of Nazi infiltration efforts in Central America. A strong and active Taft supporter in 1952, he would likely have been appointed to a higher position had Senator Taft been the Republican nominee instead of General Eisenhower and had won the election. I write about him as he would become my next boss in OGC and later my partner in private law practice.

3. Attorney in the OGC Central Office 1954-62.

In 1953 I helped Trow prepare for a Congressional hearing, and this led to my transfer in 1954 to the central office of OGC, also in the main Navy building adjoining the office of the assistant secretary of the Navy for procurement and supply management and a principal client of the office. I would report to Al Stein, then the deputy general counsel for all legal matters within the OGC's jurisdiction other than procurement which Merritt Steger, the other deputy general counsel covered. Al's variegated responsibilities included contract litigation, disposal of surplus property, fiscal matters, industrial security, intellectual property, legislation, recruitment of OGC attorneys, and much else. I would over the next several years work on most of these matters. All legal matters involving the Navy and Marine Corps were divided between OGC and the office of the Navy Judge Advocate General (JAG). JAG had responsibility for administration of the Uniform Code of Military Justice, for admiralty other than matters arising from contract, civilian personnel, international law, and tort claim matters and for litigation in the federal courts involving these matters, among other things.

I would share an office for about a year with Benjamin Lee Bird, HLS 1948, who with his wife Diana would become lifelong close friends. Lee then became counsel to the high priority Polaris program, concerned with equipping nuclear submarines with long range atomic bomb missile capabilities. Trow vom Baur in 1958 appointed Lee to the Armed Services Board of Contract Appeals (ASBCA) where he would serve as one of their ablest and most respected judges for almost 20 years.

During my years in Washington in the 1950s, each spring for several years Aunt Louise, my father's spinster older sister, would travel by overnight train from Boston to for an extended visit to her dear friend Lorna Graydon Upton, the mother of my friend Graydon Upton, at her winter place at Mathew's Courthouse in the beautiful tidewater region of Virginia. I would meet Aunt Louise's train at the Union Station and drive her there at first in my car and then in a rented one. I would spend the weekend and then go back a couple of weeks later to enable Aunt Louise's return to Boston and Duxbury. Aunt Louise was then well into her 70s and after three or four such annual visits was no longer able to continue them due to declining health. I liked Mrs. Upton immensely. She was Aunt Louise's contemporary and their close friendship had begun many years before. She knew that Graydon and Ann had become my good friends in Washington. Graydon and Ann would later have the place at Matthew's Courthouse after his mother died.

My initial assignments from Al included the initial interviewing and screening of applicants for attorney jobs in OGC. If I thought well of them and their writing sample I would refer them to a Bureau office of counsel which was seeking to fill one or more openings. If I believed an applicant was not qualified I discouraged him or her as politely as I could. If in doubt, I would refer the applicant to a Bureau counsel for a second opinion. OGC was then expanding as the result of the Korean War and the Cold War. In the course of this interviewing over the next few years, I strongly encouraged the hiring of four outstanding candidates, George H. Aldrich, HLS 1958, Martin Norr an OGC alumnus, John Riismandel, a lawyer from Estonia, and Rudolf Sobernheim, a lawyer from Berlin.

George Aldrich, who also had an LL.M. from HLS in international law, came to us when there were no openings in the Office of the Legal Advisor at the State Department. Scholarly and judicious, he was obviously very capable and OGC would benefit from his services while seeking an international law position at the State Department or elsewhere in the government. He was hired for the office of counsel for the Bureau of Ships and remained there for about two years until he accepted a job in international security affairs in the General Counsel's office of the Department of Defense. Later he transferred to the Legal Advisor's office and earned his way to becoming deputy legal advisor when Henry Kissinger was Secretary of State and was his lawyer during the negotiation of the Paris Accords with North Vietnam in 1973. In 1981 President Reagan appointed George to be a judge of the U. S.-Iran Claims Tribunal at The Hague, a position from which will retire in April 2012 as the tribunal's work winds up and about which he has written a highly acclaimed treatise. He and his wife Rosemary, a gifted watercolorist and sculptress, have long been close friends of mine. I visit them at their home at St. Michaels, Maryland, on the eastern shore of Chesapeake Bay when they are not in Holland.

The stated aim of Martin Norr, a 1930s honors' graduate of Columbia Law School, was to join the Solicitor General's office. To that end when I met with him in 1958, he said he had wanted to rejoin OGC for a year or two in order to resharpen his skills as a lawyer after having spent many years in the ladies' shoe manufacturing business with his wife. Sam Pinn, Al Stein's successor as counsel to the Bureau of Ships, warmly welcomed him.

A looming emergency was then confronting BuShips: its Long Beach Naval Shipyard was slowly and steadily sinking into the Pacific Ocean at the rate of at least an inch or two each year primarily as the result of a large scale pumping of oil from nearby wells. At this rate of subsidence, the shipyard would have to be abandoned in a few years, depriving the Navy of a major ship-repair and dry docking capability on the west coast. Trow vom Baur, Sam Pinn and I discussed this. Trow decided to send Martin to Long Beach to investigate the causes of the subsidence and how it might be abated and to evaluate what if any legal remedies the Navy might have. Martin was delighted to have this opportunity.

Some three months later he produced a comprehensive memorandum of several hundred pages and technical exhibits squarely holding the several oil companies pumping oil in areas adjacent to the shipyard as causing the subsidence and why the Navy had appropriate legal remedies against them. He also cited expert opinion that if water under high pressure was injected into areas where the oil had been removed that should both arrest further subsidence and produce what was known as "secondary recovery" of additional oil on a large scale. Here was a program of a "win-win" resolution.

Upon his return, Martin and Trow presented this memorandum to the head of the Lands Division at the Department of Justice who in due course gave a favorable and prompt response. He also hired a special counsel to bring suit against the oil companies on the basis of Martin's memorandum. Within a couple of years the government and the oil companies reached a settlement that was a "win-win". Martin Norr saved the Long Beach Naval Shipyard. It was also a major achievement for OGC.

Martin remained with OGC for another year or two. His friend Professor Stanley Surrey was also heading a program at Harvard Law School of writing books on the tax laws of the principal industrial countries. He invited Martin to join the program. Martin accepted this opportunity which enabled him to return to his family in the Boston area. He would go on to write highly acclaimed books on taxation in Sweden and in France. Sadly he died a few years later in the later 1960s. During 1959, his last year in OGC while he was persuading the Justice Department to proceed against the oil companies, he shared a house for a few months with Dennis Lyons and me on Ordway Street in the Cleveland Park NW area of Washington. He was a good friend.

John Riismandel was a post-war refugee from Estonia where he had obtained a law degree. He became an American citizen and then got another one from Columbia Law School. In applying to OGC in 1957 or 1958 he was seeking his first job as a lawyer in this country. He impressed me as bright, committed and mature. He too went to BuShips and advised on shipbuilding contracts and claims and represented BuShips in litigating contract disputes in the ASBCA, including one in which Trow was the opposing counsel.[29] Several years later, Trow's successor Meritt Steger appointed him to the ASBCA where he had a distinguished career for many years as an administrative judge.

Rudolph Sobernheim was yet another older refugee from Hitler's Germany. A lawyer in Berlin before escaping the Nazis he too had a law degree from Columbia and about in 1958 applied to OGC. He had both scholarly thoroughness and practical decisiveness. Again BuShips welcomed him. Trow appointed him to the ASBCA where he served for many years and later as the Labor Department board of contract appeals as a much respected administrative judge.

We also hired our first lady lawyer on my recommendation. She was Florence Kelly, a recent graduate of George Washington University Law School who had gone there during the evenings from her daytime job as a long-serving secretary to Justice Frankfurter. She had an enthusiastic letter of recommendation from the Justice, and Bill Sellman warmly welcomed her as did Trow vom Baur.

Florence was instrumental in persuading the Justice to be the principal speaker at the OGC annual, black-tie dinner at the Carlton Hotel on a Saturday evening in February 1959. Sinclair Armstrong, a former student of and law clerk to the Justice and then the Assistant Secretary of the Navy for Financial Matters and the next chairman of the SEC, Florence and I were the reception committee for Mr. Justice Frankfurter that evening driving him from his home in Georgetown to the hotel and back. One was at once in the presence of a towering intellect and conversationalist. His after-dinner talk on the importance of public service by lawyers was so sidetracked by his countless fascinating digressions that the overall theme was submerged. This also led to a growing friendship with Sinc Armstrong, also a friend of my brother Pat's, that would ripen a decade later when I would see him in Edgartown on Martha's Vineyard island.

---

29 *Bath Iron Works*, ASBCA No. 12382, 68-1 BCA ¶ 7050 (1968) discussed in Part Five at Note 43 and related text.

There were two other highly qualified recent law school graduates to whom I recommended that each apply elsewhere. I interviewed Joe Califano, a HLS 1955 honors graduate, early in 1961. He was disillusioned from several years of practice in one of the large Wall Street firms and thought government service as a lawyer might be more rewarding. I suggested he contact Cyrus Vance, the new general counsel of the Department of Defense whom I had met and regarded highly. Vance, a former partner in Simpson, Bartlett & Thacher, a leading New York firm, promptly hired Joe and so began his stellar career in government, a few years later becoming a principal assistant for domestic policy for President Johnson and the Secretary of Health, Education and Welfare in the Carter administration.

The other exceptional applicant was Peter Powers, also an honors' graduate from Harvard or Yale law schools, who like Joe Califano was seeking a challenging position as a lawyer in government after some years in private practice with a large firm. After some discussion, I suggested he contact my law school friend David Martin who was then an assistant to Dillon Ripley, the new Secretary of the Smithsonian Institution. Secretary Ripley promptly hired Peter as the general counsel of the Smithsonian, a position he filled with great distinction for the next 40 years. I would occasionally see him at Smithsonian chamber music concerts.

These results were gratifying. This interviewing and screening of applicants for OGC, although time-consuming, was valuable; it taught me about appraising a lawyer's potential in problem analysis, in oral and written coherence, in appearance and demeanor, and other intangible factors. During this period the office expanded from about 125 lawyers when I began in 1949 to about 165 when I left for private practice in 1962. This experience would be invaluable later in my hiring young lawyers for the vom Baur law firm starting about 1964.

Another fascinating work assignment from Al Stein would have far-reaching consequences. There was pending in the U. S. District Court in Washington, DC, the case of *Greene v. McElroy,* 150 F. Supp. 958, in which Mr. Greene alleged that he had lost his job as an aeronautical engineer when the Navy had illegally revoked his security clearance required for the performance of his job doing classified work under his employer's contract with the Navy. Anthony Lewis, later a distinguished reporter covering the Supreme Court for *The New York Times*, but then a reporter for the *Washington Daily News,* headlined "Red Rubs Off On Greene" in his news story of the case.

Al asked me to review the case and work with the Justice Department attorney in an endeavor to stipulate the facts with Mr. Greene's attorney, Carl Bereuffy. It soon became evident that the revocation of the security clearance was based on secret wiretaps and on the statements of FBI informants never disclosed to Mr. Greene and whom he had no opportunity to confront and cross-examine. The Justice Department attorney, a Miss Beatrice Rosenberg, was a bright young lady who immediately grasped the critical importance of so stipulating to the outcome of the case. She agreed to that portion of the stipulation as well as with the other material facts I had drafted and Al Stein had approved. We soon reached agreement on the stipulation with Mr. Bereuffy.

On the basis of the stipulation, both parties moved for summary judgment, and the district court granted the government's motion. On appeal, the Court of Appeals affirmed, holding that there was no "justiciable controversy" since only the Executive Branch was competent to evaluate the competing considerations in whether or not to grant or revoke security clearances and that the denial of opportunity to confront his accusers and access to the confidential reports did not deprive Mr. Greene of any "due process" rights. No one had a "right" to a security clearance. *Greene v. McElroy*, 254 F. 2d 944, 952.

The Supreme Court reversed, 350 U.S. 474 (1959). In a landmark opinion by Chief Justice Warren, the Court held that that since the challenged procedures had never been explicitly authorized either by Congress or the President resulting in Mr. Greene's loss of employment and raising fundamental Constitutional questions of procedural fairness, the revocation of his clearance was void. Justice Tom Clark, President Truman's former attorney general, was the sole dissenter.

As the result of the Court's decision, President Eisenhower issued Executive Order 10865, "Safeguarding Classified Information within Industry" on February 20, 1960. It was drafted by Philip Areeda, HLS 1954, then an exceptionally bright attorney at the White House and one of my roommates at a later bachelor household that I had joined a year or two previously. I told Phil what I knew about the case, as I also had Dennis Lyons, another of my then housemates who was clerking for Justice Brennan in the October 1958 term. The Executive Order required that before any industrial security clearance could be denied or revoked the individual would be afforded the opportunity to cross-examine persons who made adverse oral or written statements except when the agency head certified that the person was a "confidential informant" whose disclosure would be "substantially harmful to the national interest" and personally reviewed and made any decision to deny or revoke a security clearance based on the information of the "confidential informant." This was an extraordinary, procedurally fair implementation of the Court's decision.

Phil went on to a distinguished teaching career at HLS and became one of the leading national authorities on anti-trust law, having written a much admired, definitive treatise on that subject. His premature death at 65 in 1995 from leukemia was widely mourned.

The Defense Department industrial security program provided in a 1955 directive for the recovery of back pay by an individual whose security clearance had wrongfully been denied or revoked as the result of a "favorable" determination. In due course Mr. Greene applied for back pay. Al Stein and I read the directive to entitle Mr. Greene to recover back pay as the result of the "favorable" decision of the Supreme Court as implemented by the district court on remand which in effect reinstated his prior clearance. At the direction of the Department of Defense, however, Al notified Mr. Greene that he was not entitled to recover under the 1955 directive then in effect since it had been replaced by a 1960 revision made after the Court's decision that required a favorable administrative security clearance decision as a condition of entitlement to back pay, and that the Navy was willing to process the claim under the new directive.

Mr. Greene's attorney rejected that course and brought suit in the Court of Claims for the recovery of about $50K in back pay under the 1955 directive. The Court of Claims denied recovery in view of the later directive. The Supreme Court granted certiorari. There Mr. Greene was represented by Eugene Gressman, a longtime former law clerk to Justice Murphy and the respected author of the leading treatise on Supreme Court practice. Bill Doolittle, then in the Solicitor General's office, who had become my friend and neighbor on Capitol Hill, argued for the government. The Court in an opinion by Justice Goldberg decided that the 1955 directive was controlling and that the result of its prior opinion and the remand action of the district court expunging the prior clearance revocation had the effect of reinstating Mr. Greene's prior security clearance, thus entitling Mr. Greene to recover the back pay sought, a position Al Stein and I had previously taken and which the Department of Defense had overruled. *Greene v. United States*, 376 U. S. 149 (1964). Justices Harlan and White dissented on the ground that Mr. Greene should first have exhausted his remedy under the later directive. Our Navy client was not pleased.

My next assignment came from Trow vom Baur: to oversee and edit the preparation of the second edition of *Navy Contract Law*, first written and published in 1949 by OGC for internal use by OGC attorneys and naval procurement officials. Trow, himself the author of the first textbook on federal administrative law, wanted the 1949 text to be updated to reflect the many legal developments in government contract law since then. He also wanted it to be available for sale to the public as one of the first textbooks on government contract law in view of the growing importance of government procurement in the national economy. It would be in a legal textbook format with section headings, a detailed table of contents, index, and tables, and published by the Government Printing Office so as to accommodate the easy incorporation of supplements rather than pocket parts. It would be so published in 1959 as a textbook on public contract law applicable to the Navy, and only in that sense "Navy" contract law.

Getting it done was a large undertaking by about a dozen lawyers assigned one or more of the twelve chapters of the text. The organization of the chapters largely followed the sequence of the procurement cycle after a historical summary of Navy procurement during World War II and the transition to the post-war conditions. Thus there were instructive chapters on procurement by formal advertising and the body of Comptroller General decisions on that subject, and by negotiation, on the types of contracts and on the explication of the standard, required contract clauses and the leading court cases involving them. There were also such chapters on the fiscal law applicable to government contracts, on contracting for research and development and for acquisition of facilities, on the termination of contracts for the government's convenience, on the recovery of excessive contractor profits, and on the disposal of government property. For example, Lee Bird's trailblazing chapter on fiscal law—-the complex and mystifying laws governing the availability, obligation and expenditure of appropriated funds—-was particularly highly regarded, so much so that the Army even copied it verbatim and issued it as its own. In addition to editing each chapter for consistency in substance, style and citation, I was responsible for the preparation of the chapters on procurement by formal advertising and on statutes regulating excessive profits. It was for me a considerable learning experience.

While I was busy with this editing task, war over the independent survival of OGC broke out between OGC and the Navy Judge Advocate General. For several weeks that would demand my full-time attention. For many months attorneys on Capitol Hill and in the Pentagon had been engaged in a project to codify all the statutes relating to the Department of Defense and the military departments into a single new title 10 of the United States Code as the substantive law. The ground rule was that there was to be no substantive change in any of the laws so codified. We belatedly discovered to our horror that an 1880s law creating the office of the Navy Judge Advocate General would be codified so as to make that official responsible for all legal services for the Navy, a substantive departure from the original statute which was silent on that matter and left the Secretary of the Navy free to employ civilian lawyers for such purposes other than military law as he wished and which had been the long-standing administrative practice. When one of the OGC attorneys reviewed the proposed codification bill and discovered what the Navy

JAG had done, the bill had already passed the House and was pending in the Senate. We had a first-class emergency.

Trow mobilized his Republican contacts in the Senate, and W. John Kenny, a prominent Washington Democrat and with Struve Hensel a co-founder of OGC in 1942, lined up support in the House and Senate. But it was necessary to prepare a supporting memorandum establishing the prior administrative practice of Secretaries of the Navy in employing civilian attorneys going back to the early 1900s. Trow asked me to compile this history on an urgent basis which I was able to do within the next week or so, doing little else. Also helping was the General Counsel of the Department of Defense who wrote to the leaders of Congress that this was a fundamental issue of civilian control of the military. Politically, we had to overcome the strong personal support of the Navy JAG's position by Carl Vinson, the powerful, long-serving chairman of the House Naval Affairs committee. We eventually prevailed. The Senate passed a corrected codification of the Navy JAG statute which the House accepted, and new title 10 of the U. S. Code became law.

The Navy JAG, Rear Admiral Ira Nunn, a protégé of Congressman Vinson's and his naval aide during the war, retired and was replaced by Rear Admiral Chester Ward, who ended forever the efforts of the JAG to take over OGC which had persisted since 1942 when James Forrestal, as undersecretary of the Navy, established OGC despite the strongest protests of Rear Admiral Woodson, the then JAG, that he had no authority to do so. Mr. Forrestal had become convinced since 1941 that the JAG was incapable of providing on-the-spot procurement legal services because for one thing its insistence that all requests for legal advice first had to be submitted to the separately located JAG in writing. The demands of wartime procurement would not permit that.

Beginning in 1941 Secretary Forrestal had authorized the bureau chiefs to hire civilian attorneys selected by his counsel, H Struve Hensel, a former partner of the Milbank, Tweed firm in New York who had been Mr. Forrestal's attorney when he was president of Dillon Reid before FDR recruited him as the undersecretary in 1940 and persuaded Struve Hensel to join him as his lawyer. This led to the establishment of OGC in 1942 with Mr. Hensel as the founding general counsel for the duration of the war.

In 1957 Congressman Dawson of Illinois wrote to the Secretary of Defense requesting detailed responses to a series of questions on the extent to which the manifold functions of the Department of Defense (DoD) complied with rule-making, adjudication, and public information requirements of the Administrative Procedure Act. The DoD general counsel referred the request to Trow vom Baur to prepare the reply because of his knowledge of administrative law, and so advised the Congressman. Trow asked me to head up a small team of lawyers from the Army and Air Force to prepare detailed answers to the Congressman's questions. This would be another large undertaking lasting several months.

The Army and Air Force lawyers assigned to this task, Bob Herzstein and Bob Cole, were exceptionally bright recent HLS graduates discharging their military service obligations as lawyers in the general counsels' offices of the Army and Air Force, respectively. We soon became friends and worked harmoniously and enjoyably together. Bob Herzstein has remained a lifetime friend.

Identifying what activities to cover and explaining their functions was a large investigatory challenge, in the course of which we learned a great deal about the organization and various functions of the DoD and the military departments. Very few of them it turned out were subject to the rule-making or adjudication requirements of the Administrative Procedure Act or the information about their activities was exempt from public disclosure. We had substantial discussions of whether the rule-making requirements should apply to the growing body of the ASPR notwithstanding the public contracts exemption in the Act from these requirements. Unfortunately, that did not come about until legislation in the 1970s establishing the Office of Procurement Policy within the Office of Management and Budget reporting to the president.

In 1958 I became the Navy member on the editing subcommittee of the Armed Services Procurement Regulation (ASPR) with a Lt. Col. Wilkinson of the Army JAG and Louis Cox of the Air Force general counsel's office, both very able attorneys. This involved editing the draft text of proposed procurement regulations tentatively approved for adoption by the ASPR committee. One project that required considerable effort was the complete set of cost principles to be applicable to the performance of cost-reimbursement type contracts.

During the course of this work and the Dawson committee work I became friends with Dennis Lyons, HLS 1955, and assigned to the Air Force general counsel's office for his military service and slated to clerk for Justice Brennan starting that summer. He invited me to dinner at his bachelor household at 2132 R Street NW in Washington. Dennis's several housemates included the above-mentioned Phil Areeda at the White House; Wayne Barnett, HLS 1953 and clerking for Justice Harlan; Bill Doolittle, HLS 1954, then in the Army and assigned to the DoD general counsel's office and slated to clerk for Justice Frankfurter a year later; John Kaplan, HLS 1954, clerking for Justice Clark; Andy Kaufman, HLS 1954, clerking for Justice Frankfurter; and John Simon, HLS 1954 with the Army General Counsel's office for his military service. It was heady, stimulating company.

After further work encounters with Dennis, he told me that Wayne Barnett was leaving the household to get married, and I gladly accepted the invitation to replace Wayne in this bachelor household in late 1957 or early 1958. It was a house of firsts: Messrs. Areeda, Barnett and Lyons each had been first in their classes at HLS. Indeed Dennis had the highest average since Justice Brandeis as well as having been president of the *Harvard Law Review*, the leading national publication of its kind. Experiencing and participating in the interplay of these active, creative, imaginative, and wide-ranging minds was mind stretching and enhancing for me.

I also frequently played hard-fought squash at the University Club with great enjoyment with Phil Areeda and with his friend Henry Steiner, HLS 1954 and clerking for Justice Harlan. All would achieve distinction in the law: Areeda I have already covered; Barnett at the Solicitor General's office and to teach law at Stanford; Doolittle also to the Solicitor General's office and the Civil Division of the Justice Department, then General Counsel of the Air Force, and finally in private practice in Washington, first with Covington & Burling and then with his own firm; Kaplan also to teach law at Stanford, Kaufman at Harvard, and Simon at Yale after a stint at Covington & Burling in Washington.

As summer approached the household would breakup with members moving on or making other arrangements. Dennis and I agreed to find a place to live. Luckily we rented for the summer Rosamund Tirana's house at 3500 Ordway Street NW in Cleveland Park and near the Washington National Cathedral. She had remained a friend of my sister Sally from Greenwich days and was now the widow of Rifat Tirana, a prominent Albanian economist who had worked for the World Bank. They had three young sons. Rosamund, an accomplished artist and active in selling residential real estate, had a summer home in Wellfleet on Cape Cod and therefore would rent her Ordway Street house for the summer. It was just right for Dennis and me, and Rosamund rented it to us at a reasonable price. The house, a detached rambling two-storey stucco structure with an attractive garden, was built in 1918 for Samuel Gompers, one of the pioneers of the labor movement. Dennis took Rosamund's bedroom. On her dressing table was a photograph of George Gershwin with a loving inscription to her, now still a remarkably attractive woman.

That summer Dennis began his clerkship with Justice Brennan for the 1958 term. President Eisenhower had appointed him to the Court late in 1956 to replace the retiring Justice Minton, and Dennis sought employment as his clerk as an opportunity to participate in molding the new justice's approach, particularly in Constitutional litigation. Each of the Justices had two law clerks who would usually serve a one-year term. During the summer months the justices were mostly away from Washington until a few weeks before the beginning of each term on the first Monday of October.

During the summer the clerks for each justice would examine the hundreds of petitions from losing litigants in the state and federal courts for the Supreme Court to review the particular decision, each called a "petition for certiorari". The prevailing party would often file a brief opposing the request. Granting this review requires the affirmative vote of four justices. Since the Court's workload could accommodate only a small percentage of the requests the principal task of the clerks during the summer months was to sift and eliminate those petitions that did not present a substantial question meriting Court review and recommend to their justices those that did for decision early in the October term. The solicitor general's office was a major player in requesting or opposing Court review. Once review was granted there was an established timetable for filing briefs and oral argument. When discussing these petitions with Justice Brennan, Dennis told me that the justice could well follow and comprehend any technical argument, high praise from Dennis.

During the summer we found a house to rent on Ordway Street near 34th Street starting in September that belonged to a Mr. Fotich, a former ambassador to the U. S. from Yugoslavia. We signed a year's lease.

During that summer Lyttleton Fox, who had helped me obtain the job in OGC in 1949, returned on leave from his job as counsel to the Navy Purchasing Office in London to which Hal Gross had assigned him so he could be near his two children following their mother's having divorced him in 1949. It was then, as before on his occasional visits from London, and thereafter a joy to be with Lyttleton. He was the most brilliant, witty, and interesting conversationalist I ever experienced, a widely shared opinion. For example, when Trow vom Baur was appointed general counsel in December 1953, Lyttleton cabled him, "When do I report for brainwashing?" Fortunately, Trow was amused by this audacity.

With the expansion of procurement from the Korean and Cold Wars and the military build-up of NATO in Europe, Lyttleton during one of his visits said he needed an assistant in his London office and offered me the opportunity. I was sorely tempted, but declined primarily because I believed it would limit my future opportunities in OGC.

He invited me to his 50th birthday celebration his mother gave for him in Southampton, Long Island, at the Irving House that 1958 summer and where I stayed. It was a large, black-tie gathering. Lyttleton began his after dinner remarks with "Joe Clark and I were brought up to believe in the inherent wickedness of Republicans." Joe, then the Democratic mayor of Philadelphia and his wife Noel with whom I would years later have a close friendship, and Lyttleton were friends from St. Paul's School. In a mostly Republican audience, some were not amused. I enjoyed meeting Lyttleton's mother, Genevieve Fox, decidedly a grand dame of the old school, and his three sisters. Kathleen, the youngest and now married had once been courted by my brother Pat and the older two, Connie and Joyce also married, were friends of my sister Louise.

After we moved into the Fotich house in September, Lyttelon was our dinner guest a few times and Dennis too was impressed by the conversational brilliance. During that visit Lyttleton introduced me to Fanny Sedgwick, an attractive young lady from Boston working in Washington whose father was one of Lyttleton's close friends. Her grandfather was Ellery Sedgwick, long a distinguished editor of *The Atlantic Monthly*. She was also related to Endicott Peabody, the founding headmaster of Groton. She had a lovely well-mannered, quiet and yet outgoing personality, and we started seeing each other. We soon reached a crossroads: either continue the relationship with a likely marriage outcome, or end it now as incompatible with our natures and emotional commitments. With much regret we mutually chose the latter course; she was as equally involved with another woman as I was with John in Philadelphia. I would not see her again. Such is life.

During that summer I got a further assignment from Trow vom Baur to work with the Assistant Secretary of the Navy for Air on the legal aspects of a new communications system for the Navy called "Tacom". This brought me into personal working relationship first briefly with Secretary James Smith and shortly thereafter with his successor Garrison Norton. During the war then Captain Norton and Lt. Fox worked together in the Bureau of Aeronautics and became close friends. Before the war, Garry, born in 1900, a graduate of Groton and Harvard College, was a partner in the accounting firm of Arthur Young & Co. in New York. He, his wife Emily, and I would become good friends and neighbors in the apartment building at 2101 Connecticut Ave. many years later through Lyttleton.

Starting in the fall Dennis would drive his old but reliable Plymouth to take Justice Brennan to the Court. I would occasionally ride part way to the office and would have interesting chats with the Justice who was informally outgoing and friendly and amusing to both of us. This led to his recommending me to be the legal assistant to his friend Ed Mills whom President Eisenhower had recently nominated to be a member of the Federal Communications Commission. I met with Mr. Mills and he offered and I accepted this position subject to his Senate confirmation. For reasons I no longer remember Mr. Mills encountered problems in getting confirmed and withdrew. Thus ended an opportunity for me in the rapidly growing field of communications law driven by rapid technological advances and the breakup of AT&T. I was nevertheless very grateful to Justice Brennan and Dennis for doing this.

Around 1955 or 1956 I joined the Washington Cathedral Choral Society. This long-established chorus under the superb leadership of Paul Callaway, since 1940 the organist and choirmaster at the Washington National Cathedral, performed two or three concerts a year at the cathedral usually accompanied by the National Symphony Orchestra. The repertoire was the great body of choral works from Bach on. Callaway was a great musician and choral conductor, better in my opinion than G. Wallace Woodworth, the very excellent director of the Harvard Glee Club when I was a member. We would rehearse once or twice a week starting in the fall, and more frequently as a performance date approached. At these rehearsals Wayne Dirksen, the music director at the St. Alban's School which was located on the cathedral close and Paul's eventual successor, was a first-class musician in his own right. He was our rehearsal pianist. I later heard him in a magnificent series of recitals performing the then largely unknown and neglected Haydn piano sonatas. He was succeeded by Richard Roeckelein who also became a good friend.

In my several years of choral singing we performed among other masterpieces, the Bach B-Minor Mass and St. Mathew Passion, the Handel Israel in Egypt and Messiah, and the Berlioz, Brahms and Verdi Requiems. Once we were honored to have the notable German composer Paul Hindemith, then teaching at Yale, conduct his 1946 work for soloists, chorus and orchestra based on Walt Whitman's poem on the death of

Lincoln, *When Lilacs Last in the Dooryard Bloom'd*. It was a difficult if beautiful piece to learn over many rehearsals with Paul, and the composer was very pleased by the way Paul had prepared us. The piece was paired with a Bruckner mass which Mr. Hindemith also conducted. He perceptively joked that we were undoubtedly happier with the Bruckner mass than with his piece. Nevertheless we gave it our all at the performance and the audience responded enthusiastically and the composer seemed content.

One day in the spring of 1959 Dennis telephoned me at work, asking if he could borrow my tuxedo to attend a black-tie dinner that evening at the British Embassy. Justice Brennan had asked Dennis to represent him at that dinner which was given for the chief justice of Nigeria. Dennis awakened me very early the next morning to report that he had fallen in love with Ann Harvey who was visiting her aunt at the Embassy. He would follow her to New York later that day to see her before she returned to England two days later. He did, and when he returned they were engaged to be married. A rapid-fire courtship if ever there was one.

After the Supreme Court term ended in June, Dennis flew to England. They were soon married there and returned to Washington and the Ordway Street house to live until the lease expired in September. I was delighted by Ann and liked her immensely. She was strikingly beautiful with dark hair, a ruddy complexion, blue eyes, a winning personality, and high intelligence. She had been working for British Overseas Airlines (BOAC) in London and transferred to the Washington office. Justice Brennan had invited Dennis to be his clerk for the October 1959 term, an unprecedented honor, which Dennis gratefully accepted. They remained with me in the Ordway Street house until early in September whereupon they rented a nearby apartment on Idaho Avenue and I returned briefly to the University Club. With the 1960 end of the Court's term he would become an associate at the blue-ribbon firm of Arnold, Porter & Fortas in Washington, and would initially work primarily for Abe Fortas until President Johnson appointed him to the Supreme Court in 1965, succeeding Justice Goldberg whom the president persuaded to leave the Court to become the U.S. Ambassador to the United Nations. Ann and Dennis in 1960 purchased and moved to a house near Alexandria. They would have two or three children and Don Ellington and

I would enjoyably visit them. Sadly, Ann and Dennis would divorce several years later. Also sadly, Don and I lost touch with them.

By 1959 I had met Don Ellington in the Washington Cathedral Choral Society of which he had been a member for several years. We would talk at the rehearsal intermissions. Once I returned to the University Club and saw more of him we decided to live together, my having insisted that he accept my existing commitment to John Shollenberger. By the end of September I moved into his apartment on Connecticut Avenue a block or two south of Dupont Circle and above a Chinese restaurant. Don was then employed as a clerk-typist by the Air Force in a civilian personnel office in one of the temporary World War II office buildings in NW Washington. We would live together until he died in 2005.

Don, born July 18, 1927, grew up in Miami, Oklahoma, a small city in the northeast corner bordering Kansas and Arkansas. His mother was half Cherokee, his father a locomotive engineer addicted to gambling, each with little schooling. Don was about the fifth of nine or ten children, and closest to his oldest sister Opal who was ten years older and then married with young children to Fred Shouse and living in nearby Baxter Springs, Kansas. Don had an excellent education in the Miami public schools. When he graduated from high school at age eighteen in 1945 he was drafted into the Army and after basic training sent to work for about two years in an Army hospital in Munich, Germany. After that he was hired as an Army civilian employee based in Salzburg, Austria, for another two years. Both positions enabled him to travel widely in Europe to his educational benefit. About 1952 he accepted a clerical job with the Army in the Pentagon and settled in Washington. When we met in 1959 he was slim, trim, of medium height, light brown hair, brown eyes, and handsome. Although he was addicted to Lucky Strike cigarettes for many years and occasionally drank too much, he retained his youthful appearance for the rest of his life.

I found Don to be highly intelligent, well educated and spoken, good manners, and widely read. He was also skilled at carpentry and a whiz at the *New York Times* weekday and Sunday crossword puzzles. I was increasingly impressed by the intelligence and occupational variety of his friends, men and women, in Washington and elsewhere as I would come to meet them over the years. He was particularly close to Betty Winspear, perhaps ten years older than he, and then living in Georgetown next door to Chapin Leinbach and Dick Cassedy who later became our good friends. Betty, attractive, brilliant, college educated, and a mistress of the deceased writer Christopher Morley, worked in the admissions office at George Washington University. She had an old Ford coupe in which she and Don would drive into the Virginia countryside on weekends visiting antique shops and flea markets. Another close friend of Betty's and Don's was Jim Garland, equally brilliant and an honors' graduate of the excellent University of the South in Sewanee, Tennessee. Garland was an early computer whiz then working for American Airlines. Later he had in a similar role for the State of New York and would live in New York City with his partner Dick Parks, an up and coming literary agent with Curtis Brown and then flourishing on his own. Over the years we would visit them in New York and in their eventual home in Salem, NY, near Albany. I list some of Don's other good friends I now remember, other than the ones he made in Key West starting in 1978, below.[30]

---

30   Bob and Priscilla Alfandre, Bob, a wealthy house builder, later divorced, with homes in D.C., Fire Island, and Key West; Priscilla remained a close friend of Don's; Dick Alford, another Sewanee graduate with American Express in D.C.; Bob Driscoll, relocating as a bank employee in San Francisco after he and his partner, Gill McNamee, a librarian, were fired from civil service jobs in D.C. because they were gay and whom we would visit; Bill Kling and Tom Patteson, makers of curtains and quilts in D.C.; Carlin Guy, independently wealthy and his partner Chuck Gillese, a civil servant; Leonard Hamilton, an interior decorator and his partner Charles Aldridge, an assistant secretary of Agriculture, and after his death Dan Buhl in Winter Park, Florida, whom we would visit; Sally Jones, a Congressional staffer and shop keeper on Capitol Hill, who later married Markam Lewis and moved to Key West; Scott Lintz, a GSA employee and later Don's business partner; Grover Loening, a pioneer in the aircraft industry, a wealthy socialite and a friend of both of my sisters; Odette May and her husband, linguists and translators for the CIA; Dick Mohr, a producer of opera recordings for RCA Victor; Gerson Nordlinger, a philanthropist in D.C.; Alva and Molly Pilliod, Alva a high official in the Immigration and Naturalization Service, and Molly having been his beautiful secretary with mostly gay friends; Robert Ricks, an Army Air Corps navigator shot down over Italy in WW II and imprisoned in a German POW camp for two years, now a government employee; Jim Riggs, then a companion to Frank Severance, a wealthy, elderly and infirm cousin of John Walker, the director of the National Gallery of Art, who gave Don a copy of a beautiful tall teak Queen Anne screen which I now have and which in fact may be the original, later

In 1960 I was frequently preoccupied with industrial security matters. In the prevailing Cold War climate the military departments were wary of granting facility security clearances to contractors to have access to classified information needed to perform government contracts if the contractors were significantly owned or controlled by foreign interests, as several important contractors appeared to be. All foreign ownership, regardless of nationality, was suspect. Yet it was important that some of these contractors with significant ownership or control potential in their British or West European shareholders or directors be cleared to perform important work. Over the objections of the Navy intelligence community in varying degrees of concern, we advised that the use of voting trusts might allay legitimate security concerns. The foreign interest would transfer its stock to a trustworthy American trustee who would have the requisite level of security clearance and would commit to exercise the voting trust authority consistently with national security requirements.

One day Thurman Arnold, then of Arnold, Porter & Fortas, stormed into my office in high dudgeon demanding a facility security clearance for his client and outraged by the bureaucratic delay and nit-picking over the extent of foreign ownership of his client. We worked out a voting trust to his satisfaction. A more difficult case arose in 1961 involving Schlumberger, a major oil-drilling company substantially owned by French interests. Tom O'Brian, the civilian chief of the Office of Naval Intelligence with whom I closely worked on these matters, strongly opposed granting the company a facility security clearance. He said the use of a voting trust was merely a "paper bulwark" that offered no real security protection regardless of the trustworthiness of the voting trustee who had been designated. Because the Navy was internally divided, Secretary of the Navy John Connally would decide. Tom O'Brien, Al Stein, I, and others met with Secretary Connally. An experienced attorney, he listened attentively to the arguments pro and con that Tom and I presented and closely questioned each of us. Fortunately for Schlumberger, Secretary Connally knew the company and its leadership and readily authorized the granting of a facility clearance once the voting trust had been established.

relocating to New Orleans and becoming an academic; George Rinear, an employee of BOAC and friend of Ann Lyons in Washington, later relocating to San Francisco; and Buck Whittemore and Jack Lowe, the duo concert pianists.

In April 1960, Trow vom Baur submitted his resignation as general counsel to the Secretary of the Navy and recommended the appointment of Meritt Steger as his successor which the Secretary promptly did. Trow would join Struve Hensel, the founder of OGC, for the practice of government contract law under the partnership of Hensel & vom Baur. Struve was separately the Washington partner of the New York firm of Simpson, Thacher & Bartlett. I believe Trow was under considerable financial pressure to do this because he greatly enjoyed his job which paid a salary of $19,000. Yet this was inadequate to educate his two daughters at private schools and at college in addition to other reasonable living expenses. The private practice opportunity with Struve should provide the needed income.

As general counsel Trow substantially uplifted the professionalism of OGC in several ways, mostly modelled on his experience at the Milbank Tweed firm which he sought to replicate in OGC to the extent practicable. He stressed rendering on-the-spot legal advice backed up by legal research and to that end he greatly increased the coverage of the OGC law library with the acquisition of the leading textbooks in the fields of business and commercial law and litigation. He wrote memoranda for all OGC lawyers on how to look up law and write and index digest memoranda of law and insisted that legal research past and present be done in this manner and that copies of all such memoranda be filed in the OGC library as future research aids. The Practising Law Institute later published these memoranda for the Bar generally. He stressed the importance of recognizing the intellectual equality of all lawyers from the youngest to the most senior when analyzing a new legal problem to obtain the best outcome. He brought distinguished judges and lawyers to speak to OGC, including Arthur Vanderbuilt, the chief justice of the New Jersey Supreme Court, and John J. McCloy, a Milbank, Tweed senior partner, former assistant secretary of war in World War II, and former high commissioner in the occupation of West Germany. He encouraged OGC lawyers to engage in bar association work, including the American Bar and Federal Bar Associations.

Prior to producing the second edition of *Navy Contract Law* in 1959 and in making it available for sale to the public, Trow had persuaded

Commerce Clearance House in 1957 to begin publishing the decisions of the Armed Services Board of Contract Appeals with head notes and to index them. They had only been available in mimeographed copies. CCH soon added the decisions of the boards of contract appeals of the other principal government agencies as well. Trow also persuaded the ASBCA to publish rules of procedure modeled on the Federal Rules of Civil Procedure.

I have already written about the efforts of Trow and Martin Norr in saving the Long Beach Naval Shipyard from subsiding into the Pacific Ocean. Trow also made a significant contribution to the procedural fairness of contested security clearance decisions resulting in the loss of employment. He arranged for the American and the D.C. Bar Associations to provide competent counsel pro bono to Navy employees and Navy contractor employees to assure that these decisions, when adverse, would be based on reliable evidence. In one notable case in 1954 involving Abraham Chasanow who had been dismissed from his job as a security risk after 22 years at the Navy's Hydrographic Office under deficient procedures, Trow persuaded the Secretary of the Navy to grant Mr. Chasanow an evidentiary hearing. The result was Mr. Chasanow's reinstatement and recovery of back pay. In reporting this story for the *Washington Daily News,* Anthony Lewis won his first Pulitzer Prize in Journalism in 1955.

I believe Trow deserved to have, and would have, advanced further to the Secretarial level within the Navy and the Department of Defense had he not at times in meetings with his superiors given a misleading impression of being pompous, vainglorious, and overly formal. He seemed unable to put them at ease. For example, when addressing meetings of high ranking Navy officials, he would stand on a podium that many thought made him appear ridiculous. Nevertheless, all in all, Trow vom Baur was a giant among the Navy's generals counsel and made lasting contributions to OGC.[31]

---

31 *See Remembering Trow vom Baur,* six tributes to Trow who died in 2000 at 90 by several former colleagues based on his accomplishments as Navy general counsel, in private practice, and in the American Bar Association in 30 ABA Public Contract Law Journal 1-7 (Fall 2000).

Meritt Steger had to find a new deputy general counsel for procurement matters, the position he had held for the past decade. I recommended John Phelan whom Trow had made chairman of the Navy Panel of the ASBCA. Meritt accepted the recommendation and persuaded John to join him. It was a splendid choice for this position and in which John would thrive until his retirement about a decade later.

Meritt also asked me to take on the first revision of *Navy Contract Law* in view of the many changes that had occurred since late 1958 which was the cut-off date for the 1959 edition. I did, and with the help of a few others we completed and published this first Supplement late in 1961. Again, it was a large undertaking, and I did most of the research and writing to my educational benefit.

In 1961 President Kennedy by executive order created the Arms Control and Disarmament Agency. The purpose was to have a government agency whose sole focus would be to explore ways in which the U. S. and the Soviet Union could begin to negotiate and reach agreements to reduce weapons of mutual mass destruction as well as conventional armaments. This seemed to me a highly worthwhile goal. I decided to apply for a position in the general counsel's office of this new agency. I believed my opportunities for further advancement in OGC were distant because of several excellent lawyers senior to me, and none of the Bureau counsel was soon likely to move on. I had reached the position of a GS-14 with an adequate salary of $12,800 which was unlikely to be raised to a GS-15.

I had an excellent interview with George Bunn, the new general counsel. Presently he offered me a position of being the contracts attorney for the agency at a GS-15 with about a $2,000 dollar increase in salary over what I was earning in OGC. The offer was subject to obtaining the highest level of government security clearance based on a detailed full field investigation of my life and locations starting with my military service. This would take several months. I happily accepted and notified my superiors at OGC. George soon invited me to cruise on his motor sailboat up the Potomac River from its mouth to Washington so we would get to know each other. I did this very enjoyably in his and his wife's company.

By this time Don and I had contracted to purchase a small two storey, two bedroom row house being built with a small garden patio along with several other houses at 130 Duddington Place SE on Capitol Hill. We moved from an apartment in Foggy Bottom and began living there in March 1961. The price was about $25K. I also started bicycling to work which was excellent exercise.

Don had become a real estate salesman of residential real estate with the Barbara Held office on Capitol Hill after passing the challenging examination that was required by the DC government real estate commission before one could sell real estate. For the previous year he had quit the Air Force clerical job and was employed in a better paying job by Martin's gift shop on Connecticut Avenue to manage the importation of Herend china from Hungary. This enabled him to purchase a dozen beautiful place settings for us at a very low wholesale price, a fraction of their very high retail price today. I still have and treasure them. When we moved to Capitol Hill he decided to go into selling residential real estate principally on Capitol Hill which was teaming with residential restoration and new construction.

While we were living at Duddington Place that year my brother Pat was promoted to Rear Admiral in the Navy reserve. He came to Washington to receive his commission in a small ceremony at the Pentagon from his friend Albert Pratt, then serving as assistant secretary of the Navy for personnel. Pat spent the night with us resplendent in his admiral's uniform. I could tell almost at once that he and Don would not be friends.

Mother also visited us in Duddington Place that year or the next. She had been coming every few years for a few days since I moved to Washington and would stay comfortably at the Carlton Hotel which was near the University Club and St. John's Church where she liked to go with me for the Sunday morning service as she did to Trinity Church in Boston. I had discontinued going to church except for weddings and funerals. She and Don got on well, and he enjoyed her company. They shared an interest in the daily crossword puzzles in the newspapers. While staying with us she got a bad cold that turned into flu. My doctor, Bretney Miller,

Graydon Upton's brother-in-law, came to the house and prescribed some medicine and a week's rest. Since Don and I were both working weekdays, I arranged for Sally to come from her home in Newtown, Connecticut, to look after her. Luckily she and Mother could share the same bedroom. It turned out well, and they were able to leave in about a week. Sally and Don also got along, barely.

Don later met Louise and liked her when she invited us to Charlottes-vile where she was staying with Morishka Owsley, a Palm Beach friend and the fabulously wealthy Hungarian widow of the former owner of the copper mines in the Mesabi iron-ore range in Minnesota, who lived in a replica of the White House. Morshika gave Don a choice of costly paper-weights from her collection, thus inspiring him to become a collector of them which he did and I now enjoy.

At OGC my life continued as before as I awaited obtaining the security clearance for the new position. I already had a top-secret clearance for my OGC job but that was not relevant since the new one was at a higher level and had to be based on a new investigation. Meritt and Al Stein selected Bill Brown, an experienced attorney from the office of counsel of the Military Sea Transportation Service, to be my successor; and he and I pleasantly held some debriefing sessions principally about the applicant interviewing and industrial security work. In late December I learned that a problem had arisen about my security clearance. Don said that his friend Desiree Baker, our next-door neighbor and who worked with him at the Barbara Held office, told him that her unemployed and alcoholic husband had told the security investigators, "I don't know about Coburn but he sure lives with a flaming faggot."

I knew at once that that statement would quash my receiving the security clearance. I did not ask the security people for an opportunity to confront any adverse evidence they might have. I considered remaining silent in the hope that there would be no effect on my OGC job. I, perhaps foolishly, did not seek legal advice. Instead, feeling an obligation of disclosure, I told John Phelan that the clearance would not be issued because of the suspicion that I lived in a gay relationship with Don Ellington. I told John that Don and I had such a relationship. John said he would have to inform Meritt. A day or two later Meritt told me with much regret that he had no choice: he would have to cancel my security clearance and I would have to resign from OGC. OGC was not permitted to employ gay attorneys.

Indeed it was not until 1975 when President Ford removed the executive branch ban on the employment of gays, and many years later during the Clinton administration before the Department of Defense would issue security clearances to them. Meritt, meaning well, advised me to obtain help from "my pastor". I submitted my resignation early in January 1962. Al Stein said if I had come to him, he would have advised me to remain silent as he doubted that anything further would come of it. I would not receive a security clearance, and fortunately did not need one, for another 25 years. Again, such is life.

So ended my twelve years with OGC. Overall, it had been an enriching, educational, professionally rewarding experience. I was sorry to have to leave. I withdrew my civil service pension of several thousand dollars that would give us enough to live on until I found other employment. I was lucky.

President Kennedy had issued another executive order in 1961 creating the Administrative Conference of the United States[32]. The purpose was to study agency implementation of and compliance with the Administrative Procedure Act and to recommend improvements and greater uniformity in agency rule-making and adjudication procedures. The executive order established a high-level conference of academics and regulatory officials that would meet periodically and consider recommendations from various committees charged with exploring various areas of agency activity. The committee chairs, senior level government officials, were authorized to employ temporary consultants to aid in the committee work. One such committee related to government procurement and was chaired by Cyrus Vance, the DoD general counsel.

---

32 Congress enacted the Administrative Conference Act of 1964, 5 U.S.C. §§ 591-596. It ceased operations in October 1995 when Congress denied further funding. Congress renewed funding in 2010 at President Obama's request and the Senate confirmed a new chairman.

I promptly applied to him for such a consultancy. He accepted my application. He told me he had also hired Professor Stanley Metzger of Georgetown Law School, and he welcomed our recommendations for on what projects the committee should address and complete within three months. After talking it over, Professor Metzger and I recommended two that should be doable within that timeframe: unifying the three separate panels of the Armed Services Board of Contract Appeals (ASBCA) into a single board, and improving the procedural fairness of the ex parte suspensions of firms from government contracting while the government investigated suspected wrong doing on their existing contracts. Mr. Vance accepted our recommendations and repeated the importance of submitting these recommendations with supporting rationale to him within three months. Professor Metzger and I agreed that he would take the lead on the ASBCA merger, and I on the suspension reform, but each to consult the other on developments and to exchange drafts. We worked well together.

We started work early in March and finished in May 1962. I consulted several attorneys in private practice who had experience in debarment and suspension practice as well as academics who had studied and written about debarment and suspension. Among the latter was Professor Arthur S. Miller at George Washington University Law School who had published a seminal, pioneering law review article on the subject. This led to our becoming friends and with his wife Dagmar in Washington and Key West until his death many years later. Arthur was a distinguished and prolific writer, scholar and teacher of constitutional law. He was a principal legal advisor to Senator Sam Ervin during the Watergate hearings.

The suspension practices of the procurement agencies of the Department of Defense cried out for reform. There was no advance notice of the suspension, and no statement of the reasons or charges other than a general reference to an ongoing investigation of possible wrong doing involving the contractor or an indictment. The effect was to bar a contractor from the award of any further contract with any agency of the DoD and perhaps by other government agencies until the suspension and any resulting debarment were terminated.

During the pendency of the suspension there was no opportunity to present evidence of the contractor's responsibility unless the suspension was replaced by a notice of proposed debarment with a statement of charges, and an opportunity to rebut them. Worst of all were the indications of the interminable duration of suspensions. Typically they lasted many months and sometimes years while the government exhaustively investigated the employees and business associates of suspended contractors. Ultimately, the Department of Justice would determine whether or not to permit the suspending agency to give notice of specific charges warranting debarment from government contracting lest it prejudice a criminal investigation or prosecution or filing a civil fraud complaint. In the meantime, contractor employees frequently lost their jobs and contractors dependent on government business failed.

I wrote a detailed report of these findings based on a significant sampling of suspensions by the military departments. Indeed, I had had some experience of suspensions and debarments while working for Al Stein in OGC although the Navy had far fewer than the Army and the Air Force. The principal recommendation had to be to persuade the Justice Department to agree to a time limit on contractor suspensions. After getting some help from Cy Vance, we persuaded Bobby Kennedy, the Attorney General, to agree to an 18-month limit on contractor suspensions. We were not able to persuade the Department of Defense or the Justice Department also to agree to a procedure under which a contractor prior to suspension would ordinarily have an opportunity to show cause within thirty days why it should not be suspended in relation to a generalized statement of charges. Again, the concern was that this might prejudice an ongoing investigation or prosecution. Even so, achieving this time limit on contractor suspensions was an important accomplishment.[33]

---

33 The present, government-wide suspension rules and procedures are set forth in section 9.407 of the Federal Acquisition Regulation, 48 C.F.R. § 9.407 (2010). While they still authorize ex parte suspensions, they must be based on "adequate evidence" of violation of one of the many enumerated causes for suspension mostly involving fraud or criminal conduct and the notice of suspension must specify the particular cause of suspension. The Department of Justice may still prevent the administrative adjudication of disputed charges if that would prejudice an ongoing investigation or prosecution. Suspensions now may not exceed 12 months unless an assistant attorney general requests a maximum extension of an additional 6 months.

Professor Metzger's recommendation to unify the ASBCA, with which I fully concurred as did he with the suspension recommendations, was acceptable to the ASBCA and the military departments since the nature of the contract disputes had nothing to with which military department the dispute had arisen. Cy Vance was appreciative and totally supportive of both recommendations and they were later unanimously adopted by the Administrative Conference. Appropriate changes to the ASPR debarment and suspension regulations and to the charter of the ASBCA were thereafter made.

So ended my final service as a government attorney. I was fortunate soon thereafter to be employed starting in June 1962 as an associate in Hensel, vom Baur & Heller. Harry Heller, formerly director of enforcement at the SEC, recently had joined the firm to practice securities law.

This concludes Part Four of my enriching life.

Part Five Law Firm Practice 1962-92

1. Associate with Hensel, vom Baur & Heller 1962.

Struve Hensel had offices at an advantageous location at 1700 K Street NW, a large corner office building facing K Street and Farragut Square built in 1950. When I began in June 1962 I was the second associate. The other was Tom Farmer who had also graduated from HLS a year or two ahead of me and who worked mostly for Struve. First, it was necessary for me to be admitted to the DC bar, which the federal district court promptly granted on Trow's motion since I had been admitted in Massachusetts long enough for a waiver from having to take the DC bar examination. I knew very little about DC law. I would soon have to learn.

-Financing the Watergate Construction Project.

Struve said he wanted my full-time help on the Watergate construction project. The John Hancock Insurance Co. was financing the large project of constructing a luxury apartment building facing the Potomac

River and an adjacent hotel and office building on Virginia Avenue NW. The financing would be released in installments only after Struve had first certified to John Hancock that the particular construction segment fully met or would meet all applicable requirements of DC and federal law. No construction work had started. I was to assist Struve by thoroughly examining the plans and specifications and other documents for compliance with the DC and federal law applicable to the project. The living room floor in my Duddington Place house was covered with construction drawings which I would pore over in the evenings as well as during the day at the office. The project manager and the building contractors were ever impatient for the quick release of the first installment payment and blamed the lawyers for delaying the job and increasing its costs.

I soon found some major issues of noncompliance. Among other things, the height of the apartment building exceeded by one storey the height limitations on buildings of a federal statute which meant that the Fine Arts Commission and the DC government would deny required approvals before construction could start. There were issues of the sufficiency of the parking for both the apartment and office buildings. The plans for the required closing of public streets failed to comply with the procedural requirements for prior notification of the affected residents and provide them with a protest remedy with the DC government. Struve so advised John Hancock who informed the project manager there would be no release of financing until the plans and specifications were revised and they were in compliance. All this would set back the construction schedule by six months.

Working for Struve was demanding. Then in his sixties and still a dynamo of activity, he was all business. There was no small talk or pleasantries. He would question me closely and thoroughly on my findings and recommendations; and when satisfied he was implacable in resisting efforts by the project people to cut corners.

I called his attention to one further problem that looked insuperable. The Vatican was the beneficial owner of the Watergate complex. An 1880s federal statute provided that "foreign interests" could not own land in DC. Struve told me to examine the enforcement history of that law in the records of the office of the DC corporation counsel and the Justice Department if necessary as well. I first determined that enforcement of the law was the responsibility of the corporation counsel. My examination of their records and interviewing of the cognizant attorneys convinced me that there was no documentary evidence or case law that the statute had ever been enforced or applied. On this basis Struve asked me to draft a letter to him from Chester Gray, the DC Corporation Counsel, detailing this history and concluding that the statute was "obsolete" and would not be applied to the Watergate project. In the meeting Struve and I had with Chester Gray and his associates Struve was a master of persuasion. A few days later he received the requested letter signed by Chester Gray. Thereafter the project moved ahead as Struve was able to certify the work covered by the payment requests was fully compliant with law. I greatly respected Struve's imaginative solution to overcoming this statutory impediment to the project.

-Life Beyond the Office.

Lyttleton Fox visited Washington for a few days and stayed with Don and me. He had important news: He had married Thelma, an English lady employed in the Navy London office a year or two earlier who was at the opposite end of the English social ladder from Dinah Brand, his first wife. She belonged to the Labor party and would sing at party rallies. They would have a son and two daughters whom I would meet later in New York and elsewhere. Having tentatively resigned as counsel for the Navy Purchasing Office in London, he had come to Washington to answer questions about receiving a security clearance for the new job as a Defense Department base rights negotiator for which he had applied. The questions concerned his relationship to his brother-in-law, George Weisman, an avowed Trotskyite, and his wife who was Lyttleton's sister Connie. He told the security people that he rejected Weisman's political beliefs in their entirety but that he was devoted to his sister who had no interest in her husband's political views. Worried that Lyttleton in the sensitive base right negotiations in Europe and North Africa might submit to blackmail to protect his sister, the security people denied his security clearance. This was absurd as Trotsky had already been murdered by Stalin's agents in Mexico and his followers were few and politically impotent.

Don reported that Lyttleton's nervousness was evidenced by the quantities of small bits of paper, apparently unable to sleep, he had torn into smaller and smaller pieces during the night. On this trip he applied for a job at the United Aircraft Corporation in Hartford and was interviewed by Bob Beech, the general counsel. Lyttleton accepted the position of counsel for the export division of the Pratt &Whitney aircraft engine manufacturing division. He and Thelma and their children soon moved to Hartford. Lyttleton's departure was a big loss to OGC. After a few years Lyttleton resigned from Pratt & Whitney to become a professor at Seton Hall Law School in Newark, N.J. They would live in Newark and I would visit them there until his premature death in 1965 whereupon Thelma and the children returned to England to live with her twin sister Gabrielle in Brighton.

-The Departure of Struve Hensel.

Late that fall Struve told us that he would return to New York to start a new job with a real estate investment trust in January. He would turn over his government contract clients to Trow which included important matters from the New York Shipbuilding Corporation and the Western Electric Company division of the AT&T corporation. Harry Heller and Tom Farmer would remain in place as attorneys in the Washington office of Simpson, Bartlett & Thatcher. Trow and I would rent adjacent space on the same floor.

Closely working with Struve Hensel was an important, unique, educational adventure for me. I would experience his demanding, enveloping greatness. A Columbia Law School graduate about 1927, he possessed a first-class intellect and was highly seasoned as a corporate law partner in the New York Milbank Tweed firm for about a decade before coming to Washington to work for James Forrestal. FDR had appointed Forrestal as undersecretary of the Navy after the fall of France in 1940. Forrestal in turn summoned Hensel who had been his attorney when he was president of Dillon Reid in New York. Struve went on to create and lead the Navy Office of the General Counsel from 1942 in World War II to the end of the war. I learned and benefitted from Struve's insistence on the highest standards of professionalism and thoroughness as a lawyer. It was a great opportunity and intensive experience for me. I knew nothing about his personal life and relationships. It was as if his personal life was separated from his professional life by an invisible curtain. He and Trow had a professional relationship. While Struve found my work acceptable, he would have tolerated nothing less. He characterized unsatisfactory work as "sloptail". I had no social conversation with him and could not claim him as a friend. He was nevertheless an unforgettable and lasting mentor.

About that time we met Spencer Beresford, HLS 1939, who as a Congressional staffer had mostly drafted the recently enacted National Aeronautical & Space Act creating the space agency known as "NASA". He was now seeking a private practice opportunity. We liked him and decided to form a partnership as of January 1, 1963, for the practice of law. We contributed some capital, Trow and Spencer each $5,000, and I $2,500, rented the adjoining office space, purchased furniture and equipment, hired a secretary, printed stationery and business cards, and mailed announcements to possible clients and other law firms.

2. vom Baur, Beresford & Coburn 1963-66.

-Practice Before the Patent Office.

One of the first matters that Trow and I worked on involved the issue of whether non lawyers were authorized to practice law in representing patent applicants before the Patent Office. As chairman of the Committee on the Unauthorized Practice of Law of the American Bar Association, Trow was asked by the Florida Bar Association to represent it in the Supreme Court in the pending case of *Sperry v. Florida*, in which the Court had granted Mr. Sperry's petition for review of a decision of the Supreme Court of Florida that had barred his work there in representing patent applicants as the unauthorized practice of law. We had started work on this some months before in the predecessor firm in view of the demands of the Court's briefing and argument schedule. The Florida Bar brought the case because it found that Mr. Sperry was holding himself out in Tampa as a "patent attorney" and engaged in the practice of law with respect to advising on patent applications. By the time the case reached the Supreme Court, Mr. Sperry had agreed to drop claiming to be a "patent attorney".

Trow suggested that I research the statutory and regulatory history in an endeavor to establish that neither authorized the practice of law by non lawyers representing applicants before the Patent Office, while he would address the Constitutional arguments that in any event Congress was without authority to sanction such practice since regulation of the practice of law was reserved to the states under the Tenth Amendment.

The applicable statute authorized the Commissioner of Patents to "prescribe regulations governing the recognition and conduct of agents, attorneys, or other persons representing applicants before the Patent Office...."[34] The Patent Office established two separate registers, one for attorneys, the other for agents "on which are entered the names of all persons recognized as entitled to represent applicants before the Patent Office. Registration...shall only entitle persons registered to appear before the Patent Office."[35] A person may be admitted under either category by establishing "that he is of good moral character and of good repute and possessed of the legal and scientific and technical qualifications necessary to enable him to render applicants for patents valuable

---

34   35 U.S.C. § 31.

35   37 Code of Federal Regulations (CFR) §§ 1.341, 1.341 (a) and (b).

service, and is otherwise competent to assist them in the presentation and prosecution of their applications before the Patent Office."[36]

These provisions and their history, we argued, did not authorize "agents" to practice law in representing patent applicants; instead they would be needed for their "scientific and technical qualifications" to assist attorneys in the successful representation of patent applicants. We cited in support an earlier version of the regulation which stated that registration "shall not be construed as authorizing persons not members of the bar to practice law."[37]

The Court heard oral argument on March 25, 1963, which I thought Trow had the better of. Two months later, from an exhaustive examination of the legislative and regulatory history, a unanimous Court in an opinion by Chief Justice Warren rejected these arguments. He cited a current trademark regulation of the Patent Office that provided "Recognition of any person under this section is not to be construed as sanctioning the performance of any acts regarded in the jurisdiction where performed as the practice of law"[38] to show that an effort to incorporate these words in a 1948 revision of the patent regulations was rejected.[39] But we had argued that at most the regulations meant agents could practice patent law only in the District of Columbia where the patent office was located, which the Court also rejected.[40]

As to our constitutional law arguments, the Court said, "We have not overlooked respondent's constitutional arguments, but find them singularly without merit."[41] They might have found traction in the Hughes Court of the early 1930s and perhaps even now in the Roberts Court but they resoundingly fell flat in the Warren Court.

---

36 37 CFR § 1.341(c).

37 3 Fed Reg. 2429.

38 37 CFR § 2.12(d).

39 373 U.S. at 386, 387.

40 *Id.*

41 373 U.S. at 403.

In my lifetime and except for representing clients in judicial and some administrative proceedings, accounting, business, management consulting, and tax firms routinely advise their clients or customers on legal questions in the course of their work, some with attorney employees, most without, largely without objection by the bar associations. The practicalities of business life require no less.

Also since 1949 when I was first admitted to the bar, the practice of law has, to my great regret, come to be primarily a business and less a profession, a trend that was hastened by a decision of the Supreme Court upholding the rights of lawyers to advertise prices for their services as a matter of Constitutional entitlement under the First Amendment,[42] thereby undermining a century's canon of ethics that proscribed advertising by lawyers. All this calls into question whether lawyers should continue to have separate professional recognition and status under state and federal law.

-Representing Bath Iron Works and Hiring Bill Simmons.

The matters that Struve had turned over to Trow kept us busy throughout 1963 and 1964. Later in 1964, thanks to my brother Pat, Bath Iron Works, a major Navy shipbuilder in Bath, Maine, requested our help in a contract pricing dispute with the Bureau of Ships (BuShips). As above related, Pat had joined the business brokerage firm of Hubbard, Westerfeld & Motley in New York. Their clients were corporations seeking merger partners or acquisitions. John Newell, president of Bath, long a family business owned by him and his family, told Pat they were seeking a merger partner. He also told him that for the first time they were having a significant contract dispute with the Navy and could he recommend a law firm to help them. Pat then told him about Trow and me and our backgrounds with the Navy OGC. It helped that one of the members of John's board of directors was a former chief of naval operations who

---

42 *Bates v. State Bar of Arizona*, 433 U.S., 350 (1977).

remembered Trow favorably. Presently John came to see us and hired us, first to attempt to resolve the dispute with the contracting officer at BuShips; if necessary litigate the claim in the ASBCA. The dispute concerned the interpretation of a standard price adjustment clause in Navy shipbuilding contracts, specifically whether they covered price increases in the costs of employee pension, supervisor retirement and employee group health insurance plans.

To do this effectively Trow and I decided we needed to hire a qualified attorney who would go to Bath and develop the case. I called Eleanor Apple, the director of the placement office at HLS, and told her of our urgent need. She soon advised us of the availability of Bill Simmons, HLS 1959, and a magna cum laude 1952 graduate of Harvard College where he had been president of *The Harvard Crimson*. After college he had four years in the Air Force in various procurement functions and had worked his way through law school with part-time work with Harbridge House, a management consulting firm connected to the Harvard Business School, teaching various courses on procurement matters and which Bill had been doing full-time since law school. Bill was now seeking employment in private law practice. He was a member of the Massachusetts Bar.

We really had found gold. We arranged to interview Bill at the Logan Airport in Boston on our way to Bath, Maine. Trow and I were tremendously impressed by Bill and we offered him employment on the spot which he accepted. Engaged to be married and living in Boston, he would be able to start in a week or so and would be available to drive to Bath as needed. Trow would go to Bath with him on the first visit and introduce him. We later would lease office space for the firm in downtown Boston for Bill after he became a named partner with Bob Turtle in the successor firm we started in 1966.

Trow and Bill, despite the submission of an exhaustive memorandum of law articulating the basis of Bath's position, were unable to settle the case with the contracting officer and the BuShips OGC lawyers, principally John Riismandel whom I strongly recommended BuShips hire several years earlier. Trow and Bill, ably assisted by Alan Peterson of the accounting firm of Arthur Andersen and about whom I shall write further, litigated the dispute in the Armed Services Board of Contract Appeals in 1967, with John representing BuShips. The decision in May 1968 fully vindicated the Bath position on the basis that the price adjustment clause covered recovery of cost increases for the challenged fringe benefit indirect costs.[43] Bill's performance in this matter as in all others for the firm was stellar, meeting the highest standards of law practice.

The news of this decision spread rapidly through the shipbuilding industry as many had contracts with BuShips with this clause and had similar issues. But some of these shipbuilders had larger cost disputes with BuShips, and they would now come to Trow for help leading to a major expansion of the firm. I must first recount our work on the Western Electric matter that Struve had referred to Trow.

-The Western Electric Past Services Pension Costs Case.

This matter involved the recovery of past-service pension costs under the company's cost-reimbursement contracts with the Navy. In 1959 the company together with its parent, the AT&T corporation, had begun a program to amortize its unfunded cost liability for past service pension costs over 10 years. The government's position, first asserted in 1962 in denying the recovery of pension costs for past services, we thought could be overturned. We submitted a comprehensive memorandum of the merits of the allowability of the questioned costs early in 1964 to Jim Bannerman, a career civil servant with whom Trow and I had worked and respected when Jim was a high official in the Office of Naval Material, and to whom the matter had been referred in his then current position as Deputy Assistant Secretary of Defense (Procurement). We also met with him and his accounting advisor, Ken Kilgore, a former manager with Arthur Andersen.

---

43 *Bath Iron Works Corporation*, ASBCA No. 12382, 68-1 BCA ¶ 7050 (May 21, 1968).

In a letter to Trow in May 1964, Jim Bannerman concluded that he would recommend the disallowance of the questioned costs because the company had delayed the amortization program for far too many years after the liability was first incurred under the pension plan even though there was evidently little agreement about this among accounting experts. Our further efforts at reconsideration were unsuccessful and we filed an appeal to the ASBCA after the Navy contracting officer finally in August 1965 disallowed reimbursement of the past service pension costs for 1960.

We began a lengthy period of trial preparation, including the interviewing, selection of company witnesses and developing the opinion testimony development of several leaders of the accounting profession as expert witnesses. The Navy had denied the recovery of the amortization amounts to be charged to these contracts in 1960 because, in the Navy's opinion, they related to the pension costs for the services of retired employees for prior years when the company had no Navy contracts and therefore were not allocable to the costs of current work. To refute this Trow and I, after much study and consultation with Alan Peterson and others, prepared a detailed memorandum that the Navy position was not supported by the relevant contract provisions or by the applicable principles of the accounting profession on the charging of past services costs to be used in trial preparation and in post-trial briefing.

Eventually, Frank Dewey, the general counsel of Western Electric who had referred the matter to Struve Hensel, decided that our litigation of the case would be strengthened by the addition of an experienced litigator in accounting disputes, Everett Willis, from the Dewey, Ballantine firm in New York. This was a great and welcome choice. He and I worked together closely and harmoniously in trial preparation, at the trial, and in drafting the post-trial brief and reply brief. Everett thoroughly mastered the case, skilfully presented the testimony of our accounting witnesses and, conducted a devastating cross-examination of Ken Kilgore the government's sole accounting witness, since apparently no recognized outside accounting expert would support the government's accounting position. Larry Chermak, counsel to the Navy Comptroller and a friend of Trow's and mine from our OGC years, was the government trial lawyer.

His cross-examination of our experts mostly reinforced the persuasiveness of their opinions why the Navy's accounting treatment of the disputed costs was erroneous.

Past service pension costs did not relate to particular employees, whether or not currently employed, but to the pension plan as a whole and particularly to the pension security of current and future employees. Moreover, AT&T and Western Electric were industry leaders in shifting from the pay-as-you-go financing of pension costs to the funding of current pension costs since 1928, to freezing the unfunded liability in 1939, and in beginning the amortization of the unfunded in 1959. Because of the effect of earning compounding interest for many years on funded pension costs, these actions substantially reduced pension costs over the pay-as-you-go method, and when done were fully in accord with generally accepted accounting principles.

In a lengthy decision [44] the ASBCA sustained our position as compelled by the contract provisions and the accounting testimony of our experts. It was a great case and wonderful litigation training for me. As Trow would emphasize, the key to successful litigation, was preparation, preparation, and more preparation!

-Erroneous Government Testing and Condemnation of Mizokami Colorado Spinach Crop.

Mike Mizokami came to Trow for help in 1964 with a tale of woe. The son of Japanese-Americans wrongfully interned in Colorado during World War II, Mike and his family had established a thriving business of growing high quality spinach on a large farm there and exporting it in refrigerated freight cars and trucks to markets throughout the country. Each growing season federal government inspectors would test his crop as safe and suitable for human consumption. In 1963, the government test results mistakenly resulted in the rejection of the entire crop as unsalable.

---

[44] *Western Electric Company, Inc.*, ASBCA No. 11050, 68-2 BCA ¶ 7275 (September 12, 1968).

A later government test by a different method established the error of the original test. By then it was too late to save the crop and sell the spinach. He came to us for help.

He was entitled to compensation for the value of the loss of his crop as evidenced by the record of his sales for recent seasons. The problem was that there was no judicial remedy. While Congress has consented for the government to be sued in tort for the negligence of its employees acting within their authority, the Federal Tort Claims Act exempted the negligent or wrongful performance of discretionary functions such as the conducting of the spinach test.[45] And of course there was no contract remedy. What to do?

After some research we found that Congress could enact a private law to redress government wrongs for which there was no judicial remedy. This was known as "Congressional Reference Cases" (28 U.S.C. § § 1492, 2509) under which either the House or the Senate could refer such a case to the Court of Claims to conduct a hearing and then make a recommendation based on its findings to the referring chamber. We pursued that course.

With the aid of Mizokami's Congressman to pave the way, we made a presentation to the counsel of the House Judiciary Committee based on Mike's affidavit we had prepared. This in turn led to a referral by the House to the Court of Claims. Chief Judge Wilson Cowen then referred the case to Commissioner Marion Bennett to conduct a trial-type hearing with the government represented by the Department of Justice. Our witnesses were Mike Mizokami and one of his principal customers, a wholesale grocer in Philadelphia, both of whom after thorough preparation made excellent witnesses which the government attorney, not for lack of effort, was unable to weaken. We also had expert testimony to prove that the initial, and fatal, government test of the spinach was erroneous and the belated one correct.

The result was that the government dropped its opposition to recovery and did not contest our proof of the damages which came to almost

---

45 28 U.S.C. § 2680 (2006).

$1 million. The Court of Claims so recommended to the House, and Congress in due course enacted a private law which President Johnson signed for compensating the Mizokamis in that amount in 1965 or 1966. Thus Mike was enabled to remain in the spinach business.

-Clients in Chicago; Working with Alan Peterson of Arthur Andersen.

About 1963 Trow had a new client in Chicago, Cook Electric Co., which had incurred increased costs on a missile base program due to compensable acts of the government called "constructive changes". In developing a program to recover these costs Trow worked with Alan Peterson, a young manager from the accounting firm of Arthur Andersen in Chicago, the company's auditors. Trow was impressed by Peterson's ability to determine the likely amount of the company's increased costs due to these government acts. Alan in turn respected Trow's skills in finding a contractual basis for recovery, and recommended Trow to other Arthur Andersen audit clients in the Chicago area on which Alan worked with similar problems. This resulted in Trow's retention by two other Chicago firms, Webcor, and later by Communications Systems Corporation (CSC), each having incurred substantial losses from attempting to comply with faulty government specifications for the manufacture of military electronic equipment.

Trow asked me to take them on, and I began several extended trips over the next few years to Chicago to work with Alan, his team, and his clients. I too would have great respect for Alan and his associates in identifying contractor costs attributable to compensable acts of the government. This was a challenging and difficult task. Contractors rarely kept records that would enable the identification of the costs attributable to compensable acts of the government. It would require a detailed reconstruction of the actual performance of the work based on the facts and extensive interviewing of company employees to estimate which of the direct labor and material costs were properly to be charged to the government in the claim for the changed work. With detailed presentations of the acts of the government creating the increased costs, the supported accounting estimates supporting the claimed costs, and of the applicable legal precedents, we were able to resolve these claims satisfactorily without litigation.

-Constructive Change Order Claims.

For many years government procurement contracts have included a standard "Changes" clause which enabled the contracting officer by a written order to direct the contractor to make changes in the work to be performed, as usually set forth in the government drawings and/or specifications. The contractor is obligated to comply unless the ordered change is beyond the scope of the original undertaking. That compliance enables the contractor to recover an "equitable adjustment" for its increased performance time as well as its increased costs of contract performance including the increased costs of work not changed that are delayed or disrupted by performing the changed work.

If the parties do not agree on the equitable adjustment the contracting officer issues a final decision. The contractor may appeal the decision within the prescribed time to the ASBCA or other agency board of contract appeals for the contracts of the civilian agencies. Alternatively, the contractor may challenge the contracting officer's decision by a suit in the U.S. Court of Federal Claims, the successor to the trial division of the former U.S. Court of Claims which became the U.S. Court of Appeals for the Federal Circuit. Both the contractor and the agency head or his delegate may appeal to the Federal Circuit for review of adverse decisions by the boards of contract appeals or by the U.S. Court of Federal Claims.

In much of our work Trow and I found that contractors had performed changed work at the oral direction of government inspectors and technical personnel without confirming written change orders from the contracting officer and often without the knowledge of the contracting officer. These cases presented difficult questions of the contractor's entitlement to recovery when the contracting officer would not issue a confirming change order. These cases were known as "constructive" change orders when there was a legal basis for holding the government liable in the absence of the confirming change order from the contracting officer.

Frequently company \employees, unschooled in the niceties of government contract law, unquestioningly heeded the directions of government personnel to make these changes as a matter of maintaining customer relationships. They would often be unaware of the adverse cost impact of performing this changed work on fixed-price contracts, and indeed in many cases unaware that the work had been contractually changed by these directions, until much later.

Resolving these cases was partly governed by a 5-4 Supreme Court decision of 1947. An Idaho farmer had applied to the Federal Crop Insurance Corporation, an agency of the Agriculture Department, to insure his spring wheat crop mostly reseeded on winter wheat acreage. The local agent of the corporation on these facts advised the farmer that his crop was insurable and recommended acceptance by the home office. The application was accepted and several months later the crop was destroyed by drought. The agency refused payment of the claim, saying that such insurance was precluded by its regulations which had been published in the Federal Register. Both the farmer and the local agent had no knowledge of the regulation.

The Idaho Supreme Court upheld the claim on the basis that a private insurance company would be liable in these circumstances because of the apparent authority of the local agent to represent to the farmer that his crop was insurable, and that the federal government should be treated no differently when it engages in the crop insurance business. The U. S. Supreme Court reversed, *Federal Crop Insurance Corporation v. Merrill*, 332 U.S. 380 (1947).

Justice Frankfurter, writing for the 5-4 majority, ruled that "[w]hatever form in which the Government functions, anyone entering into an arrangement with the Government takes the risk of having accurately ascertained that he who purports to act for the Government stays within the bounds of his authority." Had the fact that reseeded wheat on winter acreage was not insurable been stated in the underlying statute, there would be no question of recovery for the loss since one is presumed to know the laws enacted by Congress regardless of actual knowledge. That instead the prohibition was in an authorized regulation published in the Federal Register makes no difference and will have the same effect since Congress has provided such publication "gives notice of their contents." The case illustrates that men "must turn square corners when they deal with the Government", quoting a famous aphorism by Justice Holmes in an earlier case.

Justice Jackson dissented, stating that it was absurd to expect a farmer to read the Federal Register. Instead, he would hold the government "to the same fundamental principles of fair dealing that have been found essential in progressive states to prevent insurance from being an investment in disappointment." Justice Douglas joined this dissent. Justices Black and Rutledge also dissented without written opinions.

This decision would govern the requisite authority needed for recovery for constructive change orders despite the fact delegations of contracting authority at subordinate levels are rarely published in the Federal Register. This led to creative efforts to find implied contracting authority in the government employees who directed the costly changes or to impute knowledge of them to the contracting officer or to find that the contracting officer had expressly or impliedly ratified them. These efforts would be applied also to incorrect government interpretations of contract specifications, to government acceleration of contract performance, to defective government specifications, to government withholding of superior knowledge needed for contract performance, and to government actions or omissions that hindered contract performance. All this was a then developing field of contract law without the guidance of the leading textbook on the subject published many years later.[46]

---

46   Nash and Feldman *Contract Changes* (3ʳᵈ ed., Thomson-West 2007). This magisterial 2-volume treatise fully covers all significant issues regarding this important subject.

Trow, however, would write a pioneering law review article on equitable adjustment recovery for constructive change orders in the 1960s for the *Federal Bar Journal* that reflected his experience representing clients in coping with them. This also helped educate government procurement personnel on this subject.

About the same time Hank Keiser, a Washington attorney, began publishing a monthly newsletter, *The Government Contractor,* to report significant new developments in government contract law in decisions of the federal courts, the agency boards of contract appeals, the Comptroller General in bid protests, and in procurement laws and regulations. He also began periodic regional educational programs on the major subjects of government contracting, recruiting leading practitioners in these subjects. "You will receive no compensation from me but I will give you a million dollars worth of publicity," he told them. He had many takers. Trow would teach courses on constructive change orders. All these efforts had important educational impact on the government contracting community and the legal profession as the scale of the government's annual procurement spending continued to climb into many billions of dollars, attracting increasingly more business firms and attorneys into this work.

-The Impact of Robert McNamara on Navy Shipbuilding Claims.

Robert McNamara became Secretary of Defense in 1961. He instituted new policies that greatly increased the incidence of constructive change-order claims. First, he stressed the necessity of fixed-price contracting for most of defense procurement, even if it involved research & development work, with maximum obtainable competition. Secondly, he told the Navy that they had too many shipbuilders and directed that they be weeded out by competitive bidding with award to the lowest price shipbuilder. The established practice of the Bureau of Ships (BuShips) had been to rotate the award of shipbuilding contracts among its private shipyards and have a cushion in the negotiated price to cover a variety of increased costs including informal changes in the work. The chief and deputy chief of BuShips resigned in protest of Secretary McNamara's direction.

This was also a fast developing field in several technologies, particularly electronics, and government specifications usually lagged way behind. This led to further bursts of constructive changes as the government program managers would want their contractors to incorporate the latest technologies in their work, and to accomplish this, they would intervene directly with the contractors and bypass the contracting officer to save time. Within several years constructive change order claims by Navy shipbuilders on their fixed-price contracts exceeded $1B and created a lot of work for a few law firms such as ours and for Arthur Andersen and others. Contractors from other defense programs with significant cost overruns would follow.

-New Partners.

Our practice slowly grew. About 1967 I represented a client in a protest of the Air Force contract award to the client's competitor in the General Accounting Office. We claimed that the award should be cancelled because the contractor would necessarily be using the client's proprietary data furnished by the Air Force to the contractor and which the client had previously submitted to the Air Force under a prior contract. The Air Force was represented by Bob Turtle, then a young officer completing his military service obligation in the general counsel's office. He won the case by being able to prove that the client had failed adequately so to mark the claimed proprietary data and failed to establish that it had otherwise protected the data as a trade secret. I was impressed. I learned he was an honor's graduate of Columbia Law School and on its law review despite having earned his way through college and law school by driving a taxicab. I would try to hire him for our firm when his military service would be completed several months later. We succeeded and persuaded him to join us as a partner.

About that time we also hired Dick Johnson from the same office on the recommendation of Ramsay Potts of the growing young firm of Shaw, Pittman & Potts, my predecessor as chairman of the squash committee at the University Club. I told Ramsay we were looking for a bright young lawyer. Ramsay told me about Johnson. He said his firm's policy of only hiring current law school graduates ruled out Dick whom he wanted to hire because he had graduated from HLS in 1961, first in his class and on the law review. He would soon complete his military service. I persuaded Dick to become one of our partners.

3.   vom Baur, Coburn, Simmons & Turtle 1967-79; Gage, Tucker & vom Baur 1979-84.

-Building the vom BaurFirm.

Spencer Beresford accepted an offer in 1967 to become general counsel of NASA, an agency he had helped create by drafting the legislation before joining us in 1963. His practice had been disappointing in client growth. This was probably a better opportunity for him than staying with us. We were sorry to see him go.

We now renamed the firm with Bill Simmons and Bob Turtle as the named partners in addition to Trow and me. Thus we became vom Baur, Coburn, Simmons & Turtle. In addition to Dick Johnson, we hired Alan

Washburn as a new partner. A top student at Columbia Law School some ten years earlier, he was exceptionally bright and had superb recommendations from his prior attorney employers. We found him to be outstanding and relentlessly committed to first-class work.

We also continued over the next several years to hire outstanding young associates as the work increased. All would excel practicing government contract law throughout their professional careers. Among them were Lisa Anderson, later Lisa Anderson Todd, just out of law school and later an administrative judge first at the NASA BCA and while there correctly ruled against me in a defective pricing case, and then at the ASBCA; David Cohen just out of law school; Hopewell Darneille on finishing a clerkship with a federal district judge; Rob Evers from Columbia Law School, first as a second-year summer associate; Bob Foster, an established practitioner in California who would later head our Orange County office; Mike Freeman from HLS and from about 1980 on becoming a distinguished administrative judge at the ASBCA; Peter Jones also from Columbia Law School; Jim McHale and Paul Remus from Cornell; Marty Golub, Stu Nibley, and Tom Williamson recent law school graduates; John Pachter, an Army JAG officer litigating contract disputes in the ASBCA, when he completed his military service and who would become a partner; Kim Preston, a recent law school graduate who would later specialize in construction law; Bruce Shirk from HLS who began in the Boston office with Bill Simmons; Florence Weight, our first lady associate; and Jeff Willis, another recent law school graduate.

Trow and I had started making recruiting trips to several Eastern law schools in the fall for summer jobs for students who would have completed their second year and for employment as first-year associates. The younger partners and associates would gradually take this on.

Trow and I over the years gradually built up the law library to have the court, BCA and GAO reports, services, textbooks, and our attorneys' memoranda of law that we would need to practice government contract law effectively. The increase in the number of attorneys necessitated a larger support staff of secretaries, an office manager and a comptroller, as well as more office space until we leased all of the 11th and much of the 10th floor at 1700 K Street.

-Life Away from the Office.

On the home front, in 1964 we sold the Duddington Place house profitably and bought another row house fairly near on Capitol Hill at 522 Fourth Street, SE. The house was slightly larger and the garden more spacious. Across the street was a lovely detached house on sizable grounds with a swimming pool, recently purchased by Richard Rodman, a widower with three young children. We became friends. Dick was an importer and retailer in Alexandria of top-of-the-line copperware made by Spring, a Swiss firm. Thanks to John Shollenberger in Philadelphia, I was able to find him a live-in nurse to look after the children. She was Dottie McKenna, a dear friend of John's and a divorced Main-Line social-ite a few years older than Dick. I too had met Dottie and thought she would be entirely suitable. I invited her to stay with us while she and Dick and the children could decide. She more than met their expectations and they hers. She remained with them for several years until the children were old enough not to need her. She gradually nurtured a forlorn roman-tic interest in Dick who in turn was in a relationship with Andrew Rigg, M.D., that had begun some years before in Boston. Andrew grew up in Australia and was educated there and in England. Now an American citizen, his medical training was in Boston. Dick moved to Washington because Andrew was now working as a pediatrician in Washington. We became friends with him as well as Dottie not surprisingly did not.

Don was doing well as a real estate salesman with Barbara Held on Capitol Hill. He sold Annette and Bill Doolitle who had been renting on Duddington Place across the street from us their first house. Bill had been one of my housemates in 1958 in the R street house, and he and Annette would become our good friends, and they still are for me. He did the same for Joe and Trudi Califano whom I had come to know through Dennis Lyon with whom I would share a house as I shall relate.

-Birth of Federal Contracts Report.

In 1964 the publishers of *U.S Law Week* began the publication of *Federal Contracts Report*, a weekly newspaper covering recent developments in federal procurement and grant law and policy. Its editorial offices were in Washington and Jerry Elswit became the editor for several years. An advisory board of mostly practitioners of government contract law was established. Trow was one of its members. The board would meet monthly to discuss an announced topic. I was asked to prepare these discussion papers which after the meeting and revised as appropriate would then be published in this weekly newspaper. I would assist the chairman in presenting them. The first chairman was Harold Leventhal, a very able lawyer whom a year or so later President Johnson would appoint to the Court of Appeals for the D.C. Circuit where he would serve illustriously for several years until dying prematurely while playing tennis. I greatly respected him and rank him along with Struve Hensel among the best I have known. Writing these papers on emerging topics of interest, although without financial compensation, was a valuable educational experience for me. The firm also benefitted with a complimentary subscription.

-Early American Bar Association Activities; Birth of the Section of Public Contract Law.

I began to become active in the American Bar Association which I had first joined in 1958 while still in OGC. Government contract issues were addressed by a committee within the administrative law section. There was a growing movement led by several practitioners, such as Trow, Gilbert Cuneo, Geoffrey Creyke, ASBCA chairman Louis Spector in Washington and Walter Pettit in San Francisco, that government contract law deserved greater recognition and focus within the ABA and should be created as a separate section. The hierarchy of ABA authorities approved, and the Section of Public Contract Law was established at the ABA annual meeting in Miami, Florida, in August 1965.

Administrative Judge Spector arranged for Judge Leventhal to be the principal speaker at the inaugural lunch. He also asked me to draft Judge Leventhal's speech. The topic was the relationships between administrative and government contract law. I spent the better part of a day with Judge Leventhal in his chambers as he reworked my draft and greatly strengthened it. It drew on the parallels between the issuance of procurement regulations and rule making under the Administrative Procedure Act (APA), and the felt need for procurement regulations which directly affected government contractors to be subject to public notice and comment before being issued. There were also parallels in the APA adjudication and judicial review procedures and those of the boards of contract appeals and the U.S. Court of Claims. Yet there were significant differences between regulation of business and procurement contracting by the federal government that merited establishing a separate section of the ABA to study this complex and growing area and recommend improvements. His speech was warmly received. Judge Leventhal and I reworked his speech into an article that was published in the monthly ABA Bar Journal.[47]

Don and I went to this annual ABA meeting, the first of several we attended over the ensuing years. While staying in Miami I went to see my sister Louise in Palm Beach. She was sadly in failing health from alcoholism and smoking. I would not see her again. Within the year she developed an inoperable brain tumor and died at 58.

-Visits to Barbados, Mexico and Hawaii.

During 1966 Don and I made two trips, one for an enjoyable week to Barbados to help me recover from a severe winter cold; and later in December for three weeks over the Christmas holidays to Mexico. There we had three weeks, first about a week in Mexico City where we stayed in

---

47   Leventhal, *Public Contracts and Administrative Law*, 52 A.B.A.J. 35 (1966).

a former monastery near the main Cathedral. The city even then teeming with millions was smog-ridden. It is on a lake bed about seven thousand feet above sea level, surrounded by mountains. We saw a wonderful performance of a folklore ballet at the opera house and greatly admired the Tiffany glass curtain as we also did the city's principal museum. We visited some Indian ruins south of the city. Our drive to Acapulco was delayed by snow in the passes. En route we stopped for lunch in Cuernavaca at a pricey restaurant with the celebrated peacocks wandering about. We drove on to Taxco where silver is mined and silversmiths display their wares, some of which we admired but did not buy as too costly for tourists such as we.

We stayed a week in Acapulco, a growing resort on the Pacific Ocean with visitors from Canada, Europe, Japan, as well as the U.S. We stayed in a small hotel that catered to gays and found some pleasant company for meals and outings. The ocean swimming was marvellous as was the hotel salt-water swimming pool. Later we had friends in Washington who purchased a vacation home in Acapulco. We would not return again.

For our last week in Mexico we flew across the country to Merida, the capital of Yucatan, a peninsula jutting into the Atlantic and Caribbean. Merida, a sizeable city, is a major production center of a wide variety of vegetables and fruits grown in the vast, flat surrounding agricultural areas. We stayed comfortably at the Continental Hotel which caters to foreign tourists from all over. We again rented a VW Beetle, as we had done for the drive to Acapulco, to visit the Mayan sites at Chichen Itza and Uxmal. We marvelled at the splendor and architectural beauty of the stone structures of this remarkable, advanced civilization and mourned the tragedy of its destruction by the Conquistadors in the name of Christianity.

For our final jaunt we drove south to Cozumel, then a small village on the Caribbean. The next day was an idyllic outing on a small fishing boat to an enchanting, tiny offshore uninhabited, unspoilt and verdant island to feast on freshly caught fish the boat captain had caught on the way and cooked for us on the fire he made on the beach. This entire area now sadly has lost its pristine beauty to the surrounding mega resort at

Cancun. The next day we returned to Merida for our Pan American flight to Miami, and then to a connecting flight to Washington. This was a brief encounter with a culture so far from what I had experienced before.

The ABA annual meeting in August 1966 was in the Waikiki Beach resort area of Oahu near Honolulu. This would be the first of two visits Don and I made to the beautiful Hawaiian Islands, the second some four or five years later at another ABA annual meeting. We flew in a propeller-driven United Airlines plane, and the noisy flight seemed interminable. The second visit by jet aircraft in the 1970s was far better. On the first visit, we explored much of this medium size island as it became more varied and interesting the farther one ventured from Honolulu. We also spent another several days visiting Maui and Kuai, each fetching in different ways.

- New Homes on Capitol Hill and Connecticut Avenue; Don's Business Life.

In 1970 after selling our 4th Street house handsomely, Don found a grander house for us for $75,000 on Capitol Hill at 401 6th Street SE. It had recently been restored to its original splendor by a retired Army couple, Col. and Mrs. Donovan, who for unexpected reasons reluctantly had to sell. Originally built as a small frame two-storey house in 1800, a larger brick addition was built about 1850 by the next generation of the family of James Mead, the original owner. The kitchen on the ground floor with a huge fireplace, and a sizeable bedroom, and bathroom upstairs, were in the original part of the house. In the living room, dining room, and front hall in the Victorian addition were the original plaster moldings and medallions designed by Brumidi, a contemporary and friend of the Meads and renowned for his frescoes in the Capitol. Upstairs were two bedrooms, a library and a second bathroom. There were four working fireplaces, two in the double living room, another in the dining room, and one in the library upstairs. Also there was an attractive patio and a garage where I kept my bicycle for riding to work.

We would live there very comfortably until late in 1976 when we would move to a late 1920s apartment building at 2101 Connecticut Avenue NW, recently upgraded and converted from a rental to a cooperative apartment building, for another eight years. Don had wearied of Capitol Hill after 15 years. The 6ᵗʰ Street house was only two blocks from his kitchen shop, the subway construction was creating excessive dust, and children would litter our yard with trash. We were fortunate to sell it for twice what we paid for it which in turn enabled us to purchase apartment 45 at 2101 Connecticut Avenue for $135,000 including an assigned space in the garage.

By 1968 Don had left Barbara Held, passed the difficult DC real estate broker's examination and opened Don Ellington Real Estate with a small office on 8ᵗʰ Street SE. Don's total honesty about the plusses and minuses of the houses he had listed for sale seemed to discourage some potential buyers, and this put him at a disadvantage with other brokers who were not that scrupulous.

After a few years of mediocre sales, he seized another opportunity for a business venture. A friend, Scott Lentz, who also lived on Capitol Hill and had a full-time government job with the General Services Administration, and Don conceived the idea of opening a kitchen boutique of attractive pots and pans and other kitchen items that would respond to the demand of widespread remodelling of houses on Capitol Hill and elsewhere in Washington. A friend of both of them, Sally Jones, who had a small gift shop on 7ᵗʰ street SE near the Eastern Market, was seeking a replacement tenant as she was about to marry Markham Lewis, an owner of two or three Howard Johnson franchises in Virginia, and begin life with him on his yacht cruising the eastern seaboard and the Caribbean. Her shop would be an ideal location for the kitchen boutique.

So Don and Scotty after acquiring the initial inventory soon opened "The Kitchen Cabinet". Don and I also purchased the building and rented the upstairs which provided income to cover the operating expenses of the shop. Don was there full time and Scotty worked there most Saturdays. Sunday shopping had yet to begin. By 1973 Scotty resigned from the government and moved to Majorca in the Balearic Islands of Spain.

For the first several years the shop did well and earned the partners a good income until the adjacent Metro subway construction in the later 1970s made it too difficult for customers to drive there and discouraged pedestrian traffic as well. This adversely affected other shops in the area as well. We closed the shop in 1978 and rented the lower floor as office space.

Ronnie van Schweringen, an aspiring young artist with much promise, had his studio next to Don's shop. He and Don became friends and over the next few years he gave or sold Don for the cost of framing several of his beautiful paintings, many in a neo-primitive style, which have graced our homes ever since.

-A Vacation Home near Berkeley Springs, West Virginia.

One summer weekend in 1968 Don and I spent a weekend at a delightful country inn in the village of Berkeley Springs, West Virginia, long celebrated for its year-round warm springs and spa. There was a nearby real estate office and in the window a photograph of a property with a small house set back on a large field. We arranged to see it. Some 13 miles northwest of the village and near the Potomac River, the property of some 14.5 acres belonged to a Cecil Ambrose, the county tax assessor. He had acquired it about 1960 for next to nothing in a tax foreclosure sale. He decided to plant several thousand evergreens to sell when they had grown sufficiently to sell as Christmas trees. He also extensively remodelled the 1850s frame house by adding porches and electricity and a shed. There was no running water, instead a stream nearby for drawing water as well as an outhouse.

By 1968 his wife had become ill and he had to sell. We met his asking price of $12,000. A few months later we purchased the adjoining eight acres with a small frame house leading to the B& O railroad tracks along the WV side of the Potomac River from Otis Gaither for $3,000 cash. We had a lot of work to do to make the Ambrose house more liveable which Don mostly accomplished in the ensuing months.

We had one neighbor, Bruce Light, with a wife, and children of varying ages. Bruce worked on the Baltimore & Ohio Railroad, adjacent to our land, as his father, grandfather and so forth had done since the 1850s when their house was built on more than 200 acres of land. A year or two older, Bruce and I became friends and we hired him as our caretaker of the place, an arrangement that lasted until his death more than thirty years later. The nameless ½ mile gravel lane from the paved Orleans Road leading to the driveway to each of our places was a school bus route which required the county to keep it maintained and plowed during the severe winters. All the surrounding land was mostly woods, no houses.

This was truly vanishing rural America, which I am glad to say it still remains, largely because the land is prime ground for hunting deer and other game in the late fall. After the terrorist attack on the U.S. on September 11, 2001, the federal government required that every residence must have a street address, and the gravel lane was duly named "Lightsville Lane" by Morgan County and our place assigned the address 461 Lightsville Lane.

In the next year or two we made significant improvements to the house: drilling a 150- foot well and connecting it to the kitchen and bathroom Don created; installing a propane gas space heater in the front sitting room and a propane gas cooking stove in the dining area; installing a hot water heater and shower in the bathroom; in lieu of a conventional toilet and septic tank we found and installed an incinerator toilet made by a firm in Texas which has worked wonderfully well ever since; and a Franklin wood or charcoal burning stove in the rear sitting room. We soon rented the house on the adjoining property to friends in Washington for weekend outings. To carry things back and forth from Washington we traded in our VW Beetle for a VW Squareback, an early VW version of a station wagon. All our cars thereafter until the final Passat in 1999, our last car, were VWs.

-Bath Iron Works: The "Crash Astern" Test of a Destroyer for the West German Federal Republic's Navy.

In January 1969, in connection with settling ongoing litigation with the Westinghouse Corporation over the geared turbines for a guided missile destroyer Bath was constructing for the West German Federal Republic, I was requested to go to Bath to witness a sea trial of the ship's propulsion system to determine whether Westinghouse had met the specifications as neither Bill Simmons nor Trow was available. Specifically, this meant would the turbines be able rapidly to transition from full speed ahead, which was about 33 knots, to a "crash astern" during which the propellers suddenly were reversed? If it passed this very severe test, the ship would ready for early delivery to the West German Navy under a contract Bath had with the Bureau of Ships under a foreign military aid program. This test was required because there would be operational situations when that maneuver would be urgently necessary.

On a beautiful, cold Sunday morning that month I boarded this 4,500 ton ship, to be commissioned "D 185 Luetjens" named for Admiral Guenther Luetjens who had commanded the battleship "Bismarck" and was killed when it was sunk by the Royal Navy in May 1941 off France. The "Luetjens" would proceed for about an hour from the shipyard on the Kennebec River to the Atlantic Ocean where the test would be conducted. Also aboard the ship still under Bath's direction and control were Westinghouse engineers and U.S. and West German naval officials. As we proceeded the tension and suspense grew increasingly palpable. On reaching the ocean, which was relatively calm, the Bath controller gradually increased the turbines to flank speed and maintained that speed for several minutes. Suddenly with a blast on the ship's horn he activated the crash astern reversal of the propellers. The ship rapidly slowed, vibrated severely, and within the specification time limits began to move astern. Later inspection confirmed this happened without damage to the turbines or other propulsion machinery. Westinghouse had successfully passed this very stringent test, and the litigation was settled. There was widespread rejoicing as we returned to the shipyard. The ship was commissioned by the West German Navy a couple of months later. For me it was an exhilarating experience.

-The Todd $110 Million Shipbuilding Claim on the DE-1052 Program.

One day in 1969, after word of Trow's and Bill Simmons's recovery for the Bath Iron Works in the ASBCA in 1968 spread through the shipbuilding industry, Trow was contacted by Jack Gilbride, president of Todd Shipyards. He asked for help in recovering large losses in constructing the lead ship of the "DE-1052 Class" of new destroyer escorts for anti-submarine warfare under several shipbuilding fixed-price contracts BuShips had awarded to Todd for 14 DE-1052s to built at its two shipyards on the west coast, and additional DE 1052s to a few other shipbuilders under Secretary McNamara's new policies described above. Trow and I soon met with him in New York. Mr. Gilbride said the company had already estimated a loss of about $40 million in unsuccessfully trying to meet a new BuShips specification called "shock and dynamic analysis" and had no prospect of achieving compliance. The specification required that all the ship's piping, electronics and other systems would continue to function properly following a large explosion near the ship as well as a not too distant, and possibly nuclear, explosion.

Trow advised that this sounded like a defective Navy specification for which there was an established path to recover under the "Changes" clause of the contract and that we would send a qualified attorney to Seattle to help draft the claim. I strongly recommended to Mr. Gilbride that he also employ the services of Alan Peterson, by then a partner at Arthur Andersen in Chicago, and explained why he would be necessary to help estimate the increased costs from the efforts to comply with this defective specification. Mr. Gilbride said that since Arthur Young & Co were their auditors we should arrange for Arthur Andersen to bill us instead.

Trow and our new associate Mike Freeman soon went to Seattle where Alan Peterson and Don Campbell, a bright young accountant from his office, and others from Alan's team, joined them at the Todd shipyard there. Within a few months Peterson, Campbell and Freeman prepared a claim document itemizing the estimated increased costs at both Todd Shipyards in vainly struggling to meet the requirements of this defective Navy specification totalling $110 million supported by a memorandum of law of entitlement to recovery which Mike Freeman and Trow prepared. We included as an exhibit to that memorandum a letter I had obtained from Gibbs & Cox, the naval architects for this program, written to the BuShips before any contracts for this program were awarded, which stated that the shock and dynamic specification was not ready for inclusion in fixed-price contracts to be awarded by competitive bidding.

After submitting the claim and the memorandum of law to the contracting officer at the Bureau of Ships, Trow and I called on Sam Pinn, the counsel for BuShips, whom we both knew well and respected from our OGC days, and handed him these documents. We specifically called his attention to this bombshell letter from Gibbs & Cox. We said, "Sam, this seems dispositive, and we prefer settlement to litigation." Within two months BuShips settled the $110 million claim for $96.5 million. Todd paid us a sought $500K bonus fee.

Later that year or in 1970, Melvin Laird, the Secretary of Defense, wrote to Congress that he was "surprised" to learn that this settlement had been made without the approval of the Secretary of the Navy or his office. Al Stein, Deputy General Counsel of the Navy and my former boss, issued a public statement that henceforth claims of this magnitude would be "put through the legal wringer". In fact, Todd's claimed costs were carefully reviewed by Gordon Rule who headed the contract clearance office in the assistant secretary of the Navy's office and found them sufficiently supported to the extent of the settlement amount. On legal entitlement to recover these costs, the Gibbs & Cox letter and the case-law precedents on defective government specifications were dispositive. We later learned that despite the Gibbs & Cox letter, BuShips decided to proceed, fearing it would otherwise lose the funding for this program if it awaited the completion of the shock and dynamic analysis specification.

This $110M outcome spread rapidly through the shipbuilding industry and we soon were representing Lockheed, Avondale, American Ship, Defoe, and others on their shipbuilding claims against BuShips, primarily as the result of the McNamara policy requiring award of these fixed-price contracts by competitive bidding to the lowest bidder. All, on our recommendation, also required the services of Alan Peterson and his team from Arthur Andersen, as did all the other shipbuilders with massive claims against BuShips. The concept spread to other major defense programs plagued by constructive change orders and other compensable acts of the Government. All this became a major source of new business for Arthur Andersen, entirely separate from its auditing work, and would evolve into a variety of management-consulting type services in the accounting profession. Peterson was its unquestioned leader in his areas of practice.

-Martha's Vineyard.

For the summers of 1968-70, I rented three different houses in Edgartown for about a month for Mother, Sally and John. John and I drove to Boston each time in John's father's car to Mother's apartment in Boston and then would drive her to Edgartown. Several years before, the Catherine Gibbs secretarial school had purchased her apartment building at 5 Arlington Street where she had lived since 1944, and she had to move. Again our luck held and I found a suitable apartment for her at 239 Commonwealth Avenue a converted town house which Aunt Louise remembered as belonging to the Thayer family and in which she had played as a child. It was, as I remember, between Dartmouth and Exeter Streets and next to the Algonquin Club which had a nice restaurant Mother could enjoy. John's father very generously let John keep the car for those months since by then he had retired from medical practice for health reasons, and he and his wife had a second car for their own needs.

I remembered how attractive Edgartown was from having visited Louise there in the summer of 1946. Sally was delighted to join us to look after Mother, as she and Bob had often visited there in Bob's plane and they had several friends there whom Mother would also enjoy. For John it was also an opportunity to paint the beautiful landscape scenes of that lovely island, at which he triumphed with many arresting creations. Each summer we had a cook. I gave Sally funds to cover paying for the cook and the food and other expenses. It worked out very well, all loved it. There was much bridge for Mother and Sally; and thanks to Sally she introduced John to Henry Beetle Hough, the publisher of *The Vineyard Gazette*, the island's weekly newspaper graced with the beautiful photographs of the island's birds, other wildlife and vistas. Henry, known as "the Beetle" and Mr. Martha's Vineyard, born and raised on the island, was a dear man then in his 70s. He commissioned John to paint his portrait which John accomplished wonderfully well to the Beetle's satisfaction with some dissent from his second wife, Edie Blake, a younger woman and tennis playing friend of Sally's, who had preferred the Beetle's portrait without his wearing his spectacles as the Beetle had insisted.

Thanks to Sally, John also made friends with Nancy Muir, an artist and wife of Malcolm Muir, the son of the founder of *Newsweek* magazine, and they would paint together; and also Terese Duble, an older widow who took a great interest in John and his work and would invite him to visit after Mother was no longer able to go to the Vineyard. I also introduced John to Bebee Howland, the widow of Silas Howland whom she had married as Bebee Phillips of Waterbury when Si and Mike worked there for the Chase Brass & Copper Co. as I have related in Part One. She and Si had a lovely commanding place in Vineyard haven overlooking the harbor, and John I would visit her often then and in later years. Maud and Tom Urmston from Wilmington were also friends of Sally's on the Vineyard who John and I came to like. Tom who had had a hip transplant persuaded John to have one too which he soon did on both hips successfully with the exceptionally skilled Dr. Stewart at the Bryn Mawr hospital.

Our second summer in a different house delighted Mother and Sally because one of the next neighbors was the home of James Reston, the eminent columnist for *The New York Times*, whom Mother and Sally would occasionally encounter and exchange pleasantries.

For these sojourns John also had the company of first Bobo, and then Wittles, his toy French poodles who were great companions to all of us. Either would ride in the car without complaint for the long drive from Merion and would be at first frightened by the half-hour ferry ride from Woods Hole to Oak Bluffs or Vineyard Haven. Mother and Sally too were confirmed dog lovers. For John and me one of the highlights of these summer visits was the tour of the island Bob Fulton gave us in his Stinson aircraft. Flying at low altitude, we had a commanding, stereoscopic view of this paradise, the surf at South Beach, the pink cliffs of Gay Head to the west, and Chappaquiddick Island at the eastern edge.

Our third summer in 1970 in the Todd house overlooking the light-house at the entrance to the Edgartown harbor was especially memorable for the tragedy at Chappaquiddick in which Ted Kennedy drove off a narrow bridge late at night and failed to rescue his lady companion who drowned. Our cook was the wife of the chief of police who kept us informed as the sordid story unfolded. It effectively ended Ted Kennedy's presidential prospects notwithstanding his attempt in 1980 to wrest the nomination from President Carter. He did go on to a remarkable, acclaimed career in the Senate for the next twenty-eight years until the advent of Barack Obama.

I spent some vacation time there each of these summers, flying from and to Washington after the arrival and departure visits. I am very grateful to Sally and John for the company and support they gave Mother who also treasured John. John and I would return to Martha's Vineyard for about a week for several years into the 1980s after Labor Day staying in the barn of the lovely Williamson place near Edgartown.

This was possible because my nephew, Rawn Fulton, had by then married Cynthia Williamson. Her father Clem Williamson and her step-mother were friends of Sally and Bob's, and my brother Pat and Clem had been the opposing quarterbacks on the Harvard and Yale football teams in 1929, becoming friends. Cynthia was the youngest of four sisters who would own the place after Clem died. Their mother had died many years before. Later we would rent from her older sister Gwyneth, known as "Baba", and married to Frank Smith. They lived in Houston but stayed in the Williamson house during the summers and rented out the barn to family friends such as we.

-An ABA Amicus Brief in the S&E Contractors Case in the Supreme Court.

Late in 1970, a majority of four judges of the U. S. Court of Claims decided that the Department of Justice could obtain judicial review by that court of a decision by an agency board of contract appeals or agency equivalent (in this case the commissioners of the Atomic Energy Commission) that was favorable to the contractor if that Department determined that the decision made legal errors or was not supported by substantial evidence, among the criteria that contractors could invoke in challenging adverse agency board decisions in that court.[48] Three judges dissented. This was wholly contrary to the settled understanding that the standard disputes clause made agency board decisions favorable to contractors final and conclusive absent fraud; and yet when the Supreme Court in a 1951 decision read that clause as denying contractors that right to obtain limited judicial review in the Court of Claims of an adverse decision notwithstanding the arbitrary and procedurally deficient character of the agency decision, [49] it provoked a storm of protest by industry and the GAO. The result was that in 1954 Congress enacted a law known as the "Wunderlich Act" overruling the 1951 decision and providing that agency board decisions on questions of fact were made final and conclusive unless determined by a court of competent jurisdiction to have been fraudulent, capricious or arbitrary, or so grossly erroneous as necessarily to imply bad faith, or not supported by substantial evidence.[50] It was silent on any right of the government to contest that decision if favorable to a contractor.

---

48 *S&E Contractors, Inc. v. United States*, 433 F.2d 1373 (Ct. Cl. 1970).

49 *United States v. Wunderlich*, 342 U.S. 98 (1951).

50 41 U.S.C. § 321 (1976). In addition, Section 322 adds "No Government contract shall contain a provision making final on a question of law the decision of any administrative official, representative, or board." The standard disputes clause was revised to incorporate these limitations.

In this case, the AEC Commissioners in 1964 had approved the contractor's claims in a final decision following a trial before a hearing examiner. A certifying officer asked the GAO about the propriety of paying one of them. Some 33 months later after a plenary review of the AEC decision, the GAO ruled that none of them should be paid because under the standards of the Wunderlich Act the decision made errors of law and was not supported by substantial evidence. The AEC then notified the contractor in 1967 that it would have to comply with the GAO decision to avoid GAO disallowance of any payments in the disbursing officer's accounts, thus requiring the contractor to sue in the Court of Claims to recover the $2M the AEC had awarded on its claims. The majority of the Court of Claims found nothing in the Wunderlich Act or its legislative history that denied the government in defending the suit the same scope of review that was available to contractors aggrieved by agency decisions. It remanded the case to one of its commissioners for further adversary proceedings to review the AEC decision and its underlying record under the standards of the Wunderlich Act

I strongly believed that the dissenting judges were correct and that it was vital that the contractor seek review by the Supreme Court. The contractor's lawyer was Geoff Creyke, a Washington attorney, and the first chair of the ABA Section of Public Contract Law. Trow was the current chair of the section, and he and I knew Geoff. Trow agreed with my suggestion to persuade Geoff to go to the Supreme Court, and with my further idea that we would try to get ABA authorization to file amicus briefs, one in support of the request for review, and a second on the merits if the Court granted review.

I soon met with Geoff and his able assistant, John Wiese, later an eminent judge at the successor Court of Federal Claims. Geoff was reluctant to pursue the case further either in the Court of Claims or in the Supreme Court since it was doubtful that the client would be able to pay for further legal services. Geoff and John, however, understood the importance of obtaining Supreme Court review and would file a petition, and we in turn would try to obtain ABA approval for the amicus briefs. In that way, the ABA briefs could be based on the needed legal research which we would make available to Geoff. With that green light, Trow and I mobilized a small team of first-class lawyers in our field including, Eldon "Took" Crow-ell, Gil Cuneo, Overton Currie, Marshall Doke, and John McWhorter, all friends and colleagues of Trow's and mine, to draft the briefs for our review. And Trow and other members of the team with high level ABA connections readily obtained the needed approval for us to proceed.

We timely filed the ABA amicus brief in support of granting review. To our surprise, the solicitor general, Erwin Griswold, my former dean at Harvard Law School, initially opposed the Court's acceptance of our amicus brief in support of the petition for Supreme Court review, which the Court swiftly rejected. After the petition was granted, the parties and the ABA as amicus filed briefs on the merits. After oral argument and reargument, the Court's decision upholding our position was issued in April 1972 by a 5-3 majority. Justice Douglas delivered the opinion of the Court, and Justice Blackman wrote a concurring opinion in which Chief Justice Warren and Justices Powell and Stewart also concurred. Justice Brennan, strongly dissenting, was joined by Justices Clark and Marshall. Justice Rehnquist recused himself, probably because of his then recent employment in the Justice Department.

Justice Douglas, in reversing the decision of the Court of Claims, found no authority for either GAO or the Justice Department under the contract Disputes clause[51] to apply the Wunderlich statutory crite-ria in that statute or its legislative history in reviewing the AEC deci-sion, absent fraud, when the AEC itself took no action to repudiate it on those grounds. Instead, as it informed the contractor, it was required by the GAO decision to deny payment. Indeed the case would be dif-ferent had the AEC done so, thus authorizing the Justice Department so to defend the contractor's suit. Justice Brennan's dissent provided an exhaustive history of the Disputes clause's judicial history as well as the legislative history of the Wundelich Act to show that that law and the revised Disputes clause incorporating the act's limitations on the finality

---

51   Here Justice Douglas quotes from the ABA brief "that the contractor's consent to permit a specific representative of the Government---the Commission--- should not be read as permitting any different representative of the Government to 'veto' decisions rendered by the Commission which are in favor of the contractor." 406 U.S. 1, 8 at footnote 5 (1972).

of agency decisions imposed no restrictions on the Justice Department's defense of the contractor's suit in the Court of Claims.[52]

This was a signal victory for government contractors, and it would propel me to become chair of the Section of Public Contract Law for the 1978-79 term. However, in 1978 Congress repealed the Wunderlich Act and enacted the comprehensive Contract Disputes Act of 1978 including a right of the head of the contracting agency, with the prior approval of a high level official in the Justice Department, to refer to the Court of Claims any final decision which the agency head has concluded is not entitled to finality under the act which repeats the same criteria as were in the Wunderlich Act.[53] To an extent this was the repudiation outcome foreseen by Justice Douglas as a legitimate basis for the Justice Department to apply these statutory criteria in defending against the contractor's suit. The notable difference was that under the new law the agency head usually would be acting independently of the agency board of contract appeals which would not be repudiating its decision; instead, the agency head would request an appeal based on the analysis of his lawyers who were the unsuccessful litigants in the board of contract appeals. However, experience seems to indicate that the majority of agency board decisions favorable to contractors are not appealed to the Court of Claims or its successor court, the U.S. Court of Appeals for the Federal Circuit.

-The Lockheed Navy Shipbuilding Claims and Deputy Secretary of Defense David Packard.

In 1965 and 1966 the Naval Shipbuilding Command ("NavShips", formerly BuShips) awarded Lockheed Shipbuilding & Construction Company, located in Seattle, three contracts to build seven amphibious

---

52   406 U.S. 1, at 23-69 plus 46 footnotes an appendix detailing the legislative history of the Wunderlich Act at 406 U.S. 69-90.

53   Section 14(h)(1) of Public Law 95-563, 41 U.S.C. § 601 Note (Supp. III to the 1976 edition), amending 28 U.S.C. § 2510 to add subsection (b)(1). The Contract Disputes Act of 1978 was codified at 41 U.S.C. Subtitle III by Pub. L. 111-350, enacted January 4, 2011.

transport docks, LPD 9-15, which were completed and commissioned during 1969-71. These were large ships for transporting amphibious vehicles and helicopters and personnel for Marine Corps seaborne landing operations. About 1965 NavShips awarded Lockheed an additional contract for the construction of about five DE-1052 ships. By 1969 Lockheed, with the assistance of attorneys from my office and of a Peterson team from Arthur Andersen, had submitted claims on these four contracts to NavShips aggregating $160 million. Detailed NavShips technical review of the claims by a team from NavShips at the shipyard in Seattle was scheduled to begin in August 1970, and Lockheed requested that a senior partner from our firm should participate. I was dispatched to Seattle for this purpose.

Not having participated in the preparation of the claims I had a challenging task in getting up to speed by intensive review of the claim documents, sometimes only the evening before the next day's discussion of them. This review had to address the legal basis of each claim in terms of an act or omission for which the government had contractual responsibility, as for a constructive change as discussed above. Further, it was necessary to understand the basis for the amount claimed for each such government act. The heart of most of these claims was how the increased labor hours were estimated since there were no records which distinguished between labor hours attributable to the original work and to the changed work due to a government act or omission. Alan Peterson and his team had extensively interviewed the company's engineers and personnel who had performed the changed work to arrive at their best estimates of the labor hour cost and delaying effect of each change and the extent to which each change also had disrupted and thereby increased the labor hour costs for the unchanged work. The backup for those estimates had critical importance.

These daily discussions over several weeks were intensive and exhausting. Also participating were Bob Waters, the company vice president for financial matters, and Ed James from Arthur Andersen. By December 1970, NavShips offered a tentative settlement at $58 million which Lockheed rejected. Further negotiations in January and February resulted in a tentative settlement with NavShips at $62 million subject to approval by the Navy's Contract Claims Control and Surveillance Group (CCCSG) chaired by Gordon Rule, and by the Assistant Secretary of the Navy (Installations & Logistics). As a result, the Navy made a further provisional payment of $20 million for a total of $49 million in provisional payments to Lockheed on these claims leaving a balance due of about $13 million which would be paid once the foregoing higher authorities approved the settlement.

Obtaining that approval was the responsibility of NavShips. It was never granted since the Navy responding to criticism of the Todd settlement by GAO, Senator Proxmire and Admiral Rickover[54] in April and May 1971 moved the goal posts from a settlement amount based on engineering estimates to one requiring strict proof of contemporaneous "tangible documentary evidence" that no then existing accounting system could satisfy.[55]

As a result, and after unavailing efforts by Lockheed to buttress the claims, the NavShips contracting officer in a final decision under the Disputes clause of the affected contracts notified Lockheed that under the new criteria NavShips would pay only $7.1 million on the claims and demanded that Lockheed repay the $42M NavShips had provisionally paid on them. Lockheed promptly appealed this to the ASBCA in May 1973 asserting, first, that the $62 million tentative settlement was legally enforceable against the Navy, and secondly, in any event, the value of the claims greatly exceeded $62 million. I would litigate the first claim, and Trow vom Baur the second if necessary.

Litigating the enforcement of the $62 million tentative settlement was a large endeavor. I was greatly assisted in the trial preparation by two very able Lockheed attorneys, David Bowman, the shipyard's general counsel, and Bob Gusman, a corporate attorney in Lockheed's Burbank office and whom I had known years before in the Navy OGC. From the vom Baur firm in Washington, Dick Johnson and Rob Evers provided

---

54 *See* Judge Bird's opinion in *Lockheed Shipbuilding & Construction Co.*, ASBCA No. 18460, 75-1 BCA ¶ 11.246, at 53,540, ¶ 37; 53,546, ¶ 56; 53,547, ¶ 58 (5/30/1975).

55 *Id.* at 53,543, ¶ 47, 53,548, ¶ 66.

excellent legal research and back-up support, particularly in the post-trial briefing of the case. There would be a sizeable discovery program with several depositions and a large number of trial witnesses.

Our claim of the enforceability of the settlement was based on the relationship of that settlement to the totality of the resolution of the Lockheed Corporation's pending claims of almost $1 billion on three other military programs and losses on the L-1011 commercial aircraft program, all of which threatened the corporation with bankruptcy. These other military programs, in order of financial magnitude, were the Air Force fixed-price "total package"[56] contract for the production of the C-5A transport aircraft which would be restructured under Public Law 85-804 in the interests of national defense with Lockheed absorbing a further fixed loss of $200 million; an estimated loss of $150 million on the two Army fixed-price contracts for the "Cheyenne" helicopter, a R&D contract and a production contract which would be resolved, again under Public Law 85-804, by converting the R&D contract to a cost-reimbursement contract; and the $100 million claim on the Army fixed-price SRAM missile motor program under which Lockheed was a subcontractor to Boeing and which was later settled for $20 million under normal procedures.

David Packard, one of the founders of Hewlett-Packard, during this period was the Deputy Secretary of Defense from 1969-71 and was the principal government actor in this matter, determined to keep Lockheed financially afloat not only to complete these four programs but also because of the critical importance of other Lockheed programs to the national defense such as the Polaris missile program. Also critical for Lockheed was the continued availability of its $400 million line of credit from a consortium of 24 banks, of which $50 million remained available. The banks had notified Lockheed that any further credit required that the claims on these four programs be settled at amounts consistent with the company's financial viability.

---

56   My partner, Bob Turtle, had participated extensively in the planning of this contract for the Air Force when serving his military obligation in the Air Force general counsel's office.

Before the trial, we became aware of the necessity for the imminent resolution of all four programs from reading Secretary Packard's December 30, 1970, letter to the Chairmen of the House and Senate Armed Services Committees. In that letter he reviewed the status of each of these programs. With respect to the shipbuilding claims he reported that the Navy had offered Lockheed a settlement of $58 million and would be settled for at least that amount. His letter concluded, "Our actions in settling the disputes on the four defense contracts will resolve contingent liabilities of Lockheed and, we hope, provide a degree of certainty to the overall affairs of Lockheed that will permit the banks to continue to finance the commercial programs, and avoid bankruptcy...The final details of the settlement and the documents necessary to implement the plan are now being prepared, and will be completed by the end of January 1971."[57]

On February 2, 1971, as the revised credit agreement based on the acceptance of Secretary's plan by Lockheed and the banks was being executed, the parties learned that Rolls Royce, the supplier of the engines for the L-1011 aircraft had announced bankruptcy, putting Lockheed in a critical cash position with about $700 million invested in that program. This development made the new credit agreement insufficient, and the banks in April 1971 said they would enlarge it from $600 million to $750 million to take account of this development only with a government guarantee of at least $250 million.[58]

Led by Treasury Secretary John Connally and Secretary Packard, Congress passed the Emergency Loan Guarantee Act, signed by President Nixon on August 9, 1971 as Public Law 92-70 authorizing the newly created Emergency Loan Guarantee Board to guarantee $250 million of the $750 million to be provided under the new credit agreement in return for which Lockheed accepted before tax losses of $484 million on all four defense programs at the settlement amounts contemplated by Secretary Packard.[59] While Secretary Packard, the banks, and Lockheed

---

57 *Lockheed Shipbuilding & Construction Company, supra,* 75-1 BCA at 53,534-35, ¶ 17.g.

58 *Id.* at 53,539-40, ¶¶ 33, 34.

59 *Id..* at 53,542, ¶42; 53,544-45, ¶¶ 51, 52.

understood that the $62 million ship claims had not been settled, all understood the required approvals of higher authority to be a formality and perfunctory.[60]

Before the trial we took several depositions, including Secretary Packard's during which he confirmed the foregoing. Gordon Rule came to his deposition bearing me a rose in a vase of water.

The trial of the case was held in 1974 in a federal courtroom in Los Angeles and later at the ASBCA near Washington, each before Administrative Judge Lee Bird, my former Navy OGC office roommate 20 years previously. Secretary Packard flew to Los Angeles in his corporate jet from Palo Alto. He testified as follows regarding the $62 million tentative settlement:

> I expected the Navy to implement the agreement that they assured me they had worked out, and I considered that in my discussions with the company and the bank[s]. I certainly intended to convey to them my conviction that this whole claim would be settled for $62 million. I intended to imply by my statement to the company, to the lawyers and to the Congress that a commitment was made to several Lockheed claims...It was my understanding that the Navy was going to settle the claim at that figure, at $62 million, and I intended to convey that impression to the people I dealt with on this matter.[61]

From this and his other statements in 1970 and 1971, we argued that Secretary Packard, although unfamiliar with the details of the $62 million tentative settlement or the Navy procedures for final review and approval, nevertheless committed to Lockheed, the banks, and to Congress that that settlement would be so approved and could be relied on by Lockheed and the banks as part of the total package of settlements on the four programs in order for Lockheed to agree to Secretary Packard's overall settlement plan by accepting a the tax losses of $484 million and for the banks to continue to finance Lockheed once the revised $750 million

---

60   *Id.* at 53,543 at ¶¶ 45, 46.

61   *Id.*. at 53,537, ¶ 25.e.

credit agreement with the $250 million government loan guarantee was executed on September 14, 1971.[62]

The trial in both cities had numerous witnesses. In Los Angeles, Secretary Packard was the first and principal witness. Also testifying there was Dan Haughton, the CEO of Lockheed, Ralph Osborne, a senior Lockheed executive who had also dealt with Secretary Packard, Secretary Connally and the banks on these matters, and Bob Waters, now the Lockheed corporate controller who had negotiated the $62 million tentative settlement with NavShips.

At the ASBCA hearing at its offices near Washington, other witnesses included former Secretary of the Navy John Warner who testified to his understanding of Secretary Packard's plan of settlement of the four defense programs; Rear Admiral Sonnenshein who had approved the $62 million settlement for NavShips; Rear Admiral Woodfin his contracting officer who tried to obtain the required higher approvals from higher authority and why he understood through September 14, 1971, that that approval would be forthcoming and was a formality and perfunctory and so communicated that through Admiral Sonnenshein to Secretary Packard, to Hugh McCullough, the chair of the special committee Secretary Packard established to monitor the settlement of the four programs, and to a Mr. Greene, Secretary to the Emergency Loan Guarantee Board; and Messrs. Moore and Leary of the Bankers Trust Co. who spoke for the consortium of 24 banks financing Lockheed of their understanding that the banks could count on the settlement of the ship claims for $62 million based on what Secretary Packard had told them, among others. The government defense relied primarily on cross-examining these witnesses by their trial attorney Morris Amchan, a veteran of the Nuremburg war crimes prosecution whom I had known in Navy OGC.

In the post-trial briefing of the case to Judge Bird we argued first that the acceptance of Secretary Packard's overall plan for the settlement of all four defense programs by Lockheed and the banks on September 14, 1971, following the execution of the $750 million credit agreement

---

62   *Id. at* 53,548-9, ¶ 68.

by the parties after approval of the $250 million government guaranteed loan to the banks, constituted a binding contract that required the Navy to pay the amounts due Lockheed under the $62 million "tentative" settlement notwithstanding that the required approval by higher Navy authority would never be forthcoming. In the alternative, we argued that in any event the government was estopped to deny the enforceability of that settlement. Judge Bird rejected the first argument and accepted the second, finding that the requisite elements of both promissory and equitable estoppel were present.

The Navy in its brief argued strongly that there could be no estoppel since the tentative settlement was made expressly subject to approval by higher Navy authority in accordance with published regulations having the force of law which Secretary Packard had never waived. Judge Bird rejected that argument, finding that Secretary Packard's actions as described above amounted to a waiver which was well within his plenary authority as the Deputy Secretary of Defense.

Judge Bird's decision was issued on May 13, 1975.[63] Four other members of the ASBCA participated in that decision. Three judges concurred in the decision, including Judge Richard Solibakke, the then chairman of the ASBCA, and Judge Harris Andrews, Jr., a vice chairman. Judge John Lane, Jr., dissented, arguing that Lockheed knew or should have known the true facts during the critical period that it could never meet the stricter documentation requirements for obtaining the higher Navy approval of the tentative settlement, thus not meeting one of the critical requirements, ignorance of the true facts, for an estoppel against the government.

The Navy promptly requested reconsideration of the decision and oral argument before the ASBCA. The request was granted, and the matter was argued on September 12, 1975 before all five judges who participated in the original decision. Judge Bird presided. I argued for Lockheed and Morris Amcham for the Navy. Its principal arguments were echoing Judge Lane's dissent that Lockheed was not ignorant of the true facts and that Secretary Packard did not have the authority to bypass, nor did he

63 Note 58 *supra*.

intend to bypass, the Navy regulatory requirements for higher approval of the tentative settlement. Judge Bird and the same three other judges rejected these arguments.[64] Again Judge Lane dissented as before but now suggesting that at most the ASBCA should find the Navy estopped to apply the new documentation requirements and remand the matter to the Navy for review of the merits of the tentative settlement under the prior standards.

So concluded this landmark case and the comprehensive, thorough, precedent-setting and masterful opinions of Judge Bird. At the Navy's request, the Justice Department began a year-long baseless investigation of any indications of Lockheed fraud in the presentation of the ship claims to the Navy in an effort to obtain a forfeiture of the $49 million paid and to avoid payment of the balance of $13 million. A courageous career senior attorney in the Civil Division of the Justice Department, Irving Jaffe, finally stopped this nonsense and directed that the payment be made.

In a subsequent proceeding in the ASBCA we unsuccessfully sought to recover several million dollars in interest on the delayed payment of that balance. In an opinion by Judge Lane he held, in an ironic twist, that Lockheed was estopped to challenge the finality of the $62 million settlement[65]; he further ruled that the release terms of that settlement barred the interest claims. Judge Bird did not participate in that decision.[66] By then he had retired after a distinguished career at the Board, unquestionably one of its greatest judges.

In looking back at this, I am astonished that the Navy did not challenge the Board's jurisdiction to rule on the arguments we made to enforce the tentative $62 million settlement. Had we litigated to prove the merits of the ship claims there would be no question of the Board's

---

64 *Lockheed Shipbuilding and Construction Company*, ASBCA No. 18460, 75-2 BCA ¶ 11,566 (10/24/1975).

65 This was highly questionable since there was no showing that Lockheed was "ignorant of the true facts", one of the required elements of equitable estoppel.

66 *Lockheed Shipbuilding and Construction Company*, ASBCA No. 18460, 77-1 BCA ¶ 12,458 (March 29, 1977).

jurisdiction to decide them under the terms of the contracts under which they arose.

By the terms of the standard Disputes clause of these contracts, the ASBCA had jurisdiction to decide only disputed "questions of fact arising under the contract" which the contracting officer had decided adversely to the contractor and from which the contractor had timely appealed to the Board. Our enforcement argument was that Secretary Packard's overall plan for resolution of the four troubled Lockheed programs when accepted by Lockheed and the banks contractually enforced the $62 million tentative settlement; and in any event estopped the Navy from denying the finality of that settlement. It's hard to see that these arguments come within disputed "questions of fact arising under the contract", especially the equitable doctrine of estoppel. Had the Navy so challenged the Board's jurisdiction, even at the reconsideration stage, I don't see now how we or the Board would have overcome it. As it was, one could say the ASBCA decided the case on the estoppel ground with the implied consent of the parties to the Board's jurisdiction to do so.

-The Lockheed Blue River Dam Litigation.

As I recall my first connection with the Lockheed Shipbuilding and Construction Company was in 1969 or 1970 when I went to Seattle to replace my partner Dick Johnson who for several months had prepared a changed conditions claim for Lockheed against the Army Corps of Engineers on the Blue River Dam project which Lockheed had recently completed. At that point another one of our clients had an emergency need for Dick's services based on prior work he had done, and Trow and I thought I could pinch hit for Dick in litigating the claim now that the Corps had denied it.

In addition to its shipbuilding work for the Navy, the Lockheed Company in Seattle was also engaged in construction work. It had recently completed the construction of the north-south Interstate Highway 5 through the Seattle segment, and was bidding on a variety of government construction projects.

In November 1965 the Corps had awarded a $15.6 million contract to Lockheed as the low bidder to construct this dam and complete an auxiliary dam at the Blue River Reservoir, in Lane County, Oregon, located in high wilderness some 50 miles east of Eugene. Lockheed successfully completed this civil works project of the Corps and now was concerned to recover some $4.5 million of additional costs from having to obtain some of the needed quantities of embankment materials from a more distant location than indicated on the government drawings. My job in Seattle was to prepare the case for trial before the Corps of Engineers Board of Contract Appeals several months later.

One of Trow vom Baur's great strengths was his extensive experience as a trial lawyer with the Milbank Tweed firm in New York for about a decade before WW II. One of the firm's clients was the Borden Milk Co. which faced incessant litigation by persons complaining of being harmed by Borden's horse drawn milk wagons or trucks. Learning from the firm's seasoned older jury trial lawyers, Trow soon developed and deepened his own considerable skills in trial work.

The lessons of this experience he passed on to the lawyers in his firm. The first was preparation, and more preparation, to learn all the facts of the case to be tried, those that helped and those that hurt. These facts were usually technical in diverse fields of knowledge such as accounting, various types of engineering, dam and road construction, and shipbuilding, among others. In addition to the facts, the trial lawyer had to master the applicable contract provisions and the case law applying them.

Next, this meant intensive work with each trial witness and after extensive interviewing drafting and redrafting each question and answer for careful review by each witness as needed so that the witness would be prepared for each question and would repeat the substance of each answer that the attorney has drafted as expressing what the witness had decided to answer as the whole truth called for by the question. The questions and answers would also cover the weak points in the case, often in anticipation of the likely cross-examination to minimize the harm the cross-examination might otherwise achieve.

Before trial, each witness would read these drafts of the other witnesses and would sometimes suggest necessary modifications to the other witnesses draft testimony. Finally, on the eve of trial we would have a final live rehearsal of all the witness testimony before a critical audience of the other witnesses and attorneys working on the case. All this resembled the staging of a play with the actors having to learn their lines.

Also before trial and witness preparation there would be usually extensive discovery by both sides of the documents not subject to claims of privilege such as attorney-client communications, attorney work products, and the prospective witness testimony of the other side. This often took considerable time and preparation and expense to the client as well.

I employed these methods in preparing the Lockheed witnesses for the trial of the Blue River Dam case and conducting discovery. I later did so with the many witnesses in the Lockheed ship case described above as well except for Secretary Packard with whom I had had no opportunity to prepare. Having taken his deposition, I knew pretty well what he would say. At the trial in Los Angeles I asked him one question: "Mr. Secretary, would you please tell Judge Bird about your involvement in this matter?" That was sufficient for him fully to tell the whole story. When he finished, perhaps 20 or 25 minutes later, I said "Thank you, Mr. Secretary. Mr. Amcham you may now cross-examine." The cross-examination served to reinforce the decisive persuasiveness of Secretary Packard's direct testimony. The witness was excused.

In the Blue River Dam case, the challenge for me was to learn the technical facts applicable to the contract dispute as well as the case law interpreting the "Changed Conditions" clause of the construction contract (later renamed "Differing Site Conditions") which would govern Lockheed's entitlement to recover. In preparing its bid, Lockheed from its examination of the government drawings estimated that it would be able to obtain about 1.5 million cubic yards of the approximate 4 million cubic yards of embankment material of various specified gradations of boulders, cobbles, gravel, and sand from the Middle Gravel Borrow and the balance from the more distant Upper Gravel Borrow from the dam site. In fact, Lockheed was able to recover only about 280,000 cubic yards of usable material from the Middle Gravel Borrow due to encountering rock and silt at elevations significantly above those indicated on the government drawings. It claimed further that due to a contour error on the government drawings, Lockheed was misled into estimating the availability of some 585,000 cubic yards of usable material in the Middle Gravel Borrow that did not exist.

Following the trial, Administrative Judge Ryan, with Administrative Judges Jellico and Reosti concurring, accepted the first claim and rejected the second, finding that other government drawings should have alerted Lockheed to the contour error so that its reliance was misplaced. The Board remanded the case to the contracting officer for the negotiation of an equitable adjustment in the contract price for obtaining the approximately 600,000 cubic yards of additional material from the more distant Upper Gravel Borrow due to the changed condition in the Middle Gravel Borrow.[67] The parties promptly reached a settlement.

Preparing for this trial took several months of my time in Seattle and in Portland, Oregon, where the trial took place over several days. I was greatly aided in understanding the case from the claim document my partner Dick Johnson had previously prepared for Lockheed to submit to the contracting officer at the Corps' district office in Portland, and from discussions with Ed James of Alan's Peterson's team and with our principal witnesses. They were Dick Hix, the construction manager, Dick Appuhn, the project engineer, and an expert witness on soil mechanics whose name I no longer remember. All these witnesses were excellent and were a joy to work with and to prepare and rehearse their testimony.

After trial and the availability of the trial transcript of the testimony, preparing the post-trial brief and then the reply brief to the government's brief required my further presence in Seattle. Not long after the briefing and submitting the case for decision, my return to Washington and other

---

67 *Lockheed Shipbuilding and Construction Company*, ENG BCA No. 3141, 74-1 BCA ¶ 10, 512 (February 12, 1974).

work was interrupted by the NavShips' contracting officer's final decision on the $62 million tentative settlement of the ship claims in which
he now asserted that the claims had been documented only to the extent
of some $7 million. I would again return to Seattle for that litigation as
described above.

-The ABA Annual Meeting in London in August 1971 and Travel in Europe.

This was a three-week's vacation for Don Ellington and me, my first
return to England or Europe since 1945. The previous summer Don with
his friends Betty Winspear and Bonnie Young had a wonderful few weeks
motoring through England and Scotland, including time in London
which made this visit quite familiar for him. In London we stayed very
comfortably for a week at Dukes, a small, upscale hotel at St. James's
Place and near the lovely Green Park for our early morning walks, and
then left for the second and third weeks in Munich, Salzburg, Vienna,
Siena, Rome, Bad Homburg, Paris, and home.

The American Bar Association meeting began in Westminster Hall,
first built about 1100. The Lord Chief Justice of England, attired in
a magnificent robe, wig, and the regalia of his high office, greeted us.
He began by saying, "Welcome home!" He continued with an inspiring account of how the Common Law, the law common among Englishmen, had its beginnings in this very place almost a thousand years
earlier and how it grew and spread to the American colonies and why
the common law was one of the important bonds that unites our
two countries in the rule of law.[68] It was a felicitous welcome laced
with understated learning and good humor that educated Englishmen speak so brilliantly well. John Mitchell, then our Attorney General, made his reply. He appeared unprepared, feeble, flat and dull, an
embarrassment.

---

68   *See* Churchill, *A History of the English Speaking Peoples*, vol. One, *The Birth of Britain*, ch. 13, *The English Common Law*, 215-25 (Barnes & Noble 1993).

While in London, I had bar association events most days as Don did sightseeing. Our evenings included some theater I no longer remember as well as attending a revue by the drag queen Dannie LaRue which amused us.

One day I travelled to Brighton to see Thelma Fox, Lyttleton's widow, who had returned to England with her children after his death some six years earlier to live with her twin sister Gabrielle. Thelma seemed much the same, and I was glad to meet the young son and two daughters who seemed well mannered and brought up. Sadly and suddenly, about two years later she died, whereupon Dinah, Lyttleton's first wife, now happily remarried as Dinah Bridge and with a young child, arranged to have Lyttleton's children live with her and her husband and raise and educate them, which they wonderfully did. She always loved Lyttleton but found him mentally too exhausting to live with. She had two children with Lyttleton, now grown up, Phyllis, named for her maternal grandmother Phyllis Langhorne Brand,[69] and James, named for her mother's brother who was tragically killed by enemy fire in Germany in March, 1945, near the end of the war in Europe. I would see all the Fox children in October 2001 when Don I returned to London for several days and as I will later relate in Part Six.

The second week we stayed in Munich at an old-fashioned hotel that had been rebuilt as the result of bomb damage during the war. There were still visible reminders of the severe bombing of the city during the war, and a great effort was under way to have that removed before the summer Olympic Games began in 1972. Munich still had much of its ancient charm which the ongoing restoration was determined to preserve, and there was much to see including the incomparable Meissen porcelain of which we purchased one or two pieces. One evening we went to the

---

69 One of the famous and beautiful Langhorne sisters of Virginia, one of whom, Irene, the famous and still beautiful "Gibson girl" who had married the artist Charles Dana Gibson and whom I had come to know in the summer of 1949 in Dark Harbor, Maine, as I have recounted in Part Three of these memoirs. For a splendid biography of her and her sisters, Lizzie, Nancy, Phyllis, and Nora, by the grandson of Phyllis and Robert Brand, Lyttleton and Dinah's eldest son, James Fox, please read *Five Sisters, the Langhornes of Virginia* (Simon & Schuster Paperbacks 2001).

beautifully restored opera house for a performance of Verdi's *Simon Boccanegra* magnificently done. We wore business suits, everyone else evening attire, the ladies laden with girth and dripping with jewelry, "Schmuck" in German. We went to see King Ludwig's fairy tale castle "Schloss Neuschwanstein", incomplete but beguiling.

Next we boarded a steamer at Passau for the voyage down the Danube and another river to Salzburg where Don had spent 1947 working for the Army. The annual summer Mozart festival of concerts and operas had already happened but Don and I enjoyably visited his past haunts. Then by train to Vienna which impressed me more as a museum of great architecture, fine arts, parks, and former glories than as a thriving commercial metropolis in our era.

We had arranged to visit my niece Joanie, the daughter of my brother Mike and his wife Joan, now recently married to Nicolo Casini and living near Siena in Tuscany. Joanie had spent part of her junior year at Radcliffe at the University of Florence where Nicolo as a student was lying in wait for a lovely girl such as she. They decided to marry that summer to which her parents and his mother gradually yielded. Finishing college would wait. They did marry that summer of 1969 in a church near her parent's home in Needham, Massachusetts, where Joanie had grown up. Work kept me from attending. When Don and I visited them about two years later they were living in a spacious ancient villa of Nicolo's family near Siena which they were slowly restoring with the help of two elderly family retainers who also looked after them.

We stayed several days and had a lovely encounter. Don and I loved Joanie and we liked Nicolo. He was an only child. His father, a banker, lost his life early in his marriage to Chiara leading his regiment in the war on the Eastern Front and never knew his son. She, a lady of great charm, cultivation and social position, raised Nicolo and never remarried. When Don and I visited Joanie and Nicolo, Chiara lived in a very grand apartment in the center of Siena with exquisite art and furnishings and remained there several more decades as now does one of her married granddaughters. We were disappointed to miss meeting her.

One evening we dined in a restaurant in the ancient and architecturally rich city of Siena near the Piazza del Campo where the Palio, the annual horse race around the square, takes place each summer. When the waiter presented me with the bill, Nicolo summoned the waiter and told him to resubmit it to him as a resident of Siena which reduced the price for the American by at least half and which I gladly and gratefully paid.

By then Joanie was fluent in proper Italian, and Nicolo's accented English was adequate and improving. Their five as yet unborn children would all be bilingual and have dual Italian-U.S. citizenship. After the first three daughters, the last of whom arrived about a year after our visit, Nicolo's bachelor uncle and his mother's brother told him that unless you have a son everything I have goes to the Church. Fortunately, their next child was Clemente, and when the uncle died a year or two later Nicolo inherited a great deal of property which enabled him to pursue his interests in the cultivation of grapes, production and marketing of their own label of wines on their lands with Joanie's business acumen and in the breeding of race horses.

Their fifth and last child, a daughter whom they named Maddelena ("Maggie"), arrived a few years after Clemente to join her older sisters Elisa, Rebecca, and Alessandra, all of whom were honors graduates of college, beauties, and are now wonderfully married with children. Elisa obtained a doctorate in mathematics, married her professor, and like him for a period of time taught that challenging subject to college students. Maggie, equally a brilliant student and beautiful, will earn a prestigious master's degree in finance in 2012 from the London School of Economics. Clemente, a late bloomer, has established himself running a hotel of his father's and is engaged to marry an American, Harmony Davies, in Rome in the spring of 2012. Growing up, for many summers all those children with their mother lived with Mike and Joan at their summer home in Wareham on Buzzard's Bay which I have described in Part One of these memoirs. This perfected their English and enabled them to bond with their countless Coburn and Shaw cousins.

Don and I next went to Rome for a few days of seeing the glorious art and architecture of the city and the Vatican which needs no description from me. We then flew to Frankfurt to visit Dick Coburn, brother Pat's and his wife Marty's second son, then and for the next 25 years teaching English at the International School established there primarily for the children of foreign parents residing in that part of West Germany. Dick lived in a very attractive, small rental apartment in nearby Bad Homburg with beautiful parks and trees. He showed us the magnificent cathedral at Cologne, the damage from the wartime bombing not having been fully repaired, and other interesting sights which I do not remember.

A day or two later we flew to Paris for two days and the flight home. I did not try to contact the Wengers in Maison Lafitte, the family with whom I lived for a few months in the winter and spring of 1945 as I have recounted in Part Two. There was no time, the parents were likely no longer living, and I did not know how to contact their children Hubert and Edith.

All in all, Don and I had a wonderful, event-filled, three weeks in England, West Germany, Austria, Italy and France. He and I would not return to England or Europe until September 2001 as I shall relate in Part Six.

-Life in Seattle and Elsewhere.

My Mother's older sister Elizabeth and her husband Robert Brinkley moved to Seattle about 1910, he to run a lumber business in nearby Edmonds where they first lived. Uncle Bob died in 1935, and Aunt Elizabeth thereafter lived in Seattle. In Part One I have recounted the very enjoyable summer of 1940 Mother and I had with her and their mother, my grandmother Florence Rawn, on Bainbridge Island on Seattle's Puget Sound.

By the time I returned to Seattle in 1969 or 1970, Aunt Elizabeth and her daughter Betty who had married the naval architect George Nickum had died, and George had remarried one of Betty's best friends, Mary Ann ("M.A") Eddy. By then George and Betty's several children were grown and married, the two sons Nick and Will whom I would come to know, particularly Nick and his wife Peg, were living in the Seattle area, and the daughters in Canada. Nick was or soon would be a lawyer practicing and living in Bainbridge Island while Will would join his father's firm.

My nephew David Coburn, Pat's youngest son, would soon move to the Seattle area; and later my great nephew Jed Nahum, the elder son of my niece Katherine Harding Nahum and her husband Jeremy Nahum, with his wife Carol. I would soon meet Peter Rawn, a second cousin descendant of one of my grandfather Ira Rawn's brothers, and his wife Polly. There was therefore, an abundance of family relatives for me to see in Seattle if and when I had the time on some weekends.

Because Lockheed work required my presence in Seattle throughout much of the 1970s, after initial stays in the Washington Plaza Hotel, I eventually rented a small furnished apartment on Queen Anne Hill and commuted to the shipyard from the hotel and the apartment often by bicycle which provided much needed exercise.

I would see George and M.A. Nickum who had a lovely summer home on Bainbridge Island near where I had visited during the summer of 1940 as well as an attractive one in a gated community in Seattle. I became fond of them, and their hospitality to me was generous and affectionate. George was probably the leading naval architect in the north western U. S. For example, he designed the spacious car ferries we would ride from Seattle to Bainbridge Island. At their house there on a clear day there were breathtaking views of Mt. Rainier (14,400') to the south, the Cascades to the east and the Olympics to the west, all mostly snow-capped in the summer months.

While staying at the Washington Plaza Hotel I became friends with Gary Michael Cope who worked at the front desk. A graduate of the University of Oregon in Eugene and born and raised in Juneau, Alaska, I found him at just turned 25 to be exceptionally bright and attractive, and I increasingly sought his company. He was gay. We had a memorable evening on January 27, 1972, dining at the Canlis Restaurant overlooking Lake Union and Capitol Hill. This was also my Mother's and Mozart's birthdays. So began an intimate relationship that graduated to an affectionate friendship that continues as I write this some forty years later. To my delight, he and Don liked each other when they met in Washington on a few later visits Gary made there. Gary went on to hold positions of increasing responsibility in other Westin Hotels in Seattle, Atlanta, and Los Angeles, and in the corporate offices in Seattle and Salt Lake City. Had he remained he would, I am confident, have become a senior executive of that hotel chain and its successor.

In 1993, after 23 years at Westin, he wearied of corporate life and moved to the Hawaiian island of Maui where with two friends, Mike Darlow and his partner Curt Thompson, he purchased a home. After returning to Westin for a special project in 1998-99, Gary returned to Maui but relocated in Tucson, Arizona, where he continues to live. For many years we have had enjoyable Sunday evening telephone calls.

While in Seattle Gary and I took some enjoyable trips to Vancouver in British Columbia and to Victoria on Vancouver Island to see the beautiful Buchart Gardens in an abandoned quarry. One of the trips to Victoria was on the October weekend in 1973 when President Nixon ordered the dismissal of Archibald Cox, the distinguished Harvard Law School professor whom Attorney General Eliot Richardson had appointed as a special prosecutor to investigate the Watergate affair and the president's involvement in that tawdry matter. In protest of the dismissal order, Richardson and his deputy resigned, creating the political firestorm of the "October Massacre" and leading to the president's resignation the following August.

In June 1972, after the trial in the Blue River Dam case, I went to Eugene, Oregon, for the wedding of my nephew Travis Fulton to Molly (I no longer remember her surname). Although an unusually hot weekend, I had a pleasant reunion with my brothers Pat and Mike and their wives and with Bob and Sally Fulton and their other sons Robin and Rawn and their wives. Travis, a graduate of Brooks School and Brandeis University, and a Peace Corps alumnus from having served in Tunisia, was now a sculptor and landscape artist living in Aspen, Colorado. He would go far. Sadly, the marriage did not last. There were no issue. He would later remarry briefly and have two children, Maya and Montgomery, who have grown up and are flourishing. While in Eugene I drove with Marty Coburn, Pat's wife, to see the Blue River Dam. For me, this was the only visit. The scenery was magnificent wilderness in the mountains. The embankment main and auxiliary dams on the Blue River seemed to blend into their surroundings as if nature had created them. It was a beautiful summer day and an enjoyable outing for Marty and me.

During these Seattle years I finally heeded Sally's insistent request that I look up Randolph Urmston, a young lawyer who had recently moved to Seattle. Randy was the son of her friends Maud and Tom Urmston who had a summer home on Martha's Vineyard and where Sally and I knew them. We finally met for dinner, Randy with Sheila Noonan, the attractive young lady he was courting. To my great surprise, Sheila was one of the children of my 1940 Seattle friend Catherine Baillargeon, now recently divorced after many years of marriage to Derwint Noonan and several children and now living in Seattle. I was delighted to see Catherine again, some thirty years later and resume a friendship. I sensed she hoped for more from me, and Gary Cope called us "the odd couple". She would later marry Frank Brownell, a cousin of Rawn Brinkley's wife Franny and a professor of mathematics at the University of Washington and they would live on Bainbridge Island. Sadly, Catherine died some thirty years later.

Don flew in for a visit of several days, his first to Seattle. Our drive to see the beautiful Olympic peninsula with its snow-capped mountains was marred by rain and fog; equally disappointing to him was that he never saw Mt. Rainier, being cloud-covered throughout his visit.

-Mother's Last Years.

By the summer or fall of 1972, Mother then in her later eighties required assisted living arrangements. My brother Pat found a suitable nursing home in Somers, New York, about a dozen miles from where he and Marty lived in Katonah and also accessible to my sister Sally in

Newtown, Connecticut. Pat and Mike moved her there and she was comfortably looked after. I was glad to pay the monthly fees of about $3K. This meant giving up Mother's rented apartment at 239 Commonwealth Avenue in Boston where she had lived for many years and distributing its contents which Mike, living in the suburb of Needham, was able to do. Pat received the English dining room table, chairs and corner cabinet. The rest of the furniture, the flat silver, china and glass, books and pictures were shipped to me in Washington where they greatly added to the furnishings of our lovely, spacious house on Capitol Hill at 401 6th Street SE.

We, her surviving four children and my siblings' spouses, all celebrated Mother's birthday on the Saturday nearest to her January 27, 1974, 90th birthday at a dinner gathering at Pat and Marty's house. Mother rose to the occasion and delighted us. It was a gala evening. She looked younger, no wrinkles in her face, a trim figure, good vision and hearing, far better than what we usually see in a lady of that age. She suffered somewhat from emphysema even though she had stopped smoking some ten years before, and dementia was gradually encroaching. In September when I happened to be in Washington I got word that the end was near and I would see her for the last time as did Sally. A week or so later she died peacefully in her sleep from old age. We held the funeral and burial at the beautiful Mayflower Cemetery in Duxbury in the family plot where she joined her husband and her daughter Louise. George Nickum was in Washington on business and we flew together to Boston and drove to Duxbury. It was loving of him to do this, to go to the funeral of his mother-in-law's younger sister, and we all greatly appreciated that.

Mother was a devoted wife and mother, gentle, refined, loving, to almost the end a whiz at bridge and cross-word puzzles, and a lover of European 19th century classical music and opera. She adored and somewhat spoiled her children but had a tendency to try to exert control over their activities long after she should have adjusted to new relationships with them. When living with her in Boston while I finished college and law school, I learned we got along well if I would say "Yes, Mother" when she would importune and then do pretty much what I wanted. Sally, sadly, never learned this and would argue and fight her requests on principle, which harmed their relationship. Yet Mother was a force for good in our lives, and we were thus blessed with two wonderful, caring parents until alcohol destroyed Papa.

In 1974 there occurred two other events in my life that I should recount. First, I quit smoking, mostly Kent filtered cigarettes, which I had begun while interrogating Germans for local government jobs and otherwise in the summer and fall of 1945 as I have related in Part Two. While not a heavy smoker, I became increasingly aware of the harm it would likely cause later, and so I decided to stop. While the first several weeks were difficult, I stuck to it and never smoked again. Don unfortunately continued to be a heavy smoker of Lucky Strike cigarettes for another 20 years and this undoubtedly hastened his death in 2005 although he had stopped some 10 years before.

The second event in 1974 was pure vanity on my part. I started wearing a wig to cover my bald head. I had lost most of my hair in the 1950s. A handsome young friend, Art Thomas, surprised me by saying he wore one that I would not have detected or even suspected. When he showed me I was astonished. He told me the name of his wig maker on Connecticut Avenue, and I promptly made an appointment to order one for about $600. First made of human hair, later models were synthetic material, lasted longer and became more expensive. I continued wearing wigs until about 2000 when I began shaving my head with barber's clippers. My wearing a wig did not provoke much comment one way or the other. Opinion was divided; I now think it was absurd.

-The Lockheed Icebreaker Pricing Litigation.

In July 1971 the Lockheed Shipbuilding and Construction Company was awarded a contract to build a new "Polar Class" of icebreaker for the Coast Guard, the first it had procured since 1954. It was to be a 400-foot battering ram of about 10,000 tons to be built to Coast Guard specifications, including new strengthened steel and stringent steel welding and propulsion requirements to assure the ship's thick ice-breaking capabilities. The contract was awarded after formal advertising for bids. Four shipyards submitted bids. Lockheed's bid of $46M compared with the other three at $48.7, $53.5, and $59.9M. The Coast Guard estimate was $50.3M. Each bid added a separate amount for design work, Lockheed's was $5.2M, the others between $3M and $6M. The high bid of $59.9M was by the Todd Shipyard in Seattle which had the same union labor rates as Lockheed. On request, Lockheed confirmed its bid in writing to the contracting officer.

In 1972 the Coast Guard obtained an appropriation of $66M from Congress for a second icebreaker of this class. It decided to award the contract for this second ice breaker to Lockheed on a negotiated sole-source basis to obtain the cost benefits of eliminating the cost of the design work, a higher labor learning curve, and reduced material costs. This also meant that the award to Lockheed would have to be made by the end of January 1973 to achieve these cost reductions. Because time did not permit the negotiation of a firm fixed-price by that date, the parties in January negotiated the award of an unpriced letter contract as "Modification 70" to the first icebreaker contract. In paragraph 1 it obligated the parties "to enter into negotiations to establish a firm fixed price for this modification within the time frame established in paragraph 7 herein." Each of these paragraphs also stated, "In no event shall the firm fixed price for the work described herein exceed $53,750,000", a price ceiling the parties had negotiated. Paragraph 8, drafted by the government, provided:

If agreement on price is not reached by the target date for establishment of firm fixed price as set forth in paragraph 7 above, or any extension thereof granted by the Contracting Officer in writing, the Contracting Officer may determine a reasonable price in accordance with Federal Procurement Regulation Subpart 1-3.8 and Part 1-15 subject to appeal by the contractor as provided in the 'Disputes' clause of the contract. The price shall be reasonable, considering actual costs incurred and cost projections on WAGB-10 [the first icebreaker], giving due consideration to inflationary factors, learning efficiencies and nonrecurring costs which would affect the cost of WAGB-11 [the second icebreaker], and applying 'should cost' techniques where appropriate. Profit rates shall be based on realized historical profit, considering company and industry wide experience. In any event, the contractor shall proceed with completion of the work specified herein.

In negotiating the letter contract the parties did not discuss the meaning of this paragraph 8 and its relationship, if any, to the price ceiling in paragraphs 1 and 7 which would emerge as the principal dispute between them in the ensuing litigation of the determination of a "reasonable price" by the Department of Transportation Contract Appeals Board in 1979.[70] The negotiation timetable was repeatedly extended as Lockheed submitted revised price proposals in greater amounts, each above the ceiling price.

Negotiations collapsed in October 1973 with Lockheed's price proposal of $60.5M with an estimated ship cost of about $54.7M, the first at the cost level before profit to exceed the $53.7M ceiling price. During these negotiations the application of the ceiling price to a price determination under paragraph 8 as insisted on by the Coast Guard contracting officer was rejected by Lockheed which asserted that the ceiling price only applied to the fixed price to be negotiated under paragraph 7. At the end of January 1974, the contracting officer issued a unilateral determination of a "reasonable price" under paragraph 8 of an estimated cost of $47,058, 894 plus a 9% profit for a total price of $51,294,194. Lockheed promptly appealed this decision to the Contract Appeals Board, and summoned me to Seattle to litigate it.

Bill Hunt would be our chief witness on the pricing issue. A former vice president of the shipyard for financial forecasting and cost accounting between 1963 and 1968, he then transferred to the Lockheed Georgia Company as deputy director of the troubled C-5A aircraft program with which Secretary Packard was deeply involved as I have related above in the Navy ship claim litigation. Bill and I worked well together, and in January 1975, Lockheed submitted its final detailed price proposal with supporting schedules, the labor hour portion of which he had prepared, to the contracting officer of about $66.2M with an estimated ship cost

---

70 *Lockheed Shipbuilding and Construction Company*, DOT CAB No. 73-36C, 79-2 BCA ¶ 14,080 (September 28, 1979). The Coast Guard was an agency within the Department of Transportation.

of $61.4M. The transmittal letter pointed out that if the parties were unable to negotiate a settlement this price would be Lockheed's position in the litigation. If the ceiling price applied to the Board's determination under paragraph 8, Lockheed at most could recover about $3M; if it did not, about $15M. The stakes were now high indeed.

Preparing this case for trial would become a large undertaking, requiring that I fully understand the ship construction process and the labor and material cost details of building the ship as well as the application of the criteria specified in paragraph 8 of Modification 70. Trial preparation took many months, and as I recall the trial was held in May and July 1975 in the federal court house in Seattle before Administrative Judge Gerson Kramer, the very able and seasoned chairman of the Department of Transportation's Contract Appeals Board. The courtroom on an upper floor had a panoramic, magnificent view of Eliott Bay and the snow-capped Olympic Mountains in the distance which we needlessly worried might distract Judge Kramer from the witness testimony.

In preparing the January 1975 pricing proposal, the Lockheed team became fully aware of major mistakes in underestimating the costs in pricing the first icebreaker. These mistakes related primarily to the number of direct labor hours to build and outfit the ship compounded by an underestimate of the weight and amount of steel for the hull construction that were carried forward in the several price proposals for the second ship until the final one. The mistakes were mostly faulty judgments in substantially underestimating the labor hours and learning required for the extensive welding the underestimated amount of hull steel and radiographic inspection of the steel welding and for outfitting the ship. There were other significant errors in transposing figures to the final labor hours. Whereas Lockheed's bid for the first ship was based on an estimated total of 1.9M hours and its initial proposal for the second ship was almost 2M hours, the January 1975 final proposal was for 2.74M hours, an increase of more than 700,000 hours and about $7M in direct labor costs alone. This was the principal pricing issue for Judge Kramer to decide.

At the trial Marty Ingwersen, the president of the shipyard, testified at length on how the bid estimate for the first icebreaker was prepared and how it as well as preliminary return costs on that ship influenced the initial proposals on the second ship. For one thing, as a check on the reasonableness of its cost estimate on the first ship, Lockheed then had access to the return costs on a recently constructed Canadian icebreaker, the LOUIS ST. LAURANT, which although somewhat smaller was very comparable in design to the Coast Guard icebreakers. He further testified that he had not become aware of the mistakes in the original estimate until the preparation of the January 1975 final proposal for the second ship.

He further testified about the negotiation of Modification 70 for the award of the second icebreaker. There was no question in his mind that the ceiling price in paragraphs 1 and 7 applied only to the negotiation of the contract price in accordance with paragraph 7. It would not apply to the independent unilateral reasonable price determination by the contracting officer under paragraph 8 if the parties could not reach agreement on the price under paragraph 7. Paragraph 8, he testified, protected both parties against unreasonable price positions by the other party. Because it specified objective criteria for the determination of a reasonable contract price it could not be subject to the price ceiling of paragraph 7, particularly if that price turned out to be unreasonably high or low. He saw no need to discuss this with the contracting officer before agreeing to the modification as he thought the inapplicability of the ceiling price to paragraph 8 was obvious.

Based on these disastrous mistakes in the estimate for the first ship that were now evident, it was therefore clear to him that the ceiling price of $53.750M was manifestly unreasonable in relation to the second ship cost of $61.4M as demonstrated in the January 1975 proposal.

On brief we would emphasize this testimony of Mr. Ingwersen on the inapplicability of the ceiling price to the reasonable price determination under paragraph 8 and further argue to Judge Kramer that if otherwise applicable, the ceiling price would not apply in any event because the mistakes made enforcement of the ceiling price unconscionable and because the contracting officer should have known that Lockheed's price was mistaken by comparison with the other prices, particularly Todd's which was $14M higher. In so briefing the case and on other matters covered by our briefs, I was greatly helped by my partner Dick Johnson, by two new associates in the firm, Hopewell Darneille and Jeff Willis, and by David Bowman, the shipyard's very able in-house general counsel who also was of immense help in the trial preparation. Howard Auten, a Coast Guard civilian attorney and later appointed as an administrative judge in the Department's Contract Appeals Board, competently represented the government at the trial and in the briefing. We completed the briefing of the case in February 1976.

In his decision, which he did not issue until September 28, 1979, Judge Kramer rejected all these arguments. First, he said the words "In no event" in paragraphs 1 and 7 have a broad reach, citing cases, as does the term "firm fixed price" as used in paragraphs 1 and 7, and thus apply the ceiling price to paragraph 8. Next, because the price negotiations failed from Lockheed's refusal to abide by the ceiling price, "the effect of all this [adopting Lockheed's interpretation] would be that we should hold that the ceiling price applies to nothing at all…, [an] interpretation [that] cannot be deemed reasonable [which] renders a portion of contractual language useless..[and which thus] violates one of the cardinal principles of contract interpretation and must be rejected", citing cases.[71]

Judge Kramer also rejected the unconscionability and mistake arguments for non enforcement of the price ceiling in paragraph 8, essentially because at the time of the agreement on Modification 70 neither party knew that Lockheed had made disastrous mistakes in estimating the labor hours for the first ship which were repeated in the initial pricing proposals for the second ship.[72] Nor had the Coast Guard any reason to know of those mistakes at that critical date since Lockheed had explicitly confirmed its bid price for the first ship. Relief for these mistakes cannot be premised on facts that first emerge in the course of contract performance; otherwise the concept of a binding firm fixed-price contract would be a mirage.

---

71   79-2 BCA ¶ 14,080, at 69,239-241.

72   *Id.* at 69,243-47.

In his reasonable price determination required by paragraph 8, Judge Kramer rejected the positions of both parties, the contracting officer's as too low because it ignores the effect of Lockheed's pricing mistakes on the reasonable costs of the second ship, and Lockheed's as too high because contrary to paragraph 8 it unduly relies on actual cost experience and cost projections of the second ship, whereas the paragraph 8 focus is on the costs of the first ship only. In addition, using the costs of the second ship to determine its reasonable price and adding a percentage for profit would violate the statutory prohibition of the cost-plus-a-percentage-of-cost system of contracting, citing cases.[73]

Judge Kramer next addressed the opposing positions of the parties on learning efficiencies, productivity rates and should-cost concepts as among the factors to be applied in the reasonable price determination under paragraph 8. He rejected the Coast Guard's learning curve of 85% for the second ship in the contracting officer's final decision as too low in view of the Coast Guard's own expert witness, a Mr. Mack-Forlist with wide experience in ship construction estimating, who supported a more realistic learning curve of about 92% which he accepted as reasonable. Lockheed's January 1975 final proposal, being essentially a projection of costs of the second ship at 42% completion, did not offer a learning curve factor.[74]

On productivity, the contracting officer's final decision adopted a hull steel productivity rate of 130 hours per ton. Mr. Ingwersen testified that had he known of the labor hour estimating errors in the 490,000 hours for the hull steel work he would have raised the productivity rate from the 92 hours per ton bid for the first ship to 158 hours per ton for 859,406 hours for hull steel. Judge Kramer rejected both. "The best estimate, we think, lies somewhat above the Government's estimate which is too low, and the overly pessimistic rate given by appellant's president. More certainty than this is not warranted by the evidence."[75] However, he

---

73   *Id.* at 69,248-49.

74   *Id.* at 69,249-50.

75   *Id.* at 69,251.

did find from the evidence in the record that 700,000 hours for the hull steel would be a reasonable estimate.[76]

On the application of should-cost factors Judge Kramer noted that the parties did not discuss it during the negotiation of Modification 70, or indeed thereafter, nor did paragraph 8 illuminate them. He faults each party's claim to have applied should-cost factors in arriving at their final positions: Lockheed's because based on the premise that what the second ship should cost is to be determined from projections of its actual costs at 42% completion, thus wholly ignoring labor inefficiencies on the first ship that carried over to the work on the second. The Coast Guard's final pricing decision was based on a conventional engineering cost analysis and did not address what each principal item of the work "should cost". "Accordingly, the use of 'should cost' techniques in making a reasonable price determination is beyond our reach in this case."[77]

In arriving at a reasonable price determination, Judge Kramer again rejected Lockheed's January 1975 2.7M labor hour estimate for the second ship as too high and the contracting officer's final decision of 1.85M hours as too low. He stated, "While this [Lockheed estimate] is too pessimistic, it is clear that the overruns will be large. Considering the totals even in the most optimistic light and factoring in general reductions for learning and should cost it seems clear to us that the Contracting Officer's total labor hour allowance is too low by at least 200,000 to 300,000 hours in all. Thus we find that the fair and reasonable price of the WAGB 11 [the second ship] must be fixed at the ceiling price of $53,750,000."[78]

Since adding these additional labor hours to the contracting officer's final decision of 1.5M hours would necessarily raise the reasonable price, with his allowance of 9% profit, substantially above the ceiling price, Judge Kramer apparently saw no reason to determine what the reasonable price would be in the absence of that ceiling. As a check on the reasonableness of the ceiling price Judge Kramer averaged the three other bids

---

76 *Id.* at 69,254-55.

77 *Id.* at 69,252-53.

78 *Id.* at 69,255.

on the first ship at about $54M which "adds some confirmation to our prior estimate."[79] Had he done so it would have been evident that the total costs of the second ship, "considering actual costs incurred and cost projections on WAGB-10[80], giving due consideration to inflationary factors, learning efficiencies which would affect the cost of WAGB-11, and applying should cost techniques where appropriate", would have likely exceeded the ceiling price before any addition of profit, also mandated by paragraph 8 in determining the "reasonable price" for the second ship. Although not addressed by Judge Kramer, since he expressly found the ceiling price to be "reasonable"[81], this presents the paradox of eliminating or subordinating paragraph 8 to the ceiling price provisions of paragraphs 1 and 7, the very result Judge Kramer said would follow from deciding that the paragraph 8 determination of a reasonable price was independent of the ceiling price.

To resolve this apparent conflict between the ceiling price and the reasonable price determination under paragraph 8, Judge Kramer could have decided that the requirement for a reasonable price for the second ship should prevail over a ceiling price that was not a reasonable price in the light of the cost experience on both ships that became increasingly evident after the ceiling price had been agreed to at the time of the award of the second ship. Yet it is also conceivable that Judge Kramer based his finding that the ceiling price was reasonable on his belief that Lockheed's failure to realize significant cost reductions from improved learning and labor efficiencies on the second ship should not affect what the reasonable price should be. In other words, he was probably unwilling to base that determination on the projections of the likely costs for the second ship to the extent they were attributable to Lockheed's gross errors in estimating

---

79 *Id.* at 69,256.

80 *Id.* at 69,254. As there indicated, the original total labor hour bid estimate of 1.9M for the first ship was likely to be exceeded by about another million hours at completion which would have resulted in the total costs of that ship substantially exceeding the ceiling price for the second ship. It is questionable that "giving due consideration to inflationary factors, learning efficiencies which would affect the cost of WAGB-11, and applying should cost techniques where appropriate" would have reduced the cost of the second ship below the ceiling price.

81 *Id.* at 69,255.

the labor hours for both ships. Since his decision is silent on these issues, I cannot speculate further.

Lockheed's disappointment in this outcome was somewhat offset by two other factors. Judge Kramer further ruled over the Coast Guard's strenuous objections that Lockheed was entitled to recover simple interest on the amount of its recovery of the disputed reasonable price determination in accordance with a mandatory clause, "Payment of Interest on Contractor's Claims", which was inadvertently omitted from the contract.[82] Under this clause this interest on the difference between the contracting officer's decision of $51.3M and the ceiling price of $53.750M, or about $2.4M, would run from when the contractor appealed the final decision of the contracting officer in February 1974 to the date of implementation of the Board's September 28, 1979 decision by contract modification.[83] With the interest period exceeding 5 years at a time of extraordinarily high interest rates ranging from 7.7/8% in February 1974 to 10.25% for the last 6 months of 1979 covering the period of Judge Kramer's decision on September 28, 1979 and its implementation by the Coast Guard,[84] the interest award should have added about $1M to Lockheed's recovery, thus making some reduction in the likely loss that Lockheed experienced on the second ship.

The other factor was the Coast Guard's prompt settling of Lockheed's large welding claim on the first ship shortly after the Board's decision in an amount that significantly reduced Lockheed's losses on that ship.

---

82 *Id.* at 69,256-258. Judge Kramer cited *G.L. Christian and Associates v. United States*, 312 F.2d 418, *reh'g denied,* 320 F.2d 345, *cert. denied*, 375 U.S. 594 (1963), in which the Court of Claims held that a standard clause, there the termination for convenience clause mandated by the Armed Services Procurement Regulation, must be read into a contract if procurement regulations having the force of law, here the Payment of Interest on contractor's Claims required by the Federal Procurement Regulation, mandate the incorporation of that clause into every applicable contract omitted inadvertently or even deliberately at subordinate levels of the procuring agency.

83 Federal Procurement Regulation 1-1.322, Payment of Interest on Contractor's Claims, effective September 21, 1972.

84 The interest rates were promulgated by the Secretary of the Treasury every 6 months and published in the Federal Register under Public Law 92-41, amending the Renegotiation Act of 1951, 50 U.S.C. App. § 1211 (1976).

In revisiting this case more than 30 years later as I write this, I marvel at Judge Kramer's mastery of a massive, complex record of trial exhibits and testimony. While one may disagree with particular findings or arguments in his decision, I do not see how his reasoning for rejecting our claim that the reasonable price determination under paragraph 8 was not subject to the ceiling price could have been gainsaid so long as that price itself was reasonable, as the parties certainly believed it was when they agreed to it. Had we anticipated his arguments or the reservations expressed above which I now doubt that we did, I do not see how we could have persuasively overcome them or the bases of his further rejection of the unconscionability and mistake claims for avoiding enforcement of the price ceiling had Lockheed sought judicial review of these elements of the decision in the U.S. Court of Claims which it probably correctly decided not to do. The evidence, however, was compelling for Judge Kramer to determine that a reasonable price for the second ship would necessarily exceed the price ceiling and therefore, subject to the reservations expressed above, that the ceiling price was itself reasonable. Nevertheless, as with Judge Bird in the Navy ship litigation discussed above, the parties here were fortunate to have the case decided by such an extraordinarily competent and objective judge.

-Teaching Law for Engineers.

During the mid-1970s Arthur Miller, a distinguished teacher of constitutional law at George Washington University Law School, asked me to take over a one-semester evening course in the graduate of school of engineering administration called "Engineering Law". The existing teacher would not be available for the next semester or thereafter. Arthur said the course would meet one evening a week for two and a half hours for which I would be paid a modest fee, I would be an "adjunct professor", and it would be a good teaching experience with bright students mostly in engineering jobs in government and industry. I jumped at it. I had known Arthur since 1962 when I briefly worked for JFK's Administrative Conference and wrote a report on the need to reform the government's prolonged suspension of contractors thought to have cheated the government. We had kept up and become friends.

I soon audited one of the evening classes conducted by the departing teacher. He did not impress me but the students, about 25, did. I asked for his syllabus. He said he did not have one: "I make up the coverage from week to week as we go along." "What subjects do you cover?" I asked. He said, "I lecture on various basic aspects of agency, contract, patent and tort law which I think engineers should be aware of." I thought I could do better.

In the several months remaining before I would begin, I was able to compile and photocopy a collection of appellate court decisions, mostly from state courts, in these subject matter areas which I had reproduced and assembled into a loose-leaf spiral bound case book entitled "Law for Engineers" for each student, and organized by subject matter. The objective was primarily to teach the students how judges approach deciding these strongly contested disputes, and secondarily about the legal principles involved. For the first teaching semester I assigned particular cases for each class discussion and told students they should be prepared to be called on and be able to summarize the court's decision and supporting reasons, subject to challenge by other students.

I was delighted by how well the students responded to this curriculum. One of the big challenges for them was to recognize that unlike engineering where there is usually only one correct solution to an engineering problem or issue, law is mostly very different in that in contested cases there may often be no single correct answer to what the court has to decide. Rather the answer may depend on the strength of the supporting reasons and any applicable court precedents applicable to the particular facts that appeal to the appellate judges, while a minority in dissent think other reasons and precedents should govern. Thus law is not science; rather "The life of the law is not logic but experience", as Mr. Justice Holmes once wrote in his famous lectures on the common law.[85]

---

85   Holmes, *The Common Law*, 1 (1881, 41st Printing, Little, Brown 1945).

For the second time I would teach this course and thereafter I organized most classes into four groups of at least five students. All would participate in the appeal and decision of each assigned case to a hypothetical supreme court that would review and decide the appeal of the assigned case. One group would argue the appeal, another would oppose, a third would be the deciding judges, and the fourth would be the critics. Each week the students would progress to the next group. In this way in the course of the semester each student would experience the role of an advocate for one side or the other, the role of a judge who would individually state his decision on the appeal with supporting reasons, and the role of a critic-gadfly. This innovation was a huge success, and many of the students told me this was the most educational learning experience of their academic lives. I in turn was impressed how well some of the students performed in these various roles, creating a buzz of excitement in many of their cases. This great learning experience for me also taught me the fundamental importance and necessity of interactive and participatory teaching for igniting student and teacher interest and learning.

After doing this for three or four years I had to give it up due to the press of client work. Fortunately, my partner John Pachter agreed to relieve me and kept it going well for the next several years. He in turn passed it on to Sandy Hoe, a splendid young partner at the Cuneo firm.

-Return to Key West.

In the winter of 1976, Arlene Robach, a real estate colleague and friend of Don's on Capitol Hill, Don, and I took the auto train from Lorton, Virginia, some 20 miles south of Washington, to Sanford, Florida, which is near Orlando and Disney World, and with our car drove on to Key West, stopping at Homestead for the night before driving the 100 miles over the Florida Keys to Key West the next morning. What a beautiful drive we beheld over the ocean with its contrasting shades of green on the road that runs on the road-bed of the Florida East Coast railroad built by 1912. This marvel of engineering survived the devastating hurricane of 1935 intact while the tracks in the Marathon Key area did not.

As recounted in Part Four, FDR in 1941 obtained Congressional authorization for the Army Corps of Engineers to build a dual-lane highway on the abandoned railway road-bed. It was completed and opened early in 1942, and became essential to the wartime use of Key West as a principal Navy base for combating the Nazi U-boat peril which during much of 1942 sank much of the shipping then operating off the East Coast.

This was my first return to Key West since visiting John Shollenberger and his parents there during the 1950s. With a still substantial Navy presence, there had been a great deal of restoration and upgrading of the 19th and early 20th century homes, and the place was booming with a thriving real estate and tourist economy. We stayed about a week in a centrally located motel and thoroughly enjoyed the visit and returning to Washington the way we came. We were glad to see Sally Lewis and Scottie Lentz, Don's former business partner in the Kitchen Cabinet. Each had moved to Key West a few years before. Sally, sadly, was now a widow. Shortly after she and Markam had purchased their Key West house and decided to establish their home there after living for several years on his boat cruising the East Coast and the Caribbean, they had returned to their yacht for a final cruise while awaiting completing the purchase of their house. While visiting Port au Prince in Haiti Markam suffered a fatal heart attack. Luckily, he had provided well for Sally financially. Don and I were distressed how enormously overweight Sally had become from living on their boat which she never was to lose compared to the waif she had been when marrying Markam about 6 years earlier.

Don and I repeated this experience in the winter of 1977 and the spring of 1978. During this latter visit, the day before our departure while walking back to our motel from dinner at a restaurant on Simonton and Louisa streets with Scottie, we saw that an older two-storey house with an outside staircase on Louisa Street, No. 522, was for sale. We delayed our departure to drive north the next day to check it out.

It had been built in the 1890s and now belonged to a Cuban lodge which rented out the two units. It was for sale at $45K. It had three small rooms in each unit: a sitting room facing the street, a bedroom with a north window, and a kitchen and bathroom adjoining the back yard.

There was a connecting hall from the sitting room to the kitchen which was large enough for a small dining room table and four chairs between the bedroom and the kitchen. The backyard was about 50 by 15 feet, big enough for a patio and garden. Louisa Street ran north and south for two blocks from Whitehead to Simonton. This house was midway on the east side between Duval and Simonton, the two principal east- west streets in Key West between the Atlantic on the east and the Gulf of Mexico to the west. It was three blocks from the ocean, and for us ideally situated. It was not far from John's parent's former house at 915 Johnson Street.

We bought 522 Louisa Street for cash, taking out a short-term mortgage on Don's building in the Eastern market to finance the purchase. We hired a young local attorney, later to become very prominent in Key West, to represent our interests.

We returned for the closing about a month later which went well. I managed to obtain a few weeks' leave so we could ready the upstairs apartment for rent, improve the downstairs, create the patio, and plant the garden. While we bought the house furnished much had to be replaced. We purchased all white wicker furniture throughout except for beds. We found some magnificent, sturdy Philippine rocking chairs for the front porch, new gas stoves, refrigerators, and hot water heaters for both units. We installed ceiling fans in both units.

For the patio we located heavy square concrete tiles on Stock Island, the next key, and made many trips in our VW 411 wagon hauling them to the house and lugging them through the house to create the patio and a border for the garden. The backyard had been used to raise chickens so that the soil was well fertilized. Below the 6-8 inches of the top soil was coral rock. Nevertheless, we were able to plant a rubber tree and two key lime trees which would flourish as well as various kinds of local flowers. We also planted a border hedge at the front of the house. We opened a checking account at a nearby bank and found a tenant would pay a rental of about $250 a month. It was all exhausting work. We also purchased two bicycles as the principal means of getting about the island, except for grocery and other shopping. Don preferred a woman's bicycle which he called "a step-through". We kept them locked on the front porch.

We met some of the neighbors. Alberto and Marie were next door. A middle age Cuban couple, they had lived there for many years; their children were now grown, and they became friends as well as good neighbors. Alberto would watch the house for us on this mostly Cuban block when we were away. In the 1890s a cigar business was established in Key West to be made from imported Cuban tobacco and many Cubans moved to Key West for employment in this venture. While the business moved to Tampa about 30 years later, many Cuban families remained and now had a large presence in Key West.

We would return for Fantasy Fest in late October, the Key West truncated version of the New Orleans Mardi Gras. After staying a few days, I would fly back to Washington leaving the car with Don. He would remain until late May and I would return for the Christmas, New Year's and Easter holidays, and to drive us back for the summer in late May. We would keep in touch with daily phone calls. This schedule prevailed over the next twenty years and Key West became Don's principal home where he made many friends and had a good life. The rental income would pay for much of his living expenses.

Driving there in October or returning in May, we would often spend a night with Don's friend Leonard Hamilton and his partner Dan Buehl in their attractive home in Winter Park, a suburb of Orlando, also the location of Rollins College where John had gone. On one visit in the 1980s Leonard asked me if I was related to a John Coburn. I said I have a brother John and he has a son John, Jr. He explained that a friend, Cecilia ("Cese") Chase Lasbury, had asked him if his Coburn guest were so related to bring him over for a drink as young John Coburn was formerly married to her daughter Abigail ("Abby"). I do not remember if I had met Abby's mother at her and John's wedding in Hartford on March 4, 1966, or if I went to the wedding. I did like Abby and was sorry that their marriage had not lasted despite two splendid sons, Mike and Tristram, whom I also knew.

I found Mrs. Lasbury, now a widow and more than a dozen years my senior, to be a very grand dame, confirming what Mike's wife's Joan had told me. Still beautiful and attractive, she also had a commanding, almost imperious demeanor that reminded me of the Princess Marina's, whom I discuss below. She had returned to Winter Park after her husband's death for the winters and would still go to her lovely place in Camden, Maine, for the summers where Mike and Tris would have extensive visits with their grandmother. She was very friendly to Don and me and remained, she said, very fond of her former son-in-law. When I told her that I had enjoyed visiting Rollins College, she said her father had given the land on which to build the college. I later learned that as a member of that family she had some very valuable orange groves which when she finally sold them enabled her when she died several years later to provide very well for her children and several grandsons including my great nephews Mike and Tris Coburn. I liked Cese and would not see her again.

Driving to and from Key West, Don and I would also frequently spend a night with my niece, Priscilla Harding, my sister Louise's second daughter, who was then married to her second husband Arthur Heublein and living near Jupiter on the east coast of Florida, some 50 miles north of Palm Beach. Priscilla had been married for many years to a charming Italian restaurateur, Nino Puccilo, and they had a daughter, Nina, and a son, Carlo. After divorcing Nino, whom I regret I never met, she married Arthur, also divorced and with grown children. The scion of the Heublein wines family in Hartford, Arthur had retired from that business and devoted much of his time to nursing his investments and some to listening with great approval to the political commentator Rush Limbaugh. However, he was devoted to Priscilla. They had an attractive home in the Everglades west of Jupiter and a lovely summer place on Long Island Sound at Stonington, Connecticut. When he died many years later he left Priscilla financially secure.

In Key West, to begin with, we had two friends, Sally Lewis and Scotty Lentz, both of whom had by then lived there for several years and had made, particularly Sally, many interesting friends. As a Republican, Sally would become politically active and was elected to the city council with the first elected openly gay mayor in the country, Michael Heymann. Through Sally and Scotty Don and I would also make new friends, especially Don. Among them was the young artist Jim Salem who had moved there a few years earlier from central Pennsylvania and whose landscape paintings there we later bought and have treasured. Also Judd Dolle, a mid-westerner retired from business who had recently moved to Key West and had become a close friend of Sally's. He was also her campaign manager, and produced placards to "Rally with Sally". She had hoped that this might lead to running for the state legislature and later for Congress. That was not to be.

I became impressed that Key West attracted leading artists and writers. The Gingerbread Gallery on Duval Street, owned by Michael Heymann and featuring his talented partner John Kirally's paintings, was a block away and during the season would have monthly shows of the leading local artists, including Jim Salem, most of whose work Don and I much admired. In winter residence, among others, were also the poets Richard Wilbur and James Merrill, the playwright Tennessee Williams, and the writer John Hersey, none of whom we had the good fortune to meet but whose work had rightly earned international acclaim.

A year or two later, once the terrace and the garden had become attractive, Don conceived the idea of an Easter Hat Party. We initially invited about 30 people with sufficient notice to create Easter hats in a contest for a token first prize and publicity in the following Sunday edition of the *Key West Citizen*. We engaged the services of "Marvellous Marvin", a much admired waiter at the Louis Backyard restaurant, to be the bar tender and the judge of the winning hat. By then Don had also built a covered deck at the rear fence of the terrace which made a suitable bar and serving station for Marvin. It was from the first a great success, and the imaginative variety and colorful effect of many of the Easter hat creations were truly astonishing and enjoyable. It became one of the Easter events in Key West, and invitations were sought after. Other friends have kept it going after Don and I sold the place in 1999.

In 1986, the day before Easter, about 7am, the electric blanket of our upstairs tenant caught on fire while he was in the kitchen. By the time he discovered it, his bedroom was ablaze. He quickly summoned the fire department and they arrived shortly in time to save the house. The upstairs apartment was mostly burned out, and the downstairs was water-soaked. There was no structural damage to the house. The hat party went on the next day as scheduled.

Luckily, we had a very favorable insurance settlement that enabled us to rebuild the upstairs, add an upstairs deck in back, rewire the entire house and make other improvements. We obtained the services of a first-class carpenter who did most of the work and insisted on weekly cash payments; and Don and I were able to spend most of that summer of 1986 helping getting this done. When finished, the upstairs apartment was far superior and more attractive to what it had been, and we were able to charge a considerably higher rent which would more than cover Don's living expenses in Key West.

-Litigating the Leasing of the Hunter's Point Naval Shipyard.

One of Trow's clients was the Triple A Machine Shop in the San Francisco bay area which was primarily engaged in ship repair work for the Navy and other customers. Early in 1976 the Navy publicly requested proposals for a five-year renewable lease of the 965-acre Hunter's Point Naval Shipyard in San Francisco bay south of the Bay Bridge. Triple A was the successful offeror with its proposal to use much of the facility for ship-repair work and to sublease a substantial portion to the City of San Francisco for $ 1.00 a year for development of a major port facility. The Navy awarded the lease to Triple A in May 1976. The City of San Francisco promptly challenged the Navy's award of the lease to Triple A by a suit in the federal district court there against the Navy and Triple A and individual Navy and Triple A employees seeking to cancel that award, obtaining the award for itself, or ordering Triple A to comply with its subleasing offer, and to recover $500M in damages from the defendants.

Triple A asked our help. Hopewell Darneille and I would spend the next couple of months litigating the several complex issues raised by the City's complaint. Defending the suit for the Navy was David Bancroft, an able young assistant U.S. attorney who welcomed our help and lead on the issues of government contract law that the suit presented. We worked together very well and ultimately prevailed in the district court.[86]

U.S. District Judge Spencer Williams in a comprehensive opinion ruled against the City on its claims on the grounds we had argued in our briefs and oral argument. He found that under the leasing statute, 10 U.S.C. § 2667, and the implementing regulations, the Navy's action was committed to agency discretion and was non-reviewable under the Administrative Procedure Act, 5 U.S.C. § 701(a)(2).[87] Since the alleged Triple A sublease commitment to the City was not incorporated in the Navy's lease to Triple A, the court had no jurisdiction to consider it, although the City might have a claim under state law in that respect. He also rejected the City's claims that the Navy had failed to provide an environmental impact statement for the leasing to Triple A, agreeing with the Navy's reasons why none was required, and rejecting any non-compliance with the Coastal Zone Management Act, 16 U.S.C. §§ 1451 *et seq*. On the damages claim, he ruled that none could be implied under the leasing statute against the Navy and the Triple A defendants under the criteria of a recent Supreme Court decision[88], and that in any event the court's jurisdiction for breach of an implied-contract damages against the Navy was limited by the jurisdictional limit of $10,000 under the Tucker Act, 28 U.S.C. § 1346(a)(2), and its claim for damages under the Federal Tort Claims Act was barred by the statutory bar of recovery

---

86 *City and County of San Francisco v. United States et al.*, 443 F. Supp. 1116 (N.D. Calif. 11/25/1977), *aff'd*, 615 F.2d 498 (9th Cir. 1980).

87 Otherwise, the court could review whether the award of the lease complied with the statute or whether the agency had abused its discretion under a line of cases recognizing the district courts' jurisdiction to review the merits of protests of contract awards and the standing of aggrieved plaintiffs to bring these cases under the judicial review provisions of the Administrative Procedure Act (5 U.S.C. §§ 701 *et seq*.) commencing with *Scanwell Laboratories v. Shaffer*, 424 F.2d 859 (D.C. Cir. 1970), and recognized by the 9th Circuit in *Ness Investment Corporation v. U.S. Department of Agriculture Forest Service*, 512 F.2d 706, 715 (1975).

88 *Cort v. Ash*, 422 U.S. 66, 78 (1975). The judicial review provisions of the Administrative Procedure Act only provide specific relief remedies such as injunctions and do not authorize the award of money damages which must be sought either in contract under 28 U.S.C. § 1491(a)(1) or in tort under 28 U.S.C. §§ 2674 *et seq*.

for misrepresentation by government agents.[89] The 9th Circuit affirmed the district court in all respects on the City's appeal[90] for which Triple A retained local counsel. The City pressed hard on all these issues as it was desperate to acquire this facility for the betterment of the City's attraction as a world-class port on the West Coast. It was complex litigation and a great learning experience.

-Other Shipbuilding Claims: American Shipbuilding and Defoe Shipbuilding, Two Great Lakes Shipyards.

Each of these shipyards had the usual run of ship claims during the 1970s that the vom Baur-Arthur Andersen team mostly led by Dick Johnson was able to settle after several years of work.

What was most notable about American Ship was George Steinbrenner its then president whose family had a controlling interest in the company. Long located at Loraine, Ohio, on Lake Erie, it was the principal builder of ore and cargo carriers for shipping on the Great Lakes, and the family also owned the principal Great Lakes shipping company. George was the most difficult client we had. A shrewd bully and braggart in his business life, he led by fear and intimidation with minimal regard for facts and rules unless one stood up to him which in the case of employees, accountants and lawyers meant incurring the risk of dismissal. Dick and I advised our team not to yield to any of his demands to which they had personal or professional objections.

I recall one incident with distaste. Alan Peterson and I were meeting with George at the Arthur Andersen's Cleveland office with the head of that office, Harvey Kapnick, later the chairman of the firm. Among other things, the meeting was to discuss the valuation of the company's recently filed ship claim we had prepared in its forthcoming disclosure

---

89 28 U.S.C. § 2680(h) (2006).

90 Note 86 *supra*.

to the SEC. George demanded that it be valued, as if it was an account receivable, at the face amount of the claim.

Alan and I strongly disagreed, stating that valuation would seriously mislead investors as the government would surely not settle at that amount and there was no reliable way to forecast the outcome. Instead, simply record the fact that a claim in that amount was submitted, and the company is advised that the claim has legal merit but the company makes no estimate of the amount or the timing of the recovery. George summarily rejected our arguments and alternative and renewed his demand. Harvey and George reached agreement.

A year or two later George came to our office seeking representation on a mistake in the pricing of a ship his company was building for the Coast Guard. I said, "George, we decline to represent you on this or any other matter. Good day." That was the last I saw of him. I learned that in 1983 he closed the Loraine shipyard because the union would not heed his demands and relocated the operations to Tampa. From there he went on to become the principal owner of the New York Yankees, where according to press accounts his behavior did not improve. American Shipbuilding is no longer in business.

A pleasant recollection of my occasional visits to the Loraine shipyard was hearing two concerts of the world-class Cleveland Orchestra, one at its home in Severance Hall and the other at the Blossom Festival at its outdoor summer location near Cleveland, very similar to the Boston Symphony's summer concerts at Tanglewood in the Berkshires. Each was masterfully conducted by George Szell its longtime conductor, producing glorious sound particularly in the acoustically superb Severance Hall.

As to Defoe, I remember that early in the summer of 1969 Defoe became a client thanks to Alan Peterson. We were then very short handed with other claims work and litigation. I was in Seattle on Lockheed work. Bob Turtle luckily had recruited Rob Evers, a very able, bright second-year student at Columbia Law School as a summer associate. Trow dispatched Rob to Bay City, Michigan, on Lake Huron, where the Defoe shipyard was located. There was no available lawyer to send with Rob.

Alan Peterson's team, led by Ray Ruona, was already there at work and was able to brief Rob on the magnitude of the claims' landscape involving several Navy contracts for different types of vessels, primarily guided missile destroyers (DDGs) and destroyer escorts, among others. Trow would make periodic visits. Rob and Ray drafted several claims and submitted them to the Navy before Rob returned to law school in the fall. Dick Johnson arrived later in Bay City and worked on other claims. Rob returned as an associate in the summer of 1970, and he and Dick remained there much of the time through 1974 litigating the DDG claim in the ASBCA which resulted in a negotiated settlement of all of the claims in 1975.

One unusual and interesting aspect of that litigation was a $300K concession of government liability for late government-furnished equipment in the government's brief to the ASBCA. The Navy repudiated that concession as the contracting officer had not approved it, as required by the published Navy procurement regulations. The ASBCA upheld the repudiation on that ground and denied that part of Defoe's appeal.[91]

I had limited contact with this work. I made a few trips to Bay City and came to know the Defoe brothers, Bill and Tom, who had inherited the business and its management from their father. The 1975 settlement sustained the shipyard, but not attracting replacement work it shut down in 1976. So ended another family-owned shipyard long renowned for high quality work.

-Developments at the vom Baur Firm 1977-84.

In 1977 my brother Pat became executive director of the National Association of Real Estate Investment Trust located in Washington. As a result he started spending most of the week there and going home

---

91 *Defoe Shipbuilding*, ASBCA No. 17095, 74-1 BCA ¶ 10,537 (3/11/1974). The Board noted, "There has been amassed a formidable record including fourteen volumes of statements of claim, almost 3,000 Rule 4 documents, in excess of 300 other exhibits, the transcript of 30 days of hearings and briefs in chief having more than 2,000 pages." *Id.* at p. 49,905.

weekends to his family in Katonah, New York. I got him a guest membership at the University Club where he was comfortably lodged. At the same time Trow and I and some of our other partners were becoming interested in exploring merger opportunities with another firm as we could see the end of the shipbuilding claims work in another year or two and it was important to start to grow replacement work, perhaps through merger with another firm whose practice would supplement and compliment ours.

Pat's field was corporate mergers and acquisitions and so we engaged his services, to be compensated if and when he arranged a merger. His godson, Nelson Pell, was a young corporate law partner in the Washington office of the young and rapidly expanding Omaha firm of Kutak, Rock & Houey. It already had an Atlanta office and was looking for a Washington firm with which to merge. Bob Kutak, about my age, was already a coming leader of the American Bar Association. He had the pioneering vision of creating the first national law firm with a home office and a presence in multiple cities. The big accounting firms were now doing this, and Bob saw good reasons for there to be national and international law firms as well, as has in fact become well established over the last 20 years.

Pat, through Haven Pell, introduced us to Bob Kutak and his principal partners, and we began an exchange of visits. We were scheduled for a further visit to Omaha in September or October which we had to cancel when our partner Bob Turtle said that he was not well and unable to go. He had missed the earlier visit because of work and it was critical that he go there to conclude the likely merger agreement as all indications so far had been very positive on both sides.

Bob's words were prophetic. A few days later, while putting his children to bed he had a fatal heart attack and died before he could be hospitalized. We learned he long had hypertension. He had also added excessive weight since joining us in 1968 and getting married in the early 1970s. He was only forty and left a wife, Susan, four young children and the fifth on the way. They lived near Don and me on Wyoming Avenue in a spacious house which we had visited. Bob's premature death was a great shock and loss to all of us. He was a brilliant lawyer and teacher of young associates and likely our best begetter of new clients and work. He and I had become good friends. The partnership contributed about $60K to sustain Susan and the children until Bob's life insurance and other assets became available. Fortunately, she soon remarried and life looked up for her and her children. We lost touch.

About the time of Bob's death, the Kutak firm's Atlanta office lost its principal client: a major bank there folded. These developments suspended our merger talks, and they never resumed. Sadly too Bob Kutak died a few years later, also very prematurely. The firm survives, but never realized his vision.

-Saving an Iranian Student from Deportation.

One of Trow's clients was the Princess Marina von Hohenzollern, a granddaughter of Kaiser Wilhelm II and a great, great granddaughter of Queen Victoria. She stood at about six feet, had a striking resemblance to her distant grandfather Friederich der Grosse, and had a commanding, imperious presence. I adored her. She came to Trow for a divorce from her husband, Kirby Patterson, an attorney in the Justice Department. They had three young children with German given names. During World War II, Kirby, aboard a B-17 bomber of the U.S. 8th Air Force based in Britain, was injured when his plane was shot down during a bombing mission over Germany. He was hospitalized where Princess Marina, serving as a nurse, nursed him back to health. At the end of the war he was repatriated, they married and moved to Washington, DC.

By the time we met in the later 1970s, Princess Marina, then separated from Kirby, had taken in a boarder, an Iranian student named Sadegh Asfahani. He had been tried, convicted, and sentenced to death *in absentia* by the Shah's government as an enemy of the state. It was now demanding his deportation to Iran. Princess Marina asked us to help, which we would do *pro bono*. I asked two of our bright summer associates,

Gerry and Jean Gleason, a young married couple having completed their second law school year, to devise a program to save Sadegh. We interviewed him and were persuaded that he deserved our help.

Gerry and Jean found that the State Department in threatening Sadegh with deportation had grossly violated their own published regulations requiring that each step of the deportation process meet specified safeguards of procedural fairness. They prepared a detailed memorandum of fact and law which we submitted to the office of the Legal Advisor of the State Department. This stopped the deportation momentum, and by the time of the deportation's order's compliance with the regulations, early in 1979, the Iranian revolution had intervened, the Shah had been ousted and his replacement by the Ayatollah Khomeni as the Supreme Leader of Iran as a theocracy had become an accomplished fact.

Sadegh, long a supporter of the Ayatollah Khomeni living in exile in France, returned to Iran and received a ministerial position in the Ayatollah's new government. We soon needed his help. One of Dick Johnson's clients was an Italian construction firm which had been doing major port construction under contract with the Shah's government. The new government froze all payments for this work, causing great financial hardship. We appealed to Sadegh for help. Dick also retained Dick Helms, formerly the director of the CIA and more recently our former ambassador to Iran. From their efforts the payments were released and the work went forward. Dick Johnson also sent Mr. Helms a case of his favorite wine.

We later learned to our horror and sadness that the Ayatollah's government had tried Sadegh for treason and had executed him. A moderate, accustomed to our values from long residence here, he apparently could not support the extremist, intolerant policies of his government for which he paid the ultimate price of losing his life. Like the French and the Russian revolutions, this one too begat a new tyranny as repressive as the one it overthrew. By then Princess Marina, now divorced, had moved to Scottsdale, Arizona, and we lost touch.

-Departures from the Firm.

In 1978 about a year after Bob Turtle's death, two of our remaining partners, Dick Johnson and Bruce Shirk, and about six associates left us to establish a government contracts practice in the Washington office of Seyfarth, Shaw, a Chicago labor law firm. This was another grievous blow. Other departures soon followed. Mike Freeman began his long, continuing service as an administrative judge of the ASBCA where he has rightly earned a stellar reputation for fairness, competence and dispatch. Jim McHale became a prosecutor at the SEC for which he is much admired and respected and continues to serve. Our partner, John Pachter, a highly competent litigator, also departed and would soon form his own firm in Vienna, Virginia, which many years later Dick Johnson would join.

Fortunately, we were soon approached by a leading Kansas City general practice firm, Gage & Tucker, which was looking for a Washington presence because its principal competitor had recently done so. These talks were fruitful. The managing partner, John Kraemer, was a law school classmate of mine and we remembered each other, which helped. The firm name for its Washington office became "Gage, Tucker & vom Baur". This became effective in the summer of 1979 and lasted until Trow retired in the mid-1980s. In 1984 I had moved to Sachs, Greenebaum & Tayler, a small Washington litigation firm primarily engaged in local domestic relations practice. A colleague of mine, Bob Ackerly, had left the Cuneo firm to establish a government's contract practice at Sachs, Greenebaum and recruited me and a few others to join him. Bill Tayler, a former litigator in the Civil Division of the Justice Department, was a law school classmate whom I had not then known.

The vom Baur firm had lasted about 22 years and made a notable mark in the jurisprudence of public contract law, establishing important precedents on suspension and debarment from government contracting,[92]

---

92   In *Horne Bros. v. Laird*, 463 F.2d 1268 (D.C. Cir. 1972), in a case brought by Bob Turtle, Circuit Judge Levanthal established guidelines of procedural fairness for suspensions for government contractors that exceeded 30 days, including notice of specific charges and an opportunity to rebut them unless the government's law enforcement

on protecting contract awards against bid protests,[93] and against arbitrary rejection of the winning bidder for lack of integrity without notice,[94] for equitable and promissory estoppels,[95] for imputed interest on claims,[96] and for establishing with Arthur Andersen the methodology for presenting and recovering on constructive change order claims as described above. At our height, we were recognized along with Sellers, Conner & Cuneo, Gil Cuneo's firm in Washington, then as the two leading firms in the country for resolving disputes on government contracts and protests of contract awards. Others would soon follow in this growing practice area. While we were a diverse group ranging the cultural and political spectrum and respected our private lives, we shared a commitment to the highest standards of the legal profession and a willingness to take novel and financially risky cases that pushed the boundaries of settled law to overcome arbitrary and unfair government actions in procurement and other areas.

In Part Four, I have noted the importance of Trow vom Baur's lasting contributions as the Navy's general counsel during the Eisenhower Administration. He would have a similar impact on those of us who practiced law with him. Earlier in this Part Five I have written about his strengths as a teacher of trial practice to us and of constructive change orders to us and

---

interests would be adversely affected in which event he outlined alternative procedures. These have since been mostly incorporated in FAR 9.407-3. In a debarment case, *Caiola v. Carroll*, 851 F.2d 395 (D.C. Cir. 1988), that I worked on while at Sachs, Greenebaum, the court terminated a debarment based on arbitrary and discriminatory application of imputed knowledge and reason to know criteria as discussed *infra*, starting at Note 117.

93 Note 86 *supra*.

94 *Old Dominion Dairy Products v. Secretary of Defense*, 631 F.2d 953 (D.C. Cir. 1980), *reversing* 471 F. Supp. 300 (D, D.C. 1979). Mike Freeman tried the case in the district court and soon thereafter was appointed as an administrative judge at the Armed Services Board of Contract Appeals. Our counsel, Charlie Ablard, obtained the reversal in the Court of Appeals.

95 Notes 59 and 64 *supra*.

96 *New York Shipbuilding Co.*, ASBCA No. 16,164, 76-2 BCA ¶ 11,979, *recons. denied*, 83-1 BCA ¶ 16,534 (equitable adjustment requires that contractors be compensated for equity capital used to finance change order work). My partner John Pachter was primarily responsible for this splendid result.

the Bar. But Trow added far more value to our practice of law. He believed that the practice of law was a calling, like the ministry, and only secondarily a business for the private practitioner. He established a plane of intellectual equality among all of us to incubate winning approaches to address clients' problems. He had tea in the library in the afternoons to encourage discussions of our work and to know each other better.

Trow insisted on the highest standards of conduct in our practice: legal advice grounded in thorough knowledge of the relevant law; continuously applied thought in formulating that advice and in problem resolution; clear, simple writing and speech and current and effective communications with clients and each other; civility and good manners with each other, with clients, judges, and with opposing attorneys. "Do it now", he would say. He was always available for advice and help.

Trow built a first-class library of books and subscriptions beyond public contract law materials and hired our splendid librarian, Josie Bach, to maintain it and circulate advance sheets to us on a continuing basis. He had us promptly deposit the results of our legal research and our briefs, properly indexed and digested, in the library with the index digests to be circulated frequently. He created a filing system for all client matters and hired Bernice Hogan who managed it with excellence.

Trow emphasized that we recruit second-year law students at the top law schools as summer associates as an effective way to hire new law school graduates, all without regard to gender and gender orientation, political affiliation, race or religion. He encouraged us to engage in bar association and do *pro bono* work.

In these and the other ways of his engaging, colourful personality, and immaculate attire, Trow added great value to his firm and was and is a lasting mentor to all of us.

For more on Trow, who died in 2000 in his 92nd year, please consult *Remembering Trowbridge vom Baur* in 30 ABA Public Contract Law Journal 1 (Fall 2000), where his former partners and colleagues recall his contributions as Navy general counsel, as one of the first chairs of the ABA Section of Public Contract Law, as the producer of the Model Procurement Code for state and local governments, as a person, practitioner and mentor, as a builder of a government contracts law practice, and as a pioneer in recovery for constructive change orders.

There is much to remember about Trow. He fought for the rule of law and practiced law in the grand manner.

-ABA Public Contract Law Section Activities 1976-79.

At Trow's suggestion, I became increasingly engaged in the work of the growing Public Contract Law Section that was established in 1965 at the annual ABA Meeting in Miami as I have related above in this Part. During the Section chairmanship of Paul Hannah in 1976-77, I was elected Secretary and worked closely with him in planning the Section's activities for his term. There were two principal projects: the development of the Model Procurement Code for State and Local Governments which was a joint undertaking with the ABA State and Local Government Section under Trow's leadership and financed primarily by a generous grant from the Department of Justice thanks to the efforts of Tom Madden, then a lawyer in the Justice Department concerned with the administration of government grants to the states and municipalities that were used to fund state and local procurement. He was rightly concerned with the absence from many state and local procurement laws of the fundamental requirements of procurement integrity and public competition. The development by the ABA of a uniform model code for the states and cities to enact would address this felt need. Alan Peterson also provided financing of this project.

The other principal project was the adoption of legislation recently recommended by the Commission on Government Procurement co-chaired by Congressman Chet Holifield and Comptroller General Elmer Staats. Their first recommendation was that Congress enact an Office of

Federal Procurement Policy[97] to coordinate greater uniformity in the federal procurement policies and practices among the federal agencies, particularly where they implemented uniform statutory language as then existed between the Armed Services Procurement Act of 1947 and the Federal Property and Administrative Services Act of 1949. We would work closely to achieve this with Congressman Holifield, his very capable assistant Herb Roback, and Sparky Hiestand, the Commission's superb general counsel and later a distinguished chair of the Section of Public Contract Law.

Also underway was draft legislation sponsored by Florida Senator Lawton Childs for a government-wide Contract Disputes Act that would provide statutory recognition and stature to the agency board of contract appeals and their administrative judges and would provide contractors the choice of an agency board or the Court of Claims to adjudicate any dispute that they were unable to resolve with the contracting officer. All this promised much needed change which we strongly supported.

These projects came to fruition during my term as section chair in 1978-79. We worked closely with Lester Fettig, the first Administrator of Federal Procurement Policy appointed by President Carter in 1977 under the recently enacted OFPP Act. He pushed hard with our strong support for the creation of a government-wide procurement regulation, to be called "the Federal Acquisition Regulation" (FAR), to replace so far as possible the separate and varying agency procurement regulations such as the Armed Services Procurement Regulation (ASPR) and its counterpart, the Federal Procurement Regulation (FPR) prescribed by the General Services Administration for the civilian agencies. Overcoming agency resistance required patience and fortitude. He succeeded, and the evolving FAR now covers most agencies' contracting policies and practices under a common statute, the Competition in Contracting Act of 1984 which repealed the predecessor statutes.[98]

---

97 This was done in 1977 and is now codified at 41 U.S.C. § 1101 by Pub. L. 111-350 enacted January 4, 2011.

98 10 U.S.C. §§ 2302-2338 (2006) for the procurements by the Department of Defense and the military departments; and 41 U.S.C. Subtitle I, Federal Procurement

The Contract Disputes Act was also enacted in 1978,[99] and we worked closely with the FAR subcommittee concerned with drafting the implementing FAR provisions.[100] The enacted statute gave the government a right of appeal from agency board of contract appeals adverse to the government's interest, thus overruling the Supreme Court's decision in the *S&E Contractors* case discussed above. However, this right of government appeal was safeguarded against excessive use by requirements for high level approvals within the agency and the Department of Justice.[101] In 1982 I would write a book about this new law for the Practising Law Institute which would publish it later that year.[102] After several years it lost its usefulness because I did not publish supplements to keep abreast of the rapidly developing case law interpreting the act.

Three other principal projects concerned me as the Section chair: enlarging the section's committees to cover much of the field of government contract law; creating quarterly educational programs to coincide with section regional council meetings in addition to the annual meeting's educational program; and encouraging government lawyers to participate in the section's activities. In all of these the results were encouraging and lasting.

Finally, during my year the Section Council and the ABA House of Delegates approved the Model Procurement Code for State and Local Governments, a signal and remarkable achievement under Trow's leadership. It has borne fruit as an increasing number of states and cities have enacted it or its later revisions.[103]

Policy, as codified by Pub. L. 111-350 enacted January 4, 2011 for procurements by other agencies of the federal government.

99   Now codified at 41 U.S.C. Subtitle III by Pub. L. 111-350.

100 FAR 33.201-215.

101 41 U.S.C. § 7107(a)(1)(B) as codified by Pub. L 111-350. Agency board decisions are not final on questions of law, nor on questions of fact if found on review to be fraudulent, arbitrary, or capricious, or so grossly erroneous as to necessarily imply bad faith, or not supported by substantial evidence. 41 U.S.C. § 7107(b).

102 Coburn, *The Contract Disputes Act of 1978*, Practising Law Institute (Jan. 4, 1982).

103 The 2000 edition of the Model Procurement Code has been adopted by at least 17 states and by hundreds of state local jurisdictions.

All this was happening during a busy time in my law practice, much of it then based in Bismarck, ND, as I shall next relate.

-The Anatomy of Unsuccessful Construction Contract Claims Litigation for Ray Clairmont and the Logans of Bismarck, North Dakota.

Trow had as clients from his teaching recovery for constructive change orders for Hank Kaiser's education programs, the Clairmont brothers, William and Ray, of Bismarck, North Dakota. William, the older brother, had a construction firm and asked Trow in the early 1970s to litigate a differing site conditions claim on an Army contract which Trow asked me to take on. The claim involved the additional costs of rock excavation which the government drawings and a site inspection had failed to disclose. It was a routine case, and we prevailed.[104] Ray Clairmont was the project manager. In 1974 he had formed his own company, Rayco, Inc.

In January 1976 Rayco was awarded a $3.6M contract by the Albuquerque District of the Army Corps of Engineers for the construction of a 10-mile access road, called "the Tetilla Peak Access Road", leading to camping and boating recreation facilities adjacent to Cochiti Lake recently formed by the Cochiti dam in Sandoval County, New Mexico, approximately midway between Albuquerque and Santa Fe. Rayco was also to construct the roads and various facilities in the recreation area.[105] The 6 other bids for this "Tetilla Peak Project" ranged from $3.9 to $6.8M, and the government estimate was about $5M. Rayco's bid was based on completing the road work and the subcontracted recreation area facilities construction before the onset of winter and finishing the planting and seeding work the following spring notwithstanding that the invitation for bids permitted completion of the project in the third

---

104 *William Clairmont*, ASBCA No. 15497, 73-1 BCA ¶ 9927.

105 I base this account mostly on the facts and the decision of the Corps of Engineers Board of Contract Appeals in *Rayco, Inc., Contractor, and Russell E. Logan and Terry E. Logan, Surety*, ENG BCA Nos. 4169, 4248, 84-1 BCA ¶ 17055 (December 30, 1983).

construction season. The required Miller Act payment and performance bond sureties on Ray's contract were two individuals, his friend Terry Logan, and Terry's father, Russell Logan, also of Bismarck.

Work in the recreation area was delayed starting in May until late August 1976 by the discovery of Indian archaeological sites requiring the relocation and deletion of some of the roads and facilities. In July, in constructing the access road up a steep hill to the required depth of 30 feet to the recreation area, Rayco encountered large boulders which proved difficult to excavate and severely damaged the excavation equipment.

Although not disclosed by the government drawings, some of these boulders would have been partly visible from a site examination prior to bidding which Rayco did not conduct in that part of the project area. By mid-August, this encounter with "the rock hill" stopped the road work there pending relaxation of the 30' excavation depth of the road going up the hill. Rayco informally then asserted a differing site condition claim as well as requesting relief from the excavation depth requirement, both of which the contracting officer's representatives said they would consider. At a meeting with the contracting officer in late September, he told Ray Clairmont that he would have to submit a formal differing site condition claim. Ray then summoned me to Albuquerque for help in preparing that claim.

By mid-December we submitted a 138-page claim with 14 exhibits to the contracting officer. We requested relief ranging from $720K to $826K depending on various alternate proposals for completing the access road in the Rock Hill area. From September to late November, Rayco's progress on the Access Road was further greatly reduced because its principal lender, the First National Bank of Bismarck, which had loaned Rayco some $882K, insisted, because of Rayco's deteriorating financial condition, that Rayco sell its earth-moving equipment which it had pledged to the bank as security for the loan. The auction of the equipment in late September yielded about $480K for the bank. In November and December Rayco was able to borrow an additional $231K from a bank in Minneapolis, most of which had to be repaid by August 1977. By the end of 1976, Rayco reported an overall loss of over $500K, much of it on a 1975 channel improvements project for the Corps of Engineers in Minot, ND. In addition, there was as of January 1977 a cost overrun of about $544K on the Tetilla Peak project. In November 1976 Rayco projected project completion in July 1977. In February 1977 the contracting officer met with Rayco and said he would not approve the differing site condition claim. His reasons were that some boulders were partly visible in the Rock Hill, the IFB described the excavation as "unclassified" which implied that rock excavation might be necessary; and the IFB further provided for blasting and for using rock fill in the embankment work. I advised Ray Clairmont that this would be difficult to overcome in litigation.

Rayco then in March 1977 submitted separate claims to the contracting officer for the changes in the recreation area from the discovery of numerous Indian archaeological sites which totalled about $1.3M, including about $392K in costs of delaying the recreation area work into 1977 which had also been included in the differing site condition claim. On the basis that the combination of the changes in the recreation area and the boulder excavation in the Rock Hill prevented completion of virtually all of the project in 1976 as planned, Rayco repriced all the remaining work on the basis of its estimated costs of performing that work in the 1977 construction season. It further requested about a year's extension of the contract completion date for the same reasons. In April the contracting officer rejected these claims. The parties then met on May 2-4, 1977 in an effort to resolve their differences. Rayco did not request my involvement in the resulting discussions or agreement.

The parties reached an agreement in principle to provide Rayco an additional $400K, $50K of which was to be paid promptly and the balance of $350K, if confirmed by government audit of the Rayco's certified cost data in support of that amount, would be paid pro rata as the work progressed. This audit requirement delayed the execution of the implementing contract modification for the $350K until October 7, 1977. That modification provided full compensation for all changed work in the recreation area and for all government-caused delays encountered by Rayco through May 5, 1977. It also substantially relaxed the excavation depth requirement in the Rock Hill to about the depth actually achieved and extended the contract completion date by 120 days. Finally, by this modification Rayco released all claims against the Corps of Engineers under the contract existing as of the May 5 date. Since the Corps estimated the net additional costs of the changed work in the recreation area at about $29K and rightly believed that Rayco's financial difficulties and the entirely inadequate production of base course material for the access road had at least equally prevented project completion in 1976 it could not agree to reprice the remaining work on the basis of the escalated estimated 1977 construction costs as Rayco had requested.

Rayco used much of the funds received under the contract in 1977 to pay his subcontractors on another project to construct an office facility in Bismarck. As a result his subcontractors for the recreation area work left the project for nonpayment after June until reaching a new agreement with Rayco the following May. Rayco was unable to complete the project in 1977 due to its substantially insufficient cash flow from its several projects. At a meeting with the contracting officer the following July, Rayco committed to project completion by the end of September, 1978. With Rayco having made little progress, the contracting officer terminated Rayco's right to proceed with the work on November 1, 1978.

On November 8, Terry Logan, one of the individual sureties, met with the contracting officer to work out the terms of a takeover agreement. Terry consulted me about the terms of the takeover agreement, and I returned to Albuquerque for that purpose. The takeover agreement, executed on November 9, required the completion of the production of the remaining base course for the access road by November 30 and for the recreation area roads a month later, and for the placing and priming of base course for these roads at the rate of two miles per week starting by the middle of November. In addition, paving the roads was also to start then and proceed at the rate of not less than 1,000 feet per day, "weather permitting, until such time as in the surety's opinion, with the advice and consent of the Contracting Officer, it is determined the construction season has ended and it is no longer economical to continue the paving operations. In such event paving shall recommence at the rate specified above as soon as practicable in the spring and no later than 1 April 1979."

The contract specifications further restricted the production of base course to "when atmospheric temperature is above 35 F." Before paving, a bituminous prime coat for priming the placed base course could be "applied only when the ambient temperature is 50 degrees F or above and when the temperature has not been below 35 degrees F for 12 hours immediately prior to application, unless otherwise directed."

These temperature restrictions were likely to delay completion of the road work until the spring of 1979. The surety's obligation under the takeover agreement further committed it to complete all work under the contract "as promptly and expeditiously as possible" "unless the weather becomes inordinately bad (substantially worse than normal conditions)...."

On November 17, about midday, a Corps inspector at the job site would not permit the scheduled priming of placed base course because the temperature had fallen to 26 F within the previous 12 hours and was only 31 F at 9 am. The surety's highly experienced and qualified project engineer, Wally Abbott, later that day wired the Corps: [block indent the next paragraph]

Stabilized base course was finished and ready for prime between Stations 71-00 and 109-00 (bridge) [of the access road]. Corps refused to let tanker shoot prime after it arrived at 12:30 pm. Weather was clear, sunny, 51 degrees. Project road work now shut down because of Corps weather limitations now being enforced.

In a further letter to the contracting officer on December 2 Terry Logan as surety wrote that "trying to construct the roadway under hit and miss conditions of winter weather would result in marginal construction and costs to us far out of proportion to what they otherwise should be in the spring after the weather has settled down....Therefore my decision remains not to resume roadway work until spring." The contracting officer then sought and was denied authority by his superior, the Division Engineer, to terminate the takeover agreement for default. Instead, he was told to work out an acceptable schedule for completion of the work in the spring and to obtain new performance and payment bonds as evidence of the surety's financial responsibility. The contracting officer by letter to the surety on December 15 requested the submission of a revised schedule for project completion in the spring and the submission of a performance bond of more than $1M and a payment bond of $414K by January 3 1979, or be terminated for default forthwith. Terry Logan then consulted me.

He said the projected costs of completing the project in the spring of 1979 had risen so substantially with the ongoing inflation, and that he would be unable financially to complete the project then at the 1976 prices Ray Clairmont had bid. He asked me whether there was any way out. He told me that the contracting officer, Col. Roth, had unconditionally promised him that he would promptly pay Rayco's final pay request if assigned to the surety, which Terry at the time estimated to be at least $50K, and also promptly so to pay the surety's initial pay request. Rayco's final pay request for $53.5K, now assigned to the surety, was submitted on November 13 and the surety's first pay request for an additional $86 K on December 1. By December 28 the surety had received no payment of any of these amounts.

I then advised Terry Logan and Ray Clairmont that in my opinion the surety now had the right to terminate the takeover agreement for material government breach in not making these payments and in demanding new performance and payment bonds. They asked me to draft such a letter for them to the contracting officer which I did and they signed and sent on December 28. In order to recover for Rayco's and the surety's losses and for my firm to recover its substantial unpaid fees from Rayco and the surety, we would have to litigate to overturn the Rayco default termination since the surety could recover no damages for the government's breach since the takeover agreement would have been performed at a loss. And the otherwise inevitable default termination of the takeover agreement for the surety's financial inability to complete the work necessitated terminating the takeover agreement now for material government breach loomed.

As expected, the contracting officer eventually responded to the December 28 letter on March 12, 1979, by terminating for default the surety's right to proceed under the takeover agreement. We had previously appealed the Rayco termination and now appealed the surety default termination, the appeals to be consolidated and tried together in the Corps of Engineers Board of Contract Appeals. After extensive discovery of the Corps' job records and some deposition taking, we went to trial in Washington, DC, in the fall of 1979. The die was now cast.

Ray Clairmont, Wally Abbott, and Terry Logan were well prepared and made effective witnesses. Ray and Wally testified that although a few boulders were partly visible in the Rock Hill, the government drawings gave no indication of rock problems there in relation to the required excavation depth of 30 feet, and Rayco accordingly had no reason to expect the severe extent of those problems that financially necessitated the abandonment of the road work pending the resolution of the resulting differing site condition claim. They further testified that they only agreed to the $400K settlement the following May and October because the alternative was a certain termination for default because of financial inability otherwise to proceed with the work in the spring of 1977.

Terry Logan testified that he had entered into the takeover agreement relying on explicit face-to-face discussions with Col. Roth, the contracting officer, that performing the work in the substantially escalated 1978 costs at the 1976 bid prices necessitated that he receive prompt payments of the forthcoming pay requests, and that in that context Col. Roth assured him that the Corps would promptly and unconditionally pay the surety Rayco's final pay request which would exceed $50K if assigned to the surety as well as the surety's initial pay request without any offsets. He further testified that the Rayco pay request for about $53.5K assigned to the surety was submitted on November 13, 1978, and the surety's first payment request for $86K on December 1, 1978; that when no payments of these amounts had been received by December 28, he and Ray Clairmont consulted counsel and were advised that the surety now had the legal right to terminate the takeover agreement for material government breach for failure to make these payments and for demanding new performance and payment bonds. He and Ray then requested counsel to prepare the appropriate letter which they signed and sent to the contracting officer later that day.

At the trial Col. Roth squarely contradicted Terry Logan's testimony about the payment promises, saying that he only promised to pay promptly what the Corps determined to be due on these pay requests, thus implying that deductions might be necessary.[106] In resolving this contradiction I was persuaded that Terry Logan was the more credible witness by far. The intangibles in his demeanor, conviction and truthfulness were manifest where Col. Roth seemed hesitant, unsure, and evasive, recalling only "his best recollection". I sensed that Judge Jellico thought so too.

In briefing the case, I argued that Ray Clairmont's and Wally Abbott's testimony sufficiently established a differing site condition in the Rock Hill so as to make the $400K settlement unconscionable and voidable for duress, citing cases. I argued why the government materially breached the takeover agreement by not making the promised payments and by demanding new performance and payment bonds as a condition of further performance, again citing cases. The case was finally submitted to the Board for decision after the completion of briefing some time later in 1980 or early in 1981.

On December 30, 1983, the Board finally issued its decision. To our surprise it was not made or written by Judge Jellico whom we later learned had retired shortly after the trial, but by a Judge McFadden with the concurrence of two other Board judges, none of whom had heard the witnesses and had before them only the trial transcript and the briefs. Judge McFadden rejected all our principal arguments.

In sustaining the Rayco default termination, Judge McFadden found that Rayco's failure to complete most of the project in 1976 was at least equally due to its financial incapacity and insufficient production of base course as to the Rock Hill boulders and recreation area changes, and given this mutual fault the $400K settlement was neither unconscionable nor the product of government duress. Accepting Col. Roth's testimony about what he promised to pay the surety, Judge McFadden

---

106 In fact, the Corps based on a final inventory of Rayco work performed asserted an overpayment claim of about $7K against this pay request and similarly reduced the surety's initial pay request to $18.3K which was never paid.

rejected the surety's termination of the takeover agreement for material breach, adding that while the demand for new bonds was a breach of the takeover agreement, it was not sufficiently material to justify the surety's termination of the takeover agreement which in turn justified the government's subsequent termination of the surety's right to proceed.[107] Of course, the credibility of witnesses with conflicting testimony often turns on the intangibles of witness demeanor, sincerity and other factors which a transcript of the testimony rarely reveals. We do not know whether Judge Jellico in his notes or otherwise made any input to Judge McFadden on this crucial issue.

Rayco and the Logans now faced the prospect of liability for the excess costs of the reprocurement to complete the project as well as liquidated damages for nonperformance. In a final decision of June 21, 1982, the contracting officer notified Rayco and the Logans that they owed the government $1.12M in excess reprocurement costs and $102.1K in liquidated damages, plus interest on those amounts. We promptly appealed that decision to the Corps of Engineers Board of Contract Appeals. In a decision issued not until March 31, 1988, Judge Solibakke who had participated in Judge McFadden's decision, and with the concurrence of two other Board judges who had not, significantly reduced the contracting officer's decision to $752K in excess reprocurement costs and $88.6K in liquidated damages, plus interest from the date of the contracting officer's final decision, as explained hereafter.[108]

I agreed with the government trial attorney to submit the case to the Board on the record of the relevant documents, thus dispensing the need for a trial. The parties instead would argue their positions by exchanging opening and reply briefs to the Board, which we did. I requested the Board to stay proceedings until the Board decided the earlier appeal and any appeal therefrom to the Court of Appeals for the Federal Circuit under the newly enacted Contract Disputes Act of 1978. The Board granted that request and restored the case to the active docket promptly

---

107 *Rayco, Inc., Contractor, and Russell E. Logan and Terry E. Logan, Surety*, ENG BCA Nos. 4169 and 4248, 84-1 BCA ¶ 17,055 at 84,931-939.

108 *Rayco, Inc. Contractor, and Russell E. Logan and Terry E. Logan, Surety*, ENG BCA No. 4792, 88-2 BCA ¶ 20,671 (March 31, 1988).

after the Federal Circuit summarily affirmed the Board's December 30, 1983 decision without opinion after I briefed and orally argued the appeal to a panel of three judges of the court.[109]

The Corps due to lack of funds delayed the reprocurement of most of the work to complete the access road until July 13, 1981 when it awarded a contract to the Wylie Corporation as the low bidder, some 28 months after the March 12, 1979 default termination of the surety's takeover agreement during a period of raging inflation. The Corps paid Wylie a total of $1.635M for performing that contract. With the funds on hand, the Corps in 1979 awarded a $310K contract to Neosho Construction Co., Inc., the low bidder for some of the remaining work in the recreation area, and separately awarded 13 non-competitive purchase orders to four vendors totaling $91.6K, two of which had been Rayco subcontractors for the rest of the remaining work in that area.

Judge Solibakke accepted our argument that the amount paid to the Wylie Corporation could not serve as a measure of excess costs of reprocurement since Rayco and the surety had no responsibility for the unreasonable delay in awarding that contract during a period of raging inflation. Accordingly, after allowing other credits that reduced the $1.635M to $1.497M, he applied a further inflation credit of 16% for the reprocurement delay, or about $240K, to arrive at excess costs of $1.27 M for the Wylie contract. Even so, the Rayco 1976 bid prices were at least another 16% below the Wylie prices as so reduced.

Judge Solibakke rejected our arguments that the fragmentation of the award of the remaining work in the recreation area as well as the award of the 13 non-competitive purchase orders prevented the amounts paid for that work as a proper measure of excess costs on the ground that the Corps' actions were "not unreasonable". From the totals of $!.616M of excess costs he properly deducted the unpaid balance of $863.8K from the Rayco contract price to arrive at a total excess cost liability of $781.84K, as contrasted with the contracting officer's demand for $1.124M. As for liquidated damages, Judge Solibakke correctly denied recovery of any

---

109 *Rayco, Inc., et al. v. United States*, 758 F.2d 668 (table) (Fed. Cir. 1984).

in relation to the Wylie contract, and limited them to the period from August 27, 1978, the contract completion date for the Rayco contract, to October 13, 1979, the completion date of the Neosho contract, 412 days at $15 per day, for a total of $88.58K as compared with the contracting officer's demand for $102.1K.

Thus the total liability imposed on Rayco and the surety by Judge Solibakke's decision was $840,430, plus very high interest from the June 21, 1982 decision of the contracting officer, down from the $1.226M then demanded by the contracting officer. Again, I appealed this outcome to the Federal Circuit Court on several grounds which again summarily upheld the Board's decision without opinion.

These two decisions of the Engineer Board of Contract Appeals were devastating disasters for Rayco, Ray Clairmont and the Logans. Ray Clairmont was broke, perhaps broken, Terry Logan almost, and Rayco was defunct. Terry's elderly father, Russell, was retired and exposing him to this liability would reduce him and his wife to penury. I so advised my opposing counsel. As far as I know, the government took no action to recover the excess costs and liquidated damages from Russell Logan and realized that there could be no recovery from Rayco, and very little if any from Terry Logan. There was also no prospect for the payment of more than $100K in fees and expenses I had billed them. Terry Logan moved to Nevada and we lost touch. I had no further contact with Ray Clairmont.

These cases were a dear and expensive lesson for me and my law firm in the economics of law practice. Yet as a matter of conscience and professional responsibility I could hardly withdraw once they could no longer pay and their case looked bleak.

-McCarney Ford v. Ford Motor Company.

In 1980 Ray Clairmont introduced me to Robert McCarney until recently the long-time owner of the Ford and Lincoln dealership in Bismarck.

He had told Ray he needed a good lawyer to appeal a recent decision against him in the federal district court. Ray recommended me.

Mr. McCarney explained to me that the district court for the second time had rejected his suits against Ford for forcing him to sell his dealer-ship at a ruinous price because he had refused to sell small Ford cars for which he said there was no market in the Bismarck area. I said I would study the court's decisions and get back to him on whether I could help.

In the first, unreported decision in 1979, the district court, in a suit brought under the "Automobile Dealers' Day in Court Act"[110] by Mr. McCarney and his wife as individuals, treated the defendant's motion to dismiss because the plaintiffs were individuals and not a Ford dealer as a motion for summary judgment and dismissed the suit because the McCarneys as individuals lacked standing to sue under that statute. They did not appeal that decision. In February 1980 they brought the same suit in the district court with McCarney Ford substituted as the plaintiff. The district court in an unreported decision granted Ford's motion to dismiss on the basis of res judicata and collateral estoppel.[111]

After studying the matter, I believed the second decision of the dis-trict court was erroneous and I advised the McCarneys that they had a good chance of prevailing on appeal to the U. S. Court of Appeals for the 8th Circuit. They asked me to proceed with the appeal and invited me to stay in their home for that purpose which I did for two or three months. I also had the use of the district court's law library and the excellent legal research help of three attorneys in Gage & Tucker's Kansas City office as well as that of the Bismarck attorney who had brought the cases in the district court for the McCarneys.

I enjoyed the McCarneys' company and hospitality. Elizabeth McCa-rney was a law school graduate who had not practiced law but was eager to discuss the pros and cons of the appeal.

---

110 15 U.S.C. §§ 1221 *et seq.* (2006).

111 The law precludes relitigation of the same issues in a subsequent suit by the same parties under the doctrine of "res judicata", "the thing having been decided". The doctrine of collateral estoppel is to the same effect.

I argued the appeal to a panel of three judges of the Court of Appeals in St Louis on April 18, 1981, after having submitted opening and reply briefs to the court as Ford had also done. The court issued its decision on August 27, 1981.[112] It accepted our arguments that the dismissal of the first suit for lack of the standing of the individual plaintiffs to bring that suit was not a decision on the merits of that suit and therefore the doctrines of res judicata or issue preclusion did not bar the second suit. It therefore reversed and remanded the second decision of the district court.

The McCarneys were delighted and they retained their local counsel to resume their litigation against Ford. I said farewell to the McCarneys and never learned the outcome of that litigation. For me it was a welcome litigation experience entirely unrelated to my usual public contract law practice.

-Life at 2101 Connecticut Avenue 1976-84.

As previously related, Don and I in December 1976 purchased the shares for apartment 45 in this splendid late 1920s apartment building recently transformed from a rental to cooperative shareholder ownership and substantially upgraded with central air conditioning, new kitchens, wiring, and other improvements. The price for this 2,500 SF apartment was $125K and another $10K for a parking space in the adjoining garage. We paid cash from the sale of the 6th Street house on Capitol Hill. My friend and colleague, John McWhorter, had recently purchased an attractive apartment there and encouraged us to do so. Don knew the president of the cooperative, Harry Hoskinson, and that helped persuade the board of directors who approved all new residents that we would be suitable.

The apartment had a large living room with a fireplace and with east and west windows, a dining room and adjoining sun room with west and north windows, three bedrooms with east windows, one of which became

---

112 *Robert P. McCarney and Elizabeth H. McCarney v. Ford Motor Company*, 657 F.2d 230 (8th Cir. 1981). The appeal was by the McCarneys individually as the owners and assignees of McCarney Ford, now dissolved.

our library and TV room, two baths and a powder room, a small maid's room and bath next to the kitchen which adjoined the dining room, and a large entrance foyer and gallery that extended all the way to the living room and was largely wasted space. Nevertheless, Don with his considerable decorating skills made our furniture, paintings, curtains, and rugs attractively becoming in this new setting.

We gradually met our neighbors. Next door in No. 47 were Supreme Court Justice Tom Clark and his wife who were cordial. About a year later my colleague, Eldon ("Took") Crowell, purchased the adjoining apartment No. 43. We would see him socially and we became good friends. Garrison and Emily Norton, who had been great friends of Lyttleton Fox lived in a grand apartment on the top floor and had moved there several years previously when the building had rental tenants. Through Lyttleton I had previously met the Nortons when they lived in Georgetown and I was working for the Navy OGC including some work for Garry when he was the Assistant Secretary of the Navy for Air during the Eisenhower administration which he said he remembered. We would become close friends and through the Nortons would also become friends with the widowed Carol Wakelin, Armida Colt, and Noel Train about whom I shall write in due course.

Garry Norton, born in 1900, was my chronologically oldest friend. He recalled the years 1909-13 when he father was secretary to the cabinet of President Taft and they lived in a house that later became the F Street Club in "Foggy Bottom" near the State Department's present location. Garry went to Groton and then Harvard College, Class of 1922. Later he became a partner in the accounting firm of Arthur Young in New York until his wartime service in the Bureau of Aeronautics where he and Lyttleton became friends.

Through a friend of Don's, a school teacher in Alexandria named Bob Reed, we came to know Robert Manson Myers, an eminent professor of English literature at the University of Maryland in College Park who also lived in a beautifully appointed and furnished apartment on the top floor. I shall have more to relate about Manson and his achievements as an author and teacher.

We lived enjoyably and comfortably at 2101 for the next 8 years. For most of this time I served on the 5-man board of directors. Harry Hoskinson, the president, and I became good friends as I also did with Harry Covington, the treasurer, and with Peter Halle, another board member whose wife, Carolyn Lamm, I had known in the American Bar Association of which she many years later would become president. I would be away much of the time on client business, and Don would be in Key West from late October until late May once we had purchased the house there in 1978 as I have previously written. Harry Hoskinson was an effective president, and he and the board were careful to screen prospective purchasers so as to exclude those we thought would not be compatible with the other residents. After Harry retired from the board, which was after we left in 1984, we learned that the turnover on ownership without this careful screening had created an atmosphere of strife and contention among many of the shareholders.

-A Project To Reform Government Debarment of Contractors.

In the fall of 1980 Sparks Hiestand, the incoming chair of the ABA Section of Public Contract Law and former general counsel to the Commission on Government Procurement discussed above, asked me to chair a new committee of the section he was establishing to tackle the felt need to reform the fairness of the government's procedures and organizational structure for debarring and suspending firms and individuals from government contracting. He said this was one of the projects that the Commission did not have time to address. He suggested that we undertake drafting comprehensive legislation detailing the criteria for the imposition of these sanctions and the creation of a government-wide debarment and suspension board of appointed administrative judges to impose them. He pointed out the weaknesses of the existing system. For example, within the Department of Defense, there were multiple debarring and suspension officials, one for each separate military department and for each separate defense agency, and there was insufficient coordination among them. Also the practice of ex parte suspension, even with a notice of proposed debarment, needed reform except in truly emergency conditions, and there should be a procedure for an evidentiary hearing when the facts are contested. Finally, there needed to be coordination with the Department of Justice where the agency action would interfere with ongoing criminal or civil investigations of the firm or individual being considered for debarment or suspension.

All this rang a bell with me, harking back to my work for Cy Vance and President Kennedy's Administrative Conference in 1962 as recounted in Part Four. Sparks and I recruited a strong team of about 8 or 10 lawyers mostly in private practice to serve on the committee. Among them were Andy Singer, then a bright young partner at Covington & Burling, and Pat Szervo, an attorney with the newly Congressionally established Office of Federal Procurement Policy in the executive office of the President. Andy was the principal draftsman of the debarment statute that Sparks had suggested. The committee spent many hours debating and revising its provisions. Several months later, the committee unanimously approved the draft, Pat Szervo abstaining because of her government position, and submitted it to the Section council for approval at the spring meeting in 1981. At that meeting I presented the committee's report which the council members had previously received and obtained unanimous council approval, again the government members of the council abstaining. The Section's action was then presented to the ABA Board of Governors and, if approved by the Board, to the House of Delegates for approval of this legislative proposal at its August 1981 meeting as legislation to be sponsored by the ABA. At that meeting Sparks very ably and effectively orally argued the merits first to the Board and obtaining Board approval to the House of Delegates which also approved it by a strong majority vote. Alas, thereafter we made little headway in persuading the Reagan Administration to sponsor this legislation or to achieve its principal reforms administratively.

4. Working at the Sach, Green- ebaum & Tayler Firm 1984-88.

When Sidney Sachs graduated from Georgetown Law School in Washington in 1941 prejudice against Jews excluded him from employment by the established law firms there and elsewhere despite an outstanding college and law school record and a sterling character. He opened an office in Washington and gradually built a thriving domestic relations practice. He hired able young lawyers on their merit and formed an expanding partnership. It was primarily a litigation firm focusing on local matters, including criminal defense, as distinguished from those involving the federal government. Sidney also rose to positions of increasing responsibility in the DC and American Bar Associations. He was a thoroughbred, estimable gentleman in every way. U.S. District Judge Paul Friedman in an address to the ABA Section of Public Contract Law at its annual education seminar in Annapolis in March 1998 on "Fostering Civility: A Professional Obligation" called the late Sidney Sachs "one of the great trial lawyers and personalities of the District of Columbia Bar" who once told him, "Always remember, the lawyer on the other side of the case is not your enemy. His client and your client may view themselves as enemies. But you and he are not enemies. You are friends, or, in time may become friends."[113] Sidney was like that, a splendid practitioner and mentor.

By the time I arrived in about 1984, having been recruited by Bob Ackerly to join him in building a public contract law litigation practice for the firm, it had about 20 lawyers, mostly litigators. Although Ackerly was at least a nominal partner, I was designated "of counsel", an indeterminate status of being neither a partner nor an associate. All my fees were to be billed by the firm, and the firm would deduct a percentage of each

---

113 Judge Friedman's remarks on March 13, 1998, primarily on the urgent importance of the restoration of civility and professionalism in the practice of law, are available on the website of the ABA Section of Public Contract Law.

fee payment to cover the firm's costs of housing me and providing various office services. That percentage was at least 25% for the three years I remained with the firm.

The firm had recently hired Jim Johnson, a recent Georgetown Law School graduate who would soon leave for a clerkship with one of the trial judges of the recently created U.S. Claims Court.[114] He was one of the brightest young lawyers I had encountered, superb at analysis and writing. He also was endearing, gentle, somewhat shy, and he became friends with Don and me. After his year's clerkship at the Court of Federal Claims working mostly on government contract disputes he became an attorney in the office of the Board of Contract Appeals of the General Services Administration. In performing searching edits of the Board's decisions prior to release he has earned appreciation and respect and at its successor Civilian Board of Contract Appeals as well where he continues to do this and other work assigned him by the Board's general counsel.

Jim is also a very talented artist in drawing and painting, and very knowledgeable and conversant with the great Western art. Had he made this primary interest his life's work I believe he would have achieved wide recognition and acclaim. As it was, he had to earn a living as a lawyer and could not do both. About 1986 he started living with Frank Spencer, a personable, quiet young man working at U.S. Airways. They now live in Alexandria and their domestic partnership happily endures.

I particularly recall two matters that I worked on at Sachs, Greenebaum, each involving litigation in the federal courts in Washington: one a bid protest, and the other overturning a debarment of two corporate officers from contracting with the federal government.

---

114 The Federal Court Improvements Act of 1982, transformed the U.S. Court of Claims, created in the 1860s to hear contract claims against the government, into two courts, a trial court called the U.S. Claims Court, and an appellate court to be known as the U.S. Court of Appeals for the Federal Circuit. The Claims Court, later renamed the U.S. Court of Federal Claims, primarily has jurisdiction over contract claims and later over bid protests as set forth in 28 U.S.C § 1491 (2006). The jurisdiction of the Court of Appeals for the Federal Circuit, as provided in 28 U.S.C. § 1295 (2006), was enlarged beyond that of the Court of Claims to add claims formerly brought in the Court of Customs and Patent Appeals which was abolished.

-Litigating the Protest of Maryland Shipbuilding & Drydock Co. and Prudential Lines Against a Navy Contract Award.

The bid protest involved the Maryland Shipbulding & Drydock Co. of Baltimore in a joint venture with Prudential Lines of New York competing for a Navy contract to convert an existing vessel of specified minimum capacities into a hospital ship for the Navy. The Maryland company contacted me promptly upon learning that the Navy had awarded the contract to their competitor, National Steel & Shipbuilding Co., on June 28, 1983.

I went to New York to meet with the officials of both companies. Prudential Lines was controlled by the film magnate Spiro Skouras, recently head of 20th Century Fox. His counsel for this matter was a Washington attorney, Dan Piliero. We agreed to file a suit in the federal district court in Washington challenging the contract award as contrary to what the evaluation criteria of the solicitation called for and that the Navy lacked a rational basis for finding that the Prudential-Maryland technical proposal did not meet the minimum requirements of the specifications in five areas and for determining that National Steel had the lower price and cost to the Navy.

After Prudential-Maryland filed the suit, National Steel intervened, and the parties engaged in substantial discovery of each other, involving documents and depositions. This led to our amending the complaint to allege that the National Steel technical proposal raised serious concerns as to whether its superstructure strength calculations in the planned conversion of a tanker to be acquired into a hospital ship as well as the emergency electrical generation and switchboard arrangements would meet the certification requirements of the American Bureau of Shipping (ABS) and the Coast Guard. If they did not, the required redesign would involve significant additional costs and delays.

As Prudential had the predominant interest in the joint venture as the owner of one of their passenger liners to be so converted, Mr. Piliero would orally argue the case before Judge June Green on cross motions for summary judgment as the material facts were not in dispute. What was disputed was whether, on those facts, either party was entitled to the contract award. The parties had previously exchanged briefs. At the oral argument, Dan Pilliero was not at his best. Some other client matter had kept him up the night before the oral argument and he was mentally exhausted. As a result, the excellent government attorney, Judith Bartnoff, had the better of the oral argument. I was not surprised therefore when Judge Green upheld the award the Navy had made.[115]

While for business reasons the joint venture did not appeal Judge Green's decision, it was nevertheless questionable in sustaining the award with the Navy not knowing if National Steel would meet the above ABS and Coast Guard technical requirements and having to incur the substantial additional contract costs and delays if it did not.[116] Under these circumstances, I believe she should have cancelled the award to National Steel and ordered the Navy to reopen the competition to enable the parties to correct the established or suspected design deficiencies, obtain the required ABS and Coast Guard certifications or assurance that they would be forthcoming, and to submit revised best and final proposals. Having lost this $350M contract, the long-established Maryland Shipbuilding Co. went out of business a year or so later for lack of work.

-Litigating the Debarment of Two Officers of a Debarred Contractor.

In the debarment case,[117] William Carroll, the debarring official of the Defense Logistics Agency of the Department of Defense, debarred Murdock Webbing, Inc., a Rhode Island contractor, and its chairman and vice chairman of the board of directors, from further government

---

115 *Prudential-Maryland Joint Venture Company v. Lehman et al..*, 590 F. Supp. 1390 D. D.C. (1984).

116 590 F. Supp. at 1408.

117 *Caiola et al. v. Carroll*, 851 F.2d 395 (D.C. Cir. 1988).

contracts following their criminal convictions for having submitted false testing reports on products it manufactured under contracts with DLA. He then proposed to extend the debarment to the three other officers and directors of Murdock Webbing as "affiliates" of the company for having had "reason to know" of the false test reports and for failing to take action to prevent the criminal conduct.[118] The three officers and directors were James Caiola, president, Edward Lodge, treasurer, and Elsa DeAngelis, secretary, whose husband was chairman of the board of directors and the controlling shareholder. In opposition to the proposed debarment all three showed they had no involvement in the manufacturing and testing operations and had no knowledge of, or reason to know of, the criminal conduct. The evidence showed that the manufacturing and testing operations were controlled by Mr. DeAngelis and his son Don, vice chairman of the board, each of whom had also been convicted and separately debarred.

Mr. Carroll concluded that while none of the three respondents knew of the criminal activity, Mr. Caiola because of his position as president and a director, and Mrs. DeAngelis, from her position of secretary and a director, each had reason to know of the criminal activity while Mr. Lodge, as treasurer, did not. He therefore debarred the first two from government contracting for three years and dismissed the proposed debarment of Mr. Lodge. The district court upheld this action, and Mr. Cailola and Mrs. DeAngelis, the unsuccessful plaintiffs, appealed.

Sachs, Greenebaum & Tayler did not represent the plaintiffs in the district court. Bill Tayler asked me to help him on the appeal. We needed to establish that Mr. Carroll's decision was "arbitrary and capricious" under the judicial review provisions of the Administrative Procedure Act.[119] We argued first that that the appellants were not "affiliates" since neither of them either directly or indirectly "controls or can control" the company as required by the FAR definition of "affiliate" since chairman De Angelis owned 90% of the stock and therefore "the reason to know"

---

118 That action was authorized by various subparagraphs of paragraph 9.406 of the 1985 edition of the Federal Acquisition Regulation then in effect. 48 C.F.R. 9.406.

119 5 U.S.C. § 702 (2006).

criterion was inapplicable. We argued further that in any event there was no evidentiary basis for Mr. Carroll's discriminatory and inconsistent finding that the appellants had reason to know of the criminal activity while Mr. Lodge did not, so as to impute that knowledge to the appellants but not to Mr. Lodge. The Court of Appeals accepted these arguments and reversed the district court with instructions to order the dismissal of the debarments of the appellants[120]. It was a close question.

The government had argued that Mrs. DeAngelis had "an identity of interest" in the stock ownership with her husband under Rhode Island law and thus was a "constructive owner" of the controlling shares and had the potential to control the company and prevent the criminal activity. To this the court replied, "These laws, even if correctly stated, were not considered at the administrative hearing, and would not appear to give Elsa DeAngelis a present property interest in her husband's stock sufficient to enable her to exercise any practical control over Murdock Webbing."[121] The court also rejected the government's further argument that Mr. Caiola's position as president of Murdock Webbing was a sufficient basis for imputing knowledge of the criminal activity to him since Mr. Carroll had found that he and Mr. Lodge "were not involved in the manufacturing and production end of Murdock Webbing and were not aware that the end-item testing had not been done.[122]

One of the Justice Department attorneys on the case was Mary Ellen Coster Williams in the course of which we became friends. I later recommended her to be an administrative judge at the GSA Board of Contract Appeals. After several years in that role she was appointed by the second President Bush to be a judge at the Court of Federal Claims where she continues to serve commendably. While at the GSA Board she also had a term as chair of the ABA Public Contract Law Section.

---

120 The opinion for the court was by Chief Judge Re joined by Circuit Judges Williams and Ruth Bader Ginsburg who was later appointed by President Clinton to the Supreme Court.

121 851 F.2d 395, 401.

122 851 F.2d 395, 400.

Moving to a Cooperative Apartment at 1661 Crescent Place NW in 1984.

In June 1984 Don and I received an attractive, unsolicited offer to buy the shares to our apartment at 2101 Connecticut Avenue for more than three times what we had paid for them. With an uncertain outlook on my future earnings and because Don knew about and liked the nearby apartment building at 1661 Crescent Place NW and the then availability of an apartment there, we accepted the offer and moved in July. In some ways we were sorry to leave and would miss seeing the friends we made there. Another worry was the rising costs of living there and the likelihood of some major capital expenses in the next few years that would significantly add to the monthly expenses. While we liked the apartment, the living room was difficult to arrange the furniture attractively due to the shape of the room, the location of the fireplace, and the wide entrance to the gallery leading to the entrance foyer. I have pointed out the wasted space of the gallery. By contrast, apartment 208 at 1661 Crescent Place, about the same size if one subtracts the 500 square feet of the gallery, was attractive throughout: a marble-tiled entrance hall leading to a sizeable dining room facing east with a pantry door to the kitchen, and beyond the dining room to a large living room also facing east and south with a fake fireplace at the north wall and with matching doors with pediments on either side, the east door also fake and the west leading to the two bedrooms and two baths also accessible from the entrance hall. There was also ample closet space in the apartment and a storage cage in the floor below off the lobby.

In buying the 110 shares for this apartment we again paid $125K in cash, the same amount we had paid eight years earlier for the shares for apartment 45 at 2101 Connecticut Avenue. We lucked out because the owner, Professor Robert W. Barnett, an Asian scholar and retired Foreign Service Officer, had recently married a lady with young children and there simply was not room. With great regret he had to sell. Don and I would become the 10th owner of the shares to this apartment since they were first sold in 1927. The original price for these shares then was $21,291; as of 2011 they were worth at least $800K and climbing!

Our furniture, rugs, curtains, paintings, etc., sufficed for Don to decorate the apartment attractively. We removed some of the bookcases and filled the others, particularly in the dining room with our books. Don had the rooms repainted, chiffon pie yellow in the entrance hall and living room, a pale dark orange in the dining room, white in the hall to the bedrooms, and a pale light blue in the bedrooms. Now some 27 years later, these colors are still vibrant and glow. Don replaced the kitchen cabinets, the stove and the refrigerator. We also installed Hunter fans in the ceilings of the principal rooms with two in the living room. We had no air conditioning and did not want or need window units. With the ceiling fans, and because there was no afternoon sun, the apartment has remained comfortable even on the hottest and most humid days of the summer months with the windows and the storm windows shut. In the next few years the building will have to replace the 1927 steam pipe heating system, probably with efficient individually controlled electrical units in the radiator spaces in the apartments circulating hot air and cold air from a centrally located compressor serving the building.

Crescent Place is a lovely, quiet, one-block street running east from 17th to 16th Street NW. Directly across the street from 1661 Crescent Place on the south side, are two magnificent, separated houses: a Georgian brick house of 1910 on less than an acre adjoining 16th Street to the east and Belmont Street to the south, and a French country house of 1920 to the west to 17th Street and south to Belmont Street, also on less than acre extending to the beginning of Crescent Place at 17th Street. Each of these properties extends south to Belmont Street which runs west from 16th to 17th Streets. Each house was designed by the noted architect John Russell Pope who also designed the National Gallery of Art and the Jefferson Memorial in Washington. His clients for the 1910 house were Henry White, formerly Theodore Roosevelt's ambassador to London or Paris, and his beautiful wife, Margaret Rutherford White, whose full length portrait by John Singer Sargent standing at the bottom of the splendid staircase now hangs in the Corcoran Gallery of Art in Washington. About 1934, Eugene Meyer, a wealthy New York investment banker and formerly a governor of the Federal Reserve appointed by President Hoover until replaced by FDR, having purchased *The Washington Post* then in bankruptcy, also purchased this house from the White estate. There his daughter Katherine Meyer would grow up, marry Philip Graham whom her father appointed to be the editor, and then succeed him when tragically he killed himself shortly after JFK's assassination in 1963.

The French country house next to the west Pope designed in 1920 for Irwin Laughlin, scion of the Jones & Laughlin Steel Co., who was a career foreign service officer. Several years later he conceived the idea of an apartment building across the street as a home base for foreign service families. It was built in 1927 as 1661 Crescent Place NW and for many years served that purpose. When Mr. Laughlin died about 1944 he left his house to a foundation that his will established, to be called the "Meridian House Foundation" and the house "Meridian House" since the north-south meridian is near. Its purpose was to be a place where diplomats in Washington would meet for cultural, educational and social purposes, and so it has thrived. In the 1980s the foundation acquired the Meyer House as well, so that both of these houses have since served those worthy purposes.

Crescent Place at 16th Street faces Meridian Hill Park which adjoins the east side of 16th Street from W Street and Florida Avenue on the south to Euclid Street, about two blocks to the north and east to 15th Street. The 12-acre park, the largest in Washington after Rock Creek Park, was constructed over two decades starting in 1914 after Congress acquired the land for that purpose from the importuning of Mary Foote Henderson, the wife of Missouri senator John Brook Henderson. The design included Italian Renaissance terraced fountains in the lower half and a French Baroque style of gardens and plantings in the upper half.[123] There are statues of an equestrian Joan of Arc and of Dante, and a large memorial to James Buchanan, Lincoln's hapless predecessor. There are also magnificent trees and plantings that all in all make visiting the park a memorable experience.

---

123 For an account of this lovely park see the entry on Meridian Hill Park in Wikipedia.

For many years we had to park on the street until in the 1990s, Brian Kehoe, the president of the coop, negotiated a long-term lease of the top floor of the garage building in back of our building with the Envoy apartment building, formerly the Hotel 2400 16th Street which was built in the early 1900s and converted to condominium apartments in the 1960s. To access the leased space we would have to build a driveway and entrance gate from our east garden, and ramp the driveway up to the third floor level of the garage. We would have to make improvements and repairs on the third floor level. All this required a $5K capital contribution from residents willing to lease one of the 45 available parking spaces. The monthly rental would be $45. We jumped at it and obtained a suitable space.

We gradually met residents of the building, some of whom had lived there for many years. There was also fairly steady turnover as people arrived and departed. With Don in Key West much of the year and weekends in West Virginia when he was here, and with my continuing business travel we did not do much socializing in Washington.

After a year or so later we learned from our neighbor and friend at 2101 Connecticut Avenue, Robert Manson Myers, a professor of English literature at the University of Maryland, that the five plays he had drawn from the letters he had edited and published in his landmark *The Children of Pride* in 1972 which had won the National Book award for nonfiction in1973 which cited "his creative use of historical materials as a lesson for historians", would be performed that October in Savannah over five days. We decided to go. Don had read the book and was greatly impressed as I later would be by his selective choice of family letters to create a powerful novel-like story of drama and pathos. These are the letters by the cultivated members of a Georgian plantation family living in Liberty County near Savannah wrote to each other beginning with the courtship of Charles Colcock Jones as a divinity student at the Princeton, N.J., seminary and his wife to be, his cousin Mary Jones, in 1829-30, to and from their sons later being educated at Princeton and Harvard, to each other as the Civil War approaches and darkens their lives and the Reverend Jones's death in 1863, and finally the despair and resolution of Mary

Jones to her daughter in New Orleans as the war engulfs and destroys their way of life.

We drove the 600 miles to Savannah in time for the first event on the Wednesday evening of our arrival at the Presbyterian Church which had been the Jones family church. There Manson greeted the arrivals with the words from Ecclesiastes, "Now let us praise famous men", referring to the Reverend Charles and his wife Mary Jones and movingly told us about the lives they led and the values they believed in. Performance of the five plays began on Thursday with matinee and evening performances of two of them, the same for two more on Friday, and the last on Saturday evening, largely a monologue by Mary as her world collapses. Each was riveting, beautifully staged and wonderfully acted in a Savannah theater that perhaps seated about 500. There were lectures each morning by academics on the significance of Manson's book which Don and I did not attend; instead, we visited some beautiful antebellum houses and city squares and other inviting sites of the city.

The final event, Sunday morning, was at the Midway church some 50 miles south of Savannah off U.S. highway 17, and near one of the Jones's former plantations and their local church. There Manson had arranged for Professor Arthur S. Link, a distinguished historian at Princeton and biographer of Woodrow Wilson, who gave a dazzling talk about Manson's book and plays about which he brimmed with enthusiasm and admiration for a great cultural achievement in the dramatic revealing in their own words the worthy lives the Reverend Jones, his wife Mary, and their two sons and their daughter had led. A picnic lunch followed, then good byes. We returned to Washington on Monday savoring this marvelous encounter with Manson's achievement. He later published the plays as *Quintet*.[124]

About this time the University of Maryland at its College Park site near Washington began an annual Handel Festival of performing that great composer's oratorios that he mostly began creating in the 1730s as

---

124 A Five-Play Cycle drawn from *The Children of Pride*, University of Illinois Press 1991.

his operas declined in popularity. I was delighted to accompany Manson to these concerts superbly prepared and conducted by Paul Traver with excellent student soloists, chorus and orchestra. In knowledge, skill, and great understanding and realization of Handel's oratorios, Paul Traver matched that of Paul Callaway, for many years the organist and choirmaster at the Washington Cathedral whom I had experienced and admired when I sang in the Cathedral Choral Society under Paul some thirty years earlier including memorable performances of *Messiah* and *Israel in Egypt*.

The excellence of these festivals attracted considerable notoriety and involvement with lectures by Handel scholars of which Manson was one[125] and music critics such as Andrew Porter, then for *The New Yorker* and later for *The Times Literary Supplement*. As Manson's guest at these festivals I was impressed by the evident stature and respect he received from his colleagues and high officials of the University. There he was indeed a very important personage. Sadly, before Paul Traver was able to perform more than about dozen of these oratorios, the funding of them withered and the festivals had to be discontinued.

5. On to Ropes & Gray 1988-92.

In about 1986, Mathew Simchak, formerly an attorney with the Cuneo firm in Washington and about 20 years younger than I and whom I had known through his work in editing the ABA *Public* Contract Law *Journal*, persuaded the long-established and respected Boston firm of Ropes & Gray to add a public contract law capability to its then recently

---

125 *Handel's Messiah, A Touchstone of Taste* by Robert Manson Myers, Macmillan 1948. This, his first book, was a reworking of his doctoral dissertation at Columbia University. The eminent English authority on Handel's opera and oratorios, Winton Dean, attended at least one of these festivals.

opened office in Washington which he would develop and lead. For many of the firm's corporate clients also had government contracts, mostly with the Department of Defense, giving rise to legal needs which he could service. Starting in 1987 when I was still with Sachs, Greenebaum, Matt began calling on me for help. This led to a developing relationship resulting later that year after extensive interviewing by the senior partners in Boston in my becoming "of counsel" to the firm early in 1998 under a contract that either party could cancel upon due notice. I was pleased with a fixed annual salary of $75K that was not conditioned on how much business I attracted.

-The General Electric Litigation,

Matt immediately assigned me to work on the litigation of a dispute the General Electric Company (GE) had with the Naval Air Systems Command (NavAir). It had recently appealed to the Armed Services Board of Contract Appeals (ASBCA) a final decision of a NavAir contracting officer. In a decision of November 6, 1987, the contracting officer had "vitiated" the final acceptance by the Navy under 18 fixed-price type production contracts for some 1200 F404-GE-400 (F404) jet aircraft engines already delivered or to be delivered, and finally accepted or to be so accepted by, the Navy for having a latent defect in the design of the after-burner (A/B) liner. The decision directed GE to take all corrective action to redesign, produce and replace the A/B liners in engines already delivered as well as those to be delivered to the Navy at no cost to the government. He finally directed GE to repay the Navy about $1.253M which the Navy had already paid GE for A/B liner redesign work.

About a year later, the same contracting officer, by a final decision of November 9, 1988, also "vitiated" the final acceptance of engines incorporating a redesigned A/B liner to cure the original A/B liner design defect since the Navy had found cracking in some of the stiffened redesigned A/B liners and hence a further latent defect. He directed GE to take all necessary action to correct that defective redesign and replace the A/B liners in delivered engines incorporating that redesign as well as in engines to be delivered, all at no cost to the government. GE timely appealed that decision which the ASBCA consolidated with the other appeal.

Judge Ruth Burg of the ASBCA soon requested the parties to brief the issue of whether it had jurisdiction over these appeals even though the government had not filed a motion to dismiss. The Board would have to decide that issue before reaching the merits of the disputes.

I prepared a brief which argued strongly for ASBCA jurisdiction. The Contract Disputes Act stated "All claims by the government against a contractor relating to a contract shall be the subject of a decision by the contracting officer".[126] The statute did not define "claim". The Federal Acquisition Regulation's implementation defined "claim" in part to mean "a written demand or written assertion by one of the parties seeking, as a matter of right, the payment of money in a sum certain, the adjustment or interpretation of contract terms, or other relief arising under or relating to the contract." [127] Importantly, the standard FAR Disputes clause in these GE production contracts incorporated the above FAR definition of "claim". There were ASBCA decisions that had recognized that a contract termination for default by the contracting officer was a government claim as well as others suggesting that a contractor contesting a final decision to correct defective work "should perform the work and file a claim... ."[128] There was no controlling precedent in the Court of Appeals for the Federal Circuit.

The ASBCA decided that this jurisdictional issue should be decided by its Senior Deciding Group of administrative judges. In a decision on April 23, 1991, more than three years after GE filed its principal appeal, an opinion by Judge Ruth Burg and joined by nine senior judges upheld the Board's jurisdiction as "Government claims for 'other relief' " arising under the contract and properly the subject of a contracting officer

---

126 Section 6(a) of the CDA, 41 U.S.C. § 7107(a)(1)(B) as codified by Pub. L. 111-350, enacted January 4, 2011.

127 FAR 33.201.

128 *H.B. Zachry Co.*, ASBCA No. 39202, 90-1 BCA ¶ 22,342 at p. 112,287.

decision.[129] Four senior judges dissented, primarily on the basis of the *Zachry Co.* precedent, which the majority overruled, and because of the concern of embroiling the ASBCA in disputes over ongoing contract administration. Judge Williams, the chairman of the ASBCA, concurred in the result of the majority decision.[130]

The Navy appealed the Board's decision to the Federal Circuit Court of Appeals which the CDA authorized as previously related.[131] By then I had left Ropes & Gray to become a solo practitioner and did not participate in arguing for the Board's jurisdiction. In a decision dated February 24, 1993, a panel of three judges of that court upheld the ASBCA decision, one judge dissenting.[132]

---

129 *General Electric Company*, ASBCA Nos. 36005, 38152, 91-2 BCA ¶ 23,958 at p. 119,847.

130 He wrote "While I share the dissenting judges' legitimate concerns that the Board not become embroiled in matters that are primarily contract administration, it is my opinion that revocation of 'final acceptance' can, and under the circumstances of these appeals does, exceed the bounds of ordinary contract administration resulting in a Government claim under the FAR Disputes clause definitions. To hold otherwise would, in my opinion, unduly restrict the interpretation of the disputes clause definition of claims for 'other relief arising under or relating to the contract.' ". 91-2 BCA at p. 119,947.

131 See Note 101 and related text *supra*.

132 *Garrett v. General Electric Company*, 987 F. 2d 747 (Fed. Cir.1993). The majority in finding that the ASBCA had jurisdiction noted the intention of Congress in the CDA to create jurisdictional parity between the Boards of Contact Appeals and the Court of Federal Claims. It cited the recent Federal Courts Administration Act of 1992 which amended that court's jurisdiction stated in 28 U.S.C. § 1491(a)(2) conferred by the Contract Disputes Act by adding jurisdiction over identified nonmonetary claims by or against a contractor, "and other nonmonetary disputes on which a decision of the contractor has been rendered under section 6 of that Act." Pub. L. No. 102-572. Chief Judge Nies in her dissent was persuaded by the dissenting four ASBCA judges, particularly on the point that the Board's jurisdictional decision would not have the requisite finality for judicial review until the Board had determined the merits of the appeals from the contracting officer's decisions. There is the further uncertainty of whether there would be any appeal from those decisions or which party would be the appellant. These are weighty considerations the majorities in the ASBCA and Federal Circuit decisions did not persuasively answer.

Pending the Board's jurisdictional decision, Judge Burg had the parties proceed with litigating the merits of the contracting officer's decisions. In preparing for trial we had the good fortune to find a retired NavAir senior engineer who had responsibility for the specification for the F-404 engine to be incorporated into the full scale development (FSD) contract NavAir awarded to GE as a letter contract in November 1975 and converted to a cost-plus-incentive-fee contract about a year later. Under this FSD contract, GE was to design, develop and deliver 33 F-404 engines, in compliance with Engine Model Specification CP45K006,[133] to the Navy for installation as government furnished equipment in the McDonnell Douglas Corporation (McAir) F/A twin-engine fighter known as the "Hornet". These engines were to conform to a parts list prepared by GE on the basis of the designs of the parts for the FSD engines approved by

---

133 This specification was based on MIL-E-5007D developed by the military departments to establish "the performance, operating characteristics, design features, detailed interface configuration definitions, and installation envelopes for turbojet and turbofan engines", "the demonstrations, tests, reports, inspection procedures, and other data required for satisfactory completion and acceptance by the Using Service" of the "Preliminary Flight Rating Tests (PFRT) and the Qualification Tests (QT) for the engines", and for the "satisfactory completion of the Acceptance Tests (AT) of the production units of either model engine." 91-3 BCA at pp. 121,668-669. In addition to these tests, the Engine Model Specification also included for the FSD Contract a Simulated Mission Endurance Test (SMET). Finally, MIL-E- 5007D added a requirement, at the request of the Air Force, that the engine manufacturer would continue to be responsible for design specification compliance throughout the production contracts "to the extent required by the applicable contract." That requirement was omitted from the Engine Model Specification for the F-404 FSD contract. However, that specification also incorporated by reference MIL-E-5007D which included it, thus creating an apparent conflict between the two documents. The Navy engineer who had negotiated the Engine Model Specification with GE testified that NavAir intended that GE would retain design responsibility for design defects for the life of the program, and that its omission from the Engine Model Specification was inadvertent. We were rescued by our retired NavAir witness who had negotiated the MIL-E-5007D general specification for NavAir with the Air Force and Army representatives. He testified that the Navy's omission of this requirement of design responsibility from the Engine Model Specification for the F-404 FSD contract was intentional and should not be read into it. Judge Burg accepted his testimony as the "more credible". 91-3 BCA at p. 121,669, ¶ 4. Her finding would have a crippling effect on the Navy's attempted revocation of the final acceptance of engines delivered under the production contracts for latent defects in the A/B liners.

NavAir upon GE's satisfactory completion of the required tests specified in the Engine Model Specification.[134]

The FSD contract also included comprehensive general inspection rights and various remedies for NavAir for the correction of defects. The Inspection clause provided in paragraph (d) that "Except as otherwise provided in the contract, acceptance [of each engine] shall be conclusive except as regards latent defects, fraud, or such gross mistakes as amount to fraud."[135] The Inspection and Correction of Defects clause provided in paragraph (b) that "At any time during performance of the this contract, but not later than six (6) months...after acceptance of...[the 33 engines]...to be delivered under this contract, the Government may require the Contractor to remedy by correction or replacement, as directed by the Contracting Officer, any failure of the Contractor to comply with the requirements of this contract...."[136] The government's remedies for GE's breach of the warranty that at the time of acceptance the 33 engines will be free from defects in materials and workmanship and will conform to the Engine Model Specification were similarly time limited to notice of the defect having been given "within ten (10) months after acceptance or four months after first engine flight, whichever first occurs."[137]

NavAir was well aware that notwithstanding that an engine such as F-404 satisfactorily passed all the tests required by the Engine Model Specification under the FSD contract, it could not assume that the components of the engine would not fail during operations both within the flight envelope and beyond it as would inevitably occur. Those tests were far from exhaustive and operational use and experience would determine the extent to which part and component failures needed redesign. For this reason the NavAir in the 1950s established a comprehensive Component Improvement Program (CIP) under which NavAir would fund

---

134 Paragraph 3.3.9.2 of the Engine Model Specification included in the FSD contract stated that the "parts list for the engine which successfully completed PFRT or QT shall constitute the approved parts list for any subsequent engines of the same types and model to be delivered to the Using Service." 91-3 BCA at p. 121,670, ¶ 7.

135 91-3 BCA at 121,671, ¶ 9.

136 91-3 BCA at 121,672, ¶ 9.

137 91-3 BCA at 121,673-74, ¶ 12.

its engine manufacturers such as GE and Pratt & Whitney under cost-reimbursement contracts to correct design inadequacies that adversely affect safety of flight or engine performance. NavAir awarded GE 18 CIP contracts during a 10-year period beginning in 1977 for more than $160M to match the 18 production contracts for the F-404 engines Nav-Air awarded GE during that period.[138]

In 1981 and again in 1984 GE reported various failures of the A/B liner and requested CIP coverage to correct the apparent design failures which NavAir approved.[139] In 1987 it requested NavAir approval, by an engineering change proposal, to replace at government expense the A/B liner in all F-404 engines with an improved capability to withstand buckling. By then NavAir had determined that the A/B liner failures were a latent defect for nonconformity which resulted in the final decision of the contracting officer which GE had appealed to the Board.[140] By January 1990 GE had reported a total of 26 failures of the A/B liner in relation to 1.5M flight hours of the F-404 engines, less than the 27.09 in one million flight hours which GE estimated as required before the QT under the FSD contract, although some of these failures also damaged other components of the A/B liner.[141]

The statement of work for the first three production contracts (Lots III, IV and V) awarded from 1977-80 required GE to build the F-404 engines to conform to the approved parts list.[142] This had the effect of having the Navy assume the risk of design deficiencies in the engines since it limited the Navy's post-acceptance remedies to latent defects in materials and workmanship. Starting with the negotiation of the work statement for the Lot VI production contract, NavAir apparently aware of this unwelcome risk wanted the work statement to provide that the engines would conform both to the parts list and to the Engine Model Specification, with the latter to prevail in the case of conflict. GE replied

---

138 91-3 BCA at 121,677, ¶ 24.

139 91-3 BCA at 121,677, ¶ 26.

140 91-3 BCA at p. 121,678,, ¶¶ 27, 28.

141 Note 134 and 140 *supra*.

142 91-3 BCA at 121.680, ¶ 33.

that it would increase the price of the engine threefold and it was in any event unacceptable.[143] Two years later the parties reached a compromise under which the work statement provided at no increase in price that the engines would conform to both the Engine Model Specification and the parts list with the limitation that conformance to the Engine Model Specification "shall be deemed complete and the requirements satisfactorily met when, at the time of initial installation, the engine successfully completes the engine related portion of the Aircraft Acceptance Test", or as GE expressed it, "when the aircraft flew over the fence" at McAir in St Louis.[144] Up to that point, but not thereafter, GE would remain responsible for any design defects discovered before or after acceptance of the engines. Acceptance of the engines was at GE's plant at Lynn, Mass.

Before this language was incorporated in the Lot VI production contract, GE realized that NavAir might postpone engine acceptance and payment until after the engine was delivered by the Navy to McAir and satisfactorily completed the engine portion of the aircraft acceptance test, which could be many months after engine delivery and acceptance at GE's plant. Accordingly, the parties agreed to transfer the design limitation language to the Defects clause and starting with the Lot X contract to the Warranty clause, intending no change in meaning.[145]

However, the Warranty clause for the Lot VIII contracts, one of the Lot IX contracts, and the Lot X contracts was substantially changed, to add that the government's rights under the contract for latent defects "are not limited by this clause" which GE understood to increase its exposure to latent defects in materials and workmanship and priced it accordingly.[146] Without informing GE, a senior NavAir engineer also added the words "For purposes of this Warranty" at the beginning of the design limitation language. Since GE signed the contracts with that

143 91-3 BCA at 121,680, ¶¶ 34, 35.

144 91-3 BCA at 121,681-682, ¶¶ 38, 39.

145 *Id.*., ¶ 39; and ¶ 43 at p. 122,684. In fact, a revised Warranty clause replaced the Defects clause starting with the Lot VIII contracts, one of the three Lot IX contracts, and the Lot X contracts. The Lot VII contract and two of the Lot IX contracts retained the design limitation language of the Defects clause. 91-3 BCA at p. 121,685, ¶ 44.

146 *Id.*., ¶ 46.

addition, this sleight of hand arguably had the effect of nullifying the design limitation language for latent design defects discovered after aircraft acceptance.[147]

We tried the case on both appeals to Judge Burg starting in January 1990. At the trial, in trial preparation and the post-trial briefing I was greatly assisted by Paul O'Donnell, an experienced litigator from the Boston office of Ropes & Gray, and by Clay Marsh, a bright young associate in the Washington office of the firm. On the above facts and contract provisions we argued in the first appeal that the NavAir's revocation ("vitiation") of the acceptance of the delivered F-404 engines under the production contracts because of latent defects in the design of the A/B liners was a nullity. Surprisingly, it had not done so as to the 33 engines delivered and accepted under the FSD contract. If it had, it would have arguably enabled the NavAir to claim that the parts list created under the FSD contract as to the A/B liner incorporated that latent defect so as to defeat limiting the applicability of the parts list in the work statement for the Lots III-V contracts to latent defects in materials and workmanship.

For the Lot VI, Lot VII and two of the Lot IX contracts we argued that the limitation of design liability for latent defects ended when the engine "flew over the fence at McAir", having successfully passed the engine portion of the aircraft acceptance test. The Lot VIII and subsequent contracts incorporating the deceptive addition of "For the purposes of this warranty" to the design limitation language, we argued, did not expose GE to liability for latent defects in the A/B liner first because the Navy engineer in deposition testimony had admitted no change in intent, and secondly, in any event such a deceptive contract change should be denied enforcement. Finally we argued that GE by 1984 before the delivery of those engines had alerted NavAir to numerous A/B liner failures and was conducting a CIP investigation to redesign the liner. Any design defects in the A/B liners delivered under those contracts, therefore, were not "latent".[148] For this reason GE also was not obligated to refund the

---

147 *Id.* , ¶ 45; decision at 121,691.

148 *Id.*

$1.23M NavAir had paid under the CIP contract to redesign the liner, as also demanded by the contracting officer's first final decision.

I must note that the deportment of the Navy trial attorney was unacceptable. He was without civility, excessively rude and hostile to opposing counsel, and I thought to Judge Burg as well who mostly managed to overlook it. He deserved citation for contempt, and as a former member of that office I was embarrassed that such an "attack dog" could be designated a "senior trial attorney" by the Navy OGC for practice before the ASBCA.

In a decision issued on August 21, 1991, with two judges concurring, Judge Burg on the revocation of acceptance on the production contracts found for GE on all issues and sustained that appeal, mostly accepting our arguments. She made extensive findings of fact, many of which I have referenced in the notes, carefully considered the opposing arguments, and wrote a masterly decision.[149]

The second appeal was from the November 1988 NavAir contracting officer's second final decision after the Navy during routine maintenance in August 1988 had discovered that the redesigned, stiffened A/B liner had also failed from cracking and buckling. It also characterized that failure as a latent defect in the redesigned liner, "vitiated" the final acceptance of the engines incorporating it, and directed GE at its expense redesign and retrofit them with a further redesigned A/B liner to be installed in all F-404 engines.[150] As of the date of that decision comparatively few of the redesigned liners had been installed in engines delivered beginning with the Lot X contracts.[151] In October 1988 GE proposed a solution under Engineering Change Proposal ECP-21 and offered to supply the redesigned liners to the Navy at no increase in price and the Navy

---

149 91-3 BCA ¶ 24,353 at 121,686-692.

150 *General Electric Company,* ASBCA Nos. 36005 and 38152, 91-2 BCA ¶ 23,958 at 119,941.

151 *General Electric Company,* ASBCA No. 36005, 91-3 BCA ¶ 24,353 at 121,679, ¶ 31.

to incur the expense of redesign and retrofitting consistent with NavAir's Component Improvement Program.[152]

On these facts we argued in the second appeal that NavAir had no latent defect remedy under the Lot X contracts under which some of the redesigned liners had been installed in the accepted engines. First, the words the NavAir engineer had surreptitiously added ("For purposes of this warranty") to the design limitation language made no difference since his deposition testimony was that he intended no change of meaning, and that in any case the Board should decline to enforce any change of meaning based on his deception. We argued further that had the Navy performed additional tests of the redesigned liner it would have discovered the further cracking and buckling so as to preclude the defects being "latent".

Judge Burg rejected these arguments. Instead, based on the November 1987 contracting officer's final decision in the first appeal revoking the final acceptance of engines under all of the F-404 contracts, she emphasized that that decision had directed GE at no increase in contract price to redesign, repair and replace and otherwise correct A/B liners in the production contracts in accordance with GE's earlier Engineering Change Proposal ECP-11 which had proposed a redesigned, stiffened A/B liner.[153] That direction, she held, was a "constructive change" to the production contracts although she did not need to decide which production contracts were to be retrofitted since the contracting officer's November 1987 decision had not specified which production contracts his direction covered.[154] She therefore concluded that GE thereby had contractual responsibility for redesign of the liners and because the redesigned liners had failed that failure was a latent defect as to accepted engines incorporating them since they also did not meet the "other contract requirements" of the

---

152 *Id.*, ¶ 29.

153 *Id.*, ASBCA Nos. 36005 and 38152, 91-3 BCA ¶ 24,353 at 121,678-679, ¶¶ 28, 29; decision at 121,692.

154 *Id.*

Inspection clause of the Lot X contracts under which redesigned liners had been installed.[155] She accordingly denied GE's second appeal.[156]

While we disagreed with her reasoning for finding a latent defect and a retroactive contract change in the contracting officer's November 1987 decision, the dollar costs of retrofitting the few accepted Lot X contracts incorporating the redesigned liner were minimal as compared to the Navy's costs of retrofitting the engines previously accepted under the earlier production contracts as to which Judge Burg had sustained GE's first appeal. GE did not appeal that second decision to the Federal Circuit. I imagine the parties negotiated an appropriate sharing of those costs as well as the redesign costs of the replacement A/B liners.

These appeals were challenging and difficult; and they were the most significant matters I worked on during my almost four years with Ropes & Gray.

-Joining the National Security Industrial Association and its Successor the National Defense Industrial Association.

During these years Ropes & Gray joined the National Security Industrial Association, a trade association of defense contractors established by James Forrestal during World War II when he was Secretary of the Navy. Matt Simchak encouraged me to become active. I joined the legal subcommittee of the Procurement Committee. Composed mostly of company lawyers and a few private practitioners the focus at its bimonthly

---

155 *Id.* at 121,692. The reference to the Inspection clause was to paragraph (k) of the FAR 52.246-2 standard Inspection clause and its predecessors that then provided that final acceptance would not be conclusive not only as to latent defects but also "as otherwise provided in the contract" as the redesigned liner did not conform to the contract requirements as changed by the contracting officer's November 1987 final decision.

156 *Id.* at 121,692.

meetings, mostly in Washington, was on recent significant decisions of the GAO on bid protests, and ASBCA and the Court of Claims, later the Court of Federal Claims and the Court of Appeals for the Federal Circuit, on contract disputes, as well as statutes and procurement regulations. As to the latter, the subcommittee often would be tasked to draft comments on proposed changes to the Federal Acquisition Regulation (FAR) and the DoD supplement to the FAR which merited objections or revisions from industry's perspective.[157] This was stimulating work for me in drafting some of these comments. Over time, these public comments, particularly those from this trade association and its successor the National Defense Industrial Association (NDIA) and the ABA Public Contract Section, were gradually heeded by the regulation drafters or cogent reasons provided when they did not adopt them.

After a few years I was invited to join the Procurement Policy Committee, a smaller group primarily made up of relatively senior executives of defense contractors concerned with procurement policy, contract financing and contract management. There were also subcommittees dedicated to contract pricing, financing and accounting issues and to contract management. Attending these bimonthly meetings was educational for me in coming to understand the growing financial impact of compliance with increasingly detailed regulations and contract provisions on the cost of doing business with the federal government and the risks of noncompliance and why that deterred most commercial companies from competing for government contracts, a condition Congress and the Executive Branch sought to ameliorate without much success.

For many years these associations would host annual meetings or conferences outside Washington, and Don and I enjoyably went to ones at The Homestead in Virgina, Hershey, Pennsylvania, Scottsdale, Arizona, and Amelia Island off Jacksonville, Florida, and another at Sarasota, Florida. At each of these locations there were for him interesting sights to see while I was in the meetings.

---

157 The requirement for notice and opportunity for public comment on the FAR and subordinate regulations was mandated by the OFPP Act of 1977, now codified at 41 U.S.C. § 1707 by Pub. L. 111-350 enacted on January 4, 2011.

-Final Years at Ropes & Gray.

Among the other work I was asked to do one matter involved help-ing a subcontractor on the A-12 program recover its termination charges after Secretary of Defense Cheney directed the Navy to terminate the prime contract in 1991.[158] This in turn would require my having a secu-rity clearance because the program was highly classified as some of the work required access to stealth technology. I did obtain the clearance but did not need it as this subcontractor's work did not involve that technol-ogy. We were able to negotiate a satisfactory resolution of the claim with the prime contractor.

In this I was ably assisted by Ed James, one of Alan Peterson's former colleagues in a management consulting practice Alan had started some years previously. Alan's new firms, Peterson Consulting and then Tucker Alan, had grown rapidly and established offices in the major cities of

---

158 This led to protracted litigation in the Court of Federal Claims and the Court of Appeals for the Federal Circuit. The contractor, a joint venture of General Dynam-ics and McDonnell Douglas to develop and produce the A-12 stealth fighter aircraft, claimed that the government's breach of its obligation to share the highly classi-fied stealth technology excused the default termination and entitled the contractor to recover under the termination for convenience clause. The government asserted that the state secrets defense as trumping any disclosure obligation and demanded repayment of $1.3B of progress payments. The Court of Appeals upheld the default termination on that ground which the Supreme Court reversed in a unanimous deci-sion by Justice Scalia, *General Dynamics v. United States*, No. 09-1298 (May 23, 2011). The Court held that neither party could recover from the other since "full litigation of that defense 'would inevitably lead to the disclosure of state secrets' ", citing *Totten v. United States*, 92 U.S. 105,107 (1867). Slip op. at 7, 8. However, the Court remanded to the Court of Appeals the issues of the extent of the government's obligation to share its superior knowledge of the stealth technology with the contractor, whether that extended to "highly classified information", and whether these issues "can be resolved without endangering state secrets." Slip op. at 13. The Court assumed, and did not revisit, the validity of the state secrets defense despite much criticism of its increasing use by the government to avoid liability for its breach of classified contracts. *See State Secrets Privilege* in Wikipedia. It is difficult to see how the remand will enable the con-tractor to overcome the government's likely defense that the issues cannot be resolved without endangering state secrets.

the U.S. It offered "litigation support" in a wide variety of areas in addition to government contracts as well as in other areas of management consulting. It became so successful that the London advertising firm of Saachi & Saachi acquired it for $100M in their bid to enter consulting. Several years later it sold Peterson back to Tucker, Alan for $10M when apparently the expected benefits from the acquisition did not materialize largely due to the downturn in advertising. Alan Peterson's example spread to many firms. It is extraordinary to reflect that all this may have begun with Alan's work on the Bath and Todd ship claim settlements as I have discussed earlier in this Part.

In the spring of 1992 Matt Simchak told me that Ropes & Gray had decided not to extend my contract when it would shortly expire. I believe the reasons included the fact that I was not producing new clients and did not have sufficient billable hours to earn the revenue the firm had expected from my work. Also at age 69 I was beyond the age that partners would retire from the firm and become "of counsel" with no billing requirements. So it came to pass. I decided to establish a solo practice at home in the name of "Coburn Legal Consulting" which I shall relate in Part Six, and so I conclude Part Five of my enriching life.

Part Six Solo Law Practice 1992-2011

Becoming a solo practitioner was a daunting undertaking. I did not know how to type and had no familiarity with computers, having foolishly declined the opportunity to learn how to create documents on them at Ropes & Gray. I had few law books and would face the considerable expense of subscribing to the several publications of CCH and others to stay abreast of ongoing developments in public contract law. I had no clients and faced the necessity and expense of announcing my availability. I did notify former colleagues and friends at various law firms and companies. I also acquired an IBM laptop computer and a combination printer and fax device connected to the computer on the recommendation of my knowledgeable nephew Peter Coburn. I was astonished how easy and user friendly it was to learn typing with all fingers on the laptop keyboard and how simple the correction of typing and spelling errors. Ready access to the expanding internet gradually reduced the need and the expense of subscribing to these publications.

1. The Kiplinger-Bay Litigation: EPCO v. United States.

I was rescued about a month later when a colleague at Sachs, Greenebaum, telephoned for help on a government contact matter involving his client Kiplinger, the financial publisher to which he was the outside general counsel. His client had entered a joint venture with Bob Bay, a Seattle printer, under the name Electronic Printing Co. trading as "EPCO Associates", in a contract to print and distribute the quantities of patents issued and ordered each week by the Patent Office. The ordered quantities had fallen well below the estimated quantities in the contract and it had become a substantial loss contract with several years more to go. His client was desperate for relief and he would recommend me if I were available. I gratefully said I was and would meet with the Kiplinger people at their earliest convenience. I soon met with Corbin Wilkes, the Kiplinger very able treasurer, and Bob Bay, an experienced, high-tech printer, and his attorney Bill Dickey. They outlined the situation and I said I would study the contract and the applicable precedents and advise them promptly.

After a few days I concluded that if we could establish through discovery that the government had negligently estimated the quantities of patents to be ordered each week in relation to what they then knew or had reason to know, we had a fair chance of establishing a material breach of contract that would entitle the joint venture so to terminate the contract and recover its increased costs and reasonably anticipated profits.[159] The risk was that we would have a failure of proof of negligent estimating in which event the government likely having terminated the contract for default by the joint venture would hold it liable for any excess costs of reprocurement from a successor contractor. I also advised them of a precedent by the Court of Claims which held that the government would not

---

159 *Womack v. United States*, 389 F.2d 798 (Ct. Cl. 1968).

be liable for a non-negligent estimate so long as it ordered the minimum quantities specified in the contract.[160]

In our case, I suggested, the minimum quantity was so trivial in relation to the estimated quantities so as to be meaningless, as well as the fact of likely negligence and thus a viable basis for distinguishing the Court of Claims precedent. Also we could point to helpful language in the Federal Acquisition Regulation with which the Patent Office and the contracting agency, the Government Printing Office (GPO), may not have followed.[161] I brought Bill Dickey up to speed by calling his attention to significant decisions of the Federal Circuit and its predecessor Court of Claims that recognized such a right of termination for material government breach and explained why that remedy would have to be sought in the Court of Federal Claims rather than alternatively in a board of contract appeals which was not subject to the Contract Disputes Act. In our case, the contract with the GPO, a Congressional agency, and its board of contract appeals were not subject to the Contract Disputes Act and it would not have jurisdiction over a breach of contract suit such as we would bring. Bill then fully concurred in my advice.

After obtaining authorization from the joint venture we filed suit in the Court of Federal Claims in Washington, declaring the contract terminated for material government breach of contract for negligently having prepared estimated maximum quantities of patents to be copied each week and demanding the recovery of increased costs in producing the greatly reduced quantities actually ordered as well as the reasonably anticipated profits had the government ordered substantially the estimated quantities.[162] The case was assigned to Judge Robert Hodges. Unfortunately for us, he had recently also been assigned to the A-12

---

160 *Mason v. United* States, 615 F.2d 1343, 1346 (Ct. Cl. 1980).

161 FAR 16.504(a)(1): "The contracting officer should establish a reasonable maximum quantity based on market research, trends on recent contracts for similar supplies or services, survey of potential users, or any other rational basis." FAR 16.504(a)(2) added, "To ensure that the contract is binding, the minimum quantity must be more than a nominal quantity, but it should not exceed the amount the Government is fairly certain to order."

162 *EPCO v. United States*, U.S. Court of Federal Claims No. 92-91C.

litigation which would occupy virtually all his time for many months.[163] We began discovery and amassed considerable evidence to support our claim of a negligently prepared estimate of the quantities the Patent Office was likely to order, way below the maximum quantities specified in the contract. In December 1992, the Government planned to take the deposition of Bob Bay in Seattle, and I welcomed returning there to prepare him and be available to object to his answering any questions I thought he should not answer. His deposition went well and impressed George Beasley, the senior Justice Department attorney who conducted it on how carefully the EPCO bid prices had been arrived at in relation to the estimated quantities in the solicitation.

Returning to Seattle was an opportunity to renew family ties. I happened to return in time for an 80th birthday gala for Franny Brinkley, the widow of my cousin Rawn Brinkley who had grown up in Seattle. Those present included George and MA Nickum, his sons Nick and Will with their wives, my nephew David Coburn, various Brinkley cousins, and Catherine and Frank Brownell, Frank being a cousin of Franny's. It was a grand occasion, and it marked my last visit to Seattle.

The GPO, as expected, terminated the contract for default by the joint venture and eventually asserted a claim for the excess costs of reprocurement of several million dollars. The Justice Department soon filed a motion to dismiss because we had failed to exhaust our administrative remedy before the GPO Board of Contract Appeals. We opposed that motion, calling the court's attention to decisions of that board which had held that it had no jurisdiction over breach of contract claims by a contractor.

Some months later Judge Hodges heard argument on the government's motion to dismiss. The government attorney, George Beasley, was very complimentary about my argument. Aware of Judge Hodges's unlikely unavailability for a trial anytime soon and in an effort to settle the case, I prepared and submitted to George Beasley a memorandum of law based on our discovery results why we had a valid claim entitling

---

163 *See* Part Five, Note 158, for more about this litigation.

the joint venture to terminate the contractor for material breach by the government and to recover its increased costs and reasonably anticipated profit. Eventually he told me that he was prepared to recommend a settlement of recovery of increased costs and more profit on quantities actually ordered under the termination for convenience clause but the Department never would agree to the recovery of any lost profits on quantities not ordered where much of our hopes for recovery were based.

We continued to prepare witnesses for trial, particularly, Bob Bay and Corbin Wilkes on developing the proof of the faulty estimates and increased costs and a reasonably anticipated profit on the quantities not ordered. Judge Hodges finally ruled and in an unpublished order granted the government's motion to dismiss without prejudice to resuming the suit should the GPO Board of Contract Appeals determine that it had no jurisdiction over our claim. This was very disappointing detour and we faced years of further litigation before obtaining a ruling on the merits of the breach of contract claim, particularly with Judge Hodges bogged down in the A-12 litigation. Corbin Wilkes thought I needed additional help and he asked me to bring in another attorney. I knew that Matt Simchak had recently relocated to Wiley, Rein & Fielding, a leading Washington communications law firm and Corbin was a friend and neighbor of Mr. Rein. Matt was not available, but his partner, Rand Allen who headed the government contract's practice for the firm, would work with us. This was very welcome since Bill Dickey was busy with other work, and I knew and respected Rand who also had been one of my successors as chair of the ABA Section of Public Contract Law. Rand also assigned a very able young associate, David Vogel, to the case.

As the months went by and the legal costs mounted with Rand's firm's much higher billing rates than mine, Corbin asked us to explore settlement with the government. Rand felt that recovery of reasonably anticipated profits was a long shot with sparse supporting precedent involving this type of contract. Judge Hodge's availability to hear that claim was highly uncertain and indefinite. A termination for convenience settlement began looking as an increasingly attractive alternative, and we began a preparing claim on that basis to submit to Mr. Beasley believing that he was open to persuading the Patent Office and the GPO to attempt to settle on that basis. We did so and suspended proceedings in the GPO BCA pending the outcome of the settlement discussions. He reported that the lawyer in the Department of Commerce representing the Patent Office and the lawyer for the GPO disagreed with each other on that outcome. Finally, George Beasley prevailed, and we settled the claim on that basis for an amount that was acceptable to the joint venture, particularly being relieved of any liability for the asserted excess costs of the reprocurement contract. All this took over three years. It was a very challenging case.

2. The Slingsby Aviation Litigation.

Rob Evers had left the vom Baur firm in 1975 after six years as a highly valued associate to join the GAO. By 1995 after many years with two or three Washington law firms, he also became a solo practitioner, and we resumed contact. Rob had developed several clients in England and Europe doing business with the Department of Defense as the result of his work in Europe for the GAO in connection with DoD's growing involvement with European rearmament to counter the Soviet threat during the Cold War. This base of clients was enough for him to start out on his own. He asked me if I would be available to help on some of this work from time. I expressed delight, and we agreed on an hourly rate of $75.

After the Kiplinger-Bay joint venture litigation was settled in 1995, I began doing occasional work for Rob on relatively small matters. Early in 1997 he told me that one of his U.K. clients, Slingsby Aviation Limited, was appealing the decision of an Air Force contracting officer to the Armed Services Board of Contract Appeals denying its $5.6M claim for constructive change order costs of performing an Air Force contract for the production and delivery of 133 trainer T-3 aircraft. Rob had already spent considerable time in the UK preparing that claim and now would litigate it in the ASBCA with my help if I would be available. Again, I was delighted to help, and we soon began discovery and trial preparation.

Slingsby claimed that the Air Force had changed the contract by requiring the production and acceptance of the T-3 aircraft which were mostly manufactured by Slingsby in the UK and then assembled by its subcontractor Northrop at its facility in Hondo, Texas, to conform to the very different quality control and inspection standards mandated by the Federal Aviation Agency (FAA) instead of those of the UK Civil Aviation Authority (CAA) which had certificated for production and acceptance the UK version of the trainer on which its proposal was based. Under the FAA regulations that CAA approval under a UK- US treaty was equivalent to conformity with the FAA quality control and inspection standards for aircraft production and acceptance certification.

To reach this conclusion required Rob and me to comprehend a bewildering maze of CAA and FAA regulations before we could undertake a comprehensive discovery and deposition program. As we progressed with that program Slingsby became concerned that trial preparation would benefit from more legal resources. They notified Rob that two or three experienced litigators from the Washington law firm of Jones, Day, Reavis & Pogue, headed by Peter Garvin whom I knew to be a very competent government contract trial lawyer, would be joining us. Thereafter, I had a reduced role, primarily with Rob getting the newcomers up to speed and on completing the planned depositions, and later reviewing their drafts of the post-hearing briefs. Their work was first class, and the ASBCA mostly sustained Slingsby's legal entitlement to recover on its claims.[164] The amount of the recovery remained for negotiation with the contracting officer in which Rob and I did participate some months after the entitlement decision in April 2003.

---

164 *Slingsby Aircraft Limited*, ASBCA No. 50473, 03-1 BCA ¶ 32,252.

The post-hearing briefing of the appeal was completed by early 2000 if not sooner. Yet Administrative Judge Moed, before whom the case had been tried, did not issue his decision until more than three years later, an unconscionable delay. By then it was far more difficult to reconstruct the details of the monetary claim. Key personnel had departed and recollections had faded. Yet somehow we managed to achieve an acceptable outcome in May 2005 in the nature of a "jury verdict" with the imaginative help of a government auditor who well understood the difficulties of estimating the costs of production disruption that Slingsby had incurred from the Air Force demand that it revise its detailed quality control procedures based on the UK CAA requirements to conform to the similar yet excruciatingly different ones of the FAA.

3. Family and Friends 1992-2011.

-March 18, 1995, Sally Dies.

By the early 1990s my brothers and their wives had sold their homes of many years and moved to recently built, attractive retirement communities near and south of Boston and each other: Pat and Marty from Katonah, NY, to New Pond Village in Walpole, and Mike and Joan from Needham to Fox Hill Village in Westwood.

Sally and Bob, who married in 1935 and had three sons, and had lived on "Flying Ridge" in rural Newtown, Connecticut, since 1945, sadly divorced in the 1980s from mutual incompatibility. Bob was generous in providing for Sally in establishing a sufficient principal account, in purchasing attractive apartments for her first in Southbury and then at

Kimball Farms, a retirement community, in Lenox, Massachusetts, and in providing a Plymouth station wagon. He frequently supplemented her income with gifts of travel cruises. Surprisingly they became and remained friends despite Bob's remarriage to Anne Smith, a Swiss friend of Sally's long married to Carlton Smith, both of whom Sally had introduced to Bob many years before.

Sally had growing health issues. In the 1980s she had an angioplasty procedure after gaining excessive weight. I had enjoyable visits to her in Southbury and later at Kimball Farms. In the summer months there she would go to the nearby Saturday morning rehearsals of the Boston Symphony in the Shed at Tanglewood for the weekend concerts, a wonderful experience to hear great orchestral music, frequently with piano, violin or vocal soloists, superbly performed by none better than those she heard.

On a Caribbean cruise that Bob had provided for her in the Spring of 1995 she became ill and was put ashore and hospitalized on one of the island stops. She died there on March 18, at the age of 83.

On June 10, 1995, a glorious day to remember, there was a memorial service for Sally at the Unitarian Church in Duxbury which our cousin, the Rev. Olivia Holmes, gracefully conducted. Bob and Anne, sons Bobby, Travis and Rawn, perhaps some of her grandchildren, and her brothers with wives Marty and Joan were among those present. She was buried in the family plot in the beautiful Mayflower Cemetery joining her parents and sister Louise. There I spoke of her selfless deeply caring devotion in everlasting, generous ways, to her family and her committed friends.

-May 1995: Chych Waterston Dies.

That May I had the sad news that Chych Waterston had died. In Part One I have written of his importance in my education at Brooks School and beyond. I then wrote to his four children Roberta, George, Sam, and Ellie, whom I had known when they were children:

I join you in the sadness of losing Chych. But have we known a finer or more caring father, husband, friend, teacher and scholar? These sterling qualities of his mind and character have touched me, and many others, long and deeply. Long ago as a first former at Brooks beginning in 1936 he and Alica became surrogate parents to me and as I grew older the relationship with each of them blossomed into lifetime friendship and love of great value to me and to so many Brooksians.

Chych's gifts as a teacher and scholar claim special recognition. His mastery of English and French literature opened the minds of countless Brooksians and others as did his flair for acting and directing great and lesser plays. His playing of the cello introduced us to some of the great works of chamber music. His scholarship and erudition are made manifest in *Order and Counter-Order*[165], a lasting work of extraordinary perceptiveness and range into fundamental questions confronting man.

Chych has enriched our lives in so many ways as did Alica, an enrichment that will carry on to your children and beyond. I was privileged to be his friend.

-Bob Fulton at Ninety.

April 1, 1999, was Bob Fulton's 90th birthday. Sadly, his wife Anne had died a few years before. Nevertheless, it was an occasion for me to attempt to sum up his life at a celebration at his home in Newtown:

It is given to few to achieve so much in a lifetime as has Bob. His fecundity and creativity are boundless, and there is likely more ahead. So at his youthful and vigorous 90 we hail and honor

---

165 Waterston, *Order and Counter-Order: Dualism in Western Culture* (Philosophical Library, NY, 1966). Chych wrote and published this text in French in 1965 for his Ph..D. from the Sorbonne.

him as a polymath and prodigy, as a father, brother and friend, as a world class citizen of the world.

I have been privileged to know Bob since 1935 when he married Sally Coburn, my sister, when I was but a boy of 11. We knew of Bob at first as the college roommate of our cousin Rawn Brinkley of Seattle whose mother was our mother's sister. We were told that our grandmother Nana (Florence Rawn) had decided that Bob should marry Rawn's sister Betty, and that Sally should stay away from him. But there was never romance between Bob and Betty who later happily married George Nickum.

Bob was already a hero to me from his adventure of being first around the world on a motorcycle as a young man in his early twenties after having studied architecture in Vienna. *One Man Caravan*, his book of that experience published here by Harcourt Brace and in England in 1937, with its many superb photographs, maps and drawings, all by Bob, remains one of the best one-world adventure books and best-written books in the English language as a rereading attests. It teaches that men and women of many tongues and different cultures around our world share far more in togetherness than in division and that the basic qualities of character we admire and deplore in people are universal. This book earned Bob world citizenship as have far too few others. The movie he filmed and the lectures of that journey he gave around the country sharpened his skills at public speaking and winning audiences. His talents as a movie photographer and at public relations led to his filming the maiden flight of the Pan American Airways China Clipper to the Orient in 1935, thus inaugurating transpacific commercial flights.

A strong interest in flying followed. He taught himself to fly and bought a small plane. Why not make flying easier for others? Why not develop a device that would show on a movie screen the actual elements of flying through aerial photography linked to the movements of the controls as operated by the pilot sitting in a replica of the cockpit and looking at the screen? Thus he achieved a triumph of engineering and aerial photography, and so was born the Fulton Airstructor.

The war in Europe had started and was headed our way. The need for thousands of new military pilots loomed. Bob saw the opportunity for the Fulton Airstructor as a way to proceed. He demonstrated the device in Washington at the Navy Department to a Captain Louis de Flores in the Office of Naval Research. He said if Bob could add the capability of aerial gunnery training the Navy would be very interested. Bob again surmounted this engineering challenge. A Japanese Zero fighter appears on the screen and engages in evasive maneuvers. The pilot aims the plane to follow these twists and turns and shoots at the Zero. The accuracy of the shooting is shown by beads of light. Thus emerged the Fulton GunAirstructor. Captain de Flores and the Navy were impressed, and soon Bob had a production contract to build and deliver about 25 of them!

To perform this contract Bob and Sally and son Robin, age 3, moved to Washington about 1942. Sally found a job as a secretary to General Bill Donovan, then heading the newly formed OSS. Bob had no employees, no facilities. He rented warehouse space in Northeast Washington and recruited his work force from the Yellow Pages of the telephone book and began to produce the GunAirstructor. One contract led to the next, and by the end of the war he and his team had delivered many hundreds of them to the Navy for installation at the Navy pilot training centers around the country. Captain de Flores later reported that the Fulton GunAirstructor was among the most important contributions the Office of Naval Research made to the war effort. Navy carrier pilots achieved something like a 10 to 1 kill ratio over Japanese Zero fighters and other aircraft, largely because of having been trained on the Fulton GunAirstructor. It required the personal intervention of the Secretary of the Navy to persuade Bob's draft board in Connecticut that his work in Washington as a civilian was essential to the war effort.

At the war's end in 1945, Bob and Sally acquired some land with an old barn and room for an airstrip in Newtown, Connecticut, and with the addition of sons Travis and Rawn made this their home and named it "Flying Ridge". For Bob this was to be home and the incubator of his new projects thereafter. What challenge to undertake next? Since the China Clipper days Bob had been self employed and with his own employees as needed rather than work for others.

Travelling to Navy bases during the war he wasted a lot of time going to the commercial airport and then to the base. Wouldn't it be better to have your own plane that you could also drive as a car for needed ground transportation? Thus was borne the idea of a flying automobile which Bob would create and call the Fulton Airphibian. With backing from an investor, Bob formed a team of engineers, leased a plant in Danbury and proceeded to design and develop the Airphibian. The technical problems were immense for this pioneering effort. Eventually a few were built, test flown and driven. One was certificated by the Civil Aeronautics Authority in Washington and licensed as an automobile by the State of Connecticut. The CAA was so impressed that it wanted to lease several for its own use. But then, sadly and suddenly, the investor withdrew his support for tax reasons, and the program came to an end.

There had been wonderful publicity in *Life Magazine* and on movie newsreels showing Sally and Bob driving to a Broadway theater and elsewhere; and the Smithsonian Air & Space Museum in Washington put one of the few on display along with the "Spirit of St. Louis", now relocated to a new facility near Dulles Airport. An engineering wonder in the aviation and automobile worlds, the Airphibian stands alone. Its day will come.

The next project was creating a rescue device to pick up someone on the ground or in the water and put him or her in an airplane flying between 500 and 1,500 feet. How could that be done?

Bob calculated, as a matter of physics, that at varying heights the object on the ground or in the water if attached to a nylon cord suspended from a balloon when intercepted by the plane would rise vertically for varying distances before arcing toward the plane and being winched aboard. Using his own plane with a fork in front to intercept the line and haul the dummy aboard, he tested with weighted dummies, developed a nylon cord of the proper flexibility and strength and a helium balloon with the needed lift. It worked. Would it be safe for humans? For them Bob designed coveralls with a built-in harness and backpack containing the nylon cord and an inflatable helium balloon and release mechanism. The cord was treated to glow in the dark, enabling night pickups. Repeated tests with Government personnel established the safety and feasibility of the system which Bob called the Fulton Skyhook.

Now the Government wanted Bob to produce the system in quantity and to fit various Government aircraft with this capability. So Bob acquired a facility in Danbury and began manufacturing or purchasing the several components of the system under various Government contracts. This work went on for many years including providing replacement of the components. Later Bob modified the Skyhook to enable multiple pickups simultaneously. In one of the James Bond films, *Thunderball*, the public was treated to a demonstration of Skyhook when James is rescued from a speedboat. I understand in all the years the Skyhook has been operational with countless pickups and saved lives there never has been a fatality or serious injury. Again we see a unique achievement and triumph of Bob's inventiveness in service to the nation.[166]

---

166 An account of how Bob and Skyhook achieved the retrieval of a cache of important documents at a hastily abandoned Soviet base on an Artic ice flow in June 1962 is grippingly told in Leary and LeSchack, *Project Coldfeet, Secret Mission to a Soviet Ice Station*, Naval Institute Press 1996, especially in Chapters 5-8. Chapter 5 also wonderfully tells the story of the development of the Fulton GunAirstructor and Airphibian. A few years ago, Bob and others concerned with this mission received posthumous awards from the CIA in a moving ceremony which I attended together with Bob, his sons Rawn and Travis, and his grandson Whitman Fulton, Rawn's eldest son.

In 1985 in his 77th year, Bob undertook to portray his "other self" in a collage of extraordinary drawings and sketches, photographic art, whimsy, poetry, and wisdom gathered in a book he created, privately printed, and called *The Winds of Life*. Together with his other self, "we have wandered back through the years, taken another look, and tried to express the essence of our experience." As with so much of what he has done, there is probably no book like it for it transcends the categories of books. The book ends with these luminous lines:

Oh heart of my mind,
Oh mind of my heart,
Play the strings of my spirit,
Sing the songs of my soul
    In the bosom of my being.

Talk to me of thoughts & things,
of this & that,
of desires & dreams
    & deeds & doodles,

of history & harmony,
of wonder & wind & weather,
of music & magic & marvel
    of passion & peace,

of peace & prayer,
of life & longing
& leisure & love
for they are what life is made of,

and I would live it 'til
    my cup runneth over
in praise & pride
    of being alive.

Let me grow & know
and love & laugh & cry & die
knowing I am going
   with a life full of living.

So we are privileged to hail Bob at 90 and a life of surpassing accomplishments. May I also speak of Bob's extraordinary generosity to Sally in her later years and of his nurturing and inspiring role for his three gifted sons who blaze in his path of artistic creativity? May Bob long continue to thrive with a life full of living and inspiration for the rest of us.

-Pat at Ninety.

A few years later, Pat's wife Marty succumbed to Parkinson's at their new, retirement home in New Pond Village after a valiant struggle of many years and after 58 years of fulfilling marriage. She too was a devoted, caring wife and mother and friend, remarkably well read in English literature and Anthony Trollop. She was buried in the churchyard of St. Mathews in Bedford, NY, where she and Pat had attended for many years and where Pat would soon join her.

Pat presently married Cassandra, "Sandy", Dexter, a recent widow at New Pond Village who with her husband, a Dr. Dexter who had perfected angioplasty, were friends of Pat's and Marty's. We celebrated this union in October 1999 on the occasion of a gala celebration of Pat's 90th birthday of family and friends, including his four sons. His beautiful and accomplished goddaughter, Katherine Harding Nahum, who lived in nearby Newton, sat on one side of him, Sandy on the other.

On this occasion I said this about Pat:

Groton School which Pat entered in 1923 and finished 6 years later is high among the formative experiences of his life, particularly the educational and spiritual impact on him of its Rector,

Endicott Peabody. If you read Louis Auchincloss's *The Rector of Justin*, you will see the enormous, pervasive influence the Rector had on molding the lives of many of his students in the practice of Christian truths. Apart from his parents, his siblings, and Marty, the other major influences in shaping Pat's life were and are the mental rigor of the Harvard Law School in teaching the methodology of problem solving, and the U.S. Navy in which he served with distinction and learned about command and control at sea and the vagaries of human behavior under stress and at ease.

Pat's commitment and devotion to Marty for the 58 years of their marriage and to their four sons are moving examples for us all, especially in their times of trouble and in Marty's case in the progressive illness of her last years.

Mike and I wish Mother and Papa could rejoice in Pat's accomplishments and joie de vivre over ninety years. Now a new chapter in Pat's life beckons. Blessed with the vigor and good health of those 20 years younger, he and Sandy Dexter have found a bright future together. May they go forward in happiness and hope.

-November 8, 2002, Pat Dies.

Sadly, this was not to be. A year or two later, Sandy found she had an incurable malady and died soon thereafter. Pat, devastated, was again alone. He was also increasingly bothered by a knee replacement that had stopped working properly. He decided on a second replacement of that knee, mindful at his age of the high risk to his life of such a procedure. If it came to that, he said he preferred not to go on living than to continue to suffer from the existing knee condition. So he went ahead with it at the Peter Bent Brigham Hospital in Boston. The operation was a success, but he died from a heart attack two days later while still in the hospital, on November 8, 2002, soon after his 93rd birthday.

His sons arranged a memorial service later that month at the Episcopal church in Dover. There was a large turnout of family and friends. His sons, Mike and I spoke. Again the service was beautifully conducted by our cousin, the Rev. Olivia Holmes. There was a burial service a few days later at Pat and Marty's long-time church, St. Mathew's in Bedford, NY, where Pat would join Marty.

Throughout his long life Pat fulfilled Papa's dearest, dying wish: "Burnish the name I have tarnished!"

-Mike at Eighty-Five.

Several months previously, on April 8, 2002, I saluted Mike at 85 at a family gathering at Fox Hill. I said:

> Blessed in life is Mike at 85: in roots, in upbringing, in schooling and athletics, in exemplary traits of character (among these, diligence, integrity, loyalty, neatness, organization, perseverance, rectitude, sportsmanship, thriftiness), in a marriage well prevailing beyond 60 years, in excellence in co-rearing, educating and launching three outstanding children (two sons and a daughter), in the joys of their 12 grandchildren and oncoming great grandchildren, by success and achievement in business life and service to Brooks and Harvard and in friendships, in good health, and in the prospects of future continuing bliss. So many blessings!

His prospect of good health was not to be. Less than two years later, Mike and Joan celebrated my 80th birthday at a family dinner at Fox Hill. I had not seen him for about a year, and I was shocked by how much weight he had apparently lost and by the gaunt look he had. I said, "Mike, you must have a checkup and find out what's happening to you." Neither he nor Joan seemed aware of the sum of the change in him as it had been gradual. The verdict was terminal: advanced cancer of the esophagus that had already spread and was beyond effective treatment.

Soon he encountered progressive difficulty in swallowing necessitating a diet of baby food. Nursing care was soon required, and he relocated to Clark House, the nursing facility at Fox Hill for its residents.

I again visited him for his 87th birthday on April 8, 2004. The end was near, yet he remained in good spirits and without dementia. We reminisced about growing up in Greenwich, our parents and siblings, and our experiences at Brooks from which he had graduated the year before I began. I would not see him again.

-June 10, 2004, Mike Dies.

He died peacefully at Clark House from his long battle with cancer. There was a celebration of his life on Saturday, August 14, 2004, at The Church of the Good Shepherd in Wareham, Mass. There was a large gathering of family and friends. Again our cousin, the Rev. Olivia Holmes conducted a moving, simple service and gave a beautiful homily about Mike. His sons, John and Lawrie and four of his eight grandsons gave their tributes. I said in part:

> Brooks School and principally its extraordinary and excellent headmaster Frank Ashburn were instrumental in molding Mike's way ahead in life by fostering deep and lasting commitments to Christian ethics, to truthfulness, to rectitude and sportsmanship, to good manners, to a large capacity for enduring friendships, and to other indicia of good character that would grow over a lifetime and endear him to so many in all walks of life. Indeed, Brooks and FDA were twin pillars of his life. Harvard College and Harvard Business School and military service during World War II as a communications officer in the Army Air Corps would also enlarge his education and outlook and prepare him for the successful business life to come. I should also mention his courage, particularly in battling cancer at the end, his enthusiasms and joie de vivre, his keen sense of organization and orderliness and his passion for neatness with everything to

have its proper place, all these qualities shone in abundance for his lifetime.

Mike's courtship of Joan Shaw starting in 1937, our first summer in Wareham, brightened our lives and introduced us to her lovely parents and siblings. Her younger brother Howie and I became best friends over that and succeeding summers. We all rejoiced at Joan's and Mike's marriage on June 18, 1940, a union that would prevail in love and happiness for each of them for almost 64 years. He married well, and she improved and inspirited him as a husband and as a father. They nurtured their three children to be unspotted from the world with loving care and discipline and provided them with the best of educational opportunities. The outcomes were immensely gratifying to Joan and Mike and to all who know John, Lawrie and Joanie.

Mike became a good husband, a good father and grandfather, a good brother, a good friend, a good citizen, and a good and generous provider. He enjoyed a good long and healthy life, one that he devoted to his family, to his business life, to his many friends, to Brooks, to Harvard, and to his country. We shall remember him with love, with affection, and with respect for influencing so many lives for the better by his exemplary qualities of good character. As we say farewell to Mike our prayers remain for Joan. Suffused with grief and seemingly alone, yet with the solace of happy memories and a loving family, may she now move on to beckoning stars of happiness. In the words of Arthur Hugh Cough in "Say not the struggle naught availeth":

> And not by eastern windows only,
> When daylight comes, comes in the light,
> In front the sun climbs slow, how slowly,
> But westward, look, the land is bright.

Mike was buried in the family plot at a cemetery near their Wareham home. Farewell to the last of my siblings.

-Bob Fulton at Ninety-Five.

April 15, 2004, was also the occasion of Bob Fulton's 95th birthday, recently saddened by the death of his eldest son Robin (Robert III) in a plane crash leaving a recently divorced wife and three children and an adopted son by his former wife. Robin had achieved much as an extraordinary creator of artistic films with breathtaking photography. Of his father I said:

> A one hundred gun salute to Bob at ninety-five, and may the drum roll of his extraordinary life remind us of what he has achieved in the arts and sciences: The firsts of the One World motorcycle journey, of the *One Man Caravan* account of it, of the Fulton GunAirstructor, of the Fulton Airphibian, of the Fulton Skyhook, of the art, poetry, wisdom and whimsy of *The Winds of Life,* and of new forms and styles of cinematography and sculpture, all these among others are uniquely firsts of different kinds in diverse fields of endeavor that transcend the abilities and achievements of most individuals.

> So too his and Sally's nurturing of three artistically gifted sons into new paths of creativity.

> From these large unremitting exertions and endeavors over seventy-five years comes now as the sun sets the serenity of satisfaction and repose for a life lived to the brim of possibility.

-May 2004, Bob Fulton Dies.

Bob was now in declining health and needed assistance. I would not see him again for he predeceased Mike by a month or so at Flying Ridge.

His sons Rawn and Travis hosted a splendid memorial for their father at Flying Ridge on Saturday, June 5, 2004, that would have greatly pleased him. Over a hundred were present, seated in a large tent near the house amidst rain and drizzle. As usual at these occasions, our cousin, the Rev. Olivia Holmes, a Universalist-Unitarian minister and a great granddaughter of George Martin Coburn whose name I bear, opened and closed the service and presided simply and superbly while recounting Bob and the omnipresence of God in his life and in Flying Ridge. A quartet of singers were wondrous in their a cappella renditions of early and modern music throughout the service. Travis and Rawn spoke of life with their father growing up in the adventures of his inventions and the life lessons he instilled. Ten grandchildren and Palgi (the young man from Mongolia whose emigration Bob and Sally had sponsored many years before to live with them) told of their love for GrandBob. Several of Bob's former employees recounted their unique experiences in working with him. We concluded with everyone singing all four verses of the great hymn, "Ye Watchers and Ye Holy Ones", with copies of the verses and music for everyone provided by Peter Coburn.

Other family members present in addition to all the Fultons, were Peter's wife, Joanne, David Coburn, Rawn Harding and her sister Katherine Nahum and husband Jeremy, and Olivia Holmes.

I gave this brief eulogy, saying in part:

> Let us now praise Bob, famous as a paragon, a polymath and as a hero to many, one who has in his long life inspired us among many by his unremitting creativity to achieve more than we could or would without the beckoning star of what he exemplified and did. In my experience since 1935 I have not known anyone I admired and respected more for what he accomplished. As Goethe said, "Shaffen, das ist der erste Ziel." "Creating is the first duty." Surely and truly, Bob lived that way of life. We shall remember him as a major force in all our lives all our days.

-Selling the Key West House.

Don and I sold the Key West house in the summer of 1999. A few years previously the Navy had relinquished some of the docking area at Mallory Square and this enabled cruise ships to add Key West as a port of call. Gradually throughout the winter seasons Key West was increasingly flooded in the downtown area and elsewhere with tourists from cruise ships for the several hours they had ashore. All this diminished our privacy and peace and quiet. Real estate values were also steadily rising.

Don had had enough, and we decided to sell. We soon accepted an offer for about $350K, having paid $45K for the place in 1978. With the proceeds we purchased a new VW Passat wagon when we returned to Washington after the closing. This was a splendid, high quality, fuel efficient car, now still running well with over 200K miles as I write this in 2011. We would return to Key West each winter thereafter through 2004 staying at the Spindrift Motel on Louisa Street at Simonton, half a block from our house at 522 Louisa. After a few years our purchaser sold the house for considerably more to a developer who planned to convert and upgrade the house into two condos with a projected selling price of about $500K each.

-Dick Cassedy and Chapin Leinbach.

For the last several years of our Key West life at 522 Louisa we became close friends with Dick Cassedy and his partner Chapin Leinbach who had their principal home in Georgetown. Born in 1912 and 1913, they had lived together in Georgetown since 1951.

Dick was a watercolorist but earned his livelihood primarily from real estate investments in Alexandria, Virginia, where he grew up. Chapin worked as a writer and editor for the Air Transport Association. They acquired their winter home in Key West in 1978, about the same time we did, after Chapin retired from his job. Chapin was very social and loved parties; Dick less so. Chapin was cultivated. Having received a M.A. degree in English literature from the University of Michigan, he had a strong knowledge of English literature and would participate in the annual Key West literary seminar that would attract leading writers and poets from here and abroad. He knew Richard Wilbur and James Merrill, two leading Key West and national poets.

For several years we would have weekly lunches with Chapin and Dick at a hotel restaurant overlooking the Gulf of Mexico. They and Don had many of the same friends.

Chapin also introduced us to Ferdinand Coudert, who born in 1909 lived in the grand manner in a very grand house near Chapin and Dick's on the west side of the island opposite to ours. Ferdinand was a retired lawyer and scion of the family international law firm of Coudert Brothers which began in New York and Paris before World War I. Educated with undergraduate and graduate degrees from Harvard and a law degree from Columbia, he was fluent in French, German, and Russian, among other languages.

Don and I enjoyed his highly educated, cultivated, fluent company. He married but briefly, from awareness of his opposite orientation. He had a steady stream of house guests throughout the winter season, many of whom we would meet at his frequent lunch or dinner parties. We visited him twice at his lovely, commanding summer home on the Connecticut River near Lyme, the last shortly before his death from cancer on September 15, 1997. He became a dear friend.

Chapin and Dick gave up Key West about the same time we did for reasons of their declining health. They moved into the Georgetown Retirement Residence late in 2000 in adjoining suites for living assistance. Dick asked me to become the trustee of his trust fund and executor of his will and Chapin that I become his executor, to which I agreed. Under Chapin's will I would have a power of appointment over his residual estate. Following complications from a stroke early in January Dick died on February 13, 2001, and Chapin the following January 5. Don and I repeatedly visited them in their last months.

Their deaths created a lot of work for me for which I was well compensated from each of their estates. I asked Don Green their very competent trust and estate attorney to probate their wills with ancillary proceedings in Florida and Virginia as well where they jointly owned houses and to prepare and file Dick's federal and state estate tax returns. Notwithstanding a substantial donation to a Key West charity, Dick's estate paid a substantial amount in estate taxes. Apart from some significant bequests to his three nephews, he left more than $1 million which Chapin's failing health would prevent his enjoying.

There were two jointly owned houses to sell in Key West, five in Alexandria, and their home in Georgetown as well as Dick's studio apartment in Adams Morgan. These sales, mostly concluded after Chapin's death, went well and yielded tidy sums for Chapin's estate. My friends Jim Johnson and Frank Spencer bought the most attractive of the Alexandria houses near the asking price without any friendship price reductions from me.

Before he died, Chapin had several discussions with me about my exercising the power of appointment under his will. The will made some specific educational bequests, one to his alma mater, Dartmouth College, and another to the Ashville School for boys. He told me to reward his care givers at the Georgetown and to make substantial gifts his Georgetown friends Hazel Burgess and Phyllis Ottinger for their help in looking after the Georgetown house when Dick and Chapin were spending their many winters in Key West; and to Don Ellington for his many services to them in Key West and Georgetown as their health problems multiplied. Chapin was insistent that the remainder of the estate should go to me, as he had no living relatives with whom he had any contact, and as I was perhaps his closest friend. I faithfully executed his wishes to the grateful appreciation of those he benefitted, I in particular. Chapin was especially and wonderfully generous to Don and to me, to our great surprise and delight.

-Dick Howland.

In the later 1980s Chapin introduced us to Dick Howland who had recently retired after many years in leadership positions at the Smithsonian Institution. He and I would become close friends. Born in Providence in 1910, he was a 1931 graduate of Brown and obtained a M.A. in art history from Harvard in 1933. He served in OSS in World War II and received a Ph.D. in classical archaeology from Johns Hopkins in 1946. Brown awarded him an honorary LL.D in 1958 in recognition of his contributions to classical archaeology and scholarship in excavations at Athens and Corinth for the American School of Classical Studies in Athens beginning in the 1930s and continuing into the 1970s. Richard Hubbard Howland had already achieved much in life when we became friends. All this would gradually unfold as I came to know and admire him.

Dick lived at the Westchester, a cooperative apartment complex of several buildings from the 1930s on Cathedral Avenue, NW. It had a splendid restaurant, and we began having weekly lunches there that continued for many years. I met some of his widow friends including Noel Train, Cappy Shannon, and Carol Wakelin whom I had previously met through Emily Norton. Cappy and Carol would frequently join us for these lunches. They too became my good friends whom I would continue to see for many years to come.

Dick was a large, gregarious man with a commanding bass voice. In retirement he led a very active social life. Divorced after a brief marriage in the 1930s, he was much sought after by the ladies of Washington society. He was particularly close to Noel Train, a widow living in an attractive house in Georgetown on R Street facing Montrose Park. Noel was mostly blind from an accident some years earlier. She was unable to read, and I soon started reading to her one afternoon a week for several years. In the course of that experience she and I too became close. A lady of great taste and refinement, she had known my sister Sally at Farmington a lifetime earlier. She was also an accomplished artist with several lovely paintings in her house. Her first husband, Joe Clark from the Philadelphia Main Line, had been mayor of Philadelphia when I was working for the Navy there in the late 1940s and early1950s, and she would tell me about life as the mayor's wife. Later he became for many years a senator from Pennsylvania in Congress during which their marriage ended. They had a daughter, Noel, who also with her husband Terry Miller, long a distinguished administrative law judge at the Labor Department, became my friends.

Dick was also an academic, teaching art history first at Wellesley College from 1939-42 and then after the war at Johns Hopkins where he established and chaired the Department of Art History for several years. While there with Eleanor Spencer he wrote *The Architecture of Baltimore* published in 1953 by the Johns Hopkins Press. He wrote the preface for the successor edition published in 2004. Dillon Ripley, an academic from Yale and recently appointed Secretary of the Smithsonian, appointed Dick in 1960 as chairman of the Department of Civil History until making him his special assistant a few years later and in which position he remained until they both retired in 1985 when Dick was 75. In 1956 Dick moved to Washington to become the first president of the National Trust for Historic Preservation for several years during which he procured a $1 million gift from Paul Mellon to launch its endowment. While at the Smithsonian Dick inaugurated and led for many years a program of frequent and highly coveted study tours abroad for about two weeks to the classical and archaeological world of Greece and Rome for Smithsonian associate members on which and to whom he lectured along with other scholars mostly from the Smithsonian. As president of the English Speaking Union in Washington he arranged the sculpting and erection of the statue to Winston Churchill that stands before the British embassy and for which the Queen invested him with the Order of the British Empire.

-Robert Manson Myers.

During the later 1980s after we moved to 1661 Crescent Place I kept up my friendship with Robert Manson Myers. He too left 2101

Connecticut Avenue in June 1986 when he retired from the faculty at the University of Maryland where he was a luminous, inspiriting teacher of English literature and life for many years. From the proceeds of selling his apartment at 2101 Connecticut Avenue Manson purchased two apartments: one further north on Connecticut Avenue known as "Tilden Gardens" and the other on Grosvenor Square in London where he would continue enjoyably to spend the summer and autumn months until reluctantly giving it up in November 1997. Each apartment was spacious and attractive, the one in London especially so, as I was told by Robert Ricks a friend of Don's and mine who had stayed a few days there as Manson's guest. This flat replaced ones Manson had rented for many years in London for his summer residence after completing *The Children of Pride* in the early 1970s. He preferred life in London with his cultivated and artistic friends at the summit of British life to that elsewhere.

Before leaving Washington in 1998, Manson was my guest for several seasons of Sunday evening enriching chamber concerts at the Smithsonian. Performances of Bach, Handel, Haydn, Mozart, Beethoven, Schubert, Brahms, Shostakovich, and few other masters of string quartets, string trios, and solo instruments and an occasional Schumann or Brahms piano quintet, by first-class players, mostly Smithsonian musicians, were the usual delights which we relished. They were given before a small rapt audience in the magnificent Renwick Gallery or at the concert hall in one of the Smithsonian buildings.

After giving up London, Manson briefly moved to Lynchburg, Virginia, in June 1998, buying a beautiful large house on 10 acres of land which turned out to be too much for him to manage comfortably. He donated the property to his alma mater, Vanderbilt University. When his two married nephews encouraged him to move to be near them in Charlotte, North Carolina, where they would look after him in his declining years, he acceded and rented a lovely town house in the attractive South Park residential area of Charlotte where he now continues to live in his 91st year as I write this in 2011. Sadly and inexplicably, the nephews and their wives soon abandoned him; one moved away and both have ignored him notwithstanding his generosity to each. A few dear friends and a connection with Winthrop University in nearby South Carolina have persuaded him to stay in Charlotte although its cultural life is far removed from what Manson experienced in London and Washington.

About 2001 Manson pledged $1.5M to Randolph-Macon Woman's College in Lynchburg to endow a chair in American cultural studies in memory of his mother. The celebration of this gift was scheduled for a two-day convocation starting on September 18, 2001. I accepted gladly his invitation to attend as one of his guests along with several members of his family.

The tragedy of 9/11 did not disrupt but darkened the event and required Kathleen Jameson, Dean of the Columbia School of Journalism, as the principal speaker to scrap her prepared talk for a remarkable *ad libitum tour de force*. President Kathleen Bowman extended to Manson's guests the same preferred VIP treatment she accorded to him in dining with her and in seating at the convocation events. For me it was very stimulating and enjoyable.

Sadly, a few years later, Randolph-Macon experienced its own 9/11. Confronting huge financial crises long ignored, Randolph-Macon under new and disastrous leadership, renamed Randolph College, turned coed, stressed the primacy of revenue-enhancing sports, auctioned masterpieces from its art gallery prompting censure from the American Association of Museums, reduced faculty, and cancelled a number of academic programs including Manson's course in American cultural studies and refused the return of his partly completed gift. All this was devastating to Manson and to many of the faculty and friends of the former Randolph-Macon as declining enrollment of its successor presaged its likely doom after long being regarded as one of the nation's premiere woman's colleges

Cappy Shannon.

Earlier in the summer of 2001 Cappy Shannon had invited Don and me to visit her in September for a week in Cortona in Tuscany where she had rented a villa for that month. The other house guests would be Amy

Atkinson, a retired English journalist and widow who would winter in Key West where we had become friends, as would Cappy for a shorter stay. We would meet Amy at Heathrow and board a connecting flight to Florence and drive on to Cortona. Fortunately, the events of 9/11 did not interfere with our flight to London which was scheduled about three weeks later. The flight was almost empty; we met Amy at Heathrow and made the connecting flight to Florence, arriving there in the early evening amidst pouring rain. Finding Cappy's house in Cortona in our rental Fiat was a challenge worsened by none of us speaking Italian to understand the driving directions. At length we arrived to join Cappy and her travelling companion of many years Billy Green whom Don and I had not previously met.

Cappy had rented an attractive, spacious, well-appointed house with plenty of bedrooms and baths. She made us very much at home and comfortable. We settled into a pleasant routine of exploring nearby villages in the mornings followed by splendid lunches at a variety of restaurants followed by leisurely afternoons at the house and garden and light suppers and wine which Cappy prepared and served. Thus, among several, other places we visited Arezzo in Tuscany and Assisi and Perugia, the capital city, in Umbria, all of great historical and architectural interest and importance. My niece Joanie Casini discouraged our visiting her in Siena as she and Nicolo were preoccupied with harvesting the grapes for their wine production. In the afternoons Billy Green and I took extensive walks about the extensive, hilly countryside of Cortona.

The week with Cappy hastened by, and we would have welcomed a prolongation. With Amy, Don and I returned to the Florence airport, she for London, we for Milan for an overnight visit to Lake Como and then on to Frankfurt am Main in Germany where we would spend the weekend with my nephew Dick Coburn in Bad Homburg. Lake Como met our expectations as a lovely place to stay and explore. Dick, well settled as an English teacher at the International School in Frankfurt, welcomed us warmly. He lived in an attractive rental apartment in a building adjoining a park with lovely trees. He drove us across the Rhine to see the beautiful cathedral at Cologne, restored from having been severely bombed during the war.

From Frankfurt we returned to London early in October for a few days before the flight to Washington. In London we visited Armida Colt who had a beautiful home in Chester Square where she lived half the year, the other half in Washington. We had become friends in the early 1980s through Emily Norton.

Armida was born in Trieste in 1912 and with her mother came to New York shortly before the outbreak of World War I. Her father had already established a successful trucking business in Brooklyn. After an early fruitless marriage to a Boston playboy Armida earned a good living restoring and decorating houses for the well-to-do on Long Island before World War II. Thereafter she met and married Harris Colt, divorced with grown children and a scion of the Colt Arms Company. An amateur archaeologist he was drawn to Washington to study at the Library of Congress. They purchased in the 1950s a lovely town house on P Street in Georgetown as well as the one in London. Harris died in the 1970s before I met Armida who was also friends with Chapin and Dick Howland. I continued to see Armida in Washington for many years until her mind, tragically, was afflicted by progressive dementia. Despite that she remained in remarkably good physical health until her death at 99 in Washington on July 8, 2011. She was an important benefactor of several institutions including the Diplomatic Rooms at the State Department, the Folger Shakespeare Library, the Metropolitan Museum of Art, and the National Gallery of Art. She was also an accomplished author and designer and printer of limited editions of varied and rare books in Washington and England. She was a good, generous friend.

In London Armida took us out to dinner at one of the city's great restaurants. I had invited Lyttleton Fox's son, James Fox, to join us. By then an acclaimed writer including *Five Sisters,* about the lives of the Langhorne sisters, one of whom was James's grandmother, James was an interesting and charming man for Armida to know, and he delighted her and us with witty, cultivated, top English talk. The next day I had arranged to meet James, his sister Phyllis, and their half siblings Edward, Genevieve, and another sister whose name I no longer remember at Edward's home near London. They gave me a wonderful Sunday lunch, and I told them what

I remembered of the wit and wisdom of their father. I liked them all, although none had their father's sparkle and conversational gifts.

Don and I were again Cappy's guests in Key West during one or two visits after we sold the Key West house. One of her friends there introduced me to XM satellite radio based in Washington and its enormous programming, including classical and operatic music. When I returned to Washington I became a subscriber as with cable television, but far less costly, and purchased the components to play the music through our Bose radio in the living room and in our WV house as well as through the Passat's excellent sound system. This has been a great companion ever since as I primarily listen to the Metropolitan opera channel on the Sirius XM network and online.

In the autumn of 1999 Cappy joined us on the maiden voyage of our new Passat, which ran perfectly, to visit Hugh Bonney for several days at his summer place in Ontario. We motored to Buffalo and crossed into Ontario, then north to Niagara, viewing the falls from Canada, then on to Toronto and to Hugh's place on a large lake about an hour beyond that city where Hugh also lived.

Hugh, then in his late 50s or early 60s, had retired having achieved financial success in business. He had an attractive condo fronting on the ocean in Key West for his winters for several years and this beautiful, remote, forested place for his summers. There was the rough hewn main house and a guest cabin in which Don and I stayed. Divorced, he had a grown son whom we would not meet and attractive friends whom we did during this visit. We enjoyed swimming in the lake; and one day an interesting couple took us for an all day outing on the lake on their comfortable motor boat with a tasty picnic lunch. One evening we attended a performance at the Stratford Shakespeare festival that was first rate, although I no longer remember which one of his plays. Strangely, the silence of the area surrounding Hugh's place was from the absence of birds, apparently the result of accumulated acid rain principally from our mid-west utility coal-burning emissions over many years. The American and Canadian border crossing controls and procedures were then minimal; not so since 9/11. We made it back to Washington in one go, glad to have gone.

-January 3, 2005, Don Dies.

I became increasingly concerned about Don's health after we sold the Key West house in 1999. His walking, usually with me several blocks once or twice a week to the Safeway market to stock up on food, slowed significantly and in frequency. He did stop smoking and drinking, acts of enormous will power to overcome those long addictions. In the early 2000s, we drove to his home town in Miami, Oklahoma, primarily to visit his sister Opal Shouse who, now a widow lived in nearby Baxter, Kansas. She told me she was shocked by his changed appearance. On returning I persuaded him to undergo a thorough checkup with our heath care provider, the non-profit Kaiser Permanente in Washington, a health maintenance organization we had recently joined, and had been assigned a first-rate primary care physician, Dr. Tom Tesoriero. He detected a failing kidney function due to the effects of hypertension and high blood pressure, and referred him to one of their renal specialists who prescribed a program of three-hour dialysis three times a week at a dialysis center, a convenient drive from our apartment which I was glad to do. My blood type and age rejected me as a potential donor of a replacement kidney. The kidney specialist also strongly recommended major changes in Don's diet from what he usually ate to more nutritious foods that would aid the kidney function.

Don made sufficient efforts to heed that advice that after about 6 months the doctors discontinued the dialysis program. All this Kaiser paid for, and our monthly premiums were comparatively low. There was little doubt that his health failure was primarily due to his lifetime consumption of excessive alcohol, smoking, salt and sugar in processed foods, desserts, and beverages, dairy and fried meat fats, and almost no fresh vegetables, and little exercise.

We made our last trip to Key West for a week in the winter of 2004, staying as before at the Spindrift Motel on Louisa Street. Don seemed less interested in looking up old friends with one or two exceptions, and stayed mostly by the motel pool reading, rarely going in the water. Driving north, we stopped at Auburn, Alabama, to visit Don's sister Opal, now living there in a nursing home near her son Fred Shouse and his wife Paula. Again. Opal was now even more distressed and worried about Don's health, as was I. When we returned to Washington, the doctors renewed the dialysis treatment, about a year after it had been discontinued.

Later that December with little apparent improvement in his health and experiencing occasional spasms in his right arm and leg, I persuaded Dr. Tesoriero to have him admitted to the Washington Hospital Center for more extensive testing and observation during the last week of December. When he was finally released with the tests indicating no cause for alarm, he insisted on terminating the final dialysis treatment because of exhaustion, and I took him home on December 29. He said he never had been so tired and went straight to bed without any supper.

About 6 the next morning, the day before New Year's Eve, I wakened to a loud thud from his next door bedroom. He had fallen out of his double bed on his left side facing the north window and opposite to the door in an apparent attempt to get up. He was unconscious on the floor. The ambulance came very promptly and returned him and me to the Washington Hospital Center. Because of his release the day before he quickly was admitted again to a semi-private room. He had suffered a stroke and was paralyzed on his right side. He was immediately placed on life support devices for heart, breathing and other vital functions. Because this was the New Year's holiday weekend the necessary tests could not be performed until the following Monday morning, January 3, 2005. He never regained consciousness, and I kept vigil at his bedside in the hope that he would.

Some years before he had executed an advanced care directive appointing me to act for him in making healthcare decisions should he become incapacitated. I notified his siblings of these developments and obtained their unanimous consent to terminate the life support should an acceptable recovery not be likely, which was Don's explicit wish, particularly not to become an invalid. Early that Monday afternoon, the doctors told me that that the MRI indicated a massive stroke and brain swelling with no prospect of recovery.

I promptly authorized them to discontinue the life support machines and witnessed his life ebb away peacefully and painlessly in a few minutes in his 78th year. So ended our life together with its ups and downs for both of us for over 45 years. There was an acute feeling of aloneness. I arranged for him, at his request, to be cremated with his ashes to be scattered later at our place in West Virginia as I shall relate.

There were two memorial gatherings for Don, one in a private room adjoining the dining room at the Westchester in Washington in the early evening on January 29, 2005, and the second in the late afternoon on Saturday, February 20, 2005, at the spacious home and patio of our friends Ray Baker and Joe Viana in Key West. Each was well attended. At the Washington gathering, Don's niece, Opal's daughter Sue Rouse and her husband Bob Rouse, came from Providence and stayed with me. My cousin, the Rev. Olivia Holmes from Wayland, Massachusetts, my nephews David Coburn from Seattle and Lawrie Coburn from Philadelphia, Travis Fulton from Aspen and his brother Rawn Fulton from Massachusetts were there as was my godson David Martin, a Washington lawyer, and Greg Watson, a dear friend from Philadelphia. Peter and Joanne Coburn were prevented by bad weather from flying from Boston.

Don's Washington friends covered his life here since the 1950s, among them Priscilla Alfandre, Jim Riggs, Annette and Bill Doolitle, Bob Reed, Lee Bird, Jim Johnson and Frank Spencer, Matt and Jane Simchak, Dick Howland, Cappy Shannon, Carol Wakelin, Hazel Burgess, Rob Evers, and Paul Domer, a neighbor at 1661 Crescent Place. Priscilla Alfandre and Jim Riggs spoke of knowing Don in Washington in the 1950s, and Sue Rouse about remembering her Uncle Don. After a few remarks of my own, I proposed a toast to Don, followed by a moment of silence, concluding with a benediction by cousin Olivia. We then proceeded to a buffet supper.

At the Key West gathering almost a month later, there were about 40 present, including my niece Priscilla Heublein from Jupiter, Florida, and my nephew John Coburn from Bonita Springs, on the west coast of Florida near Naples. There was an outpouring of love and affection for him from his many Key West friends. Sally Lewis, Mary Ann Worth, and Jim Salem gave happy and amusing tales of his Key West life and Easter Hat parties. Bob Alfandre recalled the young Don he and Priscilla had known in Washington in the early 1950s. Sally Lewis too spoke of knowing Don in Washington in the 1960s and 1970s before moving to Key West. Our host read a glowing message from "Momy" Ortiz Benavides who had returned from living in Key West to his family home in Mexico City. Following my remarks, a farewell toast and a moment of silence, we had the utterly delicious hors d'oeuvres and the services of a bar tender provided by the restaurant Square One.

At both gatherings, I concluded with these thoughts about Don:

> Don led a full and engaging life, blessed with many friends in Washington and Key West. He read a lot and was a whiz at crossword puzzles and Scrabble. He loved Broadway musicals and was a devoted fan of Barbara Cook. He was filled with fun. He was very talented at interior decorating and made our several homes inviting and attractive. He enjoyed cooking and over the years produced some memorable meals for friends. As for his traits of character, I would describe Don as outspokenly honest, as having a strong sense of humor, sometimes biting, as very thrifty, and as being blessed with a large uncompromising integrity. In sum, he was a worthy and irreplaceable companion to me for 45 years in the journey of life.

We had two scatterings of his ashes in our West Virginia home on Saturday, April 9, and Saturday, April 30, to accommodate those family members and friends who could come on one but not the other of these Saturdays. On that first glorious spring Saturday afternoon, my nephew and godson, Peter Coburn, his wife Joanne, and his brothers Gordy and David drove out from Washington where they had met earlier that day at the Reagan National Airport having flown there from Seattle (David), Santa Barbara (Gordy), and Boston (Peter and Joanne). They would spend that Saturday night at a motel in Berkeley Springs. After lunch at the house, we scattered some of Don's ashes in the two flower beds he had planted, one in front of the house and the other next to the shed in back. Peter then read this stanza from Swinburne's "The Garden of Proserpine":

> From too much love of living
> From hope and fear set free,
> We thank with brief thanksgiving
> Whatever gods may be
> That no life lives forever;
> That even the weariest river
> Winds somewhere safe to sea.

Gordy then read this passage from Whitman's "Leaves of Grass":

> In the dooryard fronting an old farm-house near the
>   whitewashed palings,
> Stands the lilac-bush tall growing with heart-shaped
>   leaves of rich green,
> With many a pointed blossom rising delicate, with the
>   perfume strong I love,
> With every leaf a miracle—and from the bush in the
>   dooryard,
> With delicate-color'd blossoms and heart-
>   shaped leaves of rich green,
> A sprig with its flower I break.

Don would have loved this; his spirit was omnipresent.

Four friends arrived early Saturday afternoon, April 20, in time for lunch: Jim Garland and Dick Parks drove from Salem in upstate New York whom Don and I had previously visited there and who had been our close friends for many years; and Jim Johnson and Frank Spencer from Alexandria, long our friends, who had visited us there several times over the years. Rosemary Aldrich, the artistic wife of George Aldrich, long a judge at the Iran Claims Court at the Hague, and our friends since the 1960s, could not be there. Instead, she wrote these lovely lines which I read:

Oh, that his passing
Might be a revelry
And that he might
Dwell in the Garden
With the Tree of Life
And the Rose of Love
There, in time, will we
Be with him forever
Those that loved him well.

I then read these words from A.E. Housman, first from "The rain, it streams on stone and hillock"

Good night, my lad, for nought's eternal,
No league of ours, for sure,
To-morrow I shall miss you less,
And ache of heart and heaviness
Are things that time should cure.

And then, from "My funeral":

We now to peace and darkness
And earth and thee restore
Thy creature that thou makest
And will cast forth no more.

Each of us then scattered the remaining ashes in the two flower beds and bade Don a loving farewell, we enriched by remembering him.

-Ode to Agnes.

I shall now introduce our cat who entered our lives by showing up at the West Virginia house one summer day about 2002. Don started feeding her, named her Agnes, and she decided to stay. She was young, perhaps a year old, and was already spayed when we took her to Dr. Murphy, the vet in Hancock, Maryland, some 25 miles from the house, to have that done. He pronounced her very healthy and gave her a battery of shots, some of which I renew each September. With short hair most every shade of brown and dark stripes, she attached herself to Don and largely ignored me. The first several years we would take her back and forth each weekend until the onset of cold weather in November. When we were away for an extended period during the West Virginia months, we arranged for Kay Light, our near neighbor, to feed her twice daily at the house with the cat food we provided. We had a cat door installed in one of the casement windows opening on to the front porch so she could come and go at will. Paul Domer, a nearby neighbor at 1661 Crescent Place, would feed her for us when we went to Key West and on other occasions in the winter months when I would be away. When Don had his fatal stroke she would not enter his bedroom for several months. She then shifted to me her loyalty and love which I cherish.

In 2010, I wrote this Ode to Agnes:

> To be with the Cat Don named Agnes
> Enfolds our hearts in ever gladness.
> Some years ago She came to the house,
> Perhaps even following a residing mouse.
> After having a meal She decided to stay.
> How could we say no to Her anyway?

> Mr. Eliot says a cat must have three different names,
> Imagine "[su]ch as Munkustrap, Quaxo, or Coricopat,"
> Perhaps even such an oddity as "Jennyannydots" in fact.
> But Agnes says No, there will be no such silly games,
> Please and so for evermore as Agnes she remains.

> Agnes wears her brown with many a shade
> Amidst emerald eyes to pierce the ever glade
> All the better for her in the woods to hide
> To wait for prey but there not long to abide.

Agnes is attentive and good mannered in her way
For everyone who may come to see her any day.
If you rub her head, stroke her back, squeeze her paw
She may jump in your lap, snooze and ask for more.

Agnes sits and sits and sleeps and nibbles her eats
All the while awaiting evermore wholesome treats.
At night when you are in bed trying to sleep
She will snuggle up close as She can by your side
Until she wakes you to eat despite the eventide.

Agnes likes her country house with the cat door
To be out or in as She pleases by a push of her paw.
In winter She comes to the city to be entirely indoors
Until spring and return to the evergreen moors.

So Agnes and I shall go on together,
Perhaps we are like birds of a feather
Come what may She will with me stay
Until one of us goes, then who can say?

Agnes, Amen.

-May 29, 2006, Robert Manson Myers at Eighty-Five.

To celebrate this occasion I travelled to Charlotte the month before over a weekend and stayed comfortably at the South Park Hotel located near Manson's attractive town house on Deckford Place in a beautiful residential area in the south park area of Charlotte. That Friday or Saturday evening Manson's friends Carol and Henry Pharr who lived nearby hosted a buffet dinner of friends in Manson's honor. After dinner and toasts I offered this salute to Manson:

Let us praise this estimable, erudite, gentle man at four score and five, as one deserving of the highest encomia. Ongoing in his aesthetic creativity, renowned as a man of letters, awesome as a great teacher and master of English, admirable as a large benefactor of Randoph-Macon College, Manson has enriched the education of several generations as well as those privileged by knowing his books and plays and by his friendship.

His creations traverse English literature. They begin in the 17th and 18th centuries With *Handel's Messiah: A Touchstone of Taste* (1948), then *Handel, Dryden and Milton* (1956), then *Restoration Comedy* (1956), and then surveying in a matchless spoof the entirety of the wolf motif in *From Beowulf to Virginia Woolf* (1952). Manson wrote *Beowulf* in the mid-1940s while teaching English literature at Yale as a young man. It was finally published in 1952 here and in England by the Bobbs-Merrill Company to great acclaim after having been rejected by a dozen less prescient publishers. It continued to sell well with many reprints until 1979. At the urging of the University of Illinois Press in 1980, Manson revised the book from his perspective of some 40 years on, and this "astounding and wholly unauthorized history of English Literature" was published as a new edition in 1984. Some have suggested that a choice subject of a doctoral dissertation would be an analysis of the differences in the two editions.

Then the focus of Manson's literary work shifts across the Atlantic to the examination and selection for editing and publication from some seven thousand letters involving the Rev. Charles Colcock Jones (1804-63) and his Georgia plantation family and their correspondents covering the period 1854-1868, and as selected culminating in 1972 in the publication by the Yale University Press of *The Children of Pride: A True Story of Georgia and the Civil War*, as told in some twelve hundred letters. This 20-year project of unremitting toil and perseverance by Manson began on Thanksgiving Day 1952 while he was teaching at Tulane University in New Orleans. A valued friend and older colleague at Tulane, one Dr. Seago who headed the Psychology Department, showed him a journal her great grandmother Mary Jones, the wife of Dr. Jones, and her daughter jointly had written about the coming of the Yankee troops in December 1864.

Manson read this with great interest and inquired about further writings. She told him she had a house full of these family letters and entrusted them to him for selecting and editing for publication. Most of the other Jones family letters were provided by the University of Georgia at Athens and by the Waller family of Augusta. Getting them published was a long, hard struggle. After rejection by several leading publishers including the Harvard University Press, a friend of Manson's at the Yale Library persuaded Professor C. Vann Woodward, then head of the History Department at Yale, to read the manuscript. He then insisted that the Yale University Press publish it.

When this was finally accomplished a year later early in 1972, after Manson overcame the publisher's recalcitrance to publication of the entire manuscript in a single volume, The New York Times gave it an unprecedented front-page glowing review by Madison Jones. He wrote that the book tells the story of the Old South and its destruction "as it has not been told before, in the fullness of its poignance and tragedy." Again in December of that year in a front-page article, The New York Times cited *The Children of Pride* as "one of the five significant books of 1972" and as one of the important, lasting books of the twentieth century. That year *The Children of Pride* also won the coveted Carey-Thomas Award, and in 1973 the National Book Award in History. The citation for that award read: *"The Children of Pride* is family reconstruction on a grand scale. It demonstrates how the editing of sources can become, in the hands of an imaginative scholar, the work of creative history."

That book with the author's prologue and epilogue provides 1,400 hundred pages of these selected and edited family letters followed by a 392 page Who's Who of detailed biographies of the more than a thousand individuals sending or receiving or mentioned in these letters, written by Manson in the course of seventeen summers searching archival records in Georgia and elsewhere. Page xxiii of the Preface vividly recalls some of this research over these years:

> In Georgia I have worked for weeks with the public records of Athens, Augusta, Macon, and Savannah; I have deciphered yellowing documents in remote county courthouses; I have sat on village porches sipping tea as I listened to reminiscences of the past; I have risked rattlesnakes (and mosquitoes and poison ivy) in the rank growth of forgotten graveyards. I have transcribed tombstones beneath a merciless August sun; I have even spent a darksome evening groping for markers in a private burial ground by the light of a flickering candle. In my pursuit of biographical data I have journeyed to Kentucky and Tennessee twice, to Georgia, Alabama, and Florida ten times. I have had innumerable adventures, some of them amusing, a few of them harrowing, most of them gratifying. And wherever I turned I have met with kindly assistance.

Manson wrote these biographies instead of identifying footnotes to the letters. In The Preface, he quotes Dr. Johnson's admonition more than two centuries ago, "Notes are often necessary, but they are necessary evils....The mind is refrigerated by interruption; the thoughts are delivered from the principal object; the reader is weary; he suspects not why; and at last throws away the book he has too diligently studied." In addition to these utmost taxing labors, Manson also prepared a 100-page detailed index of these individuals in the Who's Who called "The Free" and the subject matter of the letters involving them; and finally a 4- page of "The Slaves" and where each of them appears in the letters. In sum, Manson's research and scholarship evident in *The Children of Pride* have brought forth history told in the everyday letters of ordinary people in a manner that is truly grand and monumental and likely to stand alone. Its apt title is from Job 41:34, "He beholdeth all high things: He is king over all the children of pride."

Manson next published some 365 pages of further letters of the Jones family in 1976 in *A Georgian at Princeton* covering the years 1850-52 when the two sons of Dr. Jones and his wife Mary, Charles, Jr., and Joseph Jones, were students at Princeton. There followed in 1984 a 671-page abridged edition of *The Children of Pride* letters of the years 1860-68 and omitting the Who's Who and the index.

Then he worked on creating five epistolary plays entirely from these letters and published in 1991 by the University of Illinois Press and including the earlier letters from the courtship of Charles Colcock Jones and his cousin Mary Jones. Don and I had the privilege of seeing these plays produced in stirring performances in Savannah in 1985.[167] They have also performed to great acclaim at the Smithsonian Institution in Washington, DC, and by the BBC in London.

More recently, Manson has created and published plays adapted from various novels. First, in 2004, came *Sixes and Sevens, Scenes from a Marriage*, a comic trilogy drawn from three novels of the late 19th and early 20th century journalist, drama critic and novelist, Ada Leverson, a great, caring friend of Oscar Wilde, particularly in his time of trouble, whom he called "the Sphinx". The title is again from Job 5:19, "He shall deliver thee in six troubles: Yea, in seven there shall no evil touch thee." The three plays are *Lover Pro Tem*, drawn from *Love's Shadow* (1908), *Tenterhooks* and *Love at Second Sight*, the last two drawn from her novels with the same titles published in 1912 and 1916, respectively. These plays portray the comedy of the Edwardian marriage of Edith and Bruce Oxley with the wit and wisdom of Manson's prose matching that in the plays of Oscar Wilde.

---

167 See Note 124 *supra* and related text for an account of those performances over several days.

Next in 2005 Manson published two plays he adapted from novels of Henry James, one of Manson's favorite authors along with Jane Austen. First was *The Bostonians* adapted from the novel of the same title, and then *Poynton Park* adapted from *The Spoils of Poynton*. All these recent plays are published by Jostens Books in Charlotte.

* * *

In summing up Manson, one is awed by his stunning literary achievements, by his masterful teaching, by his wit and wisdom, by his exemplary character, and by his being at the summit of what an aesthetic life may achieve. By the intensity, by the thoroughness, by the persuasiveness of all he does in writing and speaking, does he not ignite the minds of his readers and listeners to know and seek perfection in what their minds do as his does and so often achieves? So we salute Manson at eighty-five and command that he may long continue so to enrich our lives.

October 24, 2006, Dick Howland Dies.

For several years Dick and I had weekly Thursday lunches at the Westchester restaurant which was also open to the public largely unaware of it, and its patrons were mostly residents. Willis Shapley and Larry Lutkins, also widower residents of the Westchester, would usually join us. They became my friends too. Each had retired at high levels from distinguished careers in government: Willis at NASA and then mostly at the Office of Management and Budget; Larry from the Foreign Service, an "old China hand". The restaurant had the advantages of a dining room of a private club, with excellent cuisine and without monthly dues. I would do my infrequent entertaining there.

By 2005 at 95, Dick's hearing had seriously deteriorated and I took him to my audiologist, Richard Brisbane, in Kensington, Maryland. A year or two earlier Richard had equipped me with two hearing aids that greatly reduced my substantial hearing loss that had also affected my mother and siblings. Don would complain that when we were driving he would hold conversations aloud with himself of which I apparently was oblivious. Richard also largely restored Dick's hearing that greatly improved the quality of his life.

He wanted to make a final trip to Greece in the fall of 2005, and would I go with him? Sadly, however, Dick's health declined that summer with no prospect of making that trip. He now required assisted living in his apartment; and I was fortunate to find a competent care giver who provided trained and caring male nurses from India that gradually expanded their service to 24/7. Dick executed a power of attorney to me to take charge of his check book and to pay the bills. I was glad to do this but insisted on his signing the checks as long as he was able to do so; and when that was no longer possible to tell him about each check I signed. We now would have our weekly lunch in his apartment which the dining room would deliver. After lunch I would attend to paying the bills. He gave up his car and donated it to a charity.

Dick had a splendid lawyer, Doris Blazek-White of Covington & Burling where she headed the trusts and estates practice. She had drawn his will with which I became familiar as she was to be the executor and Dick had insisted that I was to assist her in its execution. She and I became friends and worked well and harmoniously together. I was to arrange the sale of the contents of his apartment when the time came. Dick had no family and his will made substantial bequests to the American School of Classical Studies and to various charities associated with classical archaeology. He had previously endowed in perpetuity an annual lecture on classical archaeology at Georgetown University. Dick had arranged for his papers, including unpublished lectures and articles on art history and classical archaeology, to go to the University of Maryland, and I was to supervise the execution of that arrangement.

A small group of friends, including Doris and Wilton Dillon, a long-time colleague and friend from the Smithsonian, celebrated Dick's 96th birthday at his apartment. It was painfully evident he would not last much longer. I persuaded Doris to open a $5K trust account for Dick at her bank from which to pay the bills until the will was probated and she was granted letters testamentary by the probate court and for which I provided the funds from the sale of some securities. For from the moment of his death my power of appointment would terminate, and I would not long be able to back date checks to pay his bills.

Dick died peacefully in his apartment on October 24, and Doris, I and Hospice were promptly notified by the caregiver. Hospice arranged for the cremation. Doris would later take his ashes to a family plot in Providence. I had drafted a death notice and an obituary for the Washington Post which promptly published them. The obituary announced that a memorial gathering of friends would be held on December 14 at the Cosmos Club in Washington where Wilton had helped me make those arrangements and greatly assisted in inviting the guests and in selecting the speakers to honor him.

It was a fitting memorial occasion. I welcomed the approximately 75 guests and introduced the 6 speakers from academia and other institutions with which Dick was closely associated. I noted that the "outpouring of affection and respect from all over the country and abroad has been extraordinary as we have contacted many people he cared about...." We had a printed program of the highlights of his life and brief biographies of the speakers, and a wonderful photograph of Dick in color at the peak of good health some years earlier. Wilton also arranged for a trio of Smithsonian musicians to play classical music for violin, cello and flute during an interlude between each of the speakers. The speakers were excellent and addressed the several diverse aspects of Dick's long life, many of which seemed unrelated but had an underlying cultural unity. In the adjoining room for refreshments after the speeches there was an exhibit of Howland memorabilia including his decorations, awards, photographs assembled by Amy Ballard of the Smithsonian, and a Greek icon Dick treasured. Dick would have greatly loved this fond farewell.

The administration of Dick's estate proceeded smoothly. Doris probated the will, paid the bills and put his apartment on the market, employing the services of a real estate agent who resided at the Westchester. On the fifth floor of the Westchester building at 3900

Cathedral Avenue, Dick's apartment had a spacious living room, an adjoining sunroom, a medium size dining room, a small kitchen, and two bedrooms and baths. It was not long before a purchaser bought it at close to the asking price together with the apartment next door, then also for sale, which he combined with Dick's to form a very large apartment.

I retained John Overton to appraise and price the contents of the apartment for sale, and to conduct the sale first to residents of the Westchester and the remainder by one of the auction houses. I had previously employed John similarly to dispose of the contents of Chapin Leinbach's house in Georgetown. He was very qualified to appraise and price antiques, china and glass, rugs, books, art objects, paintings, and the usual household contents. On successive weekends in November and December John was able to sell most of the items to the Westchester residents. They included a beautiful 18th century Rhode Island grandfather clock, some lovely pieces of furniture, rugs, rare books, and pictures. He sent what was left to Sotheby's to be auctioned. John's compensation was a reasonable percentage of the gross receipts plus his expenses. Doris and I were pleased with the results of his work.

-April 2008, Rawn Harding Dies.

My sister Louise's first child born in April 1932, Rawn Harding had for many years lived in mid-town Manhattan and worked for the concert violinist Midori, assisting in the management of the Midori Foundation. Sadly, early in 2008 after having retired a few years previously, Rawn was diagnosed with incurable lung cancer, the likely result of a lifetime of smoking. She faced her few remaining months with extraordinary equanimity and courage. Her sisters Priscilla and Katherine, her brother Henry Harding, a Harding cousin, some close friends, David Coburn and I all met to celebrate her life in the attractive garden of her apartment a few months later. Dear, gentle, exemplary in many ways, Rawn was much loved and will be greatly missed by family and friends.

-May 29, 2011, Manson at Ninety.

Following his 85th birthday I began the practice of visiting Manson semi-annually in Charlotte in late April and October, staying at the Marriott South Park Hotel within comfortable walking distance to his house. I would drive the 400 miles from Washington early on a Friday morning, reaching the hotel by 4 p.m. Manson would stop for me for an early dinner with Carol and Henry Pharr who lived nearby, either at their more distant club, the beautiful Charlotte Country Club, or in their beautiful apartment. I enjoyed their company. Henry, a corporate lawyer in his sixties from an old Charlotte family with a well-established Charlotte law firm, sadly had developing health issues that would eventually lead to the necessity for kidney dialysis. Henry had grown children from a prior marriage. Carol whom he had married several years previously was vivacious, conversant with French literature and language, was utterly caring and devoted to Henry and his well being. Both of them were awed by Manson whom they had met a few years before and treasured his company, sparkling conversation and wit. They became my friends too. The conversation, mostly about current affairs, soared. All of us had very negative views of President Bush, Vice President Cheney and their policies, domestic and foreign, such a telling contrast and departure from those of his predecessor and even from his father's administration.

Saturday mornings I would work at my computer in the hotel room until meeting Manson at his house later in the morning for nonstop conversation mostly by him about his current writing project with fascinating digressions into his teaching from which I concluded that Manson taught "life" as revealed in great literature including the Bible as literature. There might be a brief lunch snack of tomato juice, celery and mixed nuts I provided each visit to him and the Pharrs. Later I would return to the hotel to change into evening attire, black tie, etc., for Manson to stop for me an hour or so later to drive me to his club for an early dinner in a private room and to which he had invited the Pharrs and usually another couple. At dinner Manson would hold forth on any number of topics, ancient and contemporary, as we savored a multi-course repast including filet mignon, choice wines, and sumptuous dessert. Sundays would be mostly a reprise of Saturdays, except that I would entertain Manson at a Chinese restaurant and in later years at the hotel for an early supper usually with the Pharrs. Monday mornings I would depart early, usually spending that night visiting Lee Bird in little Washington, Virginia, some 75 miles west of our Capitol.

In addition to these visits, I would telephone Manson monthly on Sunday afternoons, either from Washington or West Virginia, usually for at least two hours of nonstop of mostly monologue, always stimulating and provocative on a wide variety of topics, again centered on his current writing project. I sensed that he acutely missed his classroom perform-ances and the stimulation that gave him. Also he was obviously lonely, and I gradually became his confidant as there was, with one principal exception, no one else in Charlotte. That exception was Mary Clark, a highly educated lady, Phi Beta Kappa, fluent in French, mother of four lovely, well-brought up teenage daughters, and long married to Kevin, a college-educated, successful business man in Charlotte. She began a practice of weekly lunches with Manson at her house for a few hours with the children at school and Kevin at work. Mary came to fill an important need in Manson's life, and he valued her literary opinion on his works in progress which he would increasingly share with her.

In late April 2011 I again drove to Charlotte for an anticipatory cel-ebration of his 90th birthday, a month later on May 29. Again the Pharrs hosted the dinner at their lovely apartment. We were joined by Elsie and Lloyd Agnew from Lynchburg, Virginia, longtime friends of Manson from his connections to Randolph-Macon College where Elsie had taught for many years and from which she had resigned in protest of the new directions of the new leadership I have recounted. I said:

> Manson exemplifies living a long life creating in his writ-
> ing, in his teaching, in his talk, in his being a Socrates of his era
> in molding minds of all ages. Who but he could long imagine

and create a cluster of poems that tell of the joy and the pain of love, of folly and frivolity in its pursuit, of what matters for mankind, all artfully and richly expressed in a variety of poetic form with every letter beginning with the letter "a"? Ovid, perhaps, as his "Ars Amatoria" so inspired Manson to create another for our times.

Let me give one example of what Manson has wrought in this instance of man's everlasting folly. From the sonnet "Ab Aeterno",

As ancient Ammonites and Amalekites
Assault assembled ancient Adamlites;
Again as Alexander aims abroad,
And aggravates aggressions all applaud;
At Agincourt again as *Angleterre*
Avails amidst an archer's arrowed air;
Again as ace Armada abdicates,
And ardent *Angleterre* annihilates——-

Again at Austerlitz as arms attain
Autonomous ascendancy amain;
At Alamo again as apt alarms
Audaciously assert assault-at-arms;
As awed Antietam amplifies affright,
And adversaries agonize aflight;
At Appomattox anguish acerbates,
And aggrieved *angst* accelerates.

Again Americans abroad advance,
Approaching absolute *Allemagne* askance;
Again, alas, Ardennes, again Argonne,
As able Allied armies attack anon;
An armistice abortively avails.
Albeit animosity assails;
And all appease an ancient appetite,
As Armageddon answers "All aright!"

Antietam, Austerlitz, and Alamo:
Aceldama awaits an afterblow!
Armada, Agincourt, Argonne, Ardennes:
Aceldama again—alas, again!

The recognition and high praise this poem and many of the others merit will ensue as readers and critics will come to see that Manson's *Ars Amatoria* is a work of high literary purpose and poetic achievement as well as one of extraordinary novelty.

Manson has not paused from the wearying exertions of that creation. He is in headlong pursuit of writing with punctilious perfection an Anglo-American romance as he completes his first novel. It has, he tells me, taken on a life of its own as the principal characters unfold in mysterious ways beyond what their creator first imagined. Its completion looms with publication more likely in England. It should also there attract a film version with it Wildean dialog, fetching English vistas and locations, and the waltzes of Franz Lehar. It has the added fillip of a transgender love vicariously fulfilled.

As he enters his tenth decade, there are no signs of mental slackening or diminishing of creative purpose. Onward he as we continue to marvel at this fountain of truth.

For those such as I who do not know "Aceldama", Manson adds "Addenda Alphabetica" amplifying "Aceldama" as "an appalling antagonistic abattoir."

4. 1992-2011. Participation in the Procurement Activities of the National Security Industrial Association (NSIA) and its Successor the National Defense Industrial Association (NDIA).

I have written in Part Five about Ropes & Gray's joining NSIA while I was with that firm in the later 1980s, thus enabling me to participate in the meetings of its procurement legal subcommittee and later on of its procurement planning committee following my election to that body mostly comprising the chair and vice chairs of the various substantive procurement subcommittees. Thanks to my affiliation with Rob Evers who had his own membership and was active in the international committee I was able to continue to participate in these procurement legal and planning meetings without incurring the significant costs of having my own individual membership. I would pay directly for the costs of attending these meetings.

In 1997 NSIA merged with the American Defense Preparedness Association (formerly the Army Ordnance Association) to form NDIA. The procurement planning committee and its procurement subcommittees continued as before. There was usually a July meeting in Boston enabling me to visit Mike and Joan in Wareham and after 2004 Joan at Fox Hill in Westwood through 2010. When visiting Joan, my niece Katherine Nahum and her husband Jeremy who lived nearby in West Newton would join us one evening for dinner to our great enjoyment. She was a respected and tenured professor of art history at Boston College; he a leading child psychiatrist. Their married sons Jed and Erich were thriving at Microsoft and IBM, respectively, and had provided their parents with grandchildren. However and regrettably, by 2011 my hearing had deteriorated despite hearing aids so that I could no longer participate in group discussions.

In 1997 I became the vice chair of the legal subcommittee for a two-year term. A year later the chair resigned when his company discontinued its NDIA membership. I filled out his term followed by one of my own for another two years. Thus I had the privilege of leading that subcommittee for three years. In this I and other subcommittee chairs were greatly, indispensably, assisted by Ruth Franklin, the executive staff director of the procurement committee, who succeeded Ed Schiff who had long ably held that position until retirement. Ruth was utterly splendid: conscientious to a fault, knowledgeable and conversant with the significant ongoing procurement regulatory issues by screening and calling to our attention significant developments published for public comment or adopted as interim or final procurement rules in the daily *Federal Register*, and arranging the timely preparation of NDIA comments when appropriate. We became and remain friends

The legal subcommittee usually had about a dozen members who regularly attended the bi-monthly and later quarterly meetings, usually held at the Army-Navy Club in Washington. There were probably more than another fifty members who would receive the minutes of our meetings from Ruth, mostly by email attachment, together with the minutes of the procurement planning committee which she would circulate to all members of the NDIA procurement committee and its subcommittees. There was a mix of able company lawyers and lawyers in private practice who would attend the legal subcommittee meetings. They were, for the most part, unusually knowledgeable about public contract law. As chair I would prepare the meeting agenda and Ruth would distribute it by email a week or so in advance of the meeting. The agenda would include reports on case law, regulatory, and any legislative developments since the last meeting, and I would task various members to provide oral and written reports on these developments on an ongoing basis which would be distributed at the meetings and attached to or summarized in the minutes. To prepare the agenda I had to keep abreast of current case law in bid protests and performance disputes as well as important regulatory or legislative matters and select for committee discussion in our three-hour morning meetings those matters which I believed raised significant questions or new issues. All the subcommittees of at least fifty members would meet for lunch for which there was usually an invited speaker from a top government procurement position who would answer questions following his talk. Many were excellent. After lunch the procurement planning committee would meet for a couple of hours to hear reports from the subcommittee chairs and discuss and vote on various items designated by the chair of that committee. Ruth would attend and prepare and distribute the minutes.

For me chairing the legal subcommittee for three years was challenging and bracing. Ruth would occasionally forward to me requests from member companies for an amicus brief by NDIA to be filed in connection with supporting an appeal of a court decision favorable to the government. I would put these on the agenda for the next meeting when time permitted; otherwise I would summarize the issues in a memorandum to the subcommittee members with my recommendation along with the company request that Ruth would distribute by email to the full membership of the legal subcommittee and requesting a prompt response which usually concurred with my recommendation. The procurement planning committee would usually accept our recommendations on whether to support or deny the request for an amicus brief. If the decision was favorable, the next task was finding a lawyer or firm willing to draft the brief, primarily *pro bono* since NDIA would not fund it. Sometimes company members would contribute financially to the drafting effort.

I prepared detailed minutes of the legal subcommittee meetings which Ruth distributed. These included my comments on the matters discussed, often including further analyses of the cases beyond what the discussion time permitted. These were well received from the feedback I got. Unlike most other chairs I had the time to prepare these extensive comments that for me were educationally rewarding. In addition, I would report at some length on our meetings to the procurement planning committee whose membership of persons of stature in the defense industry I respected.

Perhaps as a result, on March 12, 2001, I was honored to receive a certificate of the annual Howard H. Cork Memorial Award with a citation reading "For his Distinguished Service to the Procurement Committee and his important contributions to Government and Industry in the field of Defense Procurement in the best traditions of Howard H. Cork" and signed by Stephen S. Kaye, Chairman, Procurement Committee, and LTG Lawrence F. Skibbie, President, NDIA.

I continued thereafter until 2011 to attend most of the quarterly meetings of the legal subcommittee and the procurement policy committee and eventually became one of its longest serving members. It was an experience of continuing education in public contract law which bore little resemblance to what it was when I began to practice it in 1949 as I have related in Part Four.

5. Allocation of Costs in Government Contracts.

In August 2000 I teamed up with Darrell Oyer, the immediate past chair of the finance subcommittee of the NDIA procurement committee, to write an article highly critical of recent accounting decisions of the Court of Appeals for the Federal Circuit[168] and the Armed Services Board of Contract Appeals.[169] These decisions, in our view, confused accounting issues of allocation of costs under government contracts with their

---

168 *Caldera v. Northrop Worldwide Aircraft Services, Inc.*, 192 F.3d 962 (Fed. Cir. 1999).

169 *Boeing North American, Inc.*, ASBCA No. 49994, 00-2 BCA ¶ 30,970 (June 8, 2000), *reversed and remanded, Boeing North American, Inc. v. Roche*, 298 F.3d 1274 (Fed Cir. 2002).

allowability under the procurement regulations. The article was then published as a supplement to a weekly issue of *The Federal Contracts Report* (74 FCR 332) and entitled " 'Benefit to the Government' as an Erroneous Basis of Cost Allocation under Government Contracts".

In *Northrop* the government had appealed the ASBCA decision in the case[170] which had held that the contractor's costs incurred in defending a wrongful discharge lawsuit by three former quality control inspectors were reasonable and allocable[171] to the contractor's cost-reimbursement contracts on which the terminated employees had worked, notwithstanding the jury verdict and award of punitive damages in the suit, because the government offered no evidence beyond that verdict in support of the plaintiffs' claim that their discharges were in retaliation for their refusal to participate in defrauding the government under the contact. The Federal Circuit reversed the ASBCA for failing to give preclusive effect to the jury verdict, and therefore denied that the costs were so allocable because, in light of the trial judge's instructions to the jury, the court could "discern no benefit to the government in a contractor's defense of a wrongful termination lawsuit in which the contractor is a found to have retaliated against the employees' refusal to defraud the government." [172]

In the *Boeing North American* case the ASBCA, explicitly quoting from and following the *Northrop* decision, concluded "We can discern no benefit to the Government in a contractor's defense of a third party lawsuit in which the contractor's prior violations of federal laws and regulations were an integral part of the third party's allegations."[173]

---

170 *In re Northrop Worldwide Aircraft Serv., Inc.*, ASBCA Nos. 45216, 45877, 98-1 BCA ¶ 29,654 (Mar. 26, 1998).

171 Within the meaning of FAR 31.201-4: "A cost is allocable if it is assignable or chargeable to one or more cost objectives on the basis of relative benefits received or other equitable relationship. Subject to the foregoing, a cost is allocable to a Government contract if it... (a) Is incurred specifically for the contract; (b) Benefits the contract and other work, and can be distributed to them in reasonable proportion to the benefits received; or (c) Is necessary to the overall operation of the business, although a direct relationship to any cost objective cannot be shown."

172 *Northrop, Note 168 supra*, 192 F.3d 962 at 972.

173 *Boeing North American*, Note 169 *supra*..

In that case Rockwell International Corporation, prior to its acquisition by Boeing in 1996 as a wholly owned subsidiary called "Boeing North American", had incurred about $4.6M in legal fees in defending and settling a minority shareholder's suit against its then directors. The suit alleged that the directors had failed in their fiduciary duties to prevent the company from engaging in government contract fraud and environmental violations as evidenced by a number of convictions and guilty pleas and False Claims Act civil settlements from 1982 to 1992. The court-approved settlement of the suit was without liability to Rockwell or the directors or relief to the plaintiffs beyond Rockwell's reimbursing them and the directors for their legal fees and expenses. Rockwell then allocated these and its own related costs to corporate overhead for these years. Rockwell presented the allocability of these costs in a test case before the ASBCA of the allocation of a small amount of these costs to an Air Force cost-reimbursement contract subject to the FAR cost principles including the cost-allocation principle of FAR 31.201-4 and not involved in any of the law violations alleged in the shareholder suit.

In reaching the above-quoted conclusion the ASBCA found that the costs so allocated to the Air Force contract were not "incurred specifically for the contract" under FAR 31.201-4(a), and were not allocated as indirect costs as between the Air Force contract and other work so as to benefit "both the contract and other work and can be distributed to them in reasonable proportion to the benefits received" within the meaning of FAR 31.201-4(b).

Instead of deciding whether the costs were "necessary to the overall operation of the business, although a direct relationship to any cost objective cannot be shown" within the meaning of FAR 31.201-4(c), the ASBCA addressed the issue of whether the costs would be so allocable if they would not have been incurred "but for" the antecedent contractor wrongdoing. It found that the $4.7M of legal costs would not have been so incurred notwithstanding that there was then no federal policy "to disallow legal costs arising from third party proceedings, as distinct from such costs arising from proceedings brought by federal, state, local, or foreign governments". It adopted a "guiding principle" for "federal agencies not to pay for the results of or consequences of contractor wrongdoing" in support of the above-quoted conclusion.[174]

In our article our disagreement with these decisions was primarily based on the confusion in both cases between the allocation and the allowability of costs. By equating "benefit to the government" with "benefit to government work" both decisions slipped from cost allocation into cost allowability. "Benefit to the government", unlike "benefit to government work", is not benefit to a cost objective within the meaning of the FAR cost principles and the Cost Accounting Standards.[175]

We argued further that cost accounting and government cost accounting rules in the FAR and the Cost Accounting Standards require "full absorption costing", including full allocation of all costs to a period and to final cost objectives; that benefits relate to where a cost is to be allocated, not if it is to be allocated; and that benefit means benefit of allocation to one or more objectives, not benefit to the customer which is a cost allowability concept.[176]

In violating these established principles of cost accounting, the decisions in *Northrop* and *Boeing North American*, by substituting "benefit to the government" as the test of cost allocability, contractors' costs not otherwise made unallowable by the FAR cost principles may now be disallowed on the further ground that they provide no benefit to the government and therefore may not be allocated to government contracts

---

174 This "guiding principle" was taken from a DoD committee report recommending that the FAR cost principles be amended to disallow the costs of the prosecution or defense of third-party lawsuits alleging improper contractor activities where the contractor was found liable or settled. This recommendation was not adopted.

175 "For a particular cost objective to have allocated to it all or part of a cost, there should exist a beneficial or causal relationship between the cost objective and the cost." CAS Board Statement of Objectives, Policies, and Concepts, 57 Fed Reg. 31036, 31037 (July 13, 1992). FAR 31.001 defines "cost objective" to mean "a function, organizational subdivision, contract, or other work unit for which cost data are desired and for which provision is made to accumulate and measure the cost of processes, products, jobs, capitalized projects, etc."

176 CAS Board Statement of Objectives, Note 175 *supra*; FAR 31.201-4, text at Note 175 *supra*.

either as direct or indirect costs. It is difficult to discern any limits to this ground of cost disallowance, other than continuing disputes over application of the slippery meaning of benefit to the government rather than to one or more cost objectives.

For these reasons we strongly advocated that Boeing appeal the *North American* decision to the Federal Circuit Court. Such an appeal perhaps would try to persuade the court first of its cost allocation error in *Northrop*; second, in any event the facts in *Boeing North American* differ materially from those in *Northrop* in that there is no finding or judgment of contractor or director wrongdoing in relation to the allegations of the minority shareholders' derivative suit; and third, no applicable federal procurement policy would justify invocation of the "but for" criterion of cost allocability.

Boeing did so appeal, and a panel of the federal circuit court reversed the ASBCA decision and remanded the case to determine the allowability of the now correctly allocated $4.6M of legal expenses should the Board determine that the shareholders' allegations of the directors' and Rockwell's contract fraud and environmental violations had "very little likelihood of success" of prevailing on the merits.[177]

The court pointed out, "Most significantly, neither party in *Northrop* addressed the provisions of the CAS [Cost Accounting Standards] by the CAS Board, which by statute has 'exclusive authority to make, promulgate, amend, and rescind cost accounting standards...governing...allocation of costs to contracts with the United States.'...Under our established precedents we are not bound by *Northrop* on the issue of allocability since the CAS issue was neither argued or discussed in our opinion....We must accordingly decide whether the CAS renders these legal expenses allocable. We conclude that it does"[178]:

Thus we agree with Boeing that allocability is an accounting concept and that CAS does not require that a cost directly

---

177 *Boeing North American, Inc. v. Roche*, 298 F.3d 1274 (2002), CCH 46 Contract Cases Federal (CCF) ¶ 77,930 at 9.

178 *Id.* at 5.

benefit the government's interest for the cost to be allocable. The word "benefit" is used in the allocability provisions to describe the nexus required for accounting purpose between the cost and the contract to which it is allocated. The requirement of a "benefit" to a government contract is not designed to permit contracting officers, the Board, or this court to embark on an amorphous inquiry whether a particular cost sufficiently "benefits" the government so that the cost should be recoverable from the government. The question whether a cost should be recoverable as a matter of policy is to be undertaken by applying the specific allowability regulations, which embody the government's view, as a matter of "policy," as to whether the contractor may permissibly charge particular costs to the government (if they are otherwise allocable).[179]

As there is no reported ASBCA decision on the remand, it appears that the parties settled the dispute on terms that have not been made public. In any event, the correct federal circuit decision on the cost allocability issue undoes the harm of both the earlier federal circuit decision in *Northrop* and the *Boeing North American* decision in the ASBCA as well.

6. Protecting Confidential Contractor Pricing.

Until World War II, formal advertising for sealed bids that would be publicly opened was the prevailing method of government procurement of supplies and services. During the war, as an emergency measure to speed up the award of government contracts, Congress enacted Title

---

179 *Id*. at 7.

II of the First War Powers Act[180] which authorized the Army and the Navy to enter into procurement contracts "without regard to the provisions of law relating to the making and administration of contracts." Under that authority the concept of procurement by negotiation replaced procurement by formal advertising. After the war the negotiation authority lapsed and formal advertising resumed until the enactment of the Armed Services Procurement Act of 1947[181] and the Federal Property and Administrative Services Act of 1949[182] for the civilian agencies. These statutes authorized negotiated procurement in defined specified circumstances as limited exceptions to the intended prevalence of formal advertising. For the Department of Defense and other agencies the onset of the Korean War in 1950 and the ensuing cold war and Vietnam War effectively ended the predominance of formal advertising. The Competition in Contracting Act of 1984 explicitly equated competitive negotiation with formal advertising and effectively ended the widespread use of formal advertising.[183] Under competitive negotiation the disclosure of the prices or other terms of competing proposals was forbidden in order to protect ongoing negotiations.[184] Once a contract was awarded the contract line-item prices were ordinarily publicly disclosed with the award announcement.[185]

There matters stood until the enactment of the Freedom of Information Act in 1966 and repeatedly amended through 1996.[186] Its purpose was to enable the public to access government records not classified or privileged from disclosure.[187] There was a statutory Exemption 4 for "matters that are...trade secrets and commercial or financial information

---

180 Act of December 18, 1941, 55 Stat. 838.

181 Act of February 19, 1948, 62 Stat.21, 10 U.S.C. § § 2301-2314 (1958); repealed by the Act of October 13, 1994, 108 Stat. 3296.

182 Act of June 30, 1949, 63 Stat. 377

183 10 U.S.C. § 2304(a)(1); 41 U.S.C. § 3301(b).

184 FAR 3.104-4.

185 FAR 5.503(b)(2), FAR 15.506(d)(2).

186 5 U.S.C. § 552.

187 5 U.S.C. § 552(a)(3)-(4)(A).

from a person and privileged or confidential."[188] In a landmark decision of 1974, the U. S. Court of Appeals for the D.C. Circuit, as quoted in a later decision, ruled that commercial or financial information obtained from a person "involuntarily," such as line-item contract prices, "is 'confidential' for purposes of the exemption if disclosure [would either]...impair the Government's ability to obtain necessary information in the future, or... cause substantial harm to the competitive position of the person from whom the information was obtained.[189]...We have long held the Trade Secrets Act, 18 U.S.C. § 1905, a criminal statute that prohibits Government personnel from disclosing several types of confidential information unless 'authorized by law,' is 'at least co-extensive with...Exemption 4 of FOIA.'[190]...The upshot is that, unless another statute or a regulation[191] authorizes disclosure of the information, the Trade Secrets Act requires each agency to withhold any information it may withhold under Exemption 4 of the FOIA.[192] A person whose information is about to be disclosed pursuant to a FOIA request may file a 'reverse-FOIA action' and seek to enjoin the Government from disclosing it." [193]

A contractor's showing of "substantial competitive harm" from the disclosure of contract line-item prices will now prevent the agency release of that information in response to a FOIA request by a contractor's

---

188 5 U.S.C. § 552(b)(4).

189 *Nat'l Parks & Conservation Ass'n v. Morton*, 498 F.2d 765, 770 (D.C. Cir. 1974) as quoted in *Canadian Commercial Corporation v. Department of the Air Force*, 514 F.3d 37, 38 (D.C. Cir. 2008).

190 *Chrysler Corp. v. Brown*, 441 U.S. 281, 319 n. 49 (1979); *Canadian Fin. Corp. v. Donovan*, 830 F.2d 1132, 1151 (D.C. Cir. 1987).

191 The court held in the *Canadian Commercial* case that FAR 15.506(e)(1) which states that "the debriefing [of unsuccessful offerors] shall not reveal any information... exempt from release under the Freedom of Information Act including...trade secrets" trumps other FAR provisions cited in Note 185 *supra* mandating disclosure of contract unit prices in announcements of contract awards and in debriefings.

192 *Bartholdi Cable Co., Inc. v. FCC*, 114 F.3d 274, 281 (D.C. Cir. 1997).

193 *See Chrysler Corp. v. Brown*, 441 U.S. 281, 317-18 (1979). *See also the Canadian Commercial decision cited in* Note 189 *supra* for the remainder of the text quoted there which held that contract line-item pricing, as that court had repeatedly held, is subject to Exemption 4 of the FOIA and therefore must be withheld from disclosure under FOIA on request of the contractor.

injunction suit in federal district court if the matter cannot be resolved with the agency.

A different legal issue arises when a contractor seeks that outcome in a contract dispute with the government over the interpretation of the contractor's rights in technical data delivered to the government in the course of contract performance. My partner Bob Turtle litigated that issue in the federal district court for the District of Columbia and in 1973 obtained a preliminary injunction against the Air Force's threatened release of the technical data to his client's competitors. Bob creatively persuaded District Judge Ritchie that the judicial review provisions of section 10 of the Administrative Procedure Act[194] provided such a remedy when the remedy of compensatory damages in the Court of Claims under the Tucker Act[195] is inadequate.[196] The government appealed and the D.C. Circuit reversed that decision and dismissed the preliminary injunction.[197]

Writing for a panel of the court that included Judge Leventhal, Judge Tamm wrote:

> We believe this case is a contract action falling squarely within the purview of the Tucker Act, therefore the APA is inapplicable....Moreover, we cannot accept the proposition that Congress intended to alter drastically the limited remedies and waiver of sovereign immunity embodied in the Tucker Act; adopting IEC's position would result in the destruction of the Court of Claims by implication. Finally, under any circumstance, the APA is inapplicable by its own terms because of appellee's adequate remedy before the Court of Claims.

* * *

---

194 5 U.S.C. § 702.

195 28 U.S.C. § 1346(a).

196 *International Engineering Co. v. Richardson,*, 367 F. Supp. 640 (D. D.C. 1973).

197 *International Engineering Co. v. Richardson,*, 512 F.2d 573 (D.C. Cir. 1975).

...The district court, however, concluded that damages would be an inadequate remedy because of the speculative nature of damages in light of the Government's belief, as the only potential buyer, that the information is useless except for what not to do, and that injunctive relief would be appropriate in order to vindicate the public interest in contract administration. We have already concluded that that this public interest factor should not be afforded the overriding weight that the district court gave to it. We further question whether damages are impossible to award. We see no barrier to the Court of Claims, if it decides that the Government has breached the contract, awarding IEC the fair market value of its data.[198]

I believe that Bob Turtle and Judge Ritchie were correct that injunctive relief from the district court was the appropriate remedy should the court conclude that the government had no contractual right to disclose IEC's claimed proprietary data since that remedy was not available in the Court of Claims.

The concern of the Court of Appeals that permitting the injunction suit and "adopting IEC's position would result in the destruction of the Court of Claims by implication" seems overbroad. Few breach of contract claims would qualify for injunctive or other specific relief; for most the recovery of damages which only the Court of Claims could award in claims over $10,000[199] would be the appropriate and exclusive remedy. In awarding money damages the Court of Claims may grant equitable relief incident thereto such as correction of mutual mistakes or reformation in contract formation.[200]

The harm from disclosure of a contractor's proprietary data through government error or inadvertence is no less than the disclosure of contractors' confidential line-item pricing in response to a FOIA request which

---

198 *Id.*, 21 CCF ¶ 83,870 at 3, 5.

199 28 U.S.C. § 1491(a)(1). The federal district courts have concurrent jurisdiction with the Court of Claims for contract actions against the United States up to $10,000. 28 U.S.C. § 1346(a)(2).

200 28 U.S.C. § 1491(a)(2).

that same court of appeals has staunchly protected through injunctive relief as discussed above. Prevention of the disclosure by injunctive relief is the only appropriate remedy. Perhaps one day the court of appeals may recognize the error in its reasoning in *International Engineering* and vindicate Bob Turtle as being ahead of his time.

A related thorny problem has confronted Rob Evers and me: what to do when a government agency inadvertently discloses a contractor's confidential line-item pricing in a bidders' conference about a forthcoming solicitation for the same and related items, or otherwise? The horse is now out of the barn. That the disclosure would give that contractor's competitors an irreparable advantage in that or any near term competition is inarguable. When such a solicitation issues despite the aggrieved contractor's demands for a sole-source award of all further requirements for the items for several years until the relevance of the disclosure fades, there may be an injunctive remedy in the Court of Federal Claims to achieve substantially that result.[201]

I expect my solo practice to continue, mostly work for Rob Evers as long as my mind functions properly. I now conclude this Part Six to write the final Part Seven, an attempt to sum up my long and enriching life.

---

201 28 U.S.C. § 1491(b).

Part Seven A Summing Up

As I enter my 89th year I survey a long life enriched by good health, mental and physical, and by rewarding creative activity; by ongoing great teachers of history, ancient and modern, Shakespeare and other western literature, law and life; by endless education in the liberal arts and the law; by requited and requiting gifts of love and friendship; by the infinite joy and the sorrow of the great music of Bach, Handel, Haydn, Mozart, Beethoven, Brahms, Tchaikovsky, Verdi, Wagner, Richard Strauss, among others; and by the lifetime of values from the firm foundation and the implantings of an upbringing of discipline and obedience to parental and Christian values from which derived a moral compass of right and wrong, truthfulness and good manners notwithstanding the gradual loss of my religious faith replaced by belief in the philosophy first expounded by Epicurus and Lucretius.

1. Some of the Principal Changes at Home and Abroad in My Lifetime.

The overriding fact of my life has been change: change in almost everything except human nature; some for our good, much for our ill and decline. The positive transformations have been astounding and miraculous. Among others:

+refrigeration in the early 1930's which enabled Papa to acquire Clarence Birdseye's process for freezing vegetables for General Foods, a notable addition to a healthy nutrition;

+FDR's New Deal which transformed the role of the federal government to the active regulation of business, the economy and to providing for the general welfare including the first of entitlements, the Social Security Act of 1935;

+winning World War II from the atomic ashes of which the U.S. strode the earth as the colossus into the 21st century, ending decades of isolationism;

+the creation of the United Nations in 1945 with high hopes for gradual reductions in national sovereignty and the growth of international law;

+the birth of the nuclear energy industry for the generation of electricity without environmental harm but with a high risk of widespread death and radiation from the use of atomic bombs or natural or accidental damage to nuclear power plants;

+the rise of commercial aviation for domestic and international travel in jet aircraft pioneered by the Germans in World War II with the resulting decline in rail travel in the United States;

+the arrival of instantaneous global communications with the advent of television, the computer, the personal computer, the tablet computer, the internet, cell and smart phones with texting and other applications, other digital devices for photography and filming and home entertainment, and electronic printing, resulting in increasing performance of work and recreation at home and in the decline of the printing of books, newspapers and magazines;

+the extraordinary advances in medicine in preventing polio and curing other diseases, in the prolongation of life, and in the physical and biological sciences enlarging our understanding of the universe and of the evolution and composition of life on planet Earth and the continuing search for the prevention or cure of AIDS, cancer and other maladies;

+beginning during World War II the expanding opportunities for women in higher education, in the professions, in business, in factories in the Western world if not yet elsewhere;

+the gradual decline of governmental and private discrimination against gays beginning with President Ford's executive order removing the ban on the employment of gays in the federal government not requiring a security clearance (later eliminated by President Clinton), the repeal or non-enforcement of laws criminalizing homosexual acts between consenting adults, and the advent of gay marriage in an increasing number of states coupled with the acceptance of gays in the U.S. military;

+the end of colonialism and the emergence of independent countries from former British, European, and U.S. possessions and protectorates.

The changes in my lifetime with adverse consequences are many, long-lasting, and dispiriting. They include:

-the deliberate political slaughter or starvation of untold innocent millions by Mao, Stalin, Hitler, African and Asian governments, and others during the 20th century, before and after World War II;

-the onset of the cold war after World War II rightly to contain the spread of Soviet communism but resulting in the creation of our excessive national security state for the next 50 years until the implosion of the Soviet Union in 1991 but greatly enlarged by the terrorist attack by al-Qaeda on September 11, 2001, and the resulting wars in Afghanistan and Iraq amidst tax cuts and grossly insufficient tax revenue to cover the ever expanding costs of these wars, national security, Medicare and Medicaid and arrest staggering growth of the national debt;

-the over production of energy inefficient automobiles, sports utility vehicles and trucks creating unsustainable dependence on Middle East oil production creating an unsustainable trade imbalance and the belated transition to hybrid and electric vehicles;

-the explosion of fast and processed food and beverages addicting consumers and causing obesity and major health problems from consumption of excessive sugar, salt and unhealthy meat and other fats and minimal fresh fruits and vegetables combined with sedentary life styles and resulting in unsustainable costs of health care;

-the alarming, resource-threatening increase in the world's population, particularly in the developing nations where birth control is virtually nonexistent coupled with the over exploitation and contamination of the planet's natural resources, primarily water, soil and forests, foreshadowing a Malthusian outcome and as further indicated by growing global over dependence on fossil fuels and other ecological follies resulting in climate change which unless soon arrested threatens the survival of man and much else on this planet;

-the arrival of the credit card in the 1950s resulting in the explosion of private debt, ultimately reducing consumer demand;

-the unsustainable growth of the debt of the federal government from the political failure to raise taxes to match growing outlays for wars, national security and entitlement programs and unlimited, improvident access to government guaranteed home mortgages which produced the financial collapse of 2008 and a major ongoing recession and excessive unemployment exacerbated by the uncontrolled export of manufacturing jobs starting in the 1990s and accelerating thereafter and by technology improvements, resulting in shrinking middle class income and consumer demand and employment for the young in manufacturing;

-the widening gap in the increasing wealth of the top one percent of our population coupled with the stagnation of middle class income since the 1970s threatening social unrest;

-the corruption of politics through virtually unlimited campaign financing by corporate interests constitutionally protected by the Supreme Court as the exercise of free speech;

-the polarization of the political parties resulting in legislative grid-lock;

-the steady decline in marriage, the growing divorce rate as "no-fault" divorce became readily available, and the substantial increase in children born out of wedlock and raised by single parents;

-the persistent economic and social discrimination against Blacks and to a lesser degree Hispanics notwithstanding the civil rights legislation of the Johnson Administration and the decisions of the Supreme Court;

-the alarming decline in public education, literacy, and reading and the increasing high school and college drop-out rate in the U.S. particularly in the inner cities as we face a more competitive world in much of which superior public education prevails to our growing disadvantage;

-the steep decline since the 1960s in moral values and manners throughout society and the rise of "me-firstism" and greed.

Whether Americans can or will reverse these adverse trends and consequences seems to me to be increasingly doubtful. What then?

The attack on Pearl Harbor in December 1941 quickly followed by Hitler's declaration of war on the U.S. were transforming events for the outcome of the war and for the U.S. role in world affairs thereafter. Had Hitler not done so, it is doubtful that the isolationism prevailing in Congress would have enabled FDR to put the defeat of Germany first as our national interest plainly required. The avoidance of entanglement in European wars and predominant public opinion would likely then have compelled our entire war effort to be concentrated on defeating Japan. Hitler might then have been able to defeat the Soviet Union and Great Britain as each would have been deprived of necessary U.S. aid. We would have then faced a very different world, with Hitler dominating Europe, Russia east to the Urals and the Middle East. Thanks to Hitler's hubris and gift to Japan, he and Japan were defeated over the next four years at unprecedented cost and loss to the West and the Soviet Union and to Germany and Japan.

World War II bankrupted Great Britain and brought on the sunset of its empire around the world. India and its partition with Pakistan obtained independence in 1947, Burma and Malaya soon after. Its protectorates of the former Ottoman Empire after World War I in the Middle East followed swiftly. Great Britain lost control of the Suez Canal in 1954. The African colonies and the West Indies gained independence in the 1960s. Hong Kong reverted to China in the 1980s. Only a few outposts remain. The monarchy survives. The United States, particularly our Navy, has assumed de facto responsibility for many of the burdens of the former British Empire on the high seas.

George Kennan's famous "long telegram" from Moscow to the State Department in 1946, followed by his "X" article in *Foreign Affairs* in 1947, each strongly advocating "containment" of the threatened expansion of the Soviet Union westward into Eastern Europe and perhaps beyond and the curtailment of Communist parties in Western Europe, had a major influence on U.S. foreign policy and in leading to the Marshall Plan of 1948 to rescue the failing economies of Great Britain and the countries of Western Europe. By 1949 the North Atlantic Treaty was ratified by the Senate and the North Atlantic Treaty Organization (NATO) was established with the unprecedented commitment of the U.S. to intervene militarily if any of its members were attacked. Good bye to isolationism. General Eisenhower was recalled to active duty to be its first commanding general.

There is little doubt that Stalin aided and abetted the North Korean attack on South Korea in June 1950, perhaps after learning Secretary of State Dean Acheson's speech earlier that year identifying the "strategic interests" of the U.S. in the western Pacific and omitting South Korea from the countries named, whether intentionally or inadvertently we may never know. President Truman's prompt and courageous response and obtaining a resolution from the UN Security Council authorizing military force to repel the invasion when the Soviet member was absent was a major development and sea change leading to an enormous and lasting U.S. military buildup to defeat the North Koreans and deter the Soviet Union in Europe. The revelations that the Soviet Union had developed an atomic bomb from secrets stolen from the U.S. and was embarked on a massive program to build intercontinental missiles with atomic warheads added urgency to the U.S. rearmament effort. Congress reinstated the draft.

General MacArthur's masterly landing at Inchon turned the tide of the Korean war from near defeat. His failure to heed the Chinese warning if he pursued overrunning North Korea and his public criticism of President Truman's refusal to widen the war once the Chinese intervened and drove us out of North Korea produced his recall and the stalemate leading in 1953 to an armistice at the 38th parallel which approximated the border between the two countries. An uneasy truce has persisted since without a peace treaty. We continue to station thousands of troops in South Korea and threaten war with China should they attempt forcible occupation of Taiwan, its former province until ceded to Japan following a military defeat in 1895 and regained by the Chinese nationalists after World War II and now an independent country.

The ouster of France from Indo China by 1954 and the growing North Vietnamese and Viet Cong Communist threat to overthrow the anti-communist government of South Vietman eventually escalated by 1964 into our full-scale military involvement in defending South Vietnam. In hindsight, it is evident that we erroneously and tragically misunderstood North Vietnam and the Viet Cong to be pawns of a monolithic Chinese-Soviet plan to take over southeast Asia when in fact they were not but were acting as nationalists seeking to impose their own communist system on a united Vietnam which they accomplished after our ignominious withdrawal ten years later and with which we thereafter established productive diplomatic, trade, and cultural relationships.

The cost of that war doomed President Johnson's planned War on Poverty as a centerpiece of his Great Society program, leading to his decision not to run for reelection in 1968 and paving the way for Richard Nixon and Watergate and the decline of public support for the federal government. Nevertheless, President Nixon had some important accomplishments: the enactment of the Environmental Protection Act for clean air and water; and the opening to China to counter the Soviet Union in the balance of power of international relations and creating for a time a period of "détente" with the Soviet Union that continued until the Soviet invasion of Afghanistan in 1979 whereupon we resumed our excessive defense build-up.

The Cuban missile crisis of 1962 between the U.S. and the Soviet Union over the installation of their missiles in Cuba capable of atomic bombing of some of our East Coast cities, probably as a reaction to the failed Bay of Pigs attempt by the CIA to overthrow Castro the year before, nearly resulted in the exchange of atomic intercontinental missiles which would have been catastrophic for both countries. JFK with vital backing from his brother Bobby, the Attorney General who was pursuing a back channel communication with the Soviet leadership, withstood the recommendations of his military chiefs to take out the Soviet missiles in Cuba which undoubtedly would have led to such a war. Instead, he negotiated their withdrawal in exchange for a similar, then secret withdrawal of U.S. missiles from Turkey. It was a terrifying, close call.

The end of the Vietnam war did not result in a significant "peace dividend" as the cold war with the Soviet Union and China persisted until the Nixon administration; and following the Soviet invasion of Afghanistan in 1979 there was no reduction in defense spending until the 1991 implosion of the Soviet Union followed by the growing fear of a resurgent China further preventing any significant lessening of defense appropriations.

Following the al-Qaeda terrorist attack in September 2001 defense and other national security spending and the cost of the Iraq and Afghanistan wars rose to unprecedented heights coupled with the political insanity of major income tax reductions and the explosion in the cost of Medicare and Medicaid that by 2011 created the imperative need to curb trillion dollar annual deficits and the growth of the federal debt by $10 trillion since 2001 from $4 trillion. The resulting cuts both in defense and in entitlements have yet to be enacted, and much will depend on the outcome of the 2012 election and the state of the economy.

Even worse than the financial bankruptcy of the federal government from the overreaction to the al-Qaeda attack of September 11, 2001, especially our invasion of Iraq which had no connection with al-Qaeda and the bungled occupation which attracted al-Qaeda to instigate the resulting insurgency and needlessly prolonged the war in Afghanistan, was the sacrifice of fundamental constitutional values by the government at the highest levels out of fear and resulting in widespread arrests and prolonged detention and torture, euphemistically called "enhanced interrogation", of thousands of Arabs and Muslims who disappeared to black sites to elicit information about possible further attacks and greatly enhancing al-Qaeda recruiting and damaging our reputation throughout the world.

For Arab and Muslim U.S. citizens or resident aliens detention and "protective custody" were no longer based on probable cause for belief of having planned or committed a crime, but instead could result from mere suspicion of terrorist acts or even support. There is as yet no prospect of criminal prosecution of U.S government persons or contractors who committed these crimes. We have yet to make amends as we finally did some 50 years later for the Americans of Japanese descent who were forcibly relocated from their homes on the West Coast to camps in Colorado without any evidence of disloyalty following the attack on Pearl Harbor.

The world of my professional life, the practice of government or public contract law, has also changed beyond recognition since I began in that vineyard in 1949. What was then a backwater area with minimal statutory and regulatory control has long since become a major arena of law practice by government and private attorneys alike as soaring government spending for defense and other programs since the 1950s has primarily relied on government contractors for their execution. Much of the change is attributable to the growing proliferation of statutes and regulations that govern the entirety of the contracting process and the resolution of disputes over contract awards and performance.

Increasing competition for contract awards has received major statutory and regulatory focus. Starting with the Korean War and the resulting defense build-up the use of sole source awards to the major defense contractors became a growing bipartisan political concern. Except for a series of statutes to set aside a proportion of procurement requirements for small business and minority business participation, it was not fully addressed until the Competition in Contracting Act of 1984. As I have related in Part Five, in that law Congress placed competitive negotiation on an equal footing with formal advertising with the result that formal advertising was rarely used except for construction projects. A supplemental law a few years later authorized the use of indefinite quantity contracts for several years' duration under which supplies or services would be ordered by the issuance of delivery and task orders to the winning contractor. The duration of these contracts and the size of individual orders prompted calls for competition for the larger individual orders as well which was gradually achieved.

Perhaps the major change has been the replacement of competitive awards otherwise acceptable based on the lowest price to awards based on "best value". That transition introduced during the Clinton Administration enabled contracting officers to specify in solicitations the criteria by which proposals would be evaluated with the flexibility to put technical, management, and performance factors as having greater importance than price in the scoring of acceptable proposals and indicating the extent to which discussions would be conducted in the evaluation of proposals following which "best and final" proposals would be solicited. On large procurements this process could occupy several months. For commercial-type items or services, best value awards would usually be inappropriate as compared with award to the lowest price acceptable offeror.

There was also a major effort to attract more commercial companies to compete for government contracts for commercial items and services, each broadly defined, by eliminating or reducing some of the statutes and regulations that would otherwise apply by specifically so exempting them in response to industry complaints of the deterrent effect they would otherwise have had. For procurements under $5M this effort largely succeeded.

The remedies of unsuccessful bidders and offerors to challenge the terms of the competition and the contract awards have also undergone a major transformation since 1949. Then there was a limited "bid protest" remedy in the General Accounting Office (GAO) for disappointed bidders to challenge solicitations of bids as restrictive of competition or otherwise contrary to the rules of competitive bidding and to protest awards of publicly opened bids as unresponsive to the solicitation or for having made award to a non-responsible bidder. The success rate of these protests was low as GAO would ordinarily accept the agency's version of the facts rather than conduct an independent examination. For the protesting bidder there was no discovery or hearing. In the rare instances in which the GAO would sustain a protest, the agency would comply, notwithstanding the GAO's status as an agency of the legislative branch, since the GAO had the statutory authority to deduct the amount of the award in its audit of the accounts of agency disbursing officers.

Until the 1950s protesters of solicitations and contract awards had no judicial remedy.[202] Then in 1951 the Court of Claims found that solicitations for bids created an implied contract with each bidder for the government to consider the bids fairly for breach of which the aggrieved bidder otherwise eligible for award could sue for damages, usually limited to the recovery of bid preparation costs because of the difficulty of proving loss of profits.[203] In 1970, in a landmark decision, the Court of Appeals for the D.C. Circuit found that the judicial review provisions of the 1946 Administrative Procedure Act provided a remedy of specific relief to disappointed bidders otherwise eligible for award who could establish that the solicitation or the contract award violated the applicable procurement law.[204]

The Competition in Contracting Act of 1984 also strengthened the GAO bid protest remedy by putting it on a statutory footing and

---

202 A landmark Supreme Court decision, *Perkins v. Lukens Steel Co.*, 310 U.S. 113 (1940), held that a bidder challenging the applicability of the Walsh-Healy Public Contracts Act of 1936, which regulated minimum wages and maximum hours on government contracts, had no standing to sue since the award of a government contract was a privilege and not a right. Congress promptly overruled its application to that statute. That doctrine has long since been rejected, primarily by the judicial review provisions of the Administrative Procedure Act as evidenced by the *Scanwell* decision *infra*.

203 *See Keco Industries, Inc. v. United States*, 492 F.2d 1200, 1203 (Ct. Cl. 1974).

204 *Scanwell Laboratories, Inc. v. Shaffer*, 424 F.2d 859 (D.C. Cir. 1970). This effectively overruled *Perkins v. Lukens Steel Co.*

conferring specific authority to recommend appropriate relief including the recovery of bid preparation and protest costs to aggrieved bidders or offerors, identified as "interested parties" who could establish that a solicitation or contract award for which they were otherwise eligible prejudicially violated a provision of law or abused agency discretion.[205] While agencies were not bound to accept the GAO's recommendation of the corrective action implementing the protest decision, the agency would have to report its non-acceptance to the GAO and by GAO to the concerned Congressional committees.[206] The result has been virtually unanimous agency acceptance of GAO protest decisions.

Later statutes empowered the Court of Federal Claims, the successor to the trial division of the Court of Claims which was transformed to the Court of Appeals for the Federal Circuit, to adjudicate bid protests in the same manner as the federal district courts under the Administrative Procedure Act.[207] By 2000 the concurrent jurisdiction of the federal district courts over bid protests was abolished, making the renamed Court of Federal Claims the exclusive judicial forum for bid protests independently of the GAO protest remedy and with judicial review of the protest decision of the Court of Federal Claims available to the protester and the contracting agency in the Court of Appeals for the Federal Circuit.[208]

In the last decade a substantial body of protest law has been created by these courts and by the GAO, recently renamed the "Government Accountability Office". Nevertheless, the GAO remains the primary forum for bid protests, mainly for reasons of economy, the availability

---

205 Codified at 31 U.S.C. §§ 3551-56.

206 31 U.S.C. § 3554(b)(3), (e)(1).

207 Section 133 of the Federal Courts Improvement Act of 1982, Pub. L. No. 97-164, 96 Stat. 25, 39-40; and section 12 of the Administrative Dispute Resolution Act of 1996 ("ADRA"), Publ. L. No. 104-320, 111 Stat. 3870, 3874-76; both sections of these statutes are codified at 28 U.S.C. § 1491(b)(1).

208 H.R. Rep. No. 104-841 at 10, the conference report on ADRA, explaining that the amendment to 28 U.S.C. § 1491(b)(1) would "consolidate federal court jurisdiction for procurement protest cases in the Court of Federal Claims" after a 4-year period of concurrency with the federal district courts. See also *Res. Conservation Group, LLC v. United States*, 597 F.3d 1238, 1242-43 (Fed. Cir. 2010).

of discovery of agency documents, an evidentiary hearing in limited circumstances, and because by filing a protest there the protester automatically obtains a stay of the procurement pending the GAO resolution of the protest, usually within three months, unless the agency at high levels exercises its statutory authority to override the protest which the protester can challenge in the Court of Federal Claims, and is rarely exercised. By contrast in the Court of Federal Claims, the protester has to establish entitlement to obtaining a temporary restraining order or preliminary injunction pending the decision on the merits of the protest.

It is now commonplace for the award of large contracts for which there is intensive competition to be subjected to protests by the losing competitor, causing substantial delay in the procurement process and the redoubling of agency efforts to avoid protest vulnerability in their decisions. Nevertheless, the protest remedy serves the public interest, and the GAO and the courts conscientiously explain their decisions which better the agency and the contractors' understanding of the applicable rules. There remain needs for the extension of the protest remedy in both the GAO and the Court of Federal Claims to challenge orders above a certain threshold under indefinite quantity contracts under the same standards applicable to contract awards and for exceeding the scope of the basic contract. Further, the improvement of an agency protest remedy as a speedy, economical alternative to protesting in the GAO or the Court of Federal Claims remains to be done.

I have noted in Part Five the importance of the Contract Disputes Act of 1978 to substantial procedural improvements to the resolution of performance disputes. The Boards of Contract Appeals have been consolidated into two Boards for the Executive Branch, the Armed Services Board of Contract Appeals (ASBCA) for the contracts of DoD and NASA,[209] and the Civilian Board of Contract Appeals (CBCA) for the civilian agencies.[210] The jurisdiction of the boards includes the authority to grant any monetary relief available to a litigant on a contract claim

---

209 41 U.S.C. § 7105(a).

210 The Civilian Board was established by section 847 of the National Defense Authorization Act of 2006, codified at 41 U.S.C. § 7105(b), replacing the several agency boards of contract appeals for the civilian agencies. In addition, there are the

in the Court of Federal Claims.[211] Even so, that relief, except for remand authority,[212] does not extend to declaratory judgments, to specific relief such as injunctions or specific performance decrees, or to the equitable remedy of restitution. These are significant remedies available to private litigants in contract cases, and there is no apparent reason why Congress should not amend the Tucker Act and the Contract Disputes Act of 1978 to make them available to the resolution of contract performance disputes in the ASBCA and CBCA and the Court of Federal Claims.[213]

During the Eisenhower Administration the Office of Management and Budget (OMB) issued Circular A-76 encouraging agencies to contract out to private industry "commercial type functions" that can be performed at lower cost to the government than by having them performed by government employees.[214] The explosion of contracting out the performance of government functions since the Reagan and succeeding administrations so predisposed has led to a substantial loss of the government agencies' capabilities to manage their functions as the scope of work to be contracted out expanded well beyond what was originally understood to be "commercial–type functions" to embrace virtually whatever government functions private enterprise was willing to undertake. As agency workloads increased without compensating increases in agency personnel contracts were necessarily awarded to get the work done.

Tennessee Valley Board of Contract Appeals, 41 U.S.C. § 7105(c), and the Postal Service Board of Contract Appeals, 41 U.S.C. § 7105(d).

211 41 U.S.C. § 7105(e)(2).

212 28 U.S.C. § 1491(a)(1): "…In any case within its jurisdiction, the court [of Federal Claims] shall have the power to remand appropriate matters to any administrative or executive body or official with such direction as it may deem proper and just…."

213 *See International Engineering v. Richardson,* discussed in Part Six text at Note 196 and following, for an unsuccessful attempt in federal district court litigation to obtain an injunction against threatened agency disclosure of a contractor's proprietary data in the context of a contract dispute on the ground that the Tucker Act remedy of money damages by a suit in the Court of Claims preempted the specific relief jurisdiction of the federal district courts.

214 The current version of this Circular may be found on Google.

The distinction between "inherently governmental functions" to be performed only by government employees and other governmental functions suitable for performance either by government employees or private contractor was blurred or ignored as agencies usually had more funds for the procurement of these services from contractors than for hiring agency employees to perform them. A substantial reduction of acquisition personnel during the Clinton Administration greatly exacerbated the extent of contracting out of governmental functions.

In 2009 President Obama and the 110th Congress reversed this progression.[215] Finally, in response to this direction, the Administrator of Federal Procurement Policy, Dan Gordon, a Presidentially appointed, Senate-confirmed official in the Office of Management and Budget, on September 11, 2011 issued Office of Federal Procurement Policy (OFPP) Letter 11-01, "Performance of Inherently Governmental and Critical Functions" effective October 12, 2011.[216] This Policy Letter is

---

215 Section 321 of the Duncan Hunter National Defense Authorization Act for Fiscal Year 2009, Pub. L. 110-417, requires the OMB to (i) Create a single definition of the term "inherently governmental function" that addresses any deficiencies in the existing definitions and reasonably applies to all agencies; (ii) establish criteria to be used by all agencies to identify "critical" functions and positions that should only be performed by Federal employees; and (iii) provide guidance to improve internal agency management of functions that are inherently governmental or critical. On March 4, 2009, President Obama issued a memorandum on government contracting that requires OMB to "clarify when governmental outsourcing for services is and is not consistent with section 321 of Public Law 110-417 (31 U.S.C. § 501 note)."

216 76 Federal Register 56227-42 (September 12, 2011). This Policy Letter in section 3 defined "inherently governmental function" by first incorporating the definition of that term in section 5 of the Federal Activities Inventory Reform Act, Pub. L. 105-270, as "a function so intimately related to the public interest as to require performance by Federal Government employees." The Policy Letter definition added: "(a) The term includes functions that require either the exercise of discretion in applying Federal Government authority or the making of values judgments in making decisions for the Federal Government, including judgments relating to monetary transactions and entitlements. An inherently governmental function involves, among other things, the interpretation and execution of the laws of the United States so as---(1) to bind the United States to take or not take some action by contract, policy regulation, authorization, or otherwise; (2) to determine, protect and advance United States economic, political, territorial, property, or other interests by military or diplomatic action, civil or criminal judicial proceedings, contract management, or otherwise; (3)

comprehensive and should effectively over time restore control to the
to significantly affect the life, liberty, or property, of private persons; (4) to commission, appoint, direct or control officers or employees of the United States; or (5) to exert ultimate control over the acquisition, use, or disposition of the property, real or personal, tangible or intangible, of the United States, including the collection, control, or disbursement of appropriations and other Federal funds. (b) The term does not normally include---(1) gathering information for or providing advice, opinions, recommendations, or ideas to Federal Government officials; or (2) any function that is primarily ministerial in nature (such as building security, mail operations, operation of cafeterias, housekeeping, facilities operations and maintenance, warehouse operations, motor vehicle fleet management operations, or other routine electrical services)."

The Policy Letter further defined "critical function" to mean " a function that is necessary to the agency being able to effectively perform and maintain control of its mission and operations. Typically, critical functions are recurring and long-term in duration." With these definitions, section 4 stated "the policy of the Executive Branch to ensure that government action is taken as a result of informed, independent judgments made by government officials....To implement this policy, agencies must reserve certain work for performance by Federal employees and take special care to retain sufficient management oversight over how contractors are used to support government operations and ensure that Federal employees have the technical skills and expertise needed to maintain control of the agency mission and operations. (a)...To ensure that work that should be performed by Federal employees is properly reserved for government performance, agencies shall (1) ensure that contractors do not perform inherently governmental functions (see section 5-1); (2) give special consideration to Federal employee performance of functions closely associated with inherently governmental functions and, when such work is performed by contractors, provide greater attention and enhanced oversight of the contractor activities to ensure that contractors' duties do not expand to include performance of inherently governmental functions (see sections 5-1(a) and 5-2(a) and Appendices B and C); and (3) ensure that Federal employees perform and/or manage critical functions to the extent necessary for the agency to operate effectively and maintain control of its mission and operations (see sections 5-1(b) and 5-2(b))."

Section 5-1 of the Policy Letter prescribes guidelines for determining (a) whether a function is inherently governmental and (b) whether a function is critical. Section 5-2 sets forth management responsibilities in planning and awarding contract, including documentation in the contract file of compliance with the Policy Letter. Appendix A to the Policy Letter lists 24 examples and sub examples of functions "considered to be inherently governmental."

Appendix B lists 9 examples and sub examples of functions "that are generally not considered to be inherently governmental but are closely associated with the performance of inherently governmental functions." Neither appendix, for example, discusses

Executive Branch of the Federal Government for executing the laws as agencies are able to hire or ramp up the technical skills for its employees to take over the inherently governmental functions performed by contractors in recent decades. This is long overdue.

Section 6, of the Policy Letter, "Judicial Review," states "this policy letter is not intended, and should not be construed, to create any substantive or procedural basis on which to challenge any agency action or inaction on the ground that such action or inaction was not in accordance with this policy letter." I question whether that statement will effectively foreclose suits or protests to the GAO or the Court of Federal Claims that challenge contract awards that require the performance of inherently governmental functions.

2.   Mostly About Me.

When I was dismissed from my 12-year job with the Navy Office of the General Counsel in January 1962 by the general counsel because of my admission of living in a homosexual relationship, I did not then see a bright future as a lawyer. I was very lucky that Trow vom Baur, my former boss as general counsel, and then in partnership with Struve Hensel for practicing government contract law in Washington, DC, was able to persuade Struve to take me on as an associate. I do not know whether

---

the interrogation of detainees suspected of terrorist activities or connected to Al-Qaeda which have since 9/11 primarily been conducted by contractors at home and abroad. Yet, as I read the definition of inherently governmental functions in section 3(a) which involve the interpretation and execution of the laws of the United States so as ... (3) to significantly affect the life, liberty, or property of private persons" the conclusion is inescapable that this bars the performance of that function by government contractors.

Trow knew why I left OGC; he never asked me, but I assume he did and it did not matter to him.

I have related in Part Five the importance for me of the experience in working directly with Struve Hensel on the Watergate construction project and Trow's decision to ask me to form a partnership starting in January 1963 when Struve decided to return to New York to pursue other interests. Had I remained with OGC or had I transferred as the contracts lawyer to the Arms Control & Disarmament Agency as planned I would not have had the enriching private practice experience that Parts Five and Six summarize. I would not have evolved as a trial and appellate lawyer with a wide variety of challenging and significant cases. All in all, it was a beneficial change, and I have no regrets. It enabled Don and me to purchase vacation homes in West Virginia and Key West, and achieve a very comfortable life style in Washington, which we otherwise could not have afforded.

In my youth I was conditioned to reject homosexuality and homo-sexual acts as unacceptable. That conduct I learned was diseased, degen-erate, criminal, and condemned in the Old Testament of the Bible. Also, "queers" were also said to be sissies and effeminate. These social and peer pressures and the prevailing homophobia were strong and unquestion-ably retarded the recognition and acceptance of my natural, instinctive, and likely genetic emotional preference for male love until after I had finished law school. As I have related in Part Four, my first homosexual experience was when John Shollenberger and I fell in love in 1951. Before then I had dated women enough to know that marriage and a family life were not for me if I had my druthers. My relationship with John was pri-vate and infrequent after I moved to Washington some six months later.

With Don Ellington, when we started living together in 1959 when I was almost 26, the relationship was necessarily less private; and I received family and social pressure to change my status from bachelor to married man. This of course I refused without acknowledging or explaining why to anyone. Even after I was dismissed from OGC in 1962 I was able to maintain the privacy of my relationship with Don except with his gay friends, most of whom I liked. Meeting them opened up a new world for me. His friends were highly intelligent and educated and talented. Some were the victims of the purge of gays in the government pushed by Senator McCarthy and other zealots in the 1950s who linked them to Communists. Most were in stable relationships. Before living with Don I had never known anyone besides John who to my knowledge was gay. I was surprised and delighted by their total refutation of the shibboleths about gays I had been falsely brought up to believe.

I continue at age 88 to enjoy good health, as yet unvexed by the afflictions that most elderly suffer, except for failing hearing, mild psoriasis, and an enlarged prostate which interrupts prolonged sleep, by eating right with lots of daily vitamin, mineral and herbal supplements, and daily moderate exercise, and so far without prescription medicine. I take the supplements because I believe that the nutritional value of our soil has been seriously depleted by excessive farming and chemicals compared to what it was in the 1930s and '40s when I was young and processed food did not exist.

In the spring and summer of 2011 I had successful cataract removals and lense implants performed skillfully by my regular eye doctor, Andrew Adelson. The result is greatly improved vision in each eye from what I could see naturally before the cataracts. I no longer need glasses for distance vision; I do for reading and computer work. All this was mostly paid for by Medicare as I did not use my Kaiser health plan for these procedures since the excellence of Dr. Adelson was a known fact and the residual expense to me was modest.

I have had an Amazon Kindle electronic reader for about two years and increasingly use it so that it serves most of my reading apart from the daily *Washington Post*, the *London Review of Books* and the *New York Review of Books*, which were or are not digitally available, as well as some books not on Kindle. The daily or less frequent publications on Kindle have included the Sunday *New York Times Book Review*, the weekly *Economist*, the quarterly *Foreign Affairs*, the weekly *Nation*, the bi-weekly *New Republic*, the weekly *Newsweek*, and the weekly *Times Literary Supplement*. All these I find to be excellent, highly informative and continuously educational as they have been for me for many years, and now at less expense that I had paid for the print versions. Also on Kindle I have many books, including masterpieces of English literature for which the copyright has long expired such as Shakespeare's plays and translations of some Greek and Roman classics, all at nominal cost. While I have a considerable library I have almost no room for more books; thus Kindle.

Another of my joys of recent years had been the advent of satellite radio. This among over 200 channels brings me the Metropolitan Opera channel and two other classical music channels, one for longer pieces and the other for shorter, more popular classics, all at reasonable cost. I play this music through Bose radios and through my laptop connected to high fidelity speakers, all with glorious sound. I especially enjoy hearing and rehearing some of the operas of Handel, Mozart, Berlioz, Tchaikovsky, Verdi, Wagner, Richard Strauss, and Benjamin Britten. For me, Wagner's the *Ring of the Nibelung* is one of the supreme achievements of art. Also I listen on CDs to much of the choral music and some of the keyboard, solo violin and cello music of Bach and the oratorios of Handel, from which all the rest of Western music derives and the chamber, choral and solo instrument works of Haydn, especially some of the piano sonatas and trios and quartets, and some Mozart, Beethoven and Brahms piano pieces and chamber music. Not having taken up the piano to learn to play any of this music is a lifetime regret.

Writers working in the 20th Century and later whom I have admired and learned from over the years include W. H. Auden, Saul Bellow, Isaiah Berlin, Elizabeth Bishop, Harold Bloom, Winston Churchill, Joseph Conrad, T. S. Eliot, Richard J. Evans, Scott Fitzgerald, Morgan Forster, William Gaddis, Marjorie Garber, Stephen Greenblatt, Vassily Grossman, Robert Graves, Thomas Hardy, Ernest Hemingway, John Hersey, A. E. Housman, Henry James, James Joyce, George Kennan, Maynard Keynes, Frank Kermode, Rudyard Kipling, Sinclair Lewis, Jonathon Littell, James Merrill, Robert Manson Myers, Vladimir Nabokov, Marcel Proust, Bertrand Russell, George Santayana, George Steiner, Wallace Stevens, Helen Vendler, Gore Vidal, G. C. Waterston, H. G. Wells, Edmund Wilson, Alfred North Whitehead, Richard Wilbur, P. G. Wodehouse, Leonard and Virginia Woolf, and William Butler Yeats, among the more important ones.

My reading recently is to learn more about the art of Shakespeare under the tutelage of Harold Bloom, Marjorie Garber, and the late Frank Kermode, each a Shakespearean scholar of the front rank, Bloom, long an eminent professor of literature at Yale, Garber, similarly at Harvard, in several books[217], and Kermode, perhaps the leading English literary critic of the last 50 years, in *The Age of Shakespeare* (Kindle) and *Shakespeare's Language* (Farrar Straus Giroux 2000). I continue to enjoy the exciting, well-written adventure novels of Clive Cussler and Charles McCarry.

For many years I have a weekly lunch at the attractive public dining room at the Westchester, a complex of four upscale cooperative apartment buildings on Cathedral Avenue near the Washington cathedral. The public is largely unaware of it and its patrons are mostly residents. Until the summer of 2011, our lunch group of the last few years included Larry Lutkins born in 1919, a retired foreign service officer and widower living at the Westchester and whom I had met through Dick Howland, Joan Leclerc, a widow near my age and previously married to a foreign service officer, Guiseppa Spigler, a widow from Milan who married Donald Spigler, a foreign service officer in Berlin shortly after World War II, frequently Dick Roeckelein, the retired music director at St. Albans School and an accomplished musician and teacher, also living at the Westchester with his lovely wife Linda who is in charge of the floral arrangements at the Washington Cathedral and cannot join us. All are my good friends, highly educated and intelligent which make the lunch talk exceptionally stimulating and interesting for all of us.

Sadly, Larry's health severely declined in the summer of 2011 from prior strokes. He died peacefully at home on August 26 at 92 in the company of his children. He had grown up in Rye, near where we lived in Greenwich, knew some of the same families we did, graduated from St. Mark's School in 1937 then to Yale, Class of 1941 where one of his close friends on the college newspaper was Kingman Brewster, also a friend

---

217 Bloom, *The Anatomy of Influence* (Kindle), *Shakespeare The Invention of the Human* (Riverhead Books 1998), *The Western Canon* (Harcourt Brace 1994); Garber, *Shakespeare After All* (Kindle). There is much wisdom in A.C. Bradley's *Shakespearean Tragedy, Lectures on Hamlet, Othello, King Lear, Macbeth* (Macmillan and Co., London 1937).

of mine at law school, and later president of Yale. Larry joined the foreign service after Yale rather than follow the Wall Street footsteps of this father, and thus began a very distinguished career serving mostly in the far east and retiring in 1975. He and his lovely wife Florence, whom I did not know, had two daughters and two sons. I came to know and love the daughters Pat, a widow living in New York and later in Shelter Island on Long Island, and Rita living with her husband in Madrid and on a farm in Spain, as the frequency of their visits to Larry increased. Both ladies are first class; I met but did not know the married sons Clint and Nick. Rita and husband had two grown-up daughters also living in Spain and beginning their careers. Larry's ashes were placed next to those of his wife in the lovely foreign service section amidst the beautiful stately trees of the Rock Creek Cemetery. And the family hosted a lovely memorial gathering at the Chevy Chase Club. We all miss Larry greatly. Happily, our Thursday lunch group continues.

In June 2011 I put the West Virginia property on the market with an asking price of $130K for an old small house and 17 and ½ acres of mostly woods near the Potomac River which has been spared development for more than 50 years and is likely so to continue as the land, mostly undeveloped is preserved for hunting. The place is suitable as a weekend home for persons living in the Baltimore and Washington areas as it is situated in beautiful countryside in vanishing rural surroundings affording maximum privacy. It should sell near that price but that may take a year or more. When the property sells, I will donate my car as I will no longer need one living in Washington.

As I reflect on my long life, I am astonished at the good fortune I have experienced throughout it without serious illness or injury, boredom, depression or adversity, financial hardship, and none of the other afflictions with which most suffer at some point in their lives. Having been born in America to educated, well-off parents was a huge head start. Having had first-class educational opportunities as outlined in Parts One and Three was yet another. The maturing and extraordinary experiences in the Army here and in England, France and Germany during World War II as related in Part Two were of lasting importance. The interesting and challenging work described in Parts Four, Five and Six were the additional major factors in shaping my life. The blessings of friendships throughout my long life and of the loving relationships since 1951 have further created the enriching, privileged and happy life I have had, the telling of which I now conclude in my 89th year, I believe well before I am at the exit for whencesoever. As I depart may I remember

> For while the tired waves, vainly breaking,
>   Seem here no painful inch to gain,
> Far back, through creeks and inlets making,
>   Comes silent, flooding in, the main.
>
> And not by eastern windows only,
>   When daylight comes, comes in the light,
> In front the sun climbs slow, how slowly,
>   But westward, look, the land is bright!

(A.H. Clough, *Say Not the Struggle Naught Availeth* 1849)

CITATIONS

Cases: Board of Contract Appeal and Court Decisions

Bartholdi Cable Co. v. FCC, 114 F.3d 274, 281 (D.C. Cir. 1997)   370n

Bates v. State Bar of Arizona, 433 U.S. 350 (1977)   181n

Bath Iron Works, ASBCA No. 12382, 68-1 BCA ¶ 7050
(1968) 148n,   181-83

Boeing North American, Inc., ASBCA No. 49994, 00-2 BCA ¶ 30,970,
    rev'd and remanded, *Boeing North American v. Roche*, 298 F.3d 1274
    (Fed. Cir. 2002) 363n, 364, 367-68

Brown v. *Board of Education*, 347 U.S. 483 (1953)   117

Caiola v. Carroll, 851 F.2d 395 (D.C. Cir. 1988)   261n, 285-87

Caldera v. Northrop Worldwide Aircraft Services, Inc., 192 F.3d 962
    (Fed. Cir. 1999)   363n, 364-68

Canadian Commercial Corp. v. Dep't of the Air Force, 514 F.3d 37,
    38 (D.C. Cir. 2008)   370*n*

Canadian Fin. Corp. v Donovan, 830 F.2d 1132, 1151
    (D.C. Cir. 1951)   370n

Chrysler v. Brown, 441 U.S. 282, 320 n.49 (1979)   370n

City and County of San Francisco v. U.S. et al., 443 F. Supp. 1116
    (N.D. Calif. 1977), *aff'd*, 615 F.2d 498 (9ᵗʰ Cir. 1980)   252-54

Cort v. Ash, 422 U.S. 66, 78 (1975)   253n

Defoe Shipbuilding, ASBCA No. 17095, 74-1 BCA ¶ 10,357   256n

EPCO v. U.S., U.S. Court of Federal Claims No. 92-91C (1992) 309-13

Federal Crop Insurance Corp. v. Merrill, 332 U.S. 380 (1947)   189-90

Garrett v. General Electric Co., 987 F.2d 747 (Fed. Cir. 1993)   296n
General Dynamics Corp. v. U.S., Nos. 09-1298, 09-1302
    (U.S. 5/23/2011), 55 CCF ¶ 79,580 (Commerce Clearing House) 306n
General Electric Co., ASBCA Nos. 36005, 38152, 91-2 BCA ¶ 23,958
    (April 23, 1991) and 91-3 BCA ¶ 24353 (August 21, 1991) 294-304
G.L. Christian and Associates v. U.S., 312 F.2d 418, reh'g denied,
    320 F.2d 345 (Ct. Cl.), *cert. denied*, 375 U.S. 594 (1963)   243n
Greene v. McElroy, 350 U.S. 474 (1959), *reversing* 254 F.2d 944
    (D.C. Cir. 1955) and 150 F. Supp. 958 (D. D.C. 1954)   149-51
Greene v. U.S., 376 U.S. 149 (1964)   151-52

H.B. Zachry Co., ASBCA No. 39202, 90-1 BCA ¶ 23,342
    295n, 296 *Horne Bros. v. Laird*, 463 F.2d 1268 (D.C. Cir. 1972) 260n

International Engineering Co. v. Richardson, 367 F. Supp. 640 (D. D.C.),
    rev'd, 512 F.2d. 573 (D.C. Cir. (1975)   371 -73, 387n
In re Northrop Worldwide Aircraft Serv., Inc., ASBCA Nos. 45216, 45877,
    98-1 BCA ¶ 29,654 (1998)   364

Keco Industries, Inc. v. U.S., 492 F.2d 1200, 1203 (Ct. Cl. 1974)   384n

Lockheed Shipbuilding and Construction Co., ENG BCA No. 3141,
    74-1 BCA ¶ 10,512 (1974)   221-24
Lockheed Shipbuilding and Construction Co., ASBCA No. 18460,
    75-1 BCA ¶ 11,246 (5/13/1975), *aff'd on reconsid..*, 75-2 BCA 75-2
    ¶ 11,566 (10/24/1975)   212-21, 261
Lockheed Shipbuilding and Construction Co., ASBCA
    No. 18460, 77-1 BCA ¶ 12,458 (1977)   220
Lockheed Shipbuilding and Construction Co., DOT CAB
    No. 73-73-36C, 79-2 BCA ¶ 14,080 (1979)   234-44

Marbury v. Madison, 5 U.S. (1Cranch) 137 (1803)   116

Mason v. U.S., 615 F.2d 1343, 1346 (Ct. Cl. 1980)   310n

McCarney v. Ford Motor Co., 657 F.2d 230 (8th Cir. 1981)   276-78

Nat'l Parks and Conservation Ass'n v. Morton, 498 F.2d 765, 770
    (D.C. Cir. 197)   370

Ness Investment Corp. v. U.S. Forest Service, 512 F.2d 706, 715
    (D.C. Cir. 1975)   253n

New York Shipbuilding Co., ASBCA No. 16,164, 76-2 BCA ¶ 11,979,
    (1976), reconsid. denied, 83-1 BCA ¶ 16,534 (1983)   261n

Old Dominion Dairy v. Laird, 631 F.2d 953 (D.C. Cir. 1980), *reversing*
    471 F. Supp. 300 (D. D.C. 1979)   261n

Perkins v. Lukens Steel Co., 310 U.S. 113 (1940)   384n

Plessy v. Ferguson, 163 U.S. 537 (1896)   117

Prudential-Maryland Joint Venture Co. v. Lehman, 590 F. Supp. 1390
    (D. D.C. 1994)   284-85

Rayco et al., ENG BCA Nos. 4169, 4248, 84-1 BCA ¶ 17,055 (1983),
    aff'd, 758 F.2d 668 (table) (Fed. Cir. 1984), 88-2 BCA ¶ 20,761
    (1988)   266-76

Res. Conservation Group, LLC v. U.S., \597 F.2d 1238, 1242-43
    (Fed. Cir. 2010)   385n

Scanwell Laboratories v. Shaffer, 424 F.2d 859 (D.C. Cir. 1970) 253n, 384n

Scott v. Sanford, 60 U.S. 393 (1857)   117

Slingsby Aviation Limited, ASBCA No. 50473, 03-1 BCA ¶ 32,252   313-15

S&E Contractors, Inc. v. U.S., 406 U.S. 1, 23 (1972), *reversing*
    433 F.2d 1373 (Ct. Cl. 1970)   209-12, 265

Sperry v. Florida, 373 U.S. 379 (1963)   178-80

Totten v. U.S., 92 U.S. 105, 107 (1867)   306n

U.S. v. Wunderlich, 342 U.S. 98 (1951)   209n, 212

West Coast Hotel v. Parrish, 300 U.S. 379 (1937) 117
Western Electric Co., ASBCA No. 11050, 68-2 BCA ¶ 7275
   (1968) 183-85
William Clairmont, ASBCA No. 15497, 73-1 BCA ¶ 9927 (1973) 266n
Womack v. U.S., 389 F.2d 798 (Ct. Cl. 1968) 309n

U.S. Constitution

Article III 116, 118
1st Amendment 181
7th Amendment 113
14th Amendment 117

Statutes

Administrative Conference Act of 1964, 5 U.S.C. §§ 591-96 170n
Administrative Dispute Resolution Act of 1996,
   28 U.S.C. § 1491(b)(1) 385n
Administrative Procedure Act of 1946, 5 U.S.C. §§ 701-706
   112, 155, 170, 197, 253n, 371, 384
   5 U.S.C. § 701(a)(2 253n
   5 U.S.C. § 702 286, 384-85
Armed Services Procurement Act of 1947, 10 U.S.C. §§ 2301-2314 (1958),
   repealed by 108 Stat. 3296 (10/13/1994) 124, 126, 129, 141,
   264, 369
Automobile Dealers' Day in Court Act, 15 U.S.C. §§ 1221 *et seq.* 277

Budget and Accounting Act of 1921, 31 U.S.C. §§ 3526 *et seq.* 125n

Coastal Zone Management Act, 16 U.S.C. § 1451 253
Competition in Contracting Act of 1984, as amended, 41 U.S.C.
   Subtitle 1, as codified by Pub. L. 111-356 (1/4/2011) and at 31
   U.S.C. §§ 3551-56
   (GAO bid protest sections) 264, 369, 383-85

Congressional Reference Cases, 28 U.S.C. §§ 1492, 2509   186

Contract Disputes Act of 1978, as amended, 41 U.S.C. Subtitle III,
    as so codified   212, 264-65, 295, 296n 310, 386-87

Duncan Hunter National Defense Authorization Act for FY 2009,
    § 321   388n

Emergency Loan Guarantee Act, Pub. L. 92-70 (Aug. 9, 1971)   216

False Claims Act   365

Federal Activities Inventory Reform Act, Pub. L. 105-270   388n

Federal Courts Administration Act of 1992, 28 U.S.C. § 1491(a)(2)   296n

Federal Courts Improvement Act of 1982,
    28 U.S.C. §§ 1295, 1491   283n, 385n

Federal Property and Administrative Services of 1949 (repealed)   264, 369

Federal Register Act of 1935   112

First War Powers Act of 1941, 55 Stat. 838 86,   124, 368-69

Federal Tort Claims Act, 28 U.S.C. §§ 2674 *et seq.*   186, 253, 254n

Freedom of Information Act, 5 U.S.C. § 552(b)(4)   112, 369-70

Military Leasing Act, 10 U.S.C. § 2667   253

Model Procurement Code for State and Local Governments   263, 265

National Aeronautical & Space Act   178 National Defense
    Authorization Act of 2006, § 847, 41 U.S.C. § 7105(b)   386n

Office of Federal Procurement Policy Act, 41 U.S.C. § 1101   155, 264,
    305n

Patent Act, 35 U.S.C. § 31   179

Pub Law 92-41, 50 U.S.C. App. § 1211   243n

Public Law 85-804   215

Public Law 110-417, § 321, 31 U.S.C. § 501 note   388n

Revised Statutes, § 3709   124

Trade Secrets Act, 18 U.S.C. § 1905   370

Tucker Act, 28 U.S.C. §§ 1295, 1346(a)(2), 1491(a)(1), (2), 1491(b)(1)

    253, 283n, 371, 372n, 373n, 385n, 387n

Uniform Commercial Code, Article Three   114, 119

Uniform Sales Act   114

Wunderlich Act, 41 U.S.C. §§ 321, 322 (1976)   209-12

Executive Order

No. 10865, Safeguarding Classified Information within Industry   151

Regulations

Armed Services Procurement Regulation (ASPR)   138, 155-56, 243n, 264

Cost Accounting Standards   366-67

Cost Accounting Board Statement of Objectives, Policies, and

    Concepts, 37 F.R. 31036-37 (7/13/1992)   366n

Federal Acquisition Regulation (FAR), 48 CFR   264, 305

FAR 3.104-4, 503(b)(2), 506(d)(2)   369n

FAR 506(e)(1)   370n

FAR 9.406   286n

FAR 9.407   172n

FAR 16.504(a)(1), (2)   310n

FAR 31.001   366n

FAR 31.201-4   295, 296n, 364n, 365

FAR 33.201-215   265n

FAR 52.246-2   304n

Federal Procurement Regulation (FPR)   235, 243n, 264

FPR 1-1.322, Payment of Interest on Contractor Claims   243

Federal Rules of Civil Procedure   110, 113, 166

Office of Management & Budget (OMB), Circular A-76   387
Office of Federal Procurement Policy Letter 11-01, Performance of
    Inherently Governmental and Critical Functions, 76 F.R. 56227-42
    (10/12/2011)   388

Patent Office Regulations, 37 CFR §§ 1.341(a), (b), 2.12(d)   179-80n

Authors

Ashburn, *Peabody of Groton* (1944)   60
Auchincloss, *A View from Old New York* (2011)   60
Auchincloss, *The Rector of Justin* (1964)   60

Bloom, *The Anatomy of Influence* (2011)   394n
Bloom, *Shakespeare The Invention of the Human* (1998)   394n
Bloom, *The Western Canon* (1994)   *394n*
Bragdon, *The Life of a Free People* (1970s)   45
Bragdon, *Woodrow Wilson: The Academic Years* (1967)   45

Churchill, *A History of the English Speaking Peoples,* I, 97-103   2n, 225
Clough, *Say the Struggle Naught Availeth* (1849)   327, 396
Coburn and Oyer, *"Benefit to the Government" as an Erroneous
    Basis of Cost Allocation under Government Contracts,*
74*Federal Contracts Report* 332 (BNA 2000)   364
Coburn, S. R., *Genealogy of the Descendants of Edward Coburn*
    (1913)   2n
Coburn, *The Contract Disputes Act of 1978, Practising Law Institute*
    (1982)   265n
Coburn *et al., Navy Contract Law,* 2d ed. 1959 and 1961 Suppl.
    (GPO)   152, 165, 167
Coburn and McMorries, *Purchasing,* Bureau of Supplies & Accounts
    Manual Vol. 6 (1952)   138
Coburn *et al., Remembering Trow vom Baur,* 30 ABA Pub. Cont. L. J. 1
    (Fall 2000)   166n, 262

Eliot, *Murder in the Cathedral* (1935)   50

Eliot, *The Waste Land* (1923)   56
English Book of Common Prayer (1927)   47

Fox, James, *Five Sisters; The Langhornes of Virginia* (2001)   121, 226n, 338
Fox, Lyttleton, *The Incubator of Greatness* (*Forum* Magazine 1933)   120n
Friedman, *Fostering Civility: A Professional Obligation*, ABA Section of
        Public Contract Law website (March 13, 1998)   282
Fulton, Robert, *One Man Caravan* (1937)   38, 318, 328
Fulton, Robert, *Winds of Life* (1985)   322, 328

Gerber, *Shakespeare After All* (2005)   394n

Hayakawa, *Language in Action* (1938)   52
Holmes, *The Common Law* 1 (1881)   107n, 245n
Houseman, *The Rain, It Streams on Stone and Hillock* (1922)   395
Houseman, *My Funeral* (1936)   395
Howland & Spencer, *The Architecture of Baltimore*
        (Johns Hopkins 1953)   334

Ismay, Hastings, *The Memoirs of General the Lord Ismay*
        (Heinemann 1960)   86n, 106n

Kennan, X (*Foreign Affairs* 1947)   379
Kermode, *The Age of Shakespeare* (Kindle)   394
Kermode, *Shakespeare's Language* (2000)   394
Korzybski, *Science and Sanity* (1933)   52

Leary and LeSchack, *Project Cold Feet, Secret Mission to a Soviet Ice
        Station* (Naval Institute Press 1966)   321n
Leventhal, *Public Contracts and Administrative Law*,
        52 ABA J. 35 (1966)   197n
Llewellyn, *The Cheyenne Way* (1941)   118

Morrison and Commager, *The Growth of the American Republic*   103
Myers, *A Georgian at Princeton* (1961)   351
Myers (Author Anonymous), *Ars Amatoria: An Anthology* (2009)   358-59
Myers, *From Beowolf to Virginia Wolf* (revised ed., 1984)   348

Myers, *Handel, Dryden, and Milton* (1956) 348

Myers, *Handel's Messiah, A Touchstone of Taste (1948)* 293n, 348

Myers, *Poynton Park* (a play adapted from Henry James's *Spoils of Poynton*) (2005) 352

Myers, *Quintet, A Five Play Cycle Drawn from The Children of Pride* (1991) 291-92, 351

Myers, *Restoration Comedy* (1956) 348

Myers, *Sixes and Sevens, Scenes from a Marriage* (2004) 351

Myers, *The Bostonians* (a play adapted from the Henry James novel) (2005) 352

Myers, *The Children of Pride* (1972) 291-92, 335, 348-51

 Abridged Ed. (Yale 1984) 351

Nash and Feldman, *Contract Changes* 3d ed. (2007) 190n

Ogden & Richards, *Basic English: A General Introduction with Rules and Grammar* (1930) 51

Ogden, *The General Basic English Dictionary* (1930s) 51

Ogden & Richards, *The Meaning of Meaning: A Study of the Influence of Language upon Thought and the Science of Symbolism* (1923) 51, 52

Pogue, *George Marshall: Statesman 1945-1959* 111n

Swinburne, *The Garden of Proserpine* (1866) 344

Thomas & Brown, *Reading Poems: An Introduction to Critical Study* (1941) 56

Thompson, *Thirty Years at Brooks* (1958) 55

vom Baur, *Federal Administrative Law* (1942) and 1947 Supplement 143

Waterston, *Order and Counter Order: Dualism in Western Culture* 52, 317n

Whitman, *Leaves of Grass* (1891) 344

Wilbur, *The Consolations of God: Great Sermons of Phillips Brooks* 43n

Woolverton, *The Education of Phillips Brooks* (1995) 44n

Wright, *The Growth of American Constitutional Law* 103

Made in the USA
Lexington, KY
08 June 2012